From Edison to Marconi

From Edison to Marconi

The First Thirty Years of Recorded Music

DAVID J. STEFFEN

McFarland & Company, Inc., Publishers
Jefferson, North Carolina, and London

Library of Congress Cataloguing-in-Publication Data

Steffen, David J., 1948–
    From Edison to Marconi : the first thirty years of recorded
music / David J. Steffen.
        p.   cm.
    Includes bibliographical references, discography, and index.

    ISBN 0-7864-2061-8 (softcover : 50# alkaline paper)

    1. Sound recordings — History.   2. Sound — Recording and
reproducing — History.   3. Sound recording industry — History.
I. Title.
    ML1055.S73   2005
    784.49'09–dc22   2005007356

British Library cataloguing data are available

On the front cover: Thomas Edison, 1888 (top), and
Guglielmo Marconi, 1896

Manufactured in the United States of America

McFarland & Company, Inc., Publishers
  Box 611, Jefferson, North Carolina 28640
    www.mcfarlandpub.com

For Dolly, for your love and patience.

For Caitlin, who continues to be the light of my life.

Acknowledgments

This book began in September 1999 as a research project tied to my undergraduate degree in American Studies at Fairfield University, was expanded as part of my masters work at New York University, and was completed in the months that followed. The help I received from faculty members at both schools was invaluable. I wish to thank those professors who found me regularly at their door or on the phone, and yet chose not to relocate their offices, change their phone numbers, or enter the federal witness protection program.

At Fairfield University my thanks go to American Studies chair Leo O'Connor for helping get the project started, and to numerous educators who each contributed to my writing and research (although they may not have fully appreciated the extent of their contribution at the time): Cecelia Bucki, Deb Chappell, Paul Davis, Philip Eliasoph, Marge Glick, Joy Gordon, Nancy Habetz, Nancy Haegel, Lawrence Kazura, Janet Krauss, Paul Lakeland, David McFadden, Laura Nash, Eugene Murphy, John Orman, Joan Overfield, Walter Petry, Tom Regan, Rose Rodrigues, Betsy Bowen, and Elizabeth Petrino; and to Iris Bork-Goldfield *ich sage vielen dank.*

At New York University I'd like to thank professors Karen Greenberg and Barbara Abrash, and everyone at the John W. Draper Program in Humanities and Social Thought who (I'm happy to say) helped change the direction of my graduate studies: Jessica Sewell, Robin Nagle, and Robert Dimit. Thanks also to Professor Robin Blackburn of the University of Essex.

I'm grateful to Riaz Khan at New York University for his guidance during my thesis, to Catherine Moore at New York University for building a music business program worth participating in, and to Brian Torff at Fairfield University for helping me to see the enjoyment of writing and teaching about music. Thanks also to my students at both Fairfield and NYU. Each of you has made teaching the rewarding experience I hoped it would be.

Music writers who have inspired me through their excellent work include Peter Guralnick, Nelson George, John A. Jackson, Tim Gracyk, Donald Clarke, the late Professor Eileen Southern, and the late editor of *Billboard* magazine Timothy White. Thanks to writer and friend Ellen Wolff, who has provided encouragement, friendship, and a lasting appreciation of the power of words.

This project would have been far more difficult without the people and the resources at the three libraries where I did much of my research for this book: Dimenna-Nyselius Library at Fairfield University (thanks to Christina McGowan, Angela Courtney, and everyone else there who indulged my presence in their midst ad nauseam), NYU's Bobst Library, and the Recorded Sound Reference Center at the Library of Congress in Washington, D.C.

Thanks to my industry friends who have been supportive both during my years in the music industry and after: Herb Alpert, David Anderle, Brenda Andrews, Steve Backer, Bill Berger, Howard Berman, Peter Blachley, Jay Boberg, Barbara Bolan, Rita Brennan-Freay, Louise Broderick, Gary Burden, Ernie Campagna, Harold Childs, Tony Clark, Rick Cohen, Patti Coleman, David Conrad, Terry Courier, Tony Dalesandro, Harold Davis, Henry Diltz, Michael Dornemann, Neal Edelson, Bob Fead, David Fitch, Rich Frankel, Lance Freed, Gil Friesen, Bob Frymire, David Gales, Richie Gallo, Bob Garcia, Frank Giuliano, Jim Grady, Seymour Greenspan, Chuck Gullo, John Hager, Jim Hanke, Larry Hayes, Curtis Hawkins, Wayne Isaak, Aaron Jacoves, Pete Jones, Martin Kirkup, Harold Lipsius, Jerry Love, Jasmine Madatian, Al Marks, Geoff Mayfield, Jerry Moss, Bob Mugge, Milt Olin, Arnie Orleans, Jane Palmese, Michael Parkinson, Phil Quarterero, Carl Rosenbaum, Larry Rosenbaum, John Salstone, Gene Silverman, Jayne Simon, Lee Smith, John Snyder, Russ Solomon, Pete Stocke, Joe Summers, Jim Swindel, Jack White, Suzanne White, Chris Whorf, and Adrian Workman; a special thanks to Mike Regan, who has been and continues to be as good a friend as one could wish for. And to Marv Dorfman, Duke Dubois, Mel Fuhrman, Joe Simone, John Kaplan, Milt Salstone, Ron Amann, John O'Brien, Ron Cuzner, Jan Basham, and Charlie Minor, mentors and friends who are gone but still remembered.

To my non-industry friends and family I am also indebted. Their support as I chased my academic dreams and chose writing instead of a real job was invaluable. Dean Kadlec, Janice Mattioli, Sue Ryan, John and Barbara Speare, Tony and Karen Stanol, Bob and Peggy Turchyn, Kathryn and Kevin Ward, Dave and Robin Weber, and the members of the Steffen and Marshall families: Dolly, Caitie, Laura Lee, Norman, Jan, Lee, Paul, Todd, Kerry, Dave, Sally, and Kristin. To Norman R., Betty, Rolf, Violet, and June, time doesn't pass that we don't think of you.

While I have made every effort to provide footnotes and lists of sources that were useful in the process of writing and editing this book, it is inevitable that someone's name or the name of an organization or text has been misspelled or simply fell through the fact-checking cracks. I apologize for any such errors.

Contents

Preface

This book will look at the first thirty years of recordings—but not just the recordings. It will explore the invention of the phonograph in the nineteenth century, and it will look even farther back, to people who had the desire to capture sound but did not have enough facts or the technology to do so.

While looking through fiction and nonfiction books, academic journals, consumer and music-industry newspapers and magazines, it seemed to me that there was room for a book that looked at the music industry in a different way. Instead of rehashing the current musical success stories or the numerous "flavors-of-the-month," I began to investigate the early music business. Were there performers who hit fast and died young? Were there one-hit wonders? Did the early recording artists carve out sustained careers?

The research for this book proceeded through five stages. First, lists of early recordings were prepared. Among the sources used were books, journals, and texts; archives of newspapers and magazines including *The New York Times* and music and entertainment industry trade publications such as *Billboard* magazine, *Talking Machine News*, and *Phonoscope*; record company documents, lists and archives; Internet lists and archives of American records; and resources at the Smithsonian Institution, the Library of Congress and a number of university libraries.

Second, it was necessary to locate and listen to a representative number of those original recordings, and view representative samples of the sheet music. Sources of original listening material (cylinders and discs) included archived recordings at libraries and private institutions, and primary among these was the Library of Congress. Its catalog of early recordings is one of the most extensive in the world. Additional recordings and sheet music samples are preserved at the libraries of the University of Colorado, Duke University, Yale University, and New York University. Some recordings were borrowed or purchased from private collectors and commercial sources, while additional recordings were listened to via streaming sources or downloaded from the Internet.

Third, all selected recordings were catagorized. Initially they were assigned to either a generally popular genre or an ethnic genre. Those assigned to the first group — generally popular — were also categorized within specific musical genres: ballads, comedy, dance, marches, military, novelty, parlor, patriotic, production, ragtime, regional, religious, romance, societal. Of the recordings within the ethnic group, titles were placed in genres according to ethnicity: black/Negro, Chinese, Exotic, French, German, Hawaiian, Irish, Italian, Jewish/Yiddish, Native American, Polish, and some additional, smaller groups. They were further categorized as either ethnic or pseudo-ethnic. The former category encompasses those recordings usually made by people sharing a common and distinctive racial, national, religious, linguistic, or cultural heritage, e.g., ethnic Irish performers in the United States — whether Irish-born or Irish-American. These Irish recordings may have been thematically, dialectically, or rhythmically similar to music heard in Ireland, and the recordings were often aimed at Irish immigrants (or sympathetic ears) living in America. One specific example of an *ethnic* Irish performer is tenor John McCormack (1884–1945), born in Ireland and relocated to America, who recorded songs such as "When Irish Eyes Are Smiling" (1917). The category *pseudo-ethnic* refers to recordings with an ethnic character to them but recorded by a performer from outside of that ethnic group. An example of a pseudo-ethnic recording is white performer Arthur Collins singing "Nigger Loves His Possum" (1905) in a stereotypical nineteenth-century Negro dialect.

Unlike the generally popular titles, ethnic recordings could be further broken down into sub-categories such as colloquial or racist. For example, the two recordings just cited could each later be defined using these subsets: "When Irish Eyes Are Smiling" might be deemed *colloquial*, while "Nigger Loves His Possum" could just as quickly be labeled *racist*. In some cases, a single recording might be categorized as both.[1] A sample of this apparent contradiction to the definition of *colloquial* versus *racist* is Earl Hogan's "All Coons Look Alike to Me." On the surface, when the title is juxtaposed against the writer's Irish-sounding name — Earl Hogan — it seems obviously racist. However, the song's origins are not actually the gratuitous ranting of a transplanted, racist Irishman:

> The biggest coon hit was Ernest Hogan's "All Coons Look Alike to Me" (1896), about a woman rejecting her lover for another man with more money. While a great many writers of coon songs and other hits of the era were Irish, Hogan was black. His real name was Reuben Crowder,

and he began his show business career as a child in *Uncle Tom's Cabin* in 1876....

Not only did "coon" become an obnoxious epithet, but Hogan's title became an obnoxious catch-phrase; Hogan is said to have regretted his greatest success.[2]

Since Hogan, that is to say Crowder, was black, can one conclude that his original composition was not designed as, or expected to be, a racist diatribe? His expression of "regret," cited by Clarke, suggests such a misjudgment. Therefore, it seems reasonable to conclude that Hogan/Crowder's original song and some of the multiple cover versions—and similar songs and recordings—that followed,[3] were both *colloquial* and *racist*, intentionally or not.

While it is easy for readers and listeners today to immediately see many of these recordings for what they were—racist, insulting, rude, and contemptuous—this book will attempt to discuss these recordings in the context of the period, not their present-day context. Therefore forbearance is suggested when reading some of the titles and their possible categorization as just described.

Fourth, historical and contemporary writing on these early recordings was evaluated to bring about a thorough understanding from differing views. How were these recordings accepted at the time? Were they successful and popular across the population in general, or was the success focused toward various consumer niches? In some cases can one conclude that they succeeded in both venues concurrently—general and niche popularity—or even some blended combination of the two? Many of the foregoing themes will be explained or defined further as the book's themes begin to develop.

The fifth and final stage of the analysis was to consider the influence any of the recordings may have had beyond entertainment, beyond their aesthetics. The generally popular titles obviously influenced dance crazes, brought Broadway to the public at-large, sent social messages, and made commercial or political statements. For ethnic recordings one might consider the impact of external and internal immigrants on these early recordings. New questions could be considered as musical categorization began to take shape. For example, did a recording like "When Irish Eyes Are Smiling" bring comfort to Irish immigrants living in America, or did it encourage Irish expatriates to consider returning to Ireland? Did recordings such as "Levinsky at the Wedding" provide a humorous look at Jewish life in America, or did they further existing negative ethnic stereotypes, and in the case of this ethnicity, anti–Semitism? How many of the recordings demonstrated a relationship with issues of the period, including class consciousness, politics, and ethnic identity? Did recordings become a unifying factor within one or more ethnic communities, or did they help maintain separation? Was music sometimes a divisive mechanism strengthening one group at the expense of another?

The early recording industry had no established or consistent method of charting the popularity of its output. This book attempts to take reliable measure by examining sheet music sales, vaudeville performances (including audience response and a star's billing on the theater marquee), and the subjective, and sometimes reconstructed, popularity charts of the day. The actual unit sales and success of early recordings were not a matter of record for the early companies: "No reliable sales figures exist. We do not know what record was first to sell a million copies.... [Until royalty-based agreements with artists existed], companies had no reason [or motivation] to provide artists with exact or even approximate sales figures."[4] While not scientific or even terribly accurate, reconstructed charts are still useful if they provide some understanding of the levels of popularity various recordings achieved. Keep in mind that the assertion of success by one company, even if only for bragging rights, might send a message to competitors: Hurry and record another version of this popular new song. The success that any one company was having could be mitigated by the music industry's lack of exclusive repertoire as well as its lack of technological standardization. Therefore, any of these dilemmas (or in the competitor's view, opportunities) could, in turn, lead the competition to record *cover* versions as cited in the example of "Bedelia."[5] Songs, styles, genres, niches could all be exploited by the various record companies on a nonexclusive basis.

In addition to artist and label competition, there was an effort to be first at establishing new genres of recordings to expand a company's business. Because recording diversity was limited in the first days of the recording industry, most record company catalogs contained broadly popular artists like Sousa's Band or vocalist Byron Harlan; any variety in repertoire was limited to the performing options of the times, e.g., brass band marches, vocalists, mild comedy, and later, smaller orchestras of woodwinds and brass, minstrel songs, and spoken word. In time, the tastes of the companies and the interests of the developing consumer market began to shape a larger, more diverse repertoire. The music business was inventing itself. The Columbia Phonograph Company catalog cited in Chapter 5 listed marches, polkas, waltzes, anthems, hymns, opera. At the same time, first, second, and third generation immigrant families were moving beyond these genres and embracing themes and styles of music that seemed closer to their ancestral origins.

Years before I first began putting my ideas on paper, others wrote about the origins of the phonograph. Roland Gelatt's centenary book *The Fabulous Phonograph: 1877–1977* is a great source on the invention. Others have explored Edison's invention and Edison the man with equal enthusiasm and detail. Andre Millard's *America on Record: A History of Recorded Sound* and *From Tin Foil to Stereo: Evolution of the Phonograph* by Oliver Read and Walter L. Welch are both worth your time. *Enrico Caruso: My Father and My Family* by Enrico Caruso, Jr., and Andrew Farkas was a valuable resource for information on the great tenor. *The Recording Angel: Explorations in Phonography* by Evan Eisenberg has a unique approach to the subject of recorded music and is recommended. For a look at Edison's invention in great detail, I recommend Allen Koenigsberg's *Edison Cylinder Recordings, 1889–1912.*

Research on the recordings and the performers was aided by a number of writers. Elie Siegmeister's *The Music Lover's Handbook* and Sigmund Spaeth's *A History of Popular Music*, both written in the 1940s, may be a little hard to find, but the personalization of the music found in each text helps one cut through the clutter. Tim Gracyk has written extensively on early recordings and is a great resource for information and perspective in books like *Popular American Recording Pioneers*. Pekka Gronow and Ilpo Saunio's *An International History of the Recording Industry* (translated by Christopher Moseley) and Gronow's "An Introduction" in *Ethnic Recordings in America: A Neglected Heritage* look at many of the early ethnic recordings. Additional authors and editors worth seeking out are Donald Clarke (*The Rise and Fall of Popular Music*), Barbara Cohen-Stratyner (*Popular Music, 1900–1919: An Annotated Guide to American Popular Songs*), and Eileen Southern (*The Music of Black Americans: A History.*)

Beyond these books, there was much time spent going through other sources to see if there were large pieces to the puzzle waiting to be found, or small scraps of information that might shed light on some other facet of the early recording business. Of the hundreds of sources—books, journals, articles, recordings, lists, catalogs, Internet sites—the most important and quoted sources are found in the bibliography.

I would simply add this: to appreciate the invention and the importance of the phonograph one must deal with the recordings of each age. We can hear our ancestors, and sometimes ourselves, in a song recorded a century ago or just last week. Each recorded performance contains, in some measure large or small, emotion, and almost always, the emotion strikes something inside of us. A group of people might listen to "A Day in the Life" from the Beatles' album *Sergeant Pepper's Lonely Hearts Club Band*, and each listener might respond to a different quality of the recording. It could be John Lennon's voice, the melody, or the lyrics inspired by an English newspaper's headlines. Music is usually personal, and the recorded song or voice resonates with us, reaches inside of us, connects with us. Recorded music helps us relive a moment in our mind's eye, or enables us to live the moment for the first time.

Introduction

One's age or position in time determines perspective. Consider the Great Depression–era parents and grandparents, whose views on the world differ from their children and grandchildren. For some that difference is expressed in the quantity or the quality of the food that each has to eat. For others it is seen in transportation — jet airliners versus propeller airplanes, or driving one's personal automobile instead of walking or taking the public bus, subway, or commuter train. Entertainment technology represents another of those existing generational chasms. When looking at the history of recorded music, one can look back at the gulf created by technological change as a means of separating listeners much as music itself has done throughout the twentieth century.

Alvin Toffler's 1970 landmark book *Future Shock* attempted to address change from the context of his late-twentieth century view. In various ways Toffler presented written images that enabled the reader to comprehend the compression of time, the accelerated pace of change, and the numbing effect that both compression and change bring to the human experience. In short, the march of time brings with it an acceleration of change that requires perspective. Such a perspective is also found in the writing of Kenneth Boulding. The seeming reductionist approach he brings to a linear history (at least in a few passages) is far more important than a cursory interpretation might suggest, such as when Boulding states that "the date that divides human history into two equal parts is well within living memory…. Another startling fact is that about 25% of the human beings who have ever lived are alive today…."[1] This, to put it simply, is powerful stuff. Boulding's statistics, even having originated forty years ago, lost no relevance when Toffler put his own then-contemporary spin on these thoughts: "[the twentieth century] represents the Great Median Strip running down the center of human history."[2] For all human beings except those born since the end of the recent millennium, the twentieth century is that median strip.

Looking backward through the history of the music industry, one can see that music, too, has demarcation lines. In the late 1970s digital recording became a reality, and a few years later the compact disc was introduced. From 1948 and into the early 1950s, the music industry introduced vinyl singles, the long-playing vinyl album, and a genre which became known as rock 'n' roll. In 1920 commercial, licensed radio became a reality and soon began to influence consumer-purchase decisions about music and performers. Radio also ushered in the microphone, which in turn signaled the end of the acoustic recording age. And 1889 was the effective start of an American music industry.

The effect of change in music technology is evident when we acknowledge that generations of twentieth century music buyers developed their own habits and embraced their own *conveyers* of recorded music. Cylinders disappeared in the 1920s; 78-rpm discs vanished in the 1950s; the 8-track tape was gone by the end of the 1970s. The 7" 45-rpm single, *the* post–World War II format for delivery of a single song was eclipsed by the cassette single in 1989.[3] The compact disc, introduced commercially in 1982, had a similar effect on the vinyl LP, reducing the latter from the dominant medium to a specialty business in less than ten years. In human terms, these changes separated generations of music consumers and classified and dated them. Most teenagers of the 1960s eschewed the 78s, 1980s teens never owned a turntable, and those of the 1990s grew up in a digital age. For this last group, vinyl discs and analog cassettes are, relatively speaking, technologies and formats of the ancients. Toffler illustrated the pace of change and the impact of that change on society. In the context of recorded music today, most music fans collect compact discs or amass a collection of MP3 or MP4 digital downloads (legally or illegally.) To them the older formats are just that—*old*.

In the process of developing a machine to record and playback sound, there were multiple approaches to the problems of achieving this goal. Various materials such as paper, wax, glass, rubber, and shellac were all explored by inventors, as were sizes and shapes of the playback formats— cylinders, discs, and wires. As we look back at the birth of Edison's phonograph and the recordings that launched an industry, it is worth remembering that as ancient as cylinders and shellac discs seem to most baby-boom generation collectors, the 45-rpm single, the vinyl album, and the 8-track tape seem equally ancient to the current prime consumers of music: those under thirty years of age.

There has been an oft-circulated story (and an erroneous one) about the "completion" of the American patent office's mission at the close of the nineteenth century. Bill Gates, in his book *The Road Ahead*, helped perpetuate the myth: "History is full of examples [of predictions and decisions]—the Oxford professor who in 1878 dismissed the electric light as a gimmick; the commissioner of U.S. patents who in 1889 asked that his office be abolished because 'everything that can be invented has been invented.'"[4] The fact that this last piece of misinformation continues to find an audience seems both humorous and troubling. As the 1800s moved to a close, the creative mind was far from finished.[5] Indeed, as the fruitful career of Thomas Edison (1847–1931) alone suggests, it was just getting started.

A parallel thought is reflected in the innovation and the innocence of the first thirty years of recording. Radio was just being developed by Guglielmo Marconi (1874–1937) during these years. Motion pictures with sound were on the distant horizon, and television was years away. The years 1889–1919 — years encompassing the initial production and first sales by Thomas Edison and before the granting of a government license to radio station KDKA in Pittsburgh to begin commercial broadcasting — were groundbreaking for the music business.[6] From Edison's first patent for a "talking machine"[7] to the realization of Marconi's dream of "wireless broadcasting," entertainment was ready to be brought into the home. Before radio there was no broadcast medium to generate consumer interest or consumer demand for recorded music. No films showcased a specially created soundtrack of contemporary music, and no MTV or *Ed Sullivan Show* existed to influence and shape the public's taste.

The tastemakers *were* the Edisons of the world; those first recording company entrepreneurs decided just who, what, and when to record. Long before the appearance of recording contracts containing large advances and substantial royalties for the performer, recordings were made for these kings of a new medium, the captains of a new industry. Many performers were hired for recording sessions without any commitment to royalties. The growth of the music business was, at least in part, aided by the lack of contracts and royalties. "If royalties had been paid to artists who covered popular songs [a large portion of the early repertoire] in the early years of the recording industry, several would have earned fortunes."[8] Instead, potential artist royalties were retained by the record companies, and in part fueled the companies' growth.

During the early years of recording, the public purchased whatever the music companies were willing to sell them, and as consumers they were satisfied. Ultimately, consumer preference emerged. Sometimes it was in the guise of multiple versions of the same song being recorded and sold by competing companies simultaneously; other times, particularly after 1900, it was consumer awareness of a particular performer. Real and spontaneous consumer demand would consequently appear after radio began entertaining America for free in the 1920s. A song or a performer heard on the radio could provide consumers with a specific want or musical desire (demand) to carry to their music store, ultimately changing the dynamic of prerecorded music-consumerism (supply). The demand of "I want *this* recording" from consumers entering a record store began to compete and take the place of the question "What do you have?"

On the consumer side of recorded music, it's worth remembering that the music-listening experience is always biased. Each of us listens to music and hears it through a filter that is shaped, much as our entire emotional and intellectual character is shaped, through the ever-present nature and nurture: what we are given as part of ourselves, and what we acquire as our lives progress. Therefore we respond to music heard for the first time with a liking or disliking, passion or dispassion, an emotional attachment or a cold rejection. Each person may pretend (or exaggerate) that s/he has an open mind when it comes to music, asserting that all music is welcome to their ears. One may qualify that assertion a bit by identifying American music, or pop music, or classical, or jazz — at least within a general construct — as being automatically acceptable. How open-minded, for example, a jazz-lover might appear, by stating a love for all jazz, i.e., traditional, contemporary, be-bop, avant-garde, fusion, dixieland, ragtime, blues, etc.—can be occasionally verified (or refuted) by a visit to his or her record collection, or observing the speed with which the car-radio button is pushed to find something else to listen to when any biases kick in.

The speed with which some music is rejected through the obvious changing of a radio station, or the less obvious mental tuning out of some music while it continues to play on in the background is a part of everyday life. When any of us listen to music we are likely to categorize it or critique it, regardless of our critical qualifications. Therefore, when one *reads* another's categorization, grains of salt should be readily available for the listener to take with the opinion. There is nothing wrong with opinion, but as you read this book or any book, think past your inherent musical biases (unless of course you have none). For perspective, consider a music critic, of sorts, from four centuries ago.

In the book *The Making of New World Slavery*, the experience of one observer of music within the early New World slave culture is retold. Author and historian Robin Blackburn cites sixteenth-century writer Jean de Léry's (1534–1613) *History of a Voyage to the Land of Brazil*. Blackburn presents what appears to be Léry's "recognition" of a familiar Judeo-Christian biblical reference in the life of Brazil's Tupinambá Indians: "Léry was fascinated by what he thought was ... a reference in one of their songs to waters covering the world."[9] In a longer passage, Léry described the music from a Tupinambá ceremony (concentrating less on lyrics and more on the melody and rhythmic elements):

> Such was their melody that — although they do not know what music is — those who have not heard them would not believe that they could make such harmony. At the beginning of the witch's sabbath, when I was in the women's house, I had been somewhat afraid; now I received in recompense such joy, hearing the measured harmonies of such a multitude, and especially in the cadence and refrain of the song, when at every verse all of them would let their voices trail, saying Heu, heuaure, heura, heuaure, heura, heura, oueh — I stood there transported with delight.[10]

Léry appears to apply a Euro-centric view — "they do not know what music is" — and then contrasts it with an expression of the fundamental desire of most who listen to music: to enjoy the experience, and when one is truly appreciative of that experience, to be "transported with delight." The point is that caution should be exercised when reading, hearing, or accepting another's interpretation of one culture's indigenous music by those from outside of that culture. The application of an *understanding* of music, much like Blackburn pointing out Jean de Léry's assumption of a biblical reference (Noah, the ark and the flood) within the song of the Tupinambá, or a contemporary "expert's" opinion on any type of music, is always opinion based on *their* biases. Trust your ears first, contextualize your opinion with others, and know that somewhere within each of us exist our own biases.

One must also draw a line between classical music, primarily of European origin as the recording era began, and popular music, which might simply be described as "everything else." Donald Clarke, in *The Rise and Fall of Popular Music*, touched on a pre–twentieth century definition of popular music: "[music] publishers ... looked down on popular songs as the 'trash' of the 'common' people."[11] The view of songwriter Charles Harris (1867–1930) was that "The word 'popular' ... has been employed expressly to designate the various classes of songs which are written, published and sung, whistled and hummed by the great American 'unmusical' public...."[12] Loosely translating Clarke and Harris one might infer that, at least for Americans, one's trash is another's treasure. The "unmusical public's" ability to (a) identify with common themes, (b) hum, whistle or sing melodies, and (c) adopt, adapt or embrace new ideas contained within early recordings helps make the case for separating popular music into a larger, all-encompassing category. Euro-classical music as a genre in the United States — at least during the first era of recording and certainly before the arrival of Enrico Caruso—was strictly the province of America's elite, aristocratic, upper socio-economic group. Sigmund Spaeth distilled the question to its basic answer: "The tradition of serious music has been definitely aristocratic. That of popular music ... is just as definitely democratic."[13]

If the foregoing provides some clarity as to what popular music is, one can quickly become confused by the description of a particular performer as a "pop" artist. The *genre-fication* of music will be discussed in some detail in the book, but for now one can make the confusing statement that there is popular music, and then there is *popular* or *pop* music. Popular music may be, as described earlier, "everything else"; but the *pop* category exists within popular music to identify some performers and performances whose music does not fall strictly within another more easily defined genre.

Question: Is B. B. King's 1969 recording of "The Thrill Is Gone" (BluesWay 61032) a blues recording? Some (not this author) might question its *bluesiness* due to the lush string arrangement used as a counterpoint to the traditional style of B. B. King's vocal and instrumental blues performance. If the sweat somehow seems missing to some, the rest of us can feel the drops just fine. Writer David Ritz described the success of King's recording:

> During ... January, 1970 [King's recording of] "The Thrill Is Gone" started climbing and didn't stop till it reached the Top Twenty *pop* charts, a first for King. The bluesman had crossed over, and suddenly his audience expanded into the international arena. Artistically, B. B. King achieved this without an iota of compromise. "The Thrill Is Gone" is as blue as blue can get.[14]

While accurate, Ritz's liner notes provide an example of the confusion that can result over genre, style, and popularity. King is a renowned master of blues music in general and the blues guitar in particular. "The Thrill Is Gone" landed on the pop charts as Ritz cites, "without an iota of compromise." King moved his consumer recognition and success beyond his primary audience genre, *blues*, to that generic, catch-all genre identifier, *pop*. What aspect of the performance made a transition possible? Maybe it was the string section or the overall arrangement, which included King's blues guitar playing. Or was it simply the moment in which King's stars, planets, and karma were all coming into alignment?

This book will consider the development of the phonograph and, in some detail, the earliest recordings that soon followed. It will focus on the first thirty years of recorded music for at least three reasons. First, the initial musical recordings were less about artistry and more about filling demand. Second, the music and the recorded performances changed (evolved) as recording techniques improved and *artistic* performers (and performances) replaced the lesser known and unknown performers, including vaudevillians and professional singers, who had been the logical first choice for many of these early recording companies. Third, the introduction of commercial radio in 1920 provided consumers with a free entertainment alternative to purchasing recorded music. Consequently, the period from 1889 until 1919 represents a unique time in the annals of recording.

As you read through this book you'll notice that portions of the narrative go into some detail about the music industry of the 1950s or other post–World War II decades through the end of the twentieth century. Clearly recording artists like Billy Joel, Elvis Presley, Lee Ann Womack, and Bob Dylan were not in the recording studio between 1889 and 1919. Their experience, and the experiences of others is, however, relevant to the primary theme of this text. I have chosen to use contemporary examples in an effort to clarify aspects of the music industry during its first thirty years. How music is and was categorized, how popularity has been determined, how recordings are and were produced, or what the consumers found then and now, I believe, benefit from those contemporary comparisons.

One last thought. The recordings cited in this book should not be considered to be complete, definitive, or exhaustive listings. What I have attempted to do is bring in a representative number of recordings to help the reader contextualize the types of recordings made during the first thirty years of recorded music. In some sections—like the military and patriotic, or the dance recordings found in chapter 15, titled "Most of the Music"— the list is long, while in others, rather short. There are 1,700 titles in the list of *ethnic* recordings. However, each section provides the reader with a sufficient sample of recordings to get a clear picture of the early years. For detailed listings one should check the sources listed in the footnotes and the bibliography, as well as numerous other sources in both print and online, such as *Billboard, The Complete Entertainment Discography, Pop Memories: 1890–1954, Popular Music, 1900–1919: An Annotated Guide to American Popular Songs*, the online source *The Online Discographical Project*, and of course the Library of Congress, online or in person.

1

The Ancients and the Jukebox Phenomenon

What we take for granted in one age was a seeming impossibility in another. Between those two ages, there is a moment when the impossibility becomes a plausible idea. That idea may be quickly developed, or it may linger as a concept that takes years or generations to bring to fruition. Creating the means to capture sound and later release it was just such an idea that evolved from impossibility to concept, and from plausible idea to practical invention. Once that concept became real, the practical use for captured sound took shape.

The idea of recording sound and playing it back did not begin with Thomas Edison. If one wishes to dig deeper into early variations of this theme, one can examine events taking place hundreds or even thousands of years before Edison. Recent writing on mysterious phenomena, including historical sites and early designs, gives us a glimpse of the human fascination with capturing sound:

> a small but growing number of researchers … are pioneering a new discipline that might be called "paleoacoustics" or "archaeoacoustics.…" These investigators are intrigued by the curious sound phenomena reported at many ancient sites. And unlike many archaeologists, they do not believe [the sounds] are accidental but proof that some ancient people had a sophisticated knowledge of acoustics and built it into their structures.[1]

When today's travelers visit an ancient site, e.g., one of the numerous historic sites found in the Middle East, they might learn that the origin and history of the site are well-known to locals and this information is happily passed on to visitors. Depending on the importance of the site and the scrutiny of historians, the accuracy of this local knowledge is often suspect, usually open to interpretation, and generally subject to independent verification. The desire to be informed or entertained by an inanimate object or mechanical device *in return for something of value*—music-on-demand—has a long history. I call it the *jukebox phenomenon*.

The fourteenth century B.C. structure known as the Colossi of Memnon (statues that guarded the ancient mortuary built at Thebes on the west bank of the Nile) represent such a site, and such knowledge. The colossi are believed to have been constructed in honor of Pharaoh Amenhotep III (1417–1379 B.C.) and were approximately seventy feet (twenty-one meters) high. Some have believed that the statue actually represented Greek hero Memnon[2] (who helped defend Troy). More to the point is what happened to the structure more than a millennium after it was built. Having suffered major destruction most likely as the result of an earthquake in 27 B.C., the damaged statue seemed to create the illusion of a recorded greeting from Memnon ostensibly for his mother Eos, Goddess of the Dawn. As with many a well-intentioned purpose, a restoration of the damaged site during the third century A.D. produced unfortunate results: upon completion of the reconstruction, the sounds were no longer heard. R. Drew Griffith brings some needed authenticity to the legend of Memnon and the reported sounds coming from the colossi. In the fourteenth century B.C. near Thebes, according to Griffith, Amenhotep III had

> set up two twenty-metre tall monolithic self-portraits of quartzose sandstone [built] ... facing twenty-six degrees south of east, where the sun also rises on the winter solstice.... The more northerly was broken in two either by Cambyses II of Persia during his invasion of 525 or by an earthquake, probably that of 27 for quakes are rare in Egypt. From the part that remained intact about an hour after dawn certain days came forth a sound as though of a slight blow, which one would best compare to the breaking of a guitar or lyre-string.... The odd noise drew pilgrims and tourists.... Someone later restored it.... Whoever did [the restoration], the repair was disastrous: the noise ceased abruptly, and the colossi survive to this day in silence.[3]

While the locals apparently wanted to perpetuate the idea of captured sound being played back, the Colossi of Memnon was not really the first jukebox.[4] Subsequent evaluations of the phenomenon removed any remaining romantic notions of the site and its sounds. The third-century restoration did not frighten the noise (or the noisemakers) from the stone. The reality is that the sounds were a natural occurrence. "Geological noises exist, for instance, the 'song of the sands,' the sound of cascading dunes, thought more common on the moon and Mars than in earthly deserts. Rarer but more pertinent is the sound that air makes passing through pores in solid rock as the temperature rises at sun-up."[5] So much for ancient recording devices.

Other examples of the jukebox phenomenon abound. Couples wandering the streets of Rome have deposited countless coins in the many fountains there. Some make the toss to bring love, others to elicit some benevolent power to make their dreams come true. Perhaps the Greeks and the Persians— philosophizing, if not romanticizing — were interested in a form of jukebox entertainment, sometimes created in the desire of eliciting answers in exchange for some small tribute, accepting as proof animate sounds coming from an inanimate object. Ancient citizens with questions requiring answers made the sometimes arduous journey to an oracle. (Plato makes numerous references to oracles.) Still others were satisfied that they and the statues in their midst could commune with one another. "Homeric poems attested to the belief of the Greeks in statues that spoke and later the Greeks and Persians alike consulted oracles before making important decisions."[6] Whether or not there was always a vocalizing priest or quick-thinking entrepreneur hidden behind those earthly structures (much like author L. Frank Baum's character, the Wizard of Oz, working behind the curtains to deceive Dorothy, Tin Man, Scarecrow, and Lion) the durable nature of the stories and legends attest to the interest of mere mortals in being inspired, mystified, guided, and entertained, particularly if a sound was part of the experience.

Music has long been a useful form of communication within a generation, or to convey information beyond the present to subsequent generations: music as oral history. It has been used as an immediate (real-time) messaging system, a signal to commence a celebration or ceremony, and for the "recording" of a tribe's history orally and aurally. Donald Wright speculated in his book *The World and a Very Small Place in Africa* that five centuries (or more) ago in the West African region of the Gambia River, tribes like the Niumi might have used music for any or all of these reasons, including the successful defense of their territory. "If true to a later form [of this music-based communication, the ruler] led a celebration enhanced by palm wine and called in praise-singers— a *mansa* [ruler's] equivalent of court chroniclers— to extol the gallantry of the bowmen."[7] The *mansa* enjoyed music on demand.

Beyond the messages received there were also mechanical aspects to the idea of sound. Cupping a hand behind one's ear improved listening comprehension by channeling the sound reception into the listener's ear. There are numerous indications that ear trumpets have been used for centuries to aid the hearing-impaired. Horatio Alger wrote about "Aunt Jane's Ear Trumpet" in 1865. One character in the story, Mrs. Eleanor Graves, extended a welcome to a visitor:

> "Why Aunt Jane, how do you do? What a pleasant surprise! Arabella
> and I were speaking of you only this morning."
> "Wait a minute, Eleanor," said the old lady, fumbling in her pocket.
> She produced an ear trumpet which she adjusted to her ear.
> "There," said she, "now we can talk."[8]

Historical photos document the availability of manufactured ear trumpets
during the nineteenth century, long before any hearing device could benefit
from the use of electricity. Whether a large sea shell, a manmade horn-
like device, or simply the cupping of one's hand to the ear, the end result
was helpful in focusing sound to the listener. When we see a photograph
of a gramophone (or look carefully at the Grammy Award given out annually to recording artists by NARAS®[9]) it seems unlikely that the creators of
early acoustic recording machines developed the idea of the acoustic horn
in a knowledge vacuum.

Absent a mechanical device, one might consider the church and the
well-heeled aristocracy from the medieval period onward as possessing an
ability to hear music on demand. Many of the composers who left their
mark in the form of great music were, in the most elementary sense, arti-
sans or craftspeople, not unlike painters, sculptors and others who created wonders from materials like glass, wood, metal, or porcelain. Elie
Siegmeister went so far as to compare these composers to their artistic
contemporaries:

> In the medieval Church and in the courts of the absolute monarchs of
> the seventeenth and eighteenth centuries, the musician was consid-
> ered — and to a large extent considered himself — as simply a crafts-
> man, one engaged to provide music for a given purpose just as a cook
> was hired to prepare food, or a carriage-maker to build coaches. In
> none of these cases was there a question of the artisan expressing *his*
> private joys or troubles; his job was to meet the requirements of
> churchman or prince, with the greatest skill and craftsmanship he had
> in him.[10]

Names which are well-recognized today by most people with a rudi-
mentary knowledge of the great European composers, as well as the more
obscure names associated with great music, were joined in a common relationship: at one time or another many were commissioned to create a body
of work or a single composition. Court composers and court musicians
(and those composing for the church) worked at their craft for short or
extended periods of time. For example, the composers on this brief list were
commissioned (or hired, subsidized, etc.) by an assortment of moneyed
sources: Claudio Monteverdi (1567–1643) had Vincenzo Gonzaga, the

Duke of Mantua as a patron; Domenico Scarlatti (1685–1757) spent time at the Court of Madrid; Johann Sebastian Bach (1685–1750) had Prince Cöthen as a benefactor; Josef Haydn (1732–1809) spent one-third of his life at Esterhaz under the patronage of Prince Miklós; and Frédéric Chopin (1810–1849) was aided by Baron Jacques de Rothschild.

In a sense the jukebox phenomenon can be seen in these patrons—Rothschild, Esterhaz, and the others—since they controlled early, on-demand recorded music, although the music was created and recorded in the minds of the composers and on the paper of the day, and playback was a live-and-in-person event. The names of these early recording machines were Monteverdi, Scarlatti, Bach, Haydn, Chopin, Beethoven, and Mozart. On demand, each would create or perform musical works for king, prince, or other aristocratic music lover with sufficient schillings, marks, and francs to support the composer. Orlando Di Lasso at one time served at the pleasure of Catherine de' Medici creating music which was, as Abbe' de Brantôme described, "the most melodious he had ever heard."[11] Factoring in the investment made in each of these (and other) composers, the playing of a selection cost the aristocrat much more than the 25¢ dropped into today's jukebox, but each aristocrat did operate a (human) music-on-demand apparatus.

2

Inventing the Music Industry

The Julian Calendar — that crafted, inventive, adjusted, and tweaked method of assigning markers for the passage of time — was not the first attempt at creating a matrix to organize our lives. Ancient Babylonians, Jews, Greeks, Egyptians, Native Americans, Druids, and Chinese all might legitimately claim a piece of that distinction. It is apparent that our twenty-first-century use of a calendar — at least in the western world — owes some, but not all homage to Caesar. This should serve as a reminder that inventive minds are found throughout the world, with strangers sometimes thinking concurrently about a common idea. It may be a thread that has been picked up by someone years, decades, or centuries after another had that first epiphany, or it may be an entirely new concept. The contemporary inventor might be working in solitude or as part of a team; another inventor or another team may have joined the race (knowingly or not) to be the first to achieve a breakthrough, making the idea practical. So it was with Thomas Edison's phonograph, that durable predecessor to today's digital recordings.

The nineteenth- and early twentieth-century inventors that we are familiar with worked toward a mechanical answer to the problem of recording sound. Early in the process a variety of factors took center stage in their thinking. Those factors were electricity, magnetism, mechanical energy, and the vibrations inherent in sound itself. A variety of minds were attempting to make the connections between airborne vibrations of sound, the resonance of those vibrations, and electromagnetic energy. Joseph Henry (1797–1878), who taught at both the Albany Institute and Princeton, also worked at the Smithsonian, and is credited with helping point those who followed (Thomas Edison, Alexander Graham Bell, Elisha Gray) in the right direction. The vocabulary of the following passage by

Oliver Read and Walter Welch may be somewhat dated, but is nevertheless relevant:

> The theory of electromagnets developed by [Joseph] Henry was fundamental to the telegraph of Morse, the telephone of Bell, to the speaker systems of our modern hi-fi phonographs, to our modern record changing mechanisms, or for that matter to the electric power plants which supply the energy.[1]

German inventor Philipp Reis (1836–1876) was working on the vibrations of sound against a diaphragm (in the process coining the name "telephone" before Bell patented his own ideas.)

Édouard-Léon Scott de Martinville of France (1817–1879) was also working with sound vibrations. In 1856 he developed his phonautograph — a device for tracing and analyzing sound waves. However, Scott's device only traced the vibrations, and was not designed to play back any sounds. "It was, as one historian of the phonograph describes it, 'halfway toward a talking machine.'"[2] The surface for his recording was smoked paper wrapped around a drum or cylinder. As the drum was turned, a stylus felt the vibrations captured on and transmitted from a diaphragm, leaving a wave-like impression on the paper. In addition to moving the concept in the right direction, Scott's phonautograph also provided the name that became synonymous with recorded music and records in the twentieth century: the phonograph.[3] Working in the years between Scott and Edison were F. B. Fenby and M. Charles Cros, both deserving of a brief mention here.

F. B. Fenby was an inventor working in Worcester, Massachusetts, who in 1863 "received a patent for 'The Electro Magnetic Phonograph.'"[4] While the name chosen for the inventions of Fenby and Edison were similar, the dynamics of the two designs were probably not. The other inventor carrying on at the same time as Edison was Frenchman M. Charles Cros (1842–1888). His concept was "apparently inspired by [Édouard-Léon] Scott's device, [which] envisaged a method of photoengraving the visual vibrations on the lampblacked surface."[5] Cros seemed destined for greatness but instead he took a detour through the Academie des Sciences des France, perhaps to his everlasting frustration. Having limited funds, in April 1877 Cros put his ideas (for a *paléophone*) in writing, and deposited papers with the Academie. This filing was made approximately three months before Edison filed preliminary patents with the British government, and eight months before Edison's filings with the United States Patent Office. The only significant recognition Cros received that year was on October 10, 1877, when an article was published about Cros' findings in the magazine *La Semaine du Clerge* (published 1872–1881.) By the time Cros demanded that the Academie open the sealed packet of papers and review his documents, a review which took place on December 3, 1877,[6] Edison's advantage was secure. Thomas Edison's ideas and designs were being publicized, and within days his patents would be recognized as well. While the Cros design differed significantly from Edison's, he was working toward a similar concept. Much like Elisha Gray's telephone — Gray lost out in the patent race with Alexander Graham Bell by a few hours — Cros' ideas were lost in the success of Edison. Whether the Academie forgot to open Cros' envelope or Cros neglected to leave specific instructions is, pardon the expression, academic. In the century-old debate of who gets the credit for the phonograph, "let it be resolved by giving each his due: Charles Cros for being the first to conceive the phonograph, Thomas Edison for being the first to achieve it."[7]

3

Edison's Invention

For those people who are not successful inventors, and that is most of us, it may be difficult to comprehend the process of inventing. In all likelihood, it is similar to the creative process the author of a book or the composer of a song goes through, or for that matter the vision of the artist who paints or sculpts. Two illustrations may help convey the organic nature of the process. Many years ago I participated in a short film project with producer, songwriter, musician, and performer Herb Alpert. During the interview Alpert discussed the creative process and explained that the process may at times appear complex, but it is not complicated. He pointed out that if you have someone that you believe has the ability to be a great musician, performer, or songwriter, you must keep in mind that "it's impossible to *make* things happen. You can't force a musician to play well, you can't force a writer to write great. But what you can do is create the environment for creative things to take place."[1] Paul McCartney said that he woke up one morning believing that he had heard a melody in a dream, but could not identify it even though it seemed familiar. He asked his fellow members of the Beatles about the melody, but none of them found it familiar. McCartney concluded that the melody was his original idea and put it down on paper. That was the origin of the song "Yesterday."[2]

In Thomas Edison's case, he knew the importance of ideas, and he recognized the importance of seizing the moment. One of his rules for aspiring inventors was, "When you are experimenting and you come across anything that you don't thoroughly understand, don't rest until you run it down; it may be the very thing you are looking for or it may be something far more important."[3]

Such a moment for Edison came while he was working on speeding up the telegraph, a wonder when established but nevertheless a nineteenth-century communication device. The telegraph enabled people to transmit information via telegrams over long distances by means of Morse code messages (made up of dots and dashes) that operators "keyed" or sent as electrical impulses through a wire.[4] With practical experience, the people pressing the key and sending the code, the telegraph operators or telegraphers, could achieve a certain speed and then, regardless of their dexterity or ability, could tap the key no faster; there was a finite speed attached to human ability. If, however, one could somehow record the coded message, and then speed up that recording mechanically, one could increase the speed with which messages could be sent or, said another way, one could increase the number of messages sent in the same period of time. Roland Gelatt, writing in *The Fabulous Phonograph*, explained Edison's serendipitous discovery:

> In the summer of 1877 Edison was working on an instrument that transcribed telegrams by indenting a paper tape with the dots and dashes of the Morse code and later repeated the message any number of times and at any rate of speed required. To keep the tape in proper adjustment he used a steel spring, and he noticed that when the tape raced through his instrument at a high speed, the indented dots and dashes striking the end of the spring gave off a noise which Edison described as a "light musical, rhythmic sound, resembling human talk heard distinctly."[5]

To help move the idea from telegraph to phonograph, Edison's staff "rigged up an indenting stylus connected to a diaphragm, which in turn was attached to a telephone speaker. As Edison shouted into the speaker, a strip of paraffin-coated paper was run underneath the stylus."[6] The experiment worked, as the marks and indentations on the paper confirmed the presence of the sound. Running the paper under the stylus again provided a faint reproduction of the "recording." The paper itself provided a permanent record of what was said, or in the case of the telegraph, the message that was keyed. Here then was Edison meeting a phenomenon that took him in another direction.

Edison envisioned the necessary machine and, as an average person might make a point on the back of a napkin at lunch, sketched out the idea. "It was apparently [Edison's November 29, 1877] sketch that his workman, John Kruesi, used to construct the first tin-foil model."[7] As the story goes, Kruesi returned with the machine a day and a half later. Edison wrapped a piece of tinfoil around the cylinder of the machine, and in a description that sounds vaguely familiar to aficionados of the twentieth century's analog recordings, "set the needle, turned the crank, and shouted into the mouthpiece the nursery rhyme that begins, 'Mary had a little lamb.' This was hardly the most profound quotation to utter at the birth of a great invention, but it at least gave fair warning of Edison's future lack of discrimination in the quality of phonographic repertoire."[8] In any case, Edison's idea and design, Kruesi's construction, and "Mary's Little Lamb" had made its point.

After refining his idea, Edison was prepared to make the invention public. There are a number of published dates for the actual invention of Edison's phonograph and the machine's public unveiling. The most likely timing is contained in Allen Koenigsberg's book *Edison Cylinder Recordings*. Koenigsberg lists multiple instances of publication of phonograph-related materials in 1877, including a British patent (July 18), *Scientific American* article (Dec 22), and U.S. Patent filing (December 24). In addition there is the granting of a U.S. patent on February 19, 1878 (patent number 200,521). Koenigsberg's list is plausible given the time-sensitive nature of getting an invention to the patent office and to the public, and also for the timing of Edison's visit to the offices of *Scientific American* on December 7, 1877. That visit inspired the December 22 article which said in part:

> Mr. Thomas A. Edison recently came into this office, placed a little machine on our desk, turned a crank and the machine inquired as to our health, asked how we liked the phonograph, informed us that *it* was very well, and bid us a cordial goodnight. These remarks were not only perfectly audible to ourselves, but to a dozen or more persons gathered around.[9]

4

Cylinders, Discs, and Vision

Hindsight, as the expression goes, is twenty-twenty. When one has grown up with something, it is difficult if not impossible to imagine a time without that thing. Consider recent American consumerism: an automobile for every family; telephones in every home; television, cable TV, satellite dishes, VCRs, and DVDs; personal computers and PDAs; fax machines, beepers and cellular phones; and compact discs. All of these at one time were non-existent. They were often exotic, futuristic novelties when introduced, became luxuries as consumerism expanded, and ultimately matured into necessities. Most are commonplace in the industrialized nations of today. It is appropriate within this latter context to declare Edison's late nineteenth-century vision for the phonograph as remarkably clear.

In 1878, less than one year after he filed his patent, Edison described a variety of uses for his new invention, demonstrating a belief that this would be both a business and a consumer device. Gelatt, Koenigsberg, and others maintain that his list included uses for dictation and stenography, talking books for the blind, talking dolls and music boxes, the teaching and preservation of language, the recording of lectures and instructions from teachers and professors, capturing the dying words of friends and family, voice clocks announcing the hour, and application as an attachment to Bell's still relatively new telephone. Although the telephone was first introduced in 1876, Edison already saw the connection and the need for a recording attachment. There was also the preservation of language and oral literature:

> Edison suggested from the very beginning that his invention could be used to archive the living voices of the dead: "It will henceforth be possible," he wrote, "to preserve for future generations the voices as

26

well as the words of our Washingtons, our Lincolns, our Gladstones, etc., and to have them give us their 'greatest effort,' in every town and hamlet in the country upon our holidays," their utterances "transmitted to posterity, centuries afterwards, as freshly and forcibly as if those later generations heard his living accents."[1]

Happily, Edison also identified the recording of music, although neither music nor entertainment was his preferred application—perhaps due to the fact that Edison was partially deaf from the age of fourteen.[2] Hindsight is one thing. Edison looked ahead one hundred years with clarity. His was the more difficult task.

Edison's new invention caught the imagination of the public, the scientific world, and business. None of this is to suggest that the phonograph was an overnight success. Reality was quite the contrary. It seems that Edison could not get past the novelty stage, as there were at least two immediate problems. One was the primitive voice reproduction that deteriorated significantly with a few plays, discouraging the repeated use of recordings. The other was the limited amount of playing time. Finding short pieces of music, oratory, or spoken word to be used as repertoire was not a problem; convincing a nineteenth-century businessman to dictate a letter or legal document, however, in two-minute increments—the length of the first cylinders—was clearly problematic. Furthermore, those two-minute increments would not include the time it would take to remove one cylinder and replace it with a blank to continue the dictation. Business-use was clearly a good idea in principle but a difficult idea to implement efficiently.

The bloom for the moment off the rose, Edison switched gears to devote most of his waking hours to perfecting the incandescent lamp. This was due at least in part, to a "contract made November 15, 1878 with the newly-formed Edison Electric Light Company, [forcing him] to cease work on the phonograph."[3] In the decade that followed, others would pursue the mission to perfect the recording of sound, but most of the 1880s would be without a practical phonograph. One of Edison's visions for recorded sound was to immortalize performances, language, and voices. Unfortunately, during the 1880s, the voices of president of the Confederacy Jefferson Davis; writer, philosopher and poet Ralph Waldo Emerson; American president Ulysses S. Grant; Swedish soprano Jenny Lind; Hungarian composer Franz Liszt; writer Henry Wadsworth Longfellow; and Union Army general George B. McClellan were all silenced without having been recorded.

Although Edison focused on other ideas, three competing inventors decided to press on. Alexander Graham Bell, Chichester A. Bell (Alexander's cousin), and Charles Sumner Tainter began collaborating in 1880. A new company, or working group, was created for their efforts, known as the Volta Laboratory Association, with the three principals as "associates." With the success of the telephone reasonably secure, though marginally profitable, the focus was to improve the telephone's transmission; the group would also pursue recorded sound. While Edison may have had the benefit of the research of Scott, Fenby, and (Alexander Graham) Bell, the Volta efforts could benefited, at least preliminarily, from Edison's work. Because Edison had received his patents in Britain earlier than in the United States, some of his early work had been refused patent protection in America "for the then novel reason that [Edison's own] English patent covering the same claims constituted prior publication."[4] Armed with knowledge of the British patents, the Bell-Bell-Tainter group began their work in earnest, and with design and workmanship that seemed similar to Edison's, created the graphophone.[5]

> The laboratory notebooks of Charles Sumner Tainter ... reveal that very early in the work of the [Volta] associates their attention became diverted almost exclusively to the phonograph.... The laboratory notes and the various disc and cylinder experimental devices show very clearly that the associates began with the information and sketches contained in Edison's British patent of 1878.[6]

At one point, Tainter even met with Edison. The Volta associates must have been making inroads into Edison's ideas considering that Volta "had in fact built several 'graphophones' during Edison's downtime.... 'This [graphophone] is very similar to Mr. Edison's phonograph,' A. B. Dick, the mimeograph manufacturer, wrote in curiosity to Edison's secretary. 'Perhaps it is the same machine under another name.'"[7] By 1886, the incandescent light was a reality and this left Edison free to renew his attention toward the phonograph. However, what might have provided a virtual monopoly for Edison in 1877 had become a competitive business by the late 1880s.

Both Edison and his competitors had determined that although playback volume would be quieter with wax, it might be the best material for recording and playback. "The use of wax allowed for sharper, better defined recording, though not so loud.... Wax also permitted closer grooving than had tin foil,"[8] therefore permitting a longer duration for the recording. While the next logical step would be the development of suitable recordings, there was one other technical issue to address. The concept of recording on a disc instead of a cylinder was an idea that went at least as far back as Leon Scott. Both Edison and the Volta group wrestled with the idea of using a disc (instead of a cylinder):

The use of a disc as a moving surface [was not] a patentable feature in itself. Edison had made experimental discs in 1878, the Bells and Tainter in 1885. The Phonautographs of Scott had utilized both cylinders and discs as the moving medium upon which was traced the sinuous, but mute, wave patterns of sound.[9]

The cylinder initially prevailed perhaps due in part to the tricky nature of cutting the recording to, and playing the recording back from a disc, a problem which the Bell-Tainter associates worked to solve.

For those who have grown up with a turntable and phonograph records, it takes perspective, a moment to wrap one's head around the problem of the grooves of a record and the spiraled route to the center of the disc. The question at hand is: How long does it take the stylus or needle to make one journey around the record in the first outermost groove, and then, how long to make a similar journey riding in the innermost groove? Bell and Tainter had this issue in mind. "[Their solution] was a continuously variable rpm speed turntable for recording and reproducing disc records, turning slowest when the stylus was at the outer circumference and progressively more rapidly as the stylus approached the center. This permitted a constant speed for the surface passing under the stylus."[10] While the laws of physics and engineering might give some of us a headache, Bell/Tainter solved the problem. In spite of their breakthrough and the potential for discs as a suitable format for recorded music, cylinders (with dimensions approximating two inches in diameter by four inches long) remained the preferred shape during the first decade of recording. However, in the 1890s, another inventor opted to pick up the cause of the disc.

Emile Berliner was developing the flat-disc concept long before his introduction of discs in 1895. He had already been granted a patent (in 1887) for his gramophone. His chosen direction for recording technology also pointed the way to the day of mass-produced discs from a single master recording. This was not an insignificant concept. Without mass production, the first recordings were, in a sense, all originals. The record companies needed to assemble multiple recording-phonographs in the studio, creating a dozen or more copies of each performance for consumer sale. Although Edison had attempted to perfect a molded approach to mass production, problems with the technology and a reluctance to invest the sizeable capital needed to transform cylinder manufacturing "delayed a successful molded cylinder by Edison until 1902."[11]

Berliner and another individual who will be discussed in more detail later, Eldridge Johnson, would make changes in the nature of manufacturing that would have significant implications for the phonograph record business to come, while simultaneously engineering the demise of the cylinder. Berliner was developing the stamped record, and once perfected and adopted, stamping continued to be an integral part of the manufacturing process right through the 1970s (and to a lesser degree beyond). If one considers the basic concepts incorporated into his thinking, Berliner "[was] the first to produce disc records commercially [and] the first to commercially produce stamped or molded records."[12] The shape of recorded music that we are still most familiar with is the disc, and from the earliest days until the advent of compact discs and DVDs, the stamped record has been a mainstay delivery system of recorded music.

5

A Consumer Business or
a Business Technology?

Unifying a single configuration for recorded music took time. Consider for a moment a late twentieth century technological difference of opinion. Beginning in 1979, the burgeoning home video industry debated the virtues of Matsushita's VHS versus Sony's Beta videotape formats. Although many believed that Beta was a superior technology, VHS became the consumer's videotape of choice. This was, in turn, reminiscent of the competing quadraphonic audio playback formats (the so-called discrete and matrix disc technologies) of the early 1970s, and of the competition between 8-tracks and cassette tapes of the 1960s and 1970s. It might be said that the original fight for format dominance in recorded music took place at the turn of the last century, when Berliner's disc took on Edison's cylinder. In the end, the disc carried the day.

Numerous lawsuits due to patent and/or copyright infringement (whether real or perceived) reflected the number of small companies jumping on the recording bandwagon. Fifty patents related to talking machines and phonographs had been filed between 1885 and 1899 by a variety of inventors: Vlademar Poulsen, Eldridge Johnson, Charles Tainter, Chichester Bell, Emile Berliner, Thomas Edison, and thirty others.[1] Patent battles aside, many of the established companies continued to expand, their growth sometimes coming at the expense of others.

Once refocused on his phonograph, Edison established a manufacturing operation in 1887, constructing two factories to create inventory for a new consumer business: to manufacture his talking machines. That same year, the Bell-Tainter assets were incorporated into the newly organized American Graphophone Company. Ultimately the marketing for both companies was consolidated through a common licensee, (the North American Phonograph Company), which in turn, licensed start-up regional

31

companies all over the United States (thirty in all). Consistent with Edison's vision for business use, most of these companies saw the phonograph as a business tool, not necessarily a device to bring music into the home. Ironically, although businessmen were interested, they did not embrace Edison's invention. "Opposition from stenographers, as well as some mechanical difficulties and inconveniences, combined to make the first years less successful than the capitalization of millions of dollars had led the investors to expect."[2]

There existed a reluctance by some musical performers to record for Edison or any of the other existing or soon-to-be companies, due as much to the machines' limitations as any other factor.

> Even at [Edison's] laboratory, the attempts to record produced such abominable scratching and nasal sounds that one prominent pianist turned ash white upon hearing the results, and artists almost unanimously divorced themselves from the machine because of its infidelity.... On January 10, 1891 [Edison] announced: "I have today closed my Music Room and discharged the staff."[3]

A prophetic moment, perhaps, as Edison may have been the first music industry executive to fire his A&R (music) staff for lack of critical and financial success. He did, however, continue to manufacture phonographs. The lack of interest in non-entertainment applications for the player/recorders would ultimately be offset by the gradual move to recorded entertainment, both for the public nickel-in-the-slot machines (early jukeboxes, to be discussed later), and in player/recorders for the home. Prerecorded cylinders and discs for those machines would come from a variety of sources.

Somewhat like the Baby Bell telephone companies of the late twentieth century (created by a court-ordered break-off from AT&T in 1984), early regional phonograph licensees like the Columbia Phonograph Company (headquartered in Washington, D.C.) became aggressive and creative regional marketing companies, some with eyes on an expanding universe of consumers. Music for the machines was being recorded and sold through Columbia and other recording companies. As early as 1891 "Columbia had already issued a [small, ten page] catalogue of its recordings ... which contained twenty-seven marches ... thirteen polkas ... ten waltzes ... and thirty-four items listed as miscellaneous...."[4] Included within this last group were anthems, hymns, and opera. This expanding diversity and categorization of repertoire is in sharp contrast to the first cylinders offered by the companies. During the novelty or introductory phase of the emerging phonograph, "records were sold by volume and not by subject [much less by title or artist]. The customer bought a dozen mixed records instead of choosing the songs he or she preferred."[5]

Faced with limited business support, and compounded by the Panic of 1893 (one of the worst economic depressions in American history), the companies (and the concept of business use) began to fail. In August 1894, the North American Phonograph Company went into bankruptcy. Thomas Edison stepped in to reacquire control of the Edison Company assets of North American, while Columbia acquired other North American assets. It took Edison two years to complete his re-entry into the business, a time during which competing companies gained strength. Joel Whitburn states that while Edison spent two years reorganizing, "Columbia and the regional companies [had] the cylinder record business to themselves. By decade's end, Columbia [had effectively driven] the smaller companies out of business."[6]

The Columbia company and a revitalized Edison, both already significant and recognizable brand names in the record business, were not the only strong players as the century moved toward a close. Emile Berliner started his company, the United States Gramophone Company,[7] in 1895, and began releasing "a new batch of records every month...."[8] The Consolidated Talking Machine Company, the precursor to the Victor Talking Machine Company (later to merge with Berliner and still later to become RCA Victor), was started in 1900. A "big three" group of players evolved. Edison, Victor, and Columbia would wield significant clout as the century turned, since each entered the recording business early, and each established market share through repertoire, distribution, manufacturing, and patents. Each sold machines, and each sold cylinders, discs, or both, although missing was the standardization of technology that most consumers are familiar with, i.e., today's digital compact discs which are playable on any compact disc player in the world.

Early dealers and consumers needed to be brand-loyal, and maintaining brand loyalty depended upon technical support for the players and offering a sufficiently large selection of recordings, whether cylinders or discs. Many record-buyers alive today recall the wave of *record-retailing* that took off in the 1960s. That expansion fueled by the postwar baby boom created a music buying experience that had echoes of those earliest years, where increasingly growth was built more on record selection and less on equipment. Like those early Edison (and other) dealers, many of the businesses selling records between the mid–1930s and the mid–1960s were record, phonograph, radio (and later television and *hi-fi*) stores; examples include entrepreneurs like Sam Sniderman (Sam the Record Man in Toronto,) and department stores like Bloomingdale's. These and other retailers catered to music customers by having a good selection of records and by building listening booths enabling customers to hear the music before they'd buy. Without radio, whose impact could not be felt until the 1920s, the retailers in the first thirty years sold records, cylinders, phonographs or gramophones. Beyond advertising, listening booths and word-of-mouth were essential.

The more successful the labels became the more inventory was created by those labels, and in turn, the more inventory a good store was required to carry. The more product that the record companies released, the improved opportunity for consumers to develop an expanding taste for recordings. "By 1910 the average store needed a stock of 3,000 to 5,000 records to keep pace with the output of new songs and the changing public taste."[9] The variety of recorded genres continued to expand as documented by Columbia and other companies in their printed catalogs and numerous recordings. Added to the marches, polkas, waltzes, anthems, hymns, and opera were spoken word recordings (including the words of great statesmen of the day) and foreign-language courses. William Shakespeare was represented in Columbia's A-series catalog — *Merchant of Venice* and *As You Like It*; so was Abraham Lincoln; humor was found in the guise of fictional characters named Casey, Clancy, Brady, Flanagan, Lewinsky and Cohen, each offering their ethnically charged views on life.

The established, dominant position of the Big Three perpetuated the aforementioned lack of standardization. Emile Berliner had been an early visionary (1888) and proponent of standardization (including "the interchangeability of records") before the recorded music business *was* a business. Berliner's vision, which he articulated in a speech, was, unfortunately for consumers, not quickly realized. Twenty years after Berliner's speech advocating music-industry standardization, there remained

> a confusing number of different options for the prospective customer. First there was the choice of cylinder or disc player. Discs were available in either lateral or vertical cut [groove systems]. Each company's cylinders came in different sizes and were recorded to a different number of grooves to the inch.... Recording speeds were determined by whoever was operating the machine.[10]

Without standardization of equipment and software, the Big Three companies continued to imitate one another's repertoire. This imitation can be seen in some obvious examples of artists competing with themselves, and of companies copying each other.

6

"A&R": Artists and Repertoire

Helping create the recordings for the emerging music companies was a new specialist, the A&R person. For the early music business, the phrase *artists and repertoire* reflected a duality of purpose: it represented the union of two important elements in successful recordings—the performers (artists) and the songs that they performed and recorded (repertoire). The A&R Director became the defined position within a recording company responsible for developing the actual recordings. During the early recording business owner/entrepreneurs functioned as de facto heads of A&R. Gradually other employees were given or assumed the role.

Fred Gaisberg was the Victor A&R person credited with signing young Italian tenor Enrico Caruso in 1902 (the significance of which will be discussed later in this book.) Gaisberg's music-business education took place within the evolving music industry of the 1890s. "He began in the industry as a laboratory assistant at the age of 16 and went on to work in several company labs including those of Volta, Columbia, and Berliner."[1] Gaisberg grew as an executive through his travels and through his contributions to establishing company offices, player manufacturing facilities, disc pressing plants, and recording studios; it was a personal evolution that eventually included A&R. Like many successful A&R people today, Gaisberg began as a teenaged employee and became a seasoned international executive.

The raw human material which would be transformed into the recording artists of the 1890s, and to a lesser degree throughout the first thirty years of recorded music, included singers with little or no stage experience and stage performers with no recording experience. Vaudeville, Broadway, concerts, and various theaters were sources for this recording talent. With some exceptions, professional recording artists, who often had limited fame or were relative unknowns when they started recording, pre-dated musical stars of any magnitude as the mainstay of the new world of recording. In his book *Popular American Recording Pioneers: 1895–1925* Tim Gracyk offers some rationale for the unknown performers preceding the knowns:

> It is important to recognize a distinction between stage personalities who happened to make some recordings when they found time in their busy schedules, and artists who made their living largely by recording regularly, perhaps finding a little time on the side for theatrical performances, vaudeville, or concert recitals. Few stars of the stage made records regularly.[2]

It is easy to identify recent performers who have attempted a large or small measure of so-called artistic growth and subsequently succeeded in multiple fields of entertainment. Frank Sinatra moved from 1940s band singer to actor and producer in the 1950s and 1960s, while Madonna made the transition from singer to actor and author almost forty years later. By contrast, in the early years of the recording industry, any opportunity for a career crossover was likely to be limited. Distilling some of the reasons suggests the following key points:

1. Time: Unknowns probably had few lengthy commitments to occupy their time, thus allowing them the freedom to make recordings as needed. As Gracyk suggests, obligations to their careers precluded established stage performers from committing significant time for recordings.

2. Inventory: The pre–mass production years required durable performers, singers and musicians willing to spend the time as well as the physical and mental stamina needed in the studio to create sufficient inventory, including recording the same title repeatedly as the individual recording machines were unloaded and then reloaded with blank cylinders. (See Chapter 9, "Recording and Recordings.")

3. Money: Prior to any reliable royalty system, established stage performers could make more money in the theaters than through the fees paid by the recording companies. The concomitant outcome was that recording companies made larger profits on the non-stage professionals by paying flat fees for the recording sessions (i.e., works for hire). Flat-fee sessions provided the labels with an inducement to exploit the ranks of the unknowns.

4. Repertoire: Professional recording artists could devote necessary time and energy to the many new songs coming from New York's music publishers, i.e., those who "songwriter-newspaperman Monroe Rosenfeld

[characterized as Tin Pan Alley publishers] when he was writing a series of articles for the *New York Herald....*"[3] New material was generally a fresh alternative to the reworking of familiar songs from the stage. Established stars who had developed a loyal following based on some consistency of their repertoire were less likely to record whatever songs the company executive asked (or told) them to record.

5. Competition: The unknowns were essentially employed to quickly learn and record the music, lyrics, rhythm, and style, to enable a record label to bring new recordings to the marketplace before the competition. Timing was not insignificant.

6. Career considerations: Because idiosyncracies or nuances inherent in the early machines it was often unpredictable how one's voice would sound once recorded. In the 1890s reputations were at stake. Two writers have addressed the quality of the playback and its impact on potential recordings by established artists. Andre Millard wrote that "the great stars refused to sing into the horn of the phonograph because they knew that it could not do justice to their voices."[4] Robert Conot (see Chapter 5) says that "attempts to record produced such abominable scratching and nasal sounds that ... artists almost unanimously divorced themselves from the machine because of its infidelity...."[5]

7. Understanding: Novices (to the world of recorded music) entering the recording studio in the post–World War II music industry generally knew little of the actual process involved in a recording session. Many new recording artists found it was sometimes a matter of entering the studio, learning the song to be recorded, being taught where and how to sit or stand in front of the microphones, and finally beginning to play or sing as the tape captured the moment. Even when ready, "run-throughs" were needed to insure that the performer knew the material, recording levels were properly set and so on. For the earliest recording artists there was no microphone, just a room and the recording phonographs. Stand too close and unwanted vocalized sounds could be heard; too far away and other ambient noise from the room or from outside could be recorded. Logic dictates that experienced studio performers would understand and avoid potential problems. Stage performers, regardless of expertise on stage, needed to learn the nuances associated with the recording process, because time is money.

An example of a prolific, early professional recording artist is John W. Myers. One way to document Myers' success is to look at Joel Whitburn's research. Whitburn lists thirty-one "chart"[6] recordings for Myers at a number of labels including Columbia (24), New York (1), New Jersey

(1), and Victor (6) between 1892 and 1907.[7] Allen Koenigsberg has identified twenty-two titles, all of them recorded for Edison between 1901 and 1907,[8] and Tim Gracyk has numbered Myers' recordings for the Victor Talking Machine Company (beyond Whitburn's "charted" releases) at more than one hundred. Gracyk also has biographical information on Myers. "Born in Wales, he emigrated to America at age twelve and worked at various jobs, eventually becoming a theatrical manager in New York."[9] The fact that he performed with a touring opera company should not suggest that he was a star of the stage, but rather that he had a voice worth recording. His fame therefore stemmed primarily from his success as a recording artist.

If Myers' history helps one understand the difference between a performing artist (initially an unknown) and stars of stage, other examples help illustrate the A&R duality — matching artists with repertoire. Although finding artists and matching them with repertoire was becoming a separate calling within the music industry, these new A&R professionals were not above lifting a good idea from a competitor, or in some cases lifting the artist. First, consider the case of Byron Harlan, another of the early successful recording stars. The Library of Congress contains listings for 73 separate recordings by Harlan, while the Edison catalog lists 130 solo recordings by him plus additional recordings he did with others. What is interesting, particularly considering the artist-label exclusivity inherent in today's recording industry, is the apparent lack of exclusivity for Harlan. In the course of Harlan's success during the period, he had recordings released by at least four different companies, at times competing with himself. He recorded and released those recordings through Columbia (1901–1917), Edison (1899–1919), Victor (1904–1915), and Indestructable (1909–1910).[10] Looking at one specific example in September 1905, Harlan achieved success with the recording of "A Picnic for Two" on Columbia, while another Harlan recording, "Would You Care," simultaneously appeared on Victor.

More significant than an artist competing with his or her own recordings was the copycat nature of the companies. It was not unusual for companies to imitate each other's repertoire. If one label began to have success with a particular song, another label's A&R person might seize the opportunity to record a new version of the song for their company. With a lack of standardization, it made sense for strong or proven repertoire to be offered by any and all competing companies (and competing technologies). The practice of recording cover versions[11] is still around today, although it is less likely to be a simultaneous event as was the case from the earliest days of the music business right through the 1980s. The inability of the early machines to play each other's recordings facilitated a business climate tailored for imitation. The Victor, Edison, and Columbia labels—and their retail dealers—could not afford to let customers walk out of their stores simply because another label had a popular song that they could not offer. The cover concept was easiest to exploit when the material, the song, was readily apparent (and available) to the various East Coast-based companies, usually through exposure in vaudeville, musical variety, or Broadway theater.

One can illustrate the early cover-version efforts by looking at the process surrounding a particular song. Consider "Bedelia," a song by William Jerome and Jean Schwartz that enjoyed popular success in America. Helped by its inclusion in the Broadway musical *The Jersey Lily* (1903) and its wide use in vaudeville, "Bedelia" was "the decade's first 3,000,000 seller [in sheet music form]...."[12] Apart from the stage success, vaudeville use, and sheet music sales, four separate recordings of "Bedelia" were available in January 1904 from three major labels. All four recordings—Billy Murray on Edison, George Gaskin on Columbia, and the Haydn Quartet and Arthur Pryor's Band on Victor — appear to have attained near-simultaneous release and success (based on the reconstructed 1904 popularity charts). Therefore, whichever brand of equipment that consumers owned, they could hope that their machine's retailer would have a playable version of a popular song (like "Bedelia") for their preferred brand of phonograph.

Other aspects of being competitive began to evolve. Regardless of the lack of standardization, consumer interest in recordings was growing, and with some justification. A higher standard of living and education in the sometimes newly-industrialized world often included the accumulation of personal wealth. As late nineteenth-century American wealth grew, that growth brought an increased appreciation of music; that appreciation, in turn, led some members of the wealthier families to a proficiency on a musical instrument, and consequently the piano often became the centerpiece in late nineteenth century homes. "The piano, because it cost a small fortune, became the prime status symbol of the bourgeois home. [Musical] scores could be collected, but they had to be [either] piano music or piano and voice ... since the ladies were expected to exhibit their skills after dinner."[13]

Evan Eisenberg goes on to suggest that recordings appeared at a propitious moment when performance was transformed from its exclusive existence as a "live" event to something more. He writes that "in 1877 music began to become a thing." With that evolution, music moved from the ethereal to the real, the tangible. Like books or fine art, music could take its place among the other cultural objects in one's life. Furthermore, for the question "why buy and collect recordings?" Eisenberg set down his rationale on the collectible nature of culture (music included) within society as follows:

    1. The need to make beauty and pleasure permanent. As beautiful sights and sounds go by, one tries to grab them rather than trust them ... to come around again.
    2. The need to comprehend beauty.... Certainly owning a book or a record permits one to study the work repeatedly at one's convenience.
    3. The need to distinguish oneself as a consumer. In capitalism there are first heroes of production and then (as [David] Riesman has shown) heroes of consumption.
    4. The need to belong. Considered as a feeling, this need might be called nostalgia. When one feels nostalgia for a time one has lived in or wishes one had lived in, cultural objects are a fairly dignified tonic.
    5. The need to impress others or oneself. This can be simple philistine snobbery or something subtler.[14]

This cultural repositioning of recordings (as a mass-market commodity and collectible) began as (a) the economy recovered from the 1893 Depression, (b) competition between phonograph manufacturers and record labels heated up, and (c) prices of cylinders, discs and players came down due to manufacturing efficiencies and competitive pricing.

    As a greater variety of phonograph models—and in many cases higher quality machines—were being sold, and as improved availability and quality of the recordings were perceived by the consumers, sales increased. Furthermore (and because of competition, availability of titles, cheaper phonographs and improvements to cylinder and disc quality,) the masses—not just the wealthy—could become interested in owning the machines, and could subsequently be transformed into recording *consumers* and *collectors*. In short, income was no longer an impediment to the arts. With lower prices in the late 1890s, even Edison chimed in with public statements proclaiming that no family was so poor that it could not afford a talking machine. As an early advertisement for Enrico Caruso's recordings (and for Victor recordings in general) stated, when one heard Caruso in their own home, they heard him *"just as truly as if [they] were listening to him in the Metropolitan Opera House."* One would not necessarily expect to see the masses at the opera (particularly since most could not afford the price of a ticket), but the opera could now be brought home.

    All of these companies, it must also be restated, were producing acoustic recordings, as this was the pre-electric, pre-microphone era. In these early days, the acoustic horn (not the microphone) was the center of the recording session, and often the "studio" was the room in which the talking machine, gramophone, graphophone or phonograph — cylinder or disc — happened to be placed. The acoustics of the rooms, like the machines themselves, would undergo an evolution in design. Form followed function.

Edison's expectations for the phonograph minimized any prerecorded music applications. Consequently, it should come as no surprise that his approach to recording music was not very discriminating. He did not appear to envision, for example, a need to create stars or negotiate with high-priced musical talent. Music was one of many uses for the phonograph, and the quality of what went onto the cylinder or disc was far less important to Edison than simply having a cylinder (or disc) to sell for his machines.

For the first recordings made to demonstrate the new invention, Edison chose the spoken word, not music. The original demonstration-cylinder for the phonograph brought to the offices of *Scientific American* magazine featured a "conversation" with the phonograph. Edison's first recording was a nursery rhyme. His further contributions to his company's recorded repertoire did not stray too far: he chose to read "Jack and Jill," "Rub-a-dub-dub," and "Three Blind Mice." He recorded "the first four lines from the 'Now is the winter of our discontent' speech of *Richard III*.... Other favorite pieces included excerpts from the currently popular songs 'John Brown's Body,' 'Old Uncle Ned,' 'La Grande Duchesse,' and 'The Wandering Refugee'...."[15] Edison also recorded a number of poems, including Thomas Grey's "Elegy" and Edgar Allen Poe's "Annabel Lee."

A&R evolved, companies adapted their approach to repertoire, recording artists began to understand the machines. And money was being made.

7

Speaking of Money,
and the Jukebox

Financially speaking, early recorded music consumerism was not for the faint of heart as one needed disposable income to purchase the new machines and the cylinders and discs to go with them. While the true commercialization of the machines would begin in the 1880s, as early as 1878 "the first few publicly available phonographs were coming out of [Edison's] Menlo Park machine shop at a price of $100 apiece...."[1] To put this in perspective, based on the consumer price index, a phonograph that carried an 1878 retail price of $100 would be comparable to a player selling for almost $1800 in year 2004's inflation adjusted dollars (IADs).[2] It would take twenty years for changes in technology (moving from battery operated electric machines to models that used a hand-crank and were spring-driven) to make the machines far more affordable.

Edison introduced a home model in 1896 that carried a $40 price (approximately $800 IADs), and in 1897 "came the $20 Edison Standard Phonograph [$400 IADs], which was indeed to be a standard model — with minor modifications—for over three decades."[3] By 1897, the retail price for some of Edison's machines had dropped 80 percent from the original tinfoil models of 1878, but $20 still might easily represent one month's income for a worker or the family, far too large a commitment for most. And yet expensive models were still being sold to those who could afford them. For example, an Edison advertisement in the June 1899 *Atlantic Monthly Advertiser* featured the pricey Edison Concert Phonograph. The ad copy stated: "It perfectly reproduces the human voice just as loud — just as clear — just as sweet. It duplicates instrumental music with pure-toned brilliance and satisfying intensity.... The price is $125.00 [$2600 IADs]."[4] The same ad reminded the reader that Edison manufactured six other inexpensive models including the Gem, which could be had for $7.50.[5]

   Retail prices set by Edison and other companies continued to drop as competition remained intense and refinements in design and efficiencies of manufacturing permitted. Scaled-down, stripped-down models would be developed that carried prices at or below Edison's $20.00 machine or even lower than the $7.50 Gem player of 1899. Prices for phonographs would eventually cover the consumer's economic spectrum; but the overall trend was definitely lower. Much like late-twentieth century low-price marketing by East Coast electronic and music retailers Crazy Eddies and The Wiz, price wars were not uncommon in the late 1890s or early 1900s. Once a high-end consumer item, phonograph prices dropped "as fast as new machines entered the market. Edison's final shot was the Gem introduced in 1899, a tiny (7-pound) machine that could play only records. It competed with the Columbia Company's popular Eagle cylinder player...."[6] Each company attempted to gain customers and in-turn create brand-loyal consumers by introducing players at ever-lower prices. One need only look at a model called the "Toy" and see that price was becoming *the* marketing ploy. The Toy sold for $3.00, barely qualified as a phonograph, and looking at photographs of the machine it seems the quality may have been, at best, dubious. Nevertheless, competition was here to stay.

   By 1902 the Graphophone Company was manufacturing and selling three players retailing between $15 and $30. The upper-tier customer was not ignored, nor was he expected to make price the only purchase criterion. During the late 1890s and the early 1900s, models continued to be manufactured and sold by various companies with prices between $100 and $200 ($1800 to $3600 in 2004 IADs.) Suggested list prices, both the highs and the lows, show a business pushing at the edges of consumer spending. Phonograph makers developed an evolutionary understanding of the realities of the bottom (mass market, thin profit margins) and the potential of the top (diminutive market, fat profit margins,) and of course anything in between. The growth (and the breadth) of the market for phonographs continued well into the first two decades of the twentieth century.

   The September 15, 1916 issue of *Talking Machine World* totaled more than one hundred pages of which twenty-three (one-fifth of that issue's pages) contained various size ads for twenty different phonograph manufacturers.[7] Advertised prices in this issue ranged from less than $5 ($82.50 in 2004 IADs) to at least one model retailing, according to the ad, for $2000 ($33,000 IADs.) This latter example was a very expensive model from the Aeolian Company of New York, specifically a model from their Vocalion-branded Art series. Aeolian had apparently gained a solid reputation from their manufacturing of high-end musical instruments, which must have justified their high prices.

Aeolian's ad in that issue of *Talking Machine World* described their manufacturing of "such superb productions as the Steinway Pianola, the Duo-Art Pianola, the modern Weber Piano and the Aeolian Pipe organ — the finest and costliest evolution of this most magnificent of instruments." This top-of-the-market cabinet version contained Aeolian's *Graduola*, "the Vocalion tone control [which allowed one to use] slight, instinctive pressures to shade each tone or phrase, to make the music live with your own feeling and thought.... It is the test which without exception gives a broad and instant vision of the inner and greater pleasure of music [and] brings home the gripping interest of the power of expression in music."[8] Obviously the ability of the owners to adjust the sound quality using tone controls (a precursor to treble/bass adjustment dials and the graphic equalizer) had its first incarnation in these early days of the phonograph industry.

At the turn of the last century the prices of phonographs spanned the personal income spectrum. At the entry-level one sacrificed quality — tone, resonance, adjustability, craftsmanship, durability, cabinetry, style, elegance — while at the upper reaches one chose to sacrifice nothing, at least nothing available for phonographs up to that moment in time.

The price of the software — the cylinders and discs for the phonographs, graphophones, and gramophones — also reflected the dynamics of the market. You can assume that if one could afford the high price of a phonograph in 1889 or 1890, he should also be able to afford the cylinders and discs.[9] Those early buyers found their favorite recorded singers, solo instrumentalists, vocal groups, combos, and bands could be a little pricey, some running as high as $2 each (compared to sheet music which was selling for 25¢-60¢.[10]) The real price of each such recording was the equivalent of $20 to $40 in IADs. In the age of digital downloads and CD burners, a full-length $15–20 compact disc containing twelve digitally recorded, digitally mastered, and digitally delivered musical performances seems overpriced to some. To nineteenth-century consumers contemplating the purchase of one song, recorded and played back with this new (noisy, scratchy, but still wondrous) technology the price must have seemed even higher. "Prices continued to fluctuate; the January, 1891 *Phonogram* gave the range as from $1.00 to $2.00 each, and oddly, by September of 1891, the prices had increased to $1.50 each for the Band records, and $1.50, $1.75, and $2.00 for the vocals...."[11]

By the mid-to-late 1890s prices were approximately 50¢ per disc ($10 IADs). The Columbia Phonograph Company issued a catalog in 1897 that featured almost one thousand selections. The most prolific Columbia artists were Len Spencer solo recordings (154 selections), Dan Quinn (120), George J. Gaskin (115), the Columbia Orchestra (109), the United States Marine Band (38), and Russell Hunting (35). Performances included male vocalists, orchestras, vocal quartets, trios and duos, yodeling, German dialect, French and German language, piccolo solos, banjo solos, clarinet solos, xylophone solos, cornet solos, artistic whistling, spoken word (including auctioneers), minstrel songs, marches, and humor (as in the series of Casey recordings, e.g., "Casey at Denny Murphy's Wake"). Columbia priced their entire catalog of recordings at "50 cents each, or $5.00 per dozen." In 1899 the National Gram-o-phone Company published an equally impressive catalog of recordings available for purchase at 50¢ each or $6 per dozen. With the advent of two-sided discs, prices crept a little higher: Zon-o-phone was selling two-sided discs for 65¢, according to their 1909 and 1910 catalogs.[12]

As with the introduction of many new consumer devices, a technological consumer "bell curve" can be seen during these early years. In 1889 and on into the early 1890s, individuals or families with sufficient disposable income — and a desire to be the first to own a new device — would have been the *Innovators*: those willing to be the first to adopt the talking machines or phonographs. Following this first group were the *Early Adopters*: these consumers were influenced by exposure to the new phonographs at retailers, through newspaper stories, or possibly at the homes of friends. The machines, however, continued to be too expensive for many in society. The *Pragmatists* began to enter the marketplace after they observed the phonograph's widening acceptance in society. Early pragmatists may not yet have viewed the phonograph as an absolute necessity, but any problems associated with the new technology seemed minor: their risk seemed minimal and pricing now came closer to their level of disposable income. The curve reached its peak during the *Pragmatist* phase as the market expanded, showed signs of maturity, and prices continued to fall. Finally, the *Traditionalists* purchased the phonograph. This last group now assumed that the technology was sound, its value/price ratio was reasonable, or that list prices alone were nearing the bottom; more and more people across class lines seemed to be buying, using, and enjoying the technology. You may recall parts of Evan Eisenberg's earlier (see Chapter 6) rationale: (a) "the need to distinguish oneself as a consumer," (b) "the need to belong," and (c) "the need to impress others or oneself." Human nature helped overcome economic realities.

Purchase and use of the machines in the home, as the bell-curve assessment implies, went from the wealthy (first-in) to the mass-market (last-in) consumers. In the early 1890s the price of machines remained high, appealing only to consumers in the more affluent parts of society. One can make a reasonably safe assumption that at that moment in American history, those affluent consumers would most often have been of white, European ancestry. Consequently their musical tastes would have been in two worlds: they were connected to the fine arts (from a European perspective) and the popular arts (from their American experience.) Given the expense of the machines and the cylinders—which limited the early consumer market—other options needed to be evaluated in an effort to make money from the new phonograph beyond selling players to the affluent. If people couldn't afford to purchase a phonograph, why not get them to rent one? If not actually renting a phonograph, why not get the masses to experiment with the phonograph one song at a time? It was just such an idea that led to the jukebox.[13]

The first jukebox was not a machine coming off of a production line. When the enterprising distributor, Pacific Phonograph Company (and its general manager Louis Glass) added a coin mechanism to an existing Edison phonograph it paved the way for the jukebox. If the phonograph could not yet be marketed and succeed as a mass-market consumer product, renting plays of the records for 5¢ each was the beginning of an alternative to the high cost of buying a home player. Phonograph companies in New York, Chicago and elsewhere arrived at a similar conclusion or simply adapted the idea from San Francisco, and the jukebox was born. The answer came in the form of a

> nickel-in-the-slot operating device.... On November 23, 1889, [the Pacific Phonograph Company] installed it in the Palais Royal Saloon in San Francisco. It was equipped with four listening tubes and a coin slot for each tube. Thus for each playing of the [song] the machine would take in from five to twenty cents. [It only took a matter of months for Glass to conclude that] here was the way to "coin" money.[14]

The cylinders and discs of the early business were expensive purchases for consumers, as the recorded music business had not yet developed significant methods for mass-production. Each of the first production cylinders was an original recording. Multiple machines would simultaneously begin recording and then be reloaded to record the same song again (or begin recording a new song.)[15]

Early attempts at creating multiple copies from one original cylinder progressed in stages. The first was a method best described as "acoustic master playback to recorder." Koenigsberg assumes that Edison began with "tubes [which] led from the master phonograph (as many as ten were used during the actual recording process) to blank cylinders on other phonographs.... Shortly afterwards a pantograph system was developed.... By March 18, 1892, the Edison Phonograph Works was getting 150 copies from each original."[16] The pantograph concept, as Koenigsberg described, was a system whereby the stylus tracking through the grooves in the original master cylinder was attached to multiple styluses recording that same information onto blank cylinders. While the move from all originals to (a) acoustic tubes and then (b) the pantograph copying system significantly changed the availability of inventory, there was still vast improvement to come. After all, there was the generational loss of sound quality, a common occurrence when making analog copies.[17] Poor sound quality motivated a number of individuals to improve production even further.

Eldridge Johnson worked to bring mass production to recorded music, achieving the necessary breakthrough between 1896 and 1900, when his company began work for Emile Berliner's gramophone company. Although Johnson was originally hired to manufacture parts for Berliner, he also worked on the twin concepts of improving the sound of Berliner's discs and finding a way to mass produce them — ultimately for himself and other companies.

8

Toward Mass Production

Eldridge Johnson believed that he had found a way to profoundly change at least one significant aspect of the recording industry. His idea was to bring mass production to the manufacture of music discs. In fact, Johnson's and Emile Berliner's work would provide the foundation for the mass production of discs for most of the next century. The plan was to record the performance, creating an original master recording, then carefully duplicate the master to preserve the original recording while still having a suitable copy to use during mass production; this copy would be used for stamping discs from some malleable material (rubber or wax), making the final copies which could be sold to consumers.

As the inventors envisioned it, the original disc, that is the disc that would ultimately contain the master recording, needed to be preserved by coating it with a substance to permanently preserve the vibrations. One has only to picture a finger running through the dusty surface of a neglected table or shelf to visualize the basic concept. Instead of dust, Berliner (and Johnson) experimented with ideas from lampblack (fine soot collected as burned carbon residue) to wax before settling on a fatty film.[1] Questions on how to mass produce discs were being explored even as Edison's recommitment to the cylinder phonograph was yielding results. One might say that Berliner and Johnson were thinking "outside the box," or more to the point, beyond the cylinder:

> In his original patent [1887–88] specifications, Berliner had mentioned the possibility of engraving a gramophone record by chemical action; ... Berliner proposed to coat a zinc disc with some workable substance, inscribe the recording on that surface, and then immerse the disc in an acid bath; the acid, he reasoned, would eat away the metal where the recording stylus had made its tracings, leaving a shallow groove of even depth etched into the zinc. It took several months of experimentation to find a suitable coating. Lampblack would not do

[as] it did not resist the acid solution.... Berliner developed a method of coating the zinc with a thin fatty film that responded to the stylus and yet was impervious to acid.[2]

Simply stated, during the recording process the stylus would cut through the coating leaving a semipermanent record of the sounds. When the disc was acid-washed, the area untouched by the stylus was smooth while the stylus-cut areas (the grooves, and the information inside those grooves) became permanently preserved. (Regardless of its potential, Berliner's achievement would not be utilized until the mid-1890s.) The result was the creation and, in effect, the preservation of an original master disc. Creating copies of the master — i.e., designing the steps which would enable the label's manufacturing plant to have a sufficient number of the necessary stamping discs— would eventually allow for the start of mass production.

In order to safeguard the original recording and ultimately create a stamper, the first disc (the original master disc) would need to be protected and copied, and to accomplish this multiple steps followed the creation of the original master recording. While relatively straightforward, one must remember that as the reflected image in a mirror can be true, it is also reversed. To accomplish the copying and preservation of the master disc, the disc proponents would develop a process of creating a series of alternately *positive* and *negative* copies of the master discs; in the last step, the process would create a (positive) disc for consumers to purchase.

In an effort to clarify the process, it makes sense to borrow from both early and late twentieth century disc-manufacturing terminology. The original disc was the (positive) *master recording* or *lacquer* and needed to be carefully preserved by sealing or electroplating. Making an impression from that disc would then create a mold, which was a negative copy, the aforementioned mirror image. This negative was known as the *metal* (manufacturing) *master*, or *father*. A subsequent copy made by that negative master would create a positive copy known today as the mother. From that positive came another copy known as a *stamper*, and therefore it too was a negative. The last disc in the process was the one a consumer would buy, and it was a positive made of shellac or vinyl, which could be sold to consumers. A simple flow chart of the various discs contained within the complete manufacturing process (and the designation of each as positive or negative) might look like this:

original	*manufacturing*			
lacquer disc	*metal master*			
master recording —>	*(father)* —>	*mother* —>	*stamper* —>	*shellac/vinyl disc*
(positive)	*(negative)*	*(positive)*	*(negative)*	*(positive)*

If one thinks about using the negative of a photograph to create multiple photographic prints, Johnson and Berliner wanted to create the musical negative so that multiple positive copies could be made for sale to consumers. If a stamper became worn or broken, a new stamper could be created from the "mother" without jeopardizing the original metal master recording. The result: mass production.[3]

Recalling the earlier statement from Allen Koenigsberg — "By March 18, 1892, the Edison Phonograph Works was getting 150 copies from each original" — one can see that a move toward an even more significant process of mass production could considerably change the supply and profitability of the music industry. Production costs tumbled and manufacturers lowered their prices. Sales jumped — and profits soared, since the new production costs were far below even the lowest consumer price. An Edison mass-produced cylinder cost 7 cents to make and sold for 50 cents.[4] These price reductions would be the equivalent of compact disc retail prices in the year 2003 dropping from $17.98 to $6.98, $4.98, or less. As recordings became more affordable, people were more inclined to become record consumers and collectors.

Maybe it was price after all that kept the greater part of American society from validating their own lives in some small way with recorded music — much like the idea, as Evan Eisenberg suggested earlier, that recorded music *could* replace books, or at least be on par with books. Collecting suggests that human beings have *some* interest beyond "self." Was this the early tangible evidence that our lives were not entirely insular, that something beyond ourselves had meaning and a durability beyond our own mortality? This all may sound somewhat mystical or metaphysical, but it should not be instantly dismissed or discounted. "Perfect preservation is a matter not simply of technology, but of ontology as well. A defect of preservation is a defect of reification...."[5] Whether price was connected directly to pride — a chance now for multiple castes within American society to "keep up with the Joneses" — collecting recorded music was probably inevitable.

By the second half of the twentieth century, record collections had become the norm in most homes, in some cases with two or three generations of recordings found under one roof. Mass production enabled mass consumption. From sales of about 500,000 records in 1897, numbers skyrocketed to 2.8 million in just two years.[6] Recordings had clearly begun their evolution into a mass-market, consumer product, in effect re-writing their business model. Sales in 1899 totaled almost three million units, a six-fold increase in just two years The music industry, as it was becoming an industry, was transformed. Instead of redundant recording sessions creating hundreds of copies of a particular song, the manufacturing side could now create thousands of mass-produced units, hundreds of titles, and simultaneously filling and creating consumer demand.

9

Recording and Recordings

Ready to sell the phonographs to waiting buyers and the recordings to waiting collectors were a combination of retailers, wholesalers, and direct merchants. In some cases the retail sales came from stores that were owned or licensed (on an exclusive or non-exclusive basis) by one of the three primary manufacturers. The three big music companies dominated their relatively new industry. Wholesalers would sell to a variety of phonograph dealers, furniture stores, and catalog houses. Both the Sears Roebuck and Montgomery Ward catalogs, for example, carried inexpensive machines and a selection of recordings, but as many long-distance purchasers found out the difficulty of keeping those early machines mechanically functional often influenced a local buying decision rather than a less-expensive long-distance, mail-order catalog version.

A question that the inventor or one observing the evolution of an idea might ask is: To what end? Not every inventor can see past the immediate application of the idea. For example, in Edison's case business use was his primary concept. He could also predict that music would be one application of his invention, but in 1878 he was unable to anticipate the breadth and depth of recordings to come, or the potential dollar value such a music-oriented business could generate.[1] The recording process, as well as the machines, needed to evolve. Changes in style and price of player/recorders were mirrored by changes in genres of music and the pricing of cylinders and discs.

In an earlier chapter the discussion touched on the vibrations of sound, diaphragms, and the shape and action of sound waves, all of which were associated with the initial hypotheses of Scott, Tainter, Bell, and Edison. Most of them spent time thinking about transferring the vibrations from the air to the artificial diaphragm and, in turn, to paper, paper tape, disc, wax, rubber, or tin foil. The surface onto which the information would be transferred needed to have the necessary characteristics to leave at least a semi-permanent impression of the sound or sound wave. The end result of their search was to conclude that a machine could be created to capture sound and play it back again. One of the problems that needed to be overcome was the fact that not all sounds create an equal effect — that is to say that not all sounds generate an identical sound wave within the recording process. When suggesting such an "acoustic inequality" Andre Millard described the problem and the process using wax as a recording surface:

> The wave form [which was] cut into the wax changed proportionately with the pitch of the sound during recording: high frequencies caused narrow, densely packed waves, while the low notes caused the stylus to move longer distances to create longer wave forms. Loud sounds forced the [writing or engraving] stylus to the edge of the groove and sometimes beyond it, ruining the recording. Drums were therefore excluded from recording studios, and technicians always waited with nervous anticipation as singers reached for climatic high notes. Too loud a recording made the diaphragm vibrate rapidly, causing "blasting" on the playback, which distorted the sound.[2]

In layman's terms, heavier bass notes, percussion instruments (particularly sounds coming from drums) and notes from the top end of the musical scale were difficult to record successfully.

This age of acoustic recordings relied on the music being captured solely by the phonograph's horn and then channeled to the recording stylus. For the vocal performers in particular, the "studios were often bare and stifling in those days before air conditioning. There was no audience to inspire brilliant performances, only a pianist who provided accompaniment."[3] Each musical instrument's sound reacted to, or was shaped by, the acoustic recording process and the various elements which could impact the recording: the room's size and dimensions, the recorder, the material used in the construction of the instruments and the building, noise from without and the human beings within. Consequently each of the elements made a contribution to the recording process. Sometimes the efforts faithfully captured the sound, sometimes any one (or many) of the elements distorted the sound beyond satisfactory sonic limits. As one listens today to the surviving musical recordings from the period, it is reasonable to suggest that the quality usually fell somewhere in between.

In addition to the occasionally unpredictable recording-nature of the various elements, there were also learned problems associated with certain sounds and certain musical instruments. Problems might be caused by the decibel-output, the volume or loudness of one or more instruments (due to the instrument's relative power or intensity). Other issues might arise from the unique quality or characteristic of an instrument's sound. Strings presented their own issues within the recording process. Many of these softer, more delicate instruments were troublesome for the machines to "hear," troublesome for the technology to "comprehend." Reviewing lists of titles and listening to cylinders and discs from the first wave of recordings suggests a pattern: string instruments were perhaps more problematic than any others. For recording groups small and large the procedure was the same. "Because stringed instruments didn't carry well, scores were often rearranged—bassoons substituting for cellos; tubas for double basses; and Stroh 'violins' for the higher strings."[4] Nevertheless, Edison's cylinder catalog (of recordings made between 1889 and 1912) lists forty-eight violin cylinder performances. The piano had its own issues due to its shape, weight, size, volume, and sound. In reviewing the one-time list of problem instruments—drums, strings, bass, piano—one might conclude that recording music, if not impossible, might not have been worth the trouble.

All was not lost, however, as the pool of musical instruments was deep, and creative approaches to various instruments overcame inherent weaknesses. Engineers found that some brass instruments worked better than others. Edison's catalog of cylinder recordings lists sixty-eight cornet solos, eight cornet duets, one cornet-clarinet duet, and three cornet-trombone duets. Woodwinds were represented by thirty-two clarinet-solo cylinder recordings. It is unlikely that Edison would have offered eighty cornet and thirty-two clarinet recordings for sale had there been significant, characteristic problems recording the performances or playing them back. One could choose from more than one-hundred banjo cylinder recordings (123 solo, 13 duets), in the Edison catalog as well as sixty-four xylophone cylinders.[5] There is another plausible explanation for the proliferation of some types of recordings in the early Edison repertoire. The banjo, the fiddle, and some brass instruments may have benefited from and appealed to a somewhat predisposed listener during the late nineteenth century. This could be due to the lingering affect of people's familiarity with music heard during the American Civil War and subsequently during the years of the Reconstruction. Most of this music will be explored in more detail in later chapters.

Generally speaking, each type of musical instrument and each human voice needed to overcome obstacles to both the overall recording set-up and the machines of the day; that is, obstacles that the voice and the instruments created by their characteristics: tone, octave range, and impact (e.g. vibration and volume). Different instruments suggested different solutions. Violins, for example, were sometimes adapted or completely reconstructed:

> To overcome the lack of carrying power of string instruments, John M.A. Stroh introduced new "violins" ... in the early 1900s. Stroh replaced the violin's usual wooden body with a metal resonator to produce a louder, more penetrating sound. The aluminum horn at the end of the fingerboard directed this sound ... into the recording horn.[6]

Other instruments were converted or adapted in a similar fashion. Tubas replaced the bass as the former's output was more readily picked up by the recording machines. Pianos—the classic upright models—were raised up off the floor, bringing the sound closer to ear level or horn level, and were played with the piano's back panel removed. The players gained volume and presence by these moves, giving the instrument a better chance at being recorded properly.

Critics of the early talking machines and the recordings described them in less than complimentary ways. Today's audio amplifiers and sound systems have treble and bass tone controls or graphic equalizers which allow the listener to make individualized adjustments of the playback. That ability to adjust, however, presupposes that the original recording has sufficient sonics to allow the listener to make adjustments based on personal preference. For example, consider the bass register, those deeper tones (what some refer to as the "bottom-end") of today's popular musical recordings. In early recordings, the flat, one-dimensional nature of the sound coming from finished cylinders had little if any bottom, at least as we think of that tonal quality in contemporary recordings. The term "tinny" is a descriptive that comes to mind, as it has often been used to characterize sound reproduction that tends to be thin, whether the result of a poorly-designed phonograph or radio, or a recording whose sound seems one-dimensional; today we can think of a tiny, inexpensive transistor radio from the 1960s as representing that tinny sound. One listen to an early cylinder or disc recording—particularly those made prior to 1900—helps elucidate the issue of limitations of early musical recordings. "Thin" recordings might have benefited from tonal-help from the phonographs on which they were played. However, with the exception of the expensive Aeolian-models, tone control on early phonographs was minimal to non-existent.

If the phonograph tended to produce a metallic sound, one way to improve (or provide a perceived improvement of) the recording was to use primarily those musical instruments that produced tonal qualities compatible with the phonograph's capabilities, instead of confronting its shortcomings. Assuming that listeners had heard these instruments often in live performances, they would expect to hear those same attributes during playback. In addition to the 136 banjo and 64 xylophone recordings, Edison's catalog of cylinders listed 24 whistling, 6 zither, 67 violin/violin-flute/violoncello, 57 chimes, and 16 bagpipe recordings. Most of these, due to their higher pitch, would seem to have been well-suited to the limitations of the early phonographs.

Whether one was a critic, an aspiring recording artist, or an early technician or engineer recording the music, there was a common understanding: one could not change the nature of the machines. Therefore the instruments, repertoire, performances, and recording techniques were adapted to the machines. A look through the recordings of the period suggests that the human voice was given early preference. This should come as no surprise as Edison had tested and perfected the phonograph using his own recorded voice (recall that first recording of "Mary Had a Little Lamb.") Additionally, Edison's early vision was based on a male-dominated business and academic world, which meant that dictation or stenographic devices, answering or message machines, talking books, language, lectures, instructions, voice clocks, and most other anticipated vocal uses would have presumed use by the male voice. In fact, early recordings included speeches or readings from the likes of William F. Hooley (reading "Lincoln's Speech at Gettysburg," Berliner No. 6012 in 1898),[7] as well as many recordings by politicians and statesmen like William Jennings Bryan.

It was also a difficult proposition to record large groups or ensembles due to limited space, both within the recording room and in the diameter of the phonograph's horn. The horn served as a collector of sound in the process of acoustic recording, much like the function of the microphone in electrical recordings which began in the 1920s. Because the horn attached directly to the recording machine, there was a limit to the horn's physical dimensions and weight. In short, only a limited number of vocalists or musicians could gather around the horn, enabling the machine to record the performance. When one looks at photographs of early recording sessions, it is easy to see how the location of the various players within the recording room, and the ability of some performers to move in front of and then away from the horn itself, was critical to a good recording. This positioning and subsequent repositioning can be easily illustrated. If the performance was to feature a vocalist, one can assume that the singer was in the front of the group and closest to the horn while actually singing. If during that same recording performance there was to be an instrumental solo by a musician, logic dictates that the vocalist would have to move out of the way — providing the soloist access to the horn — during those solos. After the instrumental solo, the vocalist would return to the front of the group to continue the vocal performance. If a musician was positioned off to one side, or to the back of the group, any sound from that individual's instrument would seem muted, muffled, or faint, contributing little to the moment.

A description of a nineteenth-century recording session is worth recounting, as it illustrates a music industry reality from a century ago. For those who have worked in today's music industry, the mind's eye may create an image of these early sessions that seems primitive, yet not entirely alien. What may have been a less-than-exciting experience for the participants was, from a contemporary perspective, just another low-tech step in the evolution of the recording session. In this particular case, the artist was Cappa's Seventh Regiment Band, apparently recording for the New York Phonograph Company.[8] One must picture a room filled with ten cylinder phonograph recorders (large, gramophone-like in appearance,) the members of Cappa's Band, and the recording technician, engineer:

> In the center of a large room are grouped members of Cappa's Seventh Regiment Band of New York; they are surrounded by ten phonographs in a circle, each one equipped with a giant metal horn. An attendant has checked all the batteries and has inserted a fresh wax cylinder in each machine. Now the recording engineer steps before the horn of the first phonograph, starts up the motor, and announces in [a loud, direct] tone: "'My Country 'Tis of Thee,' played by Cappa's Seventh Regiment Band, record taken by Charles Marshall, New York City." He stops the motor, steps over to the second phonograph and repeats the same announcement…. When every cylinder has been inscribed with an announcement, all ten motors are started simultaneously [and the next recording could begin].[9]

There was a practical side to the prefatory announcements: the listener was informed as to the performance they were about to hear, and it augmented the scant amount of information — if any —contained on the exterior package as well as information found on the edge of the cylinder itself. A 1907 Edison cylinder by Harry Anthony and James F. Harrison titled "Will There Be Any Stars in My Crown" contained title and selection number on the beveled edge of the cylinder, inscribed as follows: "Duet. Will There Be Any Stars In My Crown. 9491. Thomas A. Edison. Pat'd"

With the exception of Edison's name, which was a facsimile of his signature, the information along the edge of the cylinder was in block letters. As for the exterior package, only the selection number appeared on the end of the paperboard cylinder sleeve. The balance of the cylinder's exterior package, roughly 24 square inches, was devoted to graphics and text about the Edison Company (and the National Phonograph Company), copyright and patent information, and a photograph of Mr. Edison.

There was also an aesthetic side to announcing the performance, at least in keeping with the style of the times. "'A musical record,' Mr. Marshall [recording engineer] believed, 'is half made by a perfect announcement.'"[10]

The engineer, as described above, having completed his ten ritual announcements, started the ten machines simultaneously. Then the band or musical director would signal for the musicians to start, and for the next two minutes music or spoken words would fill the room. The musicians or speaker would perform and then the director would signal the performers to stop, and all would stand quietly while each of the machines was turned off. All of this recording activity occurred within the strictly allotted time, which was based on the maximum playing time of the cylinders. Having recorded the performance, the cylinders were then removed, fresh blank cylinders were inserted in each of the ten machines, and the process was repeated. Allowing for the unloading and loading of the machines, the announcements and the performance, it's reasonable to estimate that ten such cycles could be completed in an hour.[11]

In a recording session lasting three hours, the musicians would perform the selection, in this example "My Country 'Tis of Thee" by Cappa's Band, thirty times. The phonograph company would now have three hundred cylinders added to their inventory, ready for sale. These sessions, as monotonous as they must have been, were first and foremost about creating inventory; the artistry of the musicians and the quality of the performances were clearly secondary. It is surprising that one doesn't read of musicians going crazy during such extended sessions. Consider the recording of "The Laughing Song" by performer George W. Johnson, which was reportedly recorded "about 40,000 times before mass duplication of master recordings was introduced."[12]

In choosing repertoire for recording one other criterion had to be considered. As noted earlier, the cylinder and later the disc had a limited amount of recording time. This restricted any performance to the maximum allowed on that cylinder or disc. In the early recordings, this probably kept the recorded performance to approximately two minutes. More than one label's output included some spoken-word recordings during the 1890s, and among those were multiple recordings of Lincoln's "Gettysburg Address."[13] There is beauty and a powerful simplicity in Lincoln's message. There is also the simple fact that the address contained less than three hundred words, and regardless of the actual time Lincoln took to deliver it on November 19, 1863, it can be respectfully recited in two minutes. Edward Everett, who shared the platform at Gettysburg with President Lincoln and delivered the main address that November day, wrote to the president afterward and said, "I should be glad, if I could flatter myself that I came as near to the central idea of the occasion, in two hours [the length of Everett's address], as you did in two minutes."[14]

10

Sound, Quality, and Topicality

Music consumers in the last quarter of the twentieth century were witness to another audio-technology transition. Consumer music purchases moved from analog to digital—from prerecorded cassette tapes and vinyl records to digital compact discs. Digital recording was introduced for the studio side of the music business in the late 1970s. The concept put forward then was that digitization was a solution to most or all of the problems associated with unwanted ambient sound on the master recording. Vinyl lovers loathed, but nevertheless had become accustomed to cracks, pops, and scratches emanating from their records. Similarly analog tape buyers accepted a certain level of tape hiss as unfortunate yet inevitable. The noise reduction efforts of Dolby Labs[1] provided significant improvement in minimizing background tape hiss, but they did not result in completely noiseless recordings. "Beginning in 1978, the state of the-art solution to noise reduction and expanded dynamic range [was] the *digital* recording of master studio tapes."[2] The next step was digital playback formats for consumers. With the introduction of compact disc (CD) players in the early 1980s, record companies believed that these compact disc consumers would ultimately be a discerning, discriminating lot. Ironically, while many believed that the brave new entertainment world was going to be 100 percent digital, in fact most early compact discs were not all digital, as evident in the identifier placed on discs and packaging: a simple three-letter code, e.g., AAD. This code identified a CD as containing an Analog recording, with Analog mastering, and Digital playback.[3] In this example, note that only the CD was digital; earlier stages of the creative process and production had all been analog.

With the enthusiastic acceptance of recorded music buyers—in other words, with the developing consumer demand—the music industry quickly discovered that their consumers were actually far less discriminating about the titles they would purchase from the limited selection of CD recordings which were available. The strong consumer demand for CDs suggested that consumers simply wanted music for their new CD players, and they often ignored the nature (digital versus analog) of the source material. This apparent paradox — the introduction of a digital playback machine and the consumer's purchase of older, nondigital recordings — has as much to do with a shortage of available CD titles (due to the industry's limited production capacity) than with a lack of sophistication on the part of the consumers. Even though compact disc players went on sale to consumers in 1982, it would be at least another two years before a sufficient number of disc manufacturing plants came on line to allow for the introduction of entire catalogs of recordings, including some new releases with digital origins and bearing the DDD mark.

These early days of the digital recording age, the 1980s, also saw a few established recording artists delay their decision to make new digital recordings, or even release their earlier analog recordings on compact disc. They remained unconvinced that this new digital medium was an accurate and sympathetic delivery system. Digitization of the music repertoire brought subjective opinion from some of the creators and some of the critics. The term "cold" was introduced to the recording lexicon in reference to digital recording (or compact disc playback) versus "warm" for analog recording (and analog or vinyl disc playback). The position of those who intuited a warmer sound might best be explained in a brief consideration of analog and digital recording, the initial portion of which is put forward by Catherine Moore:

> The first step in the digitalization of music was the binary encoding of a master tape, which stored the audio signal from the studio or concert hall as a series of on/off, zero/one codes and allowed rapid access to any point with computerized accuracy. Unlike other significant recording and playback developments— acoustic 78s, electric 78s, monaural LPs and stereo LPs— digital recording did not improve recording quality or sound reproduction. The relative fidelities of analogue and digital chips are succinctly described in ... an article by John Markoff about analogue computer chips: "Digital chips [are] ideal for processing large amounts of data, [but] they are not suited for communicating with the real world, which is full of gray areas that lie between 1 and 0." When that real world is music, "a digital chip can only approximate the details of the curve of a sound wave.... The digital version of the music is transferred to a CD, which lacks the sonorous subtleties of an analog recording but can be copied more precisely."[4]

Allow me to offer my abbreviated lay-interpretation of Catherine

Moore's (and John Markoff's) point: Analog and digital recordings may in fact both have shortcomings, and to some degree both may be imperfect and imprecise media. How one's ear perceives a recording or playback medium determines whether the sound is warm or cold. If, for example, the nuanced area of a digitized musical work — what Markoff labels as the "gray areas [lying] between 1 and 0"—cannot be fully represented in the digital world, then for someone who believes himself able to hear such nuances, something is missing. Consequently, not all recording artists— particularly those whose ears "can hear what is missing" (or whose ears "cannot hear what should be there")— embraced digital recording or compact discs when both were first introduced. Returning to an earlier discussion of a technological consumer bell curve, the consumer innovators, and the consumer early adopters were hungry for CDs to feed to their new players. Period. Recognizing this demand, record companies released almost anything they wanted (warm or cold) into the waiting arms of these newly enfranchised music lovers with compact disc players in their homes. To these consumers the CDs were neither warm nor cold. They were digital.

Almost one hundred years before the compact disc, it was one thing to distribute and sell the recording machines, even with blank cylinders for do-it-yourself recording. (Home or business recording on cylinders was envisioned but never became the primary motivation for the success of the phonograph. Nevertheless blank cylinders for recording were available.)[5] It was another matter to create a consumer market for prerecorded music. Logically, before there was a market, there needed to be a strategy to identify and motivate it. As we know, the strategy at least in part was dictated by the design limitations of nineteenth-century recording technology. We have established a general description of the instruments used in early recordings as well as vocal characteristics, the recording machine's capabilities, and the limited playing time. The next step is to consider a logic to recorded musical repertoire.

As the record business became a genuine business, music, and for that matter spoken-word recordings, took on increasingly varied forms. Music then as today reflected the mood, the mores, and the values of the times. Within the memory of living generations, pieces of American history have been musically documented or memorialized by singer-songwriters like Woody Guthrie (1912–1967), who sang about the 1930s Dust Bowl, the Great Depression, and bank robber "Pretty Boy" Floyd. Pete Seeger (b. 1919) traveled with Guthrie and brought more than topical themes to his music, at times wearing his political and social beliefs on his sleeve. Regardless of the continual shaping or reinforcement of those beliefs, there has been a constant to the activist singer-songwriter over the years. "Seeger had joined the Young Communist League at Harvard in 1937."[6] He supported Henry Wallace's 1948 candidacy for president on the Progressive Party ticket, a campaign which "made a clean test of the power of song. 'There were times when a song lightened the atmosphere,' Seeger later reflected. 'I think it probably helped people from getting killed.'"[7] His recordings with the Weavers included "If I Had a Hammer" and the rediscovery of a song titled "We Shall Overcome." After (or because of) people like Guthrie and Seeger, other voices used music and recordings as the medium for the message. In 1965 folk singer Barry McGuire sang about Cold War angst on the hit record "Eve of Destruction." A year later Staff Sergeant Barry Sadler had a hit with the pro–Vietnam War record "The Ballad of the Green Berets."

It seems reasonable to suggest that music always reflects, in both direct and indirect ways, the times in which we live. It is just as reasonable to assume that recordings *then* reflected the times a century ago. Connections between social moods and music have been asserted by Hughson F. Mooney. In an article titled "Songs, Singers, and Society, 1890–1954," Mooney states that

> urban songs [which were] popular during the generation preceding the 1890s ... were revealing in two ways. In the first place, they showed [America's] slavish imitation of European "culture." With their languishing, sorrowful melodies, tales of dead or dying mothers. Lost lovers, or timid maidens; with their high-flown sentimentalism, these ballads reflected the dominance of an upper middle class in our Atlantic seaboard cities which harbored the cultural backwash of Europe and looked to its stale romanticism as the mode.[8]

Mooney, then, characterizes the socio-economic makeup of record and cylinder buyers during the first thirty years of recording as upper middle class and imitative of Europeans, consumers interested in "sentimentalism" and "romanticism," even if both were, as Mooney suggests, "stale." To fully appreciate the impact of daily life on the arts, including music, one can consider the events of the first thirty years of recording, and in later chapters, the music itself.

The World's Columbian Exposition opened in Chicago in 1893, simultaneously celebrating the arrival of Columbus in the New World in 1492 and showing the world America's progress in the century-plus since gaining independence from Great Britain. "President Grover Cleveland flipped a switch, lighting 10,000 electric bulbs...."[9] If America was perceived by some as a shining city on a hill, the Chicago Exposition and the bright lights seemed to affirm that perception. Unfortunately, outside the confines of the Chicago site emerged a depression in 1893 as deep as any economic upheaval the young country had ever seen, and it would last four years. If songwriters needed inspiration, they did not have to look too far. And there was more. Consider the events of the 1890s.

Populist politics were visible in the election of 1892. At the end of the nineteenth century Americans were becoming acquainted with places they knew little if anything of: the sinking of the American Navy battleship *Maine* in Havana's harbor on February 15, 1898, pushed American troops and ships toward both Cuba and the Philippines as the United States fought a successful war with Spain; as a result of the victory, Puerto Rico joined the American Empire. Winning the war against Spain turned, at least in part, into a war of independence by Filipino guerrillas (1899–1901), and any doubt that racism in America might be in decline was dismissed with the attitudes of U.S. fighting and occupation troops toward the indigenous Philippine people: "American soldiers tended to dismiss Filipinos as nearly subhuman."[10] United States Marines captured Beijing, ending the Boxer Rebellion in 1900. American dominance of the Caribbean became law with the Hay-Pauncefote Treaty (1901). The young American nation considered, and perhaps relished, its position in the world.

Automobiles began to be manufactured and sold in greater numbers in the 1890s, with early models coming out of Detroit. The Wright Brothers successfully launched the age of powered flight (1903). New York City's subway and the city's Williamsburg Bridge over the East River opened (1904). San Francisco experienced the Great Earthquake (1906). Halley's Comet made its expected appearance (1910). The Triangle Shirtwaist factory in New York City burned, killing more than one hundred workers (1911). The British ship Titanic, sank on its maiden voyage (1912). Ethnic newspapers continued to reach an immigrant audience (the *Jewish Daily Forward* began publishing in 1897).

About the same time that Edison and his competitors began to aggressively market the phonograph, moving pictures became a reality. (Edison introduced his kinetoscope in 1891.) Although the pictures moved, the sound accompanying the films consisted of the people in the audience munching on their snacks, the theater's musician playing a piano, and the noise from the projector casting images onto the screen. "For only a nickel [hence the name "nickelodeon"], patrons watched a silent screen flicker with moving images as an accompanist played music on a tinny piano."[11] Instead of hearing dialog one could read the actor's lines displayed within the dialog frames or as part of the film's subtitles. Although sound would not be added to films until the 1920s— and music moved front and center with Al Jolson's performances in 1927's *The Jazz Singer*— silent short films and features caught the attention of the public and provided escape and entertainment, e.g., *The Great Train Robbery* (1903).

Literature of the times included new works by Mark Twain (*Tom Sawyer Abroad*, 1894), John Luther Long (*Madame Butterfly*, 1897), Lyman Frank Baum (*The Wonderful Wizard of Oz*, 1900), Booker T. Washington (*Up from Slavery*, 1901), Woodrow Wilson (*A History of the American People*, 1902), W.E.B. DuBois (*The Souls of Black Folks*, 1903), Jack London (*The Call of the Wild*, 1903), George Santayana (*The Life of Reason*, 1905), Upton Sinclair (*The Jungle*, 1905), O. Henry (*The Trimmed Lamp*, 1907), Zane Grey (*Riders of the Purple Sage*, 1912), and Carl Sandburg (*Chicago Poems*, 1916).

One can still imagine, based on the literature, memoirs, photographs and historical documents of American life, the place that music occupied — literally and figuratively — within the home of late nineteenth-century Americans. Images of those pre-phonograph family members sitting around their piano and listening to or singing along with popular sheet music of the day is an image that many seem to be familiar with. Americans today continue to experience a contemporary version or re-creation of the oft-pictured concert in the park, or an afternoon of music in a New England town. Nineteenth-century musicians performed in the bandshell or the gazebo or on the lawn in the center of town. Music was performance, meaning the audience was literally in the presence of the performers— whether on stage, in the home, or on the town green.

By 1917, when America's soldiers went off to fight in World War I, "Over There" was a popular hit in sheet music and would yield multiple recorded versions. Its author, George M. Cohan, was one of many prolific — in his case, one of the premier — songwriters, whose name and musical style we continue to recognize today. They were all, the famous composers and the obscure, creating melodies and lyrics that were indicative of the times. During the first thirty years of recorded music, melody and rhythms, style and substance would evolve, and incorporated into that evolution would be musical types that would each be recognizable to these early record buyers. The types would include the ballad, romance, comedic or novelty, ethnic, production, dance, ragtime (including coon songs, cakewalks, and shouts) military, societal, political and patriotic, promotional, and more.

Consumer taste emerged with the offerings from an increasing number of manufacturing companies, an expanded variety in musical styles, and the growing number of recording performers. In addition, as pointed out in Chapter 5, there were problems created by the lack of an industry technological standard: each phonograph-maker sold machines and cylinders or discs without a standardization of technology enabling any recording to be played on any player. If dealers and consumers needed to maintain brand loyalty, the labels would have to keep a regular flow of new releases moving through the market pipeline. Dealers and consumers needed to be brand loyal.

Although the phonograph was demonstrated as practical in 1877, only sixty-three artists[12] had recorded for Edison between 1889 and 1892, and diversity in style was not necessarily a watchword. Recordings of solo violin, clarinet, xylophone, flute, and piano, and a few vocal titles made up the bulk of Edison's offerings. The industry was moving beyond "Mary Had a Little Lamb," but in steps, not leaps. That would begin to change during the next twenty years, with varied and numerous releases being offered at an accelerating rate. "By 1910, the average store needed a stock of 3,000 to 5,000 records to keep pace with the output of new songs and changing public taste."[13] How and why musicians were chosen to become recording artists, which songs were selected by and for them, and how popularity was determined is the next consideration.

11

A Popular Product and
a Consumer Market

In the recorded music business since 1950, the distinction between the delivery systems (hardware and software) and the creative forces (the artists) is clear. Hardware is a term used to describe audio systems (amplifiers, speakers, CD players, personal computers, MP3 players, iPods), while software is the product to be played on those audio systems (compact discs, MP3/MP4 files, DVDs).[1] The creative forces are usually the performers, but an equal measure of creativity often comes from the songwriters (lyricists and composers) and recording producers.

When one measures creative success, there is also a distinction to be made between critical acclaim and popularity. One might say, there are two criteria for determining success: one is qualitative, the other is quantitative. Critical acclaim is the recognition of a musical performer's works by music critics or the musical artist's peers. Either group may make public comment on whether a performer's creative work has risen to a level that is on par with the highest standards of a particular genre of music. The word *genre* in music today refers to the distinctive musical style of the performer/performance, which that performer or their record label hopes will connect with the specific taste of some music buyers. American musical genres include the following: popular, jazz, classical, rhythm & blues, country, hip-hop, rock 'n' roll, adult contemporary, bluegrass, and so on. Any artist may have success in more than one genre, but that artist's core audience is almost always centered around their strongest, usually the genre of their original success.

Genre becomes an important ingredient when attempting to critique the musical performer. For example, it is difficult to compare the work of jazz musician Charlie Parker (1920–1955) with the work of classical and Broadway composer Leonard Bernstein (1918–1990) or the music of the

"King of Rock 'n' Roll" Elvis Presley (1935–1977). One might superficially remark that these legends have only three things in common: they all achieved success in music in the twentieth century, they are all Americans, and they are all dead. That would be an unfair and unfortunate oversimplification, just as inappropriate as finding a similarly limited commonality between, for example, realist painter Edward Hopper (1882–1967) and expressionist Jackson Pollock (1912–1956).

Critical acclaim occurs within a particular context, and then one or more subsets of that context. Critics might ponder which other jazz musician, or more specifically, which alto saxophone players in jazz, could be compared with Parker, his body of work, and his lasting influence a half-century after his death? Which other twentieth-century American composer/musician has created a truly American theatrical success to compare with Bernstein's *West Side Story*? Which other performer in popular music helped bring rock 'n' roll to an emerging audience with the lasting impact of Presley? Separate and apart from music critics, there are also the critiques made by fellow recording artists (and other voting members) when it comes time to nominate and vote for the annual Grammy Awards of the music industry.[2] All of this is to suggest that a critical evaluation, therefore, represents the qualitative measure of success.

There is, in contrast, the quantitative evaluation of an artist's or a recorded song's popularity. Such an evaluation is not necessarily determined by the acclaim of a performer's peers, or the critical evaluation of learned musical members of society. Popularity is gauged today by the quantity of compact discs sold, the number of digital downloads transferred to consumers, and the number of times a recording or song is played on the radio, used on television, performed on Broadway, heard in films, or performed in public. Some critics might have difficulty characterizing the Monkees' "Last Train to Clarksville" as a performance worthy of critical acclaim. However, the fact that on September 10, 1966 it became the #1 song in America (according to *Billboard* magazine[3]) affirms its quantitative popularity. Critical acclaim and consumer popularity often operate independently. From 1889 to 1919, popularity could be determined by the number of cylinders or discs purchased by consumers, the number of performances a song received in the theater, and the number of copies of sheet music for each song that were sold.

Evidence of popularity can be inferred by finding the actual recordings or by finding references to those recordings. First, if there exist copies of multiple titles (at least three[4] or more distinct, released recordings) made by one particular performer, one might assume that this performer was sufficiently pleasing to the phonograph companies, retail stores, or consumers, to qualify as popular. Similarly, if there exist copies of multiple performers (again, three or more) recording the same song, one might assume that this song could also be categorized as popular. Verifying evidence would include actual cylinder and disc recordings from the period, or credible lists—the Library of Congress, for example—documenting that such recordings existed.

Second, and separate from the recordings themselves, is evidence that the recordings existed. If there are lists of multiple recorded versions of a song, written evidence of live performance use, or other recognition, this could confirm popularity and justify adding this song title to the list of titles to be explored in this book. Consumer-oriented books, daily or weekly newspapers containing text about or consumer advertising for recorded songs, mail-order catalogs (Sears, Montgomery-Ward), and magazine stories all prove useful.

Third, if one reviews the music trade publications of the period (*Billboard*, the *Talking Machine News*, *Talking Machine World*, the *Phonogram*, and *Phonoscope*,) there should be some information providing additional names of recording artists, or at least corroborating names already collected. These trade publications should be able to do the same for song titles. Advertisements aimed at the music trade and editorial content regarding the response to the songs or performers in various live shows would also tend to reinforce the notion of popularity.

Attempting to verify or chart the popularity of a song or a performer during the early years of recorded music — if possible — may require a mixture of sources. There were over-the-counter consumer sales (as reported to or inferred by the industry newspapers and trade publications) and unit sales (as reported by a sampling of the retail stores or the music companies themselves). However, "trade journals never systematically ranked records [although] dealers at times reported to *Talking Machine World* that certain records were selling well, but this is meaningless"[5] without some type of consistent, reliable, and credible sales data to draw from. Trade papers also reported live performances of songs in the variety theater known as vaudeville,[6] as well as other so-called "legitimate" musical theater of the period.

Billboard began publishing in 1894, although it would be years before music was incorporated into its primary mission. In 1900 its pages regularly covered activities in vaudeville, and by 1910 *Billboard*'s pages were devoted to detailed accounts of the stage, in some cases also focusing on music. For example, the magazine covered many performances around New York City on the front page of two of its sections: "Music and the Stage" and "Vaudeville Profession." In the latter section of the January 8,

1910 issue, the Plaza Music Hall, Fifth Avenue Theater, Colonial Theater, Alhambra Theater, and Hammerstein's Victoria all received editorial space. For example:

> Fifth Avenue Theater — Albert Chevalier has reached this house with his character changes and songs. He is singing by request this week his old-time success, My Old Dutch, Knocked 'Em In The Old Kent Road, and Mrs. 'Enery 'Awkins, and in addition the new ones of this season, The Workhouse Man, The Fallen Star, and Wot Vor do Ee Luv Oi?[7]

1912 brought a new feature to *Billboard*, a section titled "Song Reviews." The lead review was for the song "Sweetest Memory." *Billboard* commented that songwriter Fred Ingmar's song is "difficult to criticize because there is no way of ascertaining just what standard is sought by the writer. Is it supposed to be a high-class song? Then why confine it to the regulation two verses and a chorus...?"[8]

The entertainment industry was attempting to legitimize its success by the validation and quantification of its consumer interest. Reviews were one step in the legitimization process, and counting sales of recorded music was a method of quantification. Although in a raw infancy (and of questionable accuracy when compared to the tabulation techniques available today) one can see these early attempts at gauging popularity were a precursor to today's music charts and their current position as the high-tech arbiters of America's taste in music.

Soundata was the creator of the modern Nielsen SoundScan popularity charts. Today SoundScan's raw data contains information reflecting over-the-counter consumer sales. By tabulating point-of-sale information captured by a variety of store types, sizes and locations, SoundScan is able, at least theoretically, to transform the data into a credible and unbiased chart, giving the world a snapshot of what's hot and what's not. The raw data from all of these stores is recalculated or projected, much the same way the American television networks calculate or project the winner of an election before all of the votes have been counted, or the way public opinion pollsters survey a few hundred or a thousand people and determine that their answers are representative of the entire American population. The data may be representative, but the data is not flawless. The popularity charts are, after all, a projection of sales based on a statistical sampling. However, senior executives of American music firms such as Universal Music have stated that the information has been somewhat accurate when they have compared SoundScan's estimated sales with their own internal (confidential and proprietary) information. At least one of those same executives added that s/he has been "shocked at least once a month by the discrepancy between [SoundScan's] numbers and the company's numbers when it came to the charts."

In displaying, listing, or charting the success of popular records, the ranking order, or what might be called a "success index," is similar for both complete albums and for individual tracks or singles, but it is not identical. Today *Billboard* has two general popularity charts: one for albums—the "Billboard 200"—and one for singles—the "Hot 100." There are also numerous genre-specific charts for albums and singles to accommodate a variety of musical styles and genres prominent in North America, formats which provide insights into the issue of popularity.[9] In 2004 the format of the "Billboard 200" album chart was to list the name of the *artist/performer* first, followed by the title of the album, and then in order, label name, selection or catalog number, distributor name, and suggested list price. Conversely, the format for today's "Hot 100" singles chart is to list the *song title* first, followed by the artist/performer's name, and then in order, the name of the producer, songwriter(s), label, selection or catalog number, and distributor. It looks like this:

Album: artist name, album title, record label, (anything else)
Single: song title, artist name, producer, songwriter, record label (any-
    thing else)

The difference is subtle but not insignificant, and the rationale can be clarified to some degree by looking a little closer at what constitutes the most popular album and the most popular single in America during one particular week.

On August 30, 2003 Alan Jackson, one of the most successful performers in American Country music since the early 1990s, reached #1 on both the "Billboard 200" album chart and the "Top Country Albums" chart with *Greatest Hits Volume II and Some Other Stuff*. Jackson's album became "only the second country title to lead the *Billboard* 200 during [2003]."[10] By comparison relative newcomer Norah Jones' album *Come Away with Me* had reached #1 on February 8, 2003. Jones' album had since dropped to #9 on the "Billboard 200" album chart, although it remained #1 on the "Top Contemporary Jazz" chart in August 2003.[11]

Since the early 1990s *Billboard* has moved from a somewhat casual store estimate of units sold to a chart with improved accuracy, developed by taking a more scientific approach. One can have relative faith in the charts today because in May 1991 *Billboard* changed the way it counted the records sold at retail stores across America. Instead of *asking* stores about their sales, the music industry's leading trade newspaper switched to an increasingly more accurate method, including electronic data sharing, for tabulating its best-seller charts:

> [With] the May 25, 1991, issue, *Billboard* drew the industry's atten-
> tion — and the ire of some record company executives— when it
> adopted the point-of-sale methodology for compilation of the *Bill-
> board* 200 Top Albums and the Top Country Albums charts. In the
> seven months [following] that momentous conversion to piece-count
> data, fears that were initially expressed about the impact the new sys-
> tem would have on the *Billboard* 200 have been allayed by the chart's
> behavior.[12]

In 2004 one can comprehend a numerical certainty to chart positions. Nielsen Soundscan *projected* in August 2003 that Alan Jackson's
album sold 318,000 units one week while Norah Jones' album had sales of
57,000 units that same week. Jackson's place at the top of the "Billboard
200" (and Norah Jones' *album* at #9) are therefore quantitative rankings
of popularity.

Returning to the individual chart *listings*, we're reminded that albums
listed (and ranked) on the "Billboard 200" are focused first on the name
of the performer.[13] It is nevertheless interesting that the music fan's usual
"first impression" of a recorded work is that of the work itself, usually a
song, and not necessarily the performer. Most new music is heard for the
first time through radio airplay, and the listener's initial impression will
normally evoke one of three responses— positive, no opinion, or negative.
The second impression just as quickly will be based on the determination
of the musical performer's identity. Once the identity of the recording's
musical performer is known, a performer's popularity may convert a consumer's preliminarily negative response (or "no opinion") into a positive
response by virtue of the predisposition of a fan to a particular artist. The
success in 2000 of Madonna is a case in point. Many of those who heard
her recording of Don MacLean's classic pop composition "American Pie"
without attribution offered opinions ranging from "average" to "appalling."
When told that the recording was by Madonna, fans tended to gravitate
toward support of her and turn their opinion positive. Many others only
affirmed their original opinion. The *Times of London* stated that "Madonna
has truly murdered this lovely song."[14] This "American Pie" peaked at #29
on *Billboard*'s Hot 100 in 2000. However, with that type of exception noted,
a negative is usually just that, negative.[15]

Billboard states that its "Hot 100" chart is tabulated not simply from
retail sales. The chart represents "the most popular singles and tracks,
according to radio audience impressions measured by Nielsen Broadcast
Data Systems, sales data compiled by Nielsen SoundScan, and playlists

from select non-monitored radio stations."[16] Using this as a guide, one might accept that on the 10 April 2004 "Hot 100" chart "Yeah!" by Usher (and featuring Lil Jon & Ludacris) is the single that has amassed the greatest amount of radio play, sales at retail music stores, mass merchants and internet outlets when compared to the other ninety-nine singles.

Having explored *Billboard*'s current approach to charting popularity, we might return to the basic question of "what is popular?" and answer it — at least quantitatively — with this written equation:

consumer sales = popularity

America tends to gravitate toward the ball player who hits the most home runs, the quarterback with the most touchdown passes, the basketball player with the most points, or the recording artist who sells the greatest number of CD units. Record companies large and small succeed by selling large quantities of albums, but they may easily fail by selling insufficient numbers of albums. The quality of art in a competitive, contemporary American music business is not, unfortunately, the preferred criterion for popularity. The opinions of artistic idealists notwithstanding, when it comes to popular music we live in a quantitative consumer society more than a qualitative one.

During the first days of recorded music, the tabulating of unit sales was primitive when compared to the SoundScan charts of today. However, the motivation for the early recording artists, songwriters, publishers, theatrical performers, and chiefly for the recording companies, including the so-called Big Three (Edison, Victor, and Columbia) was to sell large quantities of cylinders, discs, and phonographs. Revenue was the key to survival. For the early music business (like the music business of today) significant unit sales and/or theatrical performances, rather than accolades, equaled revenue, and revenue equals success.

12

A&R in the Early Years
— Styles and Genres

The A&R process has always been one of recognizing the potential of a talented performer (artist) and the potential of a song worth recording (repertoire). In today's music industry, members of the A&R department include executives, directors, gophers (as in "go for this, go for that"), stringers, and other A&R "wannabees." To some degree each of these people is attempting to prove that they are "musically clairvoyant"; those in A&R must have the ability to recognize the commercial potential of music and performers, and also to recognize trends and be able to predict the future taste of consumers. The transition from unknown performer to star performer is not usually instantaneous, regardless of the myth of the overnight sensation. Consider two success stories.

In 1977 the British-American pop-rock trio known as the Police was born, and two years later the group was playing to small (but enthusiastic) audiences at clubs in the United States— primarily on the initial radio airplay success of a song called "Roxanne." Their first album entered the Top 200 in November 1979. Bryan Adams made his transition from little-known songwriter and (very briefly) club music performer in 1979 to become a rock superstar in 1983.[1] Adams had thirteen successful singles charted in *Billboard* between 1983 and 1990, five of them in the Top Ten, including "Straight from the Heart." Neither artist at first was the polished, proven, successful, and bankable commodity that each was destined to become. The Police (Sting, Stewart Copeland, and Andy Summers) and Bryan Adams had each been signed by a record label and began to make music that an A&R person had deemed years earlier would be relevant and successful in the near future. And so it is with A&R that one must be in touch with the music-consumer's taste (understand the present and anticipate the future), appreciate the quality of a song (and its potential appeal to those consumers), and believe in the viability of the artist in today's market. The A&R person must also believe in the artist's ability to grow or musically evolve to continue having commercial (and artistic) relevance and success.

Returning to the early recording industry, the direction of early recorded music would evolve based on two overriding factors. First, whatever criteria were applied to making these recordings would reflect the personal taste (and business acumen) of the original recording pioneers. In short, what Edison and his peers liked the public could purchase. In these formative years of the business of music, the owners of the companies, as often as not, were also the de facto A&R executives. Second, once the public decided that something was worth their money, thus making it popular by virtue of demand created by consumers buying copies, these early music consumers (a) reinforced their own buying habits by purchasing similar recordings (because they liked what they heard — a positive option), or (b) purchased something different (because they did *not* like what they heard or grew tired of it — a negative option.)

Either way, once the 1890s-1900s consumers had made their investment in a phonograph, they wanted — or felt compelled — to own more recordings. With those purchases consumers began to exert pressure on the record labels. In essence, the basic law of supply and demand, as it relates to the first years of recording, began to push A&R in one direction or another. One should also keep in mind that the limitations of the early recording and playback equipment determined to a large degree the type and number of instruments or voices used. However, as recording techniques improved and the manufactured discs and cylinders began to reproduce each recording with less extraneous noise, new instruments or additional musicians or voices could be added to the recording session, expanding the dimensions of sound and, in a larger sense, the recording frontier.

The dynamics of recording were as fluid as the primitive technology would allow, and the types of music that could be recorded also evolved, based at first on those techniques and company preferences, and later on the public's changing taste. "Styles, rhythms, vocal ranges, and themes went in and out of fashion as American life changed."[2] Many of the styles (genres) of music that the public embraced had names, some of them enduring through the first century of recording to remain in the lexicon. Others fell into disuse, most with no appreciable loss to society, disappearing from the language of recording, relegated instead to historical writing. New names would be given to musical styles whenever existing names no longer suited a particular style of music. Important musical styles of the first thirty years and their origins are discussed in the chapters that follow.

13

Of Places, Performers, and Songs

As the nineteenth century came to a close, New York City was becoming the epicenter of the prospering music industry. The explanation for New York's prominence can be traced to a variety of factors: East Coast entrepreneurs, performing artists, songs, venues, population, immigration, and finance. The short explanation for success in the city is that, first, New York was close to the early entrepreneurs (including Edison, who was across the Hudson River in New Jersey; Eldridge Johnson in Camden, New Jersey; and Columbia's Graphophone plant in Bridgeport, Connecticut). Second, the area had an abundance of talent, i.e., potential recording artists; third, the New York area offered companies an easy access to repertoire; fourth, the city had plenty of performance venues; fifth, the size of the population of cities like New York provided a sufficient (and growing) number of potential consumers; sixth, the immigrant population of the area added a dimension to New York's cultural life. Finally, New York and the East represented financial America with a concentration of wealth and capital, and it was also the gateway to doing business in Europe. The next few sections will explore these reasons in an effort to place the recordings and the music within the business and cultural climate of the times.

Beyond the physical location of offices, research, and manufacturing, beyond Thomas Edison, Emile Berliner, Eldridge Johnson, and the other entrepreneurs who launched the recorded music industry in the region in 1889, there were the people. The American population was concentrated mainly east of the Mississippi in 1900 and would continue as such for decades to come. The well-documented immigration waves beginning at mid-nineteenth century helped make New York a truly cosmopolitan city, and musical influences would be no exception. (The composition of the immigrant population, the music coming from that ethnic population, and its influence on music in general will be discussed in a later chapter on ethnic recordings.) Circa 1900 19.2 million people lived in just five states: New York (7.3 million), Pennsylvania (6.3 million), Massachusetts (2.8 million), New Jersey (1.9 million), and Connecticut (.9 million). One-fourth of America's population in 1900 lived in the backyards of the recording companies.[1]

What early record buyers chose to buy was tied to the venues, the performers, and the repertoire of the times. Stage performance has a long history in the United States, usually taking its shape from the participants, the material, and the audience. Theaters came, went, came again, disappeared, were razed, restored, rebuilt, and renamed. Ultimately, live performance established a permanent presence in New York City. "The Mount Vernon Gardens in New York on Broadway and Leonard Street opened [July 9, 1800] as a regularly organized summer theater, perhaps the first in the United States."[2] Throughout the nineteenth century the visual and performing arts expanded their presence beyond New York to many American cities, from Boston to New Orleans and on to the West Coast, but one looked east for change.

The legitimate stage and the modern musical-variety theater began in the Northeast, the latter with the opening of Tony Pastor's Opera House in New York's Bowery in 1865. (Pastor moved a little further uptown in 1881 to East 14th Street.) In addition to Pastor's enterprises, a sampling of theater openings in New York City alone during the 1800s suggests the acceptance of the performing arts: American Academy of Fine Arts (1808), the Park Theater (rebuilt 1820), the Chatham Theater (1825), Bowery Theater (1826), Niblo's Garden (1828), Chatham Gardens (1837), Castle Garden Theatre (1839), National Theatre, Jenny Lind Hall, and Tripler Hall (1850), Metropolitan Hall (1851), Laura Keene's Theatre (1856), Olympic Theatre (1863), San Francisco Music Hall (1875), Aberle's Theatre (1879), Hermann's Gaiety Theatre and Germania Theatre (1890), and two Wintergarden Theaters (1859, 1895).[3]

Stage performers (and their choice of music) generally took one of two distinctly prominent forms. First there were the performers in legitimate theater — those perceived as being the most accomplished artists, performing serious repertoire; at least it was considered serious from the perspective of those "legitimate" performers. Second, there was everything and everyone else. The music of the former could boast of Sir Arthur Seymour Sullivan (1842–1900) and Sir William Schwenck Gilbert (1836–1911), collaborators who were otherwise known as Gilbert and Sullivan, and whose musicals, *H.M.S. Pinafore* and *The Pirates of Penzance*, made their American debuts in 1878 and 1879 respectively. This duo, while a significant success, was not the only respected source of material during the first decades of recording. Another was Victor Herbert (1859–1924), who delivered *Babes in Toyland* (1903) and *Naughty Marietta* (1912). A third early contributor, mentioned earlier, was George M. Cohan (1878–1942), who gave the theater a variety of shows including his musical *Little Johnny Jones* (1904), which featured the songs "Give My Regards to Broadway" and "Yankee Doodle Boy." Other Cohan classics were "You're a Grand Old Flag" (1906) and "Over There" (1907).

Theaters continuing to run legitimate musicals in the early 1900s included the New York Theater, the Knickerbocker, Madison Square, Casino, Savoy, Belasco, Majestic, New Amsterdam, and the Broadway. European classical music was also to be found. Leoncavallo's opera *I Pagliacci* was first performed in America (to less than stellar reviews) at the Grand Opera House in New York City on June 15, 1893.[4] Some veterans of the legitimate stage made recordings but early on, particularly before Caruso's first recordings in 1902 and his 1903 debut with the Metropolitan Opera, most top-rated performers of classical repertoire and the Broadway stage were otherwise occupied. "Many stage personalities had only a [recording] session or two. This is true of Jessie Bartlett Davis, who won fame in Reginald de Koven's (1859–1920) *Robin Hood* (1890) and Victor Herbert's *Serenade* (1897). She was among the first stage celebrities to record, making three [recordings] on May 3, 1898."[5] Regardless of the growing number of recordings made in the 1890s, established legitimate stage performers appear to have been the exception in the recording studio, not the rule.

If one group of performers and their stages was thought of as legitimate, what was one to make of the latter category, that other music and those other musical performers? The re-invention of musical-variety theater began with Tony Pastor's theaters. The generic name for entertainment at Pastor's and the theaters that followed him (and imitated his success) would be "vaudeville," and the vaudeville circuit was hitting its stride by 1900. Although its heart is arguably in New York City, the vaudeville concept became a national theater circuit.

With the hesitation of many legit performers to commit to the new phonograph and spend the necessary time in the recording studios, early recording artists were found instead among the more successful singers, comics, orators, politicians, and musicians, particularly those musicians and others performing in vaudeville theaters in New York City. Vaudeville was stage entertainment in which the variety in the type of performances was sometimes only exceeded by the diversity in the quality of that entertainment. One might settle into a seat and be entertained by comedy, song-

and-dance routines, jugglers, trained animal acts, family acts, minstrel shows (increasingly done by whites in black face), oratory, pantomime, and popular music. The success of Pastor and those who followed him firmly established the venues that began offering variety fare as demand continued to grow. Theaters like the Alhambra, the Garden Music Hall, Haub's Saloon, and the Atlantic Gardens became destinations for both performers and audiences.

The expansion of available venues became a type of siren's call drawing customers— mostly male — to the new entertainment.[6] The vaudeville name could be heard used by the theater-going clientele as both a destination and as a definition for its particular type of entertainment. For the origin of the name "vaudeville," one must look to Europe:

> Variety was the name attached to what in later years and in a somewhat different guise would be called vaudeville — that excitingly nostalgic word whose derivation is so dull. In its original French (Vau-de-Vire — "Valley of Vire") it merely signified the locality where lighthearted love songs were performed…. As so often happens in a semantic grab-bag, the place became the name of the songs themselves…. The later rechristening of vaudeville was in keeping with moralistic attempts to remove from "variety" the smudged reputation which rubbed off on it in the Bowery [section of Manhattan] "museums" and city-wide sex palaces which were an inevitable part of the song-plugger's itinerary.[7]

Clarke echoes Meyer's explanation, but adds an important ingredient: "With the taverns and local 'opera houses' available as venues for touring talent, *and with the railways making it possible for the talent to go anywhere* [emphasis added], a variety show circuit began to develop all over the USA…. The American music hall tradition came to be called Vaudeville."[8]

One must also consider the repertoire that the performers brought to the various stages and to the recording studios. Songwriting and the music publishing business was centered in Manhattan, along a section of 28th Street (between Fifth and Sixth Avenues) known as Tin Pan Alley.[9] For observers of the early music business of vaudeville and Broadway, Tin Pan Alley was a well-traveled two-way street between performers and the songwriters. The concentration of songwriters, would-be songwriters, and musicians all hammering out new material along Twenty-eight Street generated both the noise and the controlled chaos which helped define the area's name.[10] Many turn-of-the-twentieth-century theaters (the venues for the performers), booking agents (those people finding work for the performers), and music publishing companies (sources of material for the performers) were located in, or relocated to, this general area of Manhattan. Examples of music-oriented businesses in the area are numerous. The entertainment trade paper, the *New York Clipper*, was published from 1853 to 1924 and was later merged into *Variety*. The paper's business office was located at 47 West 28th Street. The offices of William Morris, Vaudeville Agent, were a few doors down at 43 West 28th Street between Broadway and Sixth Avenue. Daly's Theatre was around the corner at 1221 Broadway, at 30th Street. Music publishers were perhaps the most common sight in the neighborhood. Examples are publishing firms like M. Witmark (1893) and Paul Dresser (1905). Witmark was located at 49 West 28th Street until 1898 when they relocated to a brownstone on West 29th. Dresser's company took space at 51 West 28th Street in 1905.[11]

Performers would go to the publishers and songwriters looking for new material and, in turn, publishers and songwriters would go to performers pitching their new songs. All three groups— performers, publishers, and songwriters— would probably agree with Hazel Meyer's assertion that the mission of the music publishers "was living music for live performance."[12] Any affinity between publishers and songwriters on one hand and performers on the other was built on an inherent dynamic tension between the two parties: quality of songs versus quality of performance. Without good material a performer could bomb with the audience, and without public performance a new song might go unnoticed (and a songwriter or publisher unrewarded).

Any recording company or A&R person could have just as easily looked for material by going directly to the music publishers of Tin Pan Alley. New material was (and still is) the lifeblood of the music industry. Finding, evaluating, and bringing new recordings to the marketplace was an ongoing effort, as the consumers who owned the phonographs undoubtedly wanted a constant supply of compelling new cylinders or discs to play at home. To that end, the record companies' representatives kept their ears to the ground for artists and repertoire. This included traveling the theater circuit, watching singers and musicians perform their material, always searching for fresh, well-received repertoire. The labels's reps spent time in these theaters performing the A&R process for their companies. They could listen both for artists who rose to the level of performance quality that the record companies were searching for, and repertoire that the public would want to hear again and again. Record company A&R people evaluated the potential sales for songs and performers by observing the theater audience's reaction: enthusiasm suggested a possible hit; sleepy indifference signalled sleepy indifference.

With all of this activity, with all of these businesses, and with all of the people moving about the area, if one was looking for fresh material to

sing or play, Tin Pan Alley was the place to begin the search. A shortage
of material was not a problem. The quality of that available material was,
however, another matter. "Competition among the publishers was fierce.
Songs were needed on a constant basis. Up and down Twenty-eighth Street,
composers sat and banged out new melodies, while lyricists stood by trying to come up with catchy phrases to fit their partners' tunes."[13] Going
directly to the source was an important option for the record executives.
After all, if a song was already being performed on stage, it might be too
late to beat the competition and become the first record label to release a
cylinder or disc version of the song.

If the A&R person came up empty in the theaters and with the music
publishers and songwriters, there was one remaining (and obvious) place
to find solid — and in some cases proven — recording repertoire: the enduring musical and oratorical repertoire of the day. Ignoring for the moment
the classical compositions of the great masters, there was material from
other segments of popular culture that provided tried-and-true repertoire.
As companies have often found throughout the first century of recorded
music, having a piece of material that the audience is already familiar with
is one way to cut through the potential clutter of so many new recordings.
Many of the familiar songs then continue to be familiar to young and old
music lovers today. For example, here is a list of thirty-four songs from
the pre-phonograph American centuries. While these songs are not all
likely to be re-recorded in the twenty-first century, each has been recorded
and remains familiar:

- "Aloha Oe" (1878)
- "America/My Country 'Tis of Thee" (1831)
- "Annie Laurie" (1838)
- "Auld Lang Syne" (18C)
- "Aura Lee" (1861)
- "Barbara Allen" (1780)
- "Battle Cry of Freedom" (1862)
- "Battle Hymn of the Republic" (1862)
- "Beautiful Dreamer" (1864)
- "Buffalo Gals" (1848)
- "Blue Tail Fly/Jimmy Crack Corn" (1846)
- "Bury Me Not on the Lone Prairie"/"The Ocean Burial" (1850)
- "Camptown Races" (1850)
- "Carry Me Back to Old Virginny" (1878)
- "(O My Darling) Clementine" (1883)
- "Columbia the Gem of the Ocean" (1844)

- "Drink to Me Only with Thine Eyes" (1789)
- "Home on the Range" (1873)
- "Home Sweet Home" (1823)
- "I Wish I Was in Dixie's Land" (1859)
- "Jeannie with the Light Brown Hair" (1854)
- "Mary Had a Little Lamb" (1831)
- "My Bonnie"/"Bring Back My Bonnie to Me" (1881)
- "My Old Kentucky Home" (1853)
- "Nearer My God to Thee" (1856)
- "Oh! Promise Me" (1889)
- "Oh! Susanna" (1848)
- "Old Folks at Home"/"(Way Down Upon the Swanee River)" (1851)
- "Silent Night" (1818)
- "Star Spangled Banner" (1814)
- "Turkey in the Straw" (1834)
- "The Wedding March" (1843)
- "Yankee Doodle" (c. 1767 Est.)
- "Yellow Rose of Texas" (1858)[14]

Some of these were written by two familiar nineteenth-century songwriters, Daniel Decatur Emmett (1815–1904) and Stephen Foster (1826–1864). Foster's contributions to the above list and to nineteenth-century songwriting in general are legendary: "Oh Susanna," "Old Uncle Ned," "Old Folks at Home," "Jeannie with the Light Brown Hair," and "Camptown Races." Emmett wrote many songs including "Blue Tail Fly," but the composition considered to be his crowning moment was "I Wish I Was in Dixie's Land," later shortened to simply "Dixie." Familiarity with a song does not automatically suggest that the audience has or will become sufficiently bored with the melody, lyrics, or both to ignore a new recorded version. Classic songs endure even as times and tastes change. There are always new examples to add to the list of classics, and one from the twentieth century is worth citing to make the point.

In 1934 Richard Rogers and Lorenz Hart wrote "Blue Moon." Beyond the numerous recorded versions of the song that have long since been forgotten, five recordings received sufficient success in the pre-rock 'n' roll era to be recognized by *Billboard* magazine: Glen Gray and the Casa Loma Orchestra on Decca Records, Benny Goodman and His Orchestra on Columbia Records, and Al Bowlly with Ray Noble's Orchestra on Victor in 1935; and Mel Torme on Capitol Records and Billy Eckstine on MGM Records in 1949. The Torme version was also featured in the motion picture *Words and Music*. Pop and rock artists also recorded "Blue Moon" after the dawn of rock 'n' roll: Elvis Presley for RCA Victor Records in 1956, followed by the Marcels on Colpix Records, Herb Lance and the Classics on Promo Records, and the Ventures on Dolton Records in 1961. A reinterpretation or simply a new voice attached to an old song can be successful.

When looking through the history of popular recordings and moving past the so-called classics, there are also the unexpected diamonds in the rough. These surprises are regularly found in the world of songwriting, as are the moments when someone chooses to record the song. In 1987 songwriter Julie Gold wrote a song which she titled "From a Distance." While receiving some attention prior to 1990—singer Nanci Griffith recorded a strong early version—it was the confluence of two events that year that propelled the song to a permanent place in both the psyche and cultural legacy of the United States. One of these events was producer Arif Mardin's and vocalist Bette Midler's decision to record Gold's song. Regardless of how the composition came to be included in Midler's 1990 recording session, it stands today as a great example of one of those diamonds at one of those key moments.

This was the second event that cemented the song's standing: On August 2, 1990, troops and tanks from Iraq invaded Kuwait, setting the stage for an international confrontation. By the end of the year almost 500,000 American troops would be heading for, or were already stationed in the Persian Gulf region, and war was imminent. On October 6, 1990, during the build-up to the war, Bette Midler's single "From a Distance" on Atlantic Records debuted on *Billboard*'s Hot 100 singles chart. It rose to #2 and spent a total of twenty-six weeks on that chart. Supplementing the general level of radio airplay, many television and radio stations all over the world used Midler's hit recording, with its poignant and hopeful lyrics, to underscore reports of the world's march toward war. The end of the fighting in February 1991 virtually coincided with Julie Gold receiving Song of the Year honors at the 1991 Grammy Award® ceremonies.

In and around the music industry are songs that have yet to be recorded and ultimately achieve greatness, and others that may achieve success a second, third, or fourth time through the recording studio. If a song has been popular once, there is always the possibility that it can be popular and successful again, particularly as each new generation hears the song as new for the first time. One might add to all of this musical repertoire, the recordings of speeches and oratory of the period. In the early years of the record business spoken-word recordings were not unusual. And one more point about the early recordings: reading through the record company catalogs it becomes apparent that the earliest group of recording artists was dominated by males. The sections of individual vocal performers in the 1897 Columbia catalog of recordings featured George Graham, Fred Valmore, George Gaskin, Len Spencer, Dan Quinn, Edward Favor, George W. Johnson, Billy Golden, Russell Hunting, and others— and no women.

14

Type, Style, Genre, Tempo

Nature and nurture. What's in a preference? What's in a name? Simple questions most adults (and probably most children) have dealt with, or at least faced. In American society — perhaps every society — naming can be an empowering force, or simply a voiced recognition of choice. Consider some of those choices, some of those names: big, fat, small, smart, ignorant, immigrant, white, black, Coke, Dr. Pepper, Jeep, Audi, homeless, helpless, Christian, Muslim. Is it human nature when one of us, almost instinctively, elects to apply a label, or is it thoughtful consideration? When listening to music, is it instinctive? Does one have a natural affinity for country music? Is Euro-classical music an acquired taste? When giving some thought to new recordings, descriptive terms are applied in two specific ways: a recording is usually placed in (a) a genre based on the artist and the performance, and (b) consideration is also given that same recording due to its tempo. Once the recording is heard or named does the listener simply articulate another's opinion (accepting it at its face value) or search for a name s/he believes is more appropriate?

Genre

The norm in the music industry is to apply a descriptive label, any label, to all new music. Every new song, new recording, and new performance is categorized, quantified, classified, and pigeonholed. While this is done for a variety of reasons, the most obvious — from a music industry vantage point — are: to know where (within which music section) to place recordings in a retail store or online catalog list; to decide on which *Billboard* magazine (or other magazine's) popularity chart to rank the recording; to determine which radio stations or video outlets need to be targeted for airplay; to choose which print, broadcast, cable, or Internet media to invest marketing dollars in; to decide which general music types this recording, if necessary, should be compared to; even to assign an informal designation to the label releasing the recording, e.g., "a rap record label," which may be useful for the company's image in the music marketplace.

The various recording-labelers come from the ranks of songwriters, singers, musicians, producers, executives, critics, radio and video programmers, reviewers, entertainment writers, and of course, consumers. Each has a perspective and often those perspectives are in general agreement. On occasion, the genre-assessment among some members of the group may differ significantly. One or more may choose to simply shade the categorization. For example, is the band known as the Eagles (who first appeared on the Hot 100 singles chart in 1972) a rock 'n' roll band, a country-rock band, or a country music band? Probably not the last, but certainly one of the others. The fact that their records have appeared on *Billboard*'s Top Country singles *and* Hot 100 singles charts does suggest a hybrid.[1]

When reflecting on genre, one may choose from various descriptive terms. In musical terms, however, a significant number of artists do not fit neatly inside one pure music genre. Therefore, creative flexibility, not unlike the hybrid example with the Eagles, may be introduced. But which terms are relevant? Which genre names are genuine)? Where did these genre names come from? For example, who receives credit for assigning the genre-defining names "rap," "hip-hop," and "rock 'n' roll," as specific, evolving, styles of music? As with most names applied to contemporary genres, these three designations were generally evolutionary in nature. Once a genre name is accepted (and after it has fallen into common usage), how far back does one have to look to discover the name origin which has been applied to one or more existing or evolving music-genre names? Exploring three genre origins should clarify the concept of genre categorization.

Was the origin of the term "rock 'n' roll" as simple as listening to a song or a string of songs, and then finding a convenient phrase of the moment? To work toward an answer to this question, mull over this list of pre-1950 recordings:

(1) Allstar Trio: "I Want a Daddy Who Rocks Me" (1919);[2]
(2) Trixie Smith: "My Daddy Rocks Me (with one steady roll)" (1922; 34);
(3) Banjo Ikey Robinson Band: "Rock Me Mama" (1929);
(4) Duke Ellington: "Rockin' in Rhythm" (1932);
(5) Chick Webb & His Orchestra: "Rock It for Me" (1937);

(6) Washboard Sam (Robert Brown): "Rockin' My Blues Away" (1942);
(7) Arthur "Big Boy" Crudup: "Rock Me Mama" (1945);
(8) Wynonie Harris: "Good Rockin' Tonight" (1948);
(9) Little Son Jackson: "Rockin' and Rollin'" (1949);
(10) Jimmy Preston: "Rock the Joint" (1949).

These ten records seem to suggest the coming of rock 'n' roll as far back as 1919, yet none of them has been universally documented as the origin of the genre-defining phrase. In addition to these pre-1950s recordings and their performers, other individuals from the early 1950s have been given some credit for applying the genre name. Disc jockey Alan Freed (like musicians Louis Jordan, Bill Haley, and Little Richard) was present and undeniably a willing participant in the coming movement "moment" in which rock 'n' roll became a genre, but should any one person receive sole credit for the naming? Alan Freed laid a claim to the first public declaration of the genre name "rock 'n' roll." Unfortunately, irrefutable and independent validation of Freed as the first to coin the phrase is elusive.

Many adults, particularly those parents raising the generation known as the baby-boomers, believed there might be something within rock 'n' roll to be concerned about. Any worry they may have had was probably not assuaged after Elvis Presley began his long-remembered appearances on America's growing new 1950s phenomenon known as television. The flaws in our cultural memory often connect Presley's first prime-time gyrations with Ed Sullivan. In fact he appeared on television programs hosted by the Dorsey Brothers and by Steve Allen prior to his Sullivan appearances, making the human pelvis a hot topic of conversation in 1956. Was this the first connection of sex and rock 'n' roll?

More than one rock 'n' roll historian will be happy to correct the notion that 1956 was the launch year when sex and rock 'n' roll were united. Nick Tosches writes that "it is difficult to say precisely when the words 'rock 'n' roll' came to describe a genre of music or what was going on within that music. The phrase itself is immemorial. It had been popular for its sexual connotations in music of the 1920s."[3] Writer John A. Jackson, in his book *Big Beat Heat: Alan Freed and the Early Years of Rock & Roll*, provides a similar view and interpretation:

> The phrase "rock & roll" appears repeatedly as a euphemism for sexual intercourse in the bluntly sexual lyrics of race, or rhythm and blues records. If the celebrated phrase is not quite as old as "race" records themselves, the separate use of either *rock* or *roll* to denote sexual intercourse certainly is…. By 1950 at least a dozen rhythm and blues songs a year mentioned "rock" or "rockin'" in their titles and some,

like Little Son Jackson's "Rockin' and Rollin'" came right out and said it all.... Although [Alan Freed] maintained that the phrase "rock & roll" came to him in an "inspirational flash" as a "colorful and dynamic" description of the "rolling, surging beat of the music," in all likelihood Freed appropriated the phrase from the rhythm and blues music he listened to.[4]

Considering the views of both Tosches and Jackson, one can safely conclude that the sequence of events and rock 'n' roll's linear history are important in the general discussion of genre-name evolution. The weight of various cultural facets found in popular music—double entendre, sex, culture, melody, rhythm, ethnicity, language, lyric, convenience, and timing—culminated in the phrase "rock 'n' roll" being applied quickly to the music and accepted, if not uniformly embraced, as a new genre and a specific type of American music. It is not likely that all of the other genre names have had as long an evolution as one finds in the case for rock 'n' roll, but logic suggests a premise: most genre-names have, in their origin, some measure of the ingredients listed above. Having established that the music world's arrival at an appellation for one new genre of music, rock 'n' roll, has its underpinnings—in no small part—in the music itself, are there other examples to confirm the premise? Exploring another contemporary musical form may affirm the general origin of genre declaration.

Three writers, Eileen Southern, K. Maurice Jones, and Nelson George, seem to maneuver us into an understanding of genre origin. Southern traced urban genres in her book *The Music of Black Americans: A History.* She followed the origins of rap and hip-hop music (and the use of their genre-defining names) through Afrika Bambaataa, Clive Campbell, and many other musicians whose stretching of the accepted definitions of 1970s music and performance—particularly rhythm and blues—expanded the boundaries of genre identity. Bambaataa's early-1970s legitimization of new musical genres emerged through his belief that, as Southern notes, "the arts could be used to combat the rampant street violence of the youth gangs in his community (which included the Bronx River project)."[5] Worth noting is that Bambaataa's efforts did not directly or immediately create or define a musical genre or style, but rather he became an enabler who facilitated artistic freedom. In time that artistic freedom would push the envelope of urban music outward, and additional genres could evolve.

There was also, explained Southern, another contribution: "In 1975 the young Jamaican Clive Campbell began his disc-jockeying career in the South Bronx area of New York City under the name Kool DJ Herc. He introduced some of the practices that contributed to the development of rap as a bona fide music genre."[6] With the rise of the rap genre, spinning records at clubs took on a new appearance, a new rapport with the audience:

> In 1975 [Kool DJ] Herc started deejaying [sic] at Bronx teen clubs, community centers, and parties. At his gigs Herc began spinning short sections of different records and talking over them.... Soon Herc played records on two turntables at the same time.... He developed the technique of mixing passages from one song into another. He would pick the most recognizable part of a hit or a soul classic and play it over and over again, integrating pieces of other songs while rhyming over them.[7]

From here one can begin to connect the dots. Once again, individuals began to explore and expand music's boundaries. The result was that these young musicians and DJs were about to go where no music had gone before. Nelson George, in his book *Hip Hop America*, adds further perspective to the origins of hip-hop:

> One of the prevailing assumptions around hip hop is that it was, at some early moment, solely African-American created, owned, controlled, and consumed. It's an appealing origin myth—but the evidence just isn't there to support it. Start with who "invented" hip hop: In its days as an evolving street culture, Latino dancers and tastemakers—later internationally known as breakers—were integral to its evolution, because of the synergy between what the mobile DJs played and what excited the breakers. Also, Caribbean culture clearly informed hip hop's Holy Trinity—Afrika Bambatta, Grandmaster Flash, and Kool Herc. Two of them, Flash and Herc, were either born in the Caribbean or had close relatives from there. In Bam's case, non-American black music had been essential to his aesthetic.
> More heretically, on the owner front, I'd argue that without white entrepreneurial involvement hip hop culture wouldn't have survived its first half decade on vinyl.[8]

The individual elements that ended up as core ingredients in the arrival of rap and hip-hop as genres were (a) the DJ's elevation from background entertainer to foreground performer, (b) the splitting of performance responsibilities between DJ and MC, (c) the presentation of lyrics and rhymes, i.e., rapping, (d) the necessary stage presence/personality of the performers, (e) street culture including ethnic backgrounds, and (f) the use of existing (older) recordings and new music. Rap and hip-hop started as a performance experience and evolved into genres of music. Following the trail documented by writers Southern, Jones, and George, one might safely conclude that rap and hip-hop were products of a chain of events, and like rock 'n' roll, the events began with the music.

Having explored these genres, it becomes obvious that defining or naming a genre "rap" or "hip-hop" (or "rock 'n' roll") is not necessarily a reference to the original moment that the genre was created. The creation moment may have occurred months or even years before a genre name is finally applied to the music and the performers and the public choose to embrace it. Music's genre names therefore reflect, to varying degrees, the music itself. Revisiting the earlier question of whether labeling a genre is a simple matter, the answer seems quite obvious: once a style of music is consistently performed and accepted by an audience, naming it does become a relatively simple matter (as long as the name sticks). But first, the audience and those making the music must feel that this style of music is truly new, and that it can be readily differentiated from its music-genre contemporaries. There is also the reality of whether those outside of the new genre objectively come to the same conclusion. Finally, a lack of acceptance by a broad-based audience does not delegitimize a new genre; it merely indicates that the audience, at least for the time being, is a niche audience.

Tempo

Clearly genres become defined as music reaches beyond its currently prescribed or accepted limits, but music — whether written, performed, or recorded — is also labeled by its tempo. While two people may not always agree on which genre a particular performance or recording embodies, it is difficult to debate the tempo of that performance or recording. Expressed formally in a language that is both uniform and Italian—*largo, adagio, moderato, andante, allegro, allegretto, presto, prestissimo,*[9] tempo helps define the mood of the song and the mood of the performance. When one speaks of a recording in terms of tempo, there is usually an inference made, based on a contemporary understanding of popular music. A ballad is a slower-tempo piece of music, whereas, dance music is likely to be mid-to-uptempo.[10] Lyrical themes are often consistent within chosen tempos. Recordings of ballads will usually take on more serious themes— love, beauty, romance, break-up, dying, and death. Uptempo recordings may also tackle love and romance, but their topics are just as likely to be light-hearted as serious. Social issues have been addressed in a variety of tempos.

Without exception, these two classifications— tempo and genre —can be applied to every recording. Consequently any recording can be placed within the context of a genre, and every recording's performance adhere's to one or more tempos within the earlier defined speeds of music. Some recordings have a change in tempo that lasts through one section or for the balance of the performance, as in "A Day in the Life" by the Beatles from the album *Sgt. Pepper's Lonely Hearts Club Band* (Capitol 2653, 1967). Even a spoken-word recording has its own tempo, created by the style of the speaker, or dictated by the rhyme of related words or the meter of a poem. While two people may not always agree on precisely which *genre* or which *tempo* a particular recording may embody, these two ideas are applied to every recording. The earlier look at the chart success of the Eagles provides one example of music that can be defined and yet whose musical boundaries may be blurred.

Once the difference between, and the connection of, genre and tempo is clear, personal taste or bias enters the discussion. After all, if none of us had an opinion about the music, then what would there be to debate? From a thoughtful consideration of genre and tempo one can conclude that recordings are both intuitive and interpretive. Regardless of the music that they have already recorded and experienced commercial success with, the musicians' or performers' inner voices may be pushing them to move their music into unexpected directions. They may move from one genre to another, i.e., from *country* to *folk* or vice versa, or incorporate a contrasting tempo to a known performance style. Either idea — genre-shift or new tempo — represents a revised understanding of the song. The intuitive performance is what the recording artist chooses to create. What the listener infers from the recording itself represents the interpretive performance. Much like the question of an A&R person's vision, what the performer believes s/he is recording may or may not be in sync with what the listener is presently hearing or wishes to hear. Consumers may or may not purchase the new recordings regardless of artistic vision or critical acclaim.

Bob Dylan's unexpected vocal style on his 1969 album *Nashville Skyline* caught many listeners, critics, and fans off guard, but did not result in a collapse of his career. Dylan stated in a June 1969 *Rolling Stone* interview that the change happened because "I stopped smoking. When I stopped smoking, my voice changed ... so drastically, I couldn't believe it myself. That's true. I tell you, you stop smoking those cigarettes ... and you'll be able to sing like Caruso."[11] Dylan's intuitive exploration of a new vocal style — whether the result of his decision to stop smoking or not — and his genre-shift from folk to a country-flavored album did not cost him unit sales of his new album. Dylan's core audience interpreted the effort positively, and with the help of a duet with country legend Johnny Cash, Bob Dylan most likely brought a few believers from country music along as well. *Nashville Skyline* peaked at #3 in *Billboard*'s Top 200 Albums (1969), as high or higher than seven of his previous eight albums. To put this in perspective, the ten noncompilation studio albums by Dylan after *Nashville Skyline* peaked well inside the Top Twenty, including half appearing in the Top Five, with three of those reaching #1.[12] To restate the obvious, Dylan's flirtation with country music did not hurt his career.[13]

Tempo, genre, style, and type can be defined, yet almost immediately any definition can be challenged; like chameleons, recording artists can adapt and change as their vision or life experience dictates.

15

Most of the Music

If one now understands the labeling or partitioning of music into genres, it then becomes easier to organize and discuss each musical style. What follows is just such a breakdown of the music into these genres, and a brief discussion of the genres during the early recording industry. In addition, a representative list of recordings within each genre made between 1889 and 1919 is provided to help the reader's understanding. (All of the recordings discussed in this chapter are included within Appendix I.)

Ballads, Romance, and the Parlor

When we think of a ballad today it is usually in the simple context of a romantic or sentimental theme, performed in a slower time signature. During the first thirty years of the music industry, many recorded ballads could be described as mini-soap operas, or two-minute dramas. In 1900 "these songs were plotted, often encapsulating the story of a popular stage melodrama or novel."[1] Today's music listeners have also, at times, looked wistfully back to the early years of recording and songwriting with a desire to recapture some of that simple, innocent, delicate, poignant nature of composition, arrangement, and production.

Publisher and songwriter Charles K. Harris (1864–1930) wrote two popular songs that are representative of the early era. In "After the Ball" (1893) Harris told the story "of a man at a dance who sees his sweetheart kissing another man; he walks out, but never gets over it, and finds out years later that the other man was her brother. His other big hit, 'Hello Central, Give Me Heaven' (1901), began with a news item about a child whose mother had died and who tried to phone her."[2] Considering the latter song, it's obvious that Harris' preternatural theme would continue to be reflected in various ways during the twentieth century. Fifty years after Harris, Oscar Hammerstein and Richard Rogers wrote "You'll Never Walk Alone," for the Broadway production of *Carousel*. Lead character Billy Bigelow's message to his daughter was meant to provide comfort to her; it was particularly effective since the message arrived as a long-distance spiritual (extrasensory and wireless) message — Bigelow was dead and looking down and communicating with his daughter from heaven.

Beyond Hammerstein, Rogers, and Harris' direct heaven-to-earth connection, death and dying continued to find a home with popular songwriters and performers. Mark Dinning's 1959 ballad "Teen Angel" has a girlfriend getting killed when a train hits the boyfriend's car as she hunts for an elusive high school ring. In 1999 the group Pearl Jam recorded Wayne Cochran's song "Last Kiss,"[3] which also used teenage death as a centerpiece: following a traffic accident, a boy wakes up to rain, blood, and a dying girlfriend. Death and the ballad are not uniformly or unconditionally linked, but the ballad — often including sad lyrics— has been a staple of recordings throughout the long history of the music business, turning up in numerous releases. Here is clear evidence of consumer acceptance and consumer demand.

An alternate option for the ballad might include a military storyline. The idea of going off to fight for God and country is not easily dismissed. In the early years of recording it was not fashionable to be cynical about patriotism as might have been the case during the late-1960s or in post-Vietnam America. In the nineteenth century, the United States was a country accepting immigrants who, in many cases, believed that the land they had left behind paled in comparison to the land they had adopted. Therefore, their sense of duty, one could assume, was genuine. Military themes (discussed in a general context later) represent another ballad type.

Many ballad recordings in which the central character died in the middle of the song depicted the grieving, surviving, lover carrying on bravely, often alone. Another common ballad theme was love and relationships— including marriage; these subjects would be developed in these mini-sagas. The characters would sing (or speak) of love: the performer would propose marriage or resign himself to living without it; a relationship would become complete, or the lonely, spurned or lost love would "whither on the vine." As with "Teen Angel" and "Last Kiss," in the recordings of the early 1900s "characters died between verses, and the refrains served as both love songs and dirges."[4] Many ballads existed without any particular context other than the theme of love, and often these were the odes being offered from one lover to another.

While some of us may occasionally wax nostalgic recalling popular recordings from the 1950s or 1960s, the fact is that even in the late nineteenth century there was a look backward to earlier music and musical styles. Whether one chooses to use the term ballad to describe genre, or tempo, or style, ballads appealed to early recording artists, songwriters, and consumers. One of the best (and best-known) examples of the ballad genre was set in the South: Stephen Foster's "Old Folks at Home" (which is also known and more widely recognized by its emblematic lyric "Way Down upon the Swanee River"). Another 1890s classic often used for wedding ceremonies, though not strictly a southern-themed song, was Reginald DeKoven's "Oh Promise Me." Ballads filled with nostalgic themes, and some with a country or rural setting, would endure well into the first thirty years of recording.

True soap-opera characteristics were found in a song written by Gussie Davis and W. H. Windom titled "The Fatal Wedding." Sigmund Spaeth said of "The Fatal Wedding" that "even [its] monumental silliness could not destroy the song's appeal to a public [in the mid-1890s] that doted on vicarious infidelity, sudden death and artificial melodrama in general."[5] Although most patriotic and military themes will be discussed in a later section, one such title is also representative of the ballad style. "Till We Meet Again" was written and published during World War I and became a popular recording after the November 1918 armistice was signed. (Two versions were listed by Whitburn as "chart" records in February and March 1919.) The lyrics expressed a longing for a postwar reunion of two lovers, either in this world or the next. It contained sighs, goodbyes, tears, fears, clouds, skies, thoughts, and prayers as the lovers looked to a day when they actually might meet once more.

"Hello Central Give Me Heaven," the Charles Harris song, also brought out both the tears and the handkerchiefs. A little girl missing her deceased mother was irresistibly heartbroken and wanted to use the relatively new invention — the telephone — to speak with her:

> *Papa I'm so sad and lonely, sobbed a tearful little child,*
> *Since dear mama's gone to heaven, papa darling you've not smiled,*
> *I will speak to her and tell her that we want her to come home*
> *Just you listen and I'll call her through the telephone*
> *Hello Central, give me heaven, for my mama's there*
> *You can find her with the angels on the golden stair*
> *She'll be glad it's me who's speaking, call her won't you please*
> *For I want to surely tell her that we're so lonely here.*[6]

The illustration on the cover of the sheet music for Harris' song left almost nothing to the imagination. One sees the little girl, telephone in hand, looking toward heaven; seven or eight angels look down (although, unfortunately, none appear to be holding a telephone); in between the angels and the girl is a switchboard with telephone operators.

Most lists of songs from the era contain examples of recordings and familiar songs which fall within the general ballad genre. These include songs sometimes employing a traditional ballad tempo, and sometimes arranged as a barbershop quartet number, e.g., "Let Me Call You Sweetheart." Perhaps a slightly faster tempo than many ballads but still thematically appropriate in this category is Ren Shields' (1868–1913) "In the Good Old Summer Time." Its lyrics painted a happier picture (happier, at least, than some of the aforementioned serious themes):

> *In the good old summer time, in the good old summer time,*
> *Strolling through shady lanes, with your baby mine,*
> *You hold her hand and she holds yours and that's a very good sign,*
> *That she's your tootsey-wootsey in the good old summer time.*[7]

Nostalgia was the order of the day, as evinced by the aging couple looking back on their life together and their romance in the song "When You Were Sweet Sixteen," with lyrics by Harry Williams (1872–1922):

> *Put on your gingham gown dear, and come on to town with me,*
> *Let's make believe we're young again, just as we used to be,*
> *I'll be your bashful beau, dear, you'll be my village queen,*
> *As in days when I was twenty-one, and you were sweet sixteen.*[8]

Mooney pointed to the mood heard in many early ballad recordings and the rationale for themes present in some slower-tempo popular songs of the 1890s and early 1900s. Songs like "'When You and I Were Young, Maggie' reflected not only aesthetic values, but also the social thinking of a nation dominated by males and built upon the sanctity of marriage, prenuptial chastity, and perennial passivity of women."[9]

While romance themes are obvious in the examples already cited, other romantic songs became popular as well. Most of the songs in this category would be simple love songs, found at the romantic genre's two extremes: a very long lifetime love or, borrowing a contemporary description, a one night stand. Initial success may have found them categorized as songs about spooning, an early euphemism for otherwise amorous behavior such as kissing, caressing or, perhaps, more. Some of the recordings were shared in performance by male or female performers, representing imaginary lovers or on occasion the performers themselves. "Many of the most popular songs were invitations, descriptions, or even instruction manuals on 'spooning', among them 'By the Light of the Silvery Moon', 'Shine on Harvest Moon', and 'Row, Row, Row.'"[10]

Other popular compositions were described as parlor songs. The more affluent homeowners would have a parlor, a room reserved for entertaining visitors. One will recall the earlier description of families enjoying the performance of a singer or pianist in the family entertaining guests and family members gathered around the piano or the performer to listen to an impromptu performance or to participate by singing along. In pre-phonograph America, songs had long been a staple within the home; musical successes from the Broadway stage, popular operas, vaudeville, or musical theater were at first brought into the family home via sheet music, and ultimately by the phonograph. Songs like "Moonlight Bay," written in 1912, were recorded staples throughout much of the twentieth century. Here is a sampling of the ballad genre, and the related romance and parlor styles among the early recordings:

Song	Performer	Record	Release Year
The Picture Turned Toward the Wall	Manhansett Quartette	North American	1892
The Fatal Wedding	George Gaskin	New Jersey	1893
Sweeet Marie [sic]	George Gaskin	New Jersey	1894
When You Were Sweet Sixteen	Jere Mahoney	Edison 7410	1900
To the End of the World	Reed Miller	Victor 17026	1901
Hello Central Give Me Heaven	Byron Harlan	Edison 7852	1901
In the Good Old Summer Time	Haydn Quartet	Victor 16125	1903
Oh Promise Me	Henry Burr	Edison 8929	1905
Will You Love Me in December as You Do in May?	Harry MacDonough	Edison 9198	1906
Shine On Harvest Moon	Walton & MacDonough	Victor 16259	1908
I Wonder Who's Kissing Her Now	Henry Burr	Columbia 707	1909
By the Light of the Silvery Moon	Ada Jones	Edison 10362	1910
It's Hard to Kiss Your Sweetheart When the Last Kiss Means Goodbye	Arthur C. Clough	Edison 10251	1910
Down by the Old Mill Stream	Arthur C. Clough	Edison (4) 796	1911
Drink to Me Only with Thine Eyes	Frank Stanley	Edison (4) 615	1911
I Want a Girl (Just Like the Girl That Married Dear Old Dad)	American Quartet	Victor 16962	1911
Let Me Call You Sweetheart	Columbia Quartet	Columbia 1057	1911
I Love You Truly	Elsie Baker	Victor 17121	1912
Till the Sands of the Desert Grow Cold	Donald Chalmers	Edison 1043	1912
Row, Row, Row	Arthur Collins	Columbia 1244	1912
Moonlight Bay	Dolly Connolly	Columbia 1128	1912
I'd Rather Be Kissed 'Neath the Mistletoe Bough Than Spoon under Any Old Tree	Campbell & Burr	Victor 17274	1913
Your Eyes Have Told Me What I Did Not Know	Enrico Caruso	Victor 8719	1913
When I Lost You	Manuel Romain	Columbia 1288	1913
M-O-T-H-E-R (A Word That Means the World to Me)	George Wilton Ballard	Edison 50325	1916

Song	Performer	Record	Release Year
Till We Meet Again	James & Hart	Victor 18518	1919
You're a Million Miles from Nowhere	Charles Harrison	Victor 18645B	1919
Old Folks at Home	Columbia Stellar Quartet	Columbia 6082	1919

Regional

Regional references and themes in popular recordings were not unusual. In some cases the writing was heartfelt and credible due to the writer's experience living in or visiting a particular part of the country. In other cases the writing was a product of only the writer's imagination (as often seen in the exotic and other themes found in Chapter 17, "Culture Swing: The Reality of Ethnic Recordings.") There were songs like "Carry Me Back to Old Virginny" which sold millions of copies in sheet music form and became an early hit cylinder recording. The song "Dixie,"[11] written by Daniel Decatur Emmett, has long been associated with and by American citizens born in, or adopting as their own, the American South. Emmett's story of the song's origin provides some insight into the craft and business of songwriting:

> Like almost everything else I ever did, ["Dixie"] was written because it had to be done. One Saturday night in 1859, as I was leaving Bryant's Theater [in New York City], where I was playing, Bryant called after me "I want a walk-around[12] for Monday, Dan." The next day it rained and I stayed indoors. At first when I went after the song I couldn't get anything. But a line, "I wish I was in Dixie," kept repeating itself in my mind, and I finally took it for my start. The rest wasn't long in coming.... It made a hit at once, and before the end of the week everybody in New York was whistling it. I sold the copyright for five hundred dollars, which was all I ever made from it.[13]

Many of Stephen Foster's songs, while not necessarily titled with an obvious regional reference, nevertheless evoke regionality, including southern thoughts and dreams. Two examples of Foster's so-called "regionality" are the mid-nineteenth century songs "Oh Susanna" (which mentions Alabama) and "Old Folks at Home (Way Down upon the Swanee River)" (which is set in Georgia/Florida; the Swanee (Suwannee) River flows from Georgia to Florida's Gulf Coast). A promotional song, written in conjunction with the Saint Louis Exposition of 1904, became famous and successful apart from the fair. "Meet Me in Saint Louis, Louis" stayed around long after the fair disappeared.

Song	Performer	Record	Release Year
Carry Me Back to Old Virginny	Edison Male Quartette	Edison 2237	1896
My Old New Hampshire Home	George Gaskin	Berliner 068	1898
The Girl I Loved in Sunny Tennessee	Albert Campbell	Edison 5718	1899
Dixie	Edison Grand Concert Band	Edison 8133	1902
O Susanna	Unknown Tenor w/Chorus		1904
Meet Me in Saint Louis, Louis	S. H. Dudley	Victor 2807	1904
Old Folks at Home	Louise Homer	Victor 81077	1905
My Old Kentucky Home	Geraldine Farrar	Edison 2223	1910
Below the Mason Dixon Line	Arthur Collins	Edison (4) 698	1911
On the New York, New Haven, & Hartford	Edward Meeker	Edison (4) 882	1912
Sailing Down the Chesapeake Bay	Henry Burr & A. Campbell	Columbia 1378	1913
Hello Frisco	Sam Ash	Columbia 1801	1915
For Dixie and Uncle Sam	Nora Bayes	Victor 45100	1916
Beale Street Blues	Earl Fuller's Novelty Orch.	Victor 18369	1917
Rock-A-Bye Your Baby with a Dixie Melody	Al Jolson	Columbia 2560	1918
Beautiful Ohio	Sam Ash	Emerson 9132	1919

Comedy/Novelty

The comedy and novelty genres played a significant part in early popular recordings— musical and non-musical, and the category is larger than one might expect. Vaudeville continued as a mainstay of entertainment until the advent of radio and motion pictures. Theaters large and small became entertainment stops across the United States. In many cities, venues adopted or simply shared the name of vaudeville's most famous venue, New York's Palace Theater. Numerous namesake Palace Theaters opened in cities including Los Angeles (1911), Manchester, New Hampshire (1915), Cleveland (1922), Waterbury, Connecticut (1922), Lockport, New York (1925), Greenburg, Pennsylvania (1926), Stamford, Connecticut (1927), Louisville (1928), and Albany, New York (1931). At the peak of vaudeville's popularity there were between 4,000 and 5,000 vaudeville-style theaters in the United States. Live theater performance contributed music (including thematic songs), monologues, and humor to the recording companies (including thematic songs), and to some degree, beyond the repertoire, vaudeville delivered some of their predisposed audience as potential record consumers.

Comedy/novelty was a natural extension of the growing recording types, given the popularity of vaudeville, and its use of comedians either as opening acts or performing in between more serious performers. As for content, some of the comedy recordings were virtually generic in nature, while other recordings were topical, sometimes aimed at a sport, celebrity, current event, or ethnic group; and still there were some monologues, routines, and performances that could not be classified in any of those. For example, there was George Johnson's "The Laughing Song" and Jay Laurier's "Sneezing." (Johnson, by the way, may have been the first African-American recording star, as he preceded even the great Bert Williams into the recording studio by ten years.) While not necessarily a comedy song or recording, one has to consider the theme of the song "Casey Jones" a novelty. The namesake, Casey Jones,

> took the Cannonball Express [train] out of Memphis on a Sunday night, April 29, 1900, substituting as engineer for a sick friend. Near Vaughn, Miss., the train crashed into another, very much as described in the song. Jones was killed "with his hand on the throttle, scalded to death by the steam." He became a symbol of courage in railroading....[14]

Lacking another category, this genre may best be defined by looking through the recordings listed below. Once defined, and once understood, the comedy/novelty genre can be explored in some detail. However, due to the nature of the recordings, the genre will be split into two "explorations." The second exploration will be to look at this genre within the context of ethnic popular recordings as found in Chapters 16 and 17 ("Immigration and Recordings" and "Culture Swing—The Reality of Ethnic Recordings"). These later chapters will take a closer look at the ethnically oriented (and ethnically charged) words, lyrics, and dialects which were found in some early recordings. The first group (below) contains samples (and general variations) of the themes of comedy and novelty found in the widely popular early recordings:

Song	Performer	Record	Release Year
The Laughing Song	George Johnson	Columbia (unknown)	1891
Casey on the Bowery	Russell Hunting	Edison 3824	1897
Reuben Haskins from Skowhegan, Maine	Len Spencer	Columbia 31582	1901
Two Rubes in a Tavern	Frank Stanley	Columbia 938	1902
If Money Talks, It Ain't on Speaking Terms with Me	Arthur Collins	Victor 1631	1902
Uncle Josh on an Automobile	Cal Stewart	Columbia 1518	1903
Any Rags	Arthur Collins	Victor 2519	1903
Everybody Works but Father	Lew Dockstader	Columbia 3251	1905
Take Me Out to the Ball Game	Haydn Quartet	Victor 5570	1908
No News, or What Killed the Dog	Nat Wills	Victor 5612	1909
Casey Jones	Billy Murray	Edison (Amberol) 450	1910
Cohen on the Telephone	Joe Hayman	Columbia 1516	1914

Song	Performer	Record	Release Year
The Baseball Game	Weber & Fields	Columbia 2092	1917
I'm Forever Blowing Bubbles	George W. Ballard	Edison 3948	1919
Sneezing	Jay Laurier	unknown	

Ragtime

In the context of early recordings, ragtime was less a fad and more a genuine genre of music to be exploited. It had some of its roots in the novelty song genre, but ragtime was clearly a distinct musical style. "As the Gay Nineties began, the industrial technological revolution and its accompanying urbanization and mass commercialization were forcing drastic changes in American life. Ragtime would become a musical reflection of these changes in two separate ways: as entertainment and as art."[15]

Musical styles can sometimes prove difficult to explain, especially to the uninitiated. But Donald Clarke seems to have turned the right phrase conveying the essence of ragtime in his characterization of the New Orleans music scene in the nineteenth century:

> In their dancing, in minstrelsy and then in ragtime, black Americans were insisting on setting European-style music free by refusing to be restricted to a ground beat. The dancing in [New Orleans'] Congo Square was described as in "ragged" time in 1886; in 1888 a banjo player in Nebraska wrote to a music magazine requesting music in "broken time" like the "ear-players" played, but none had been printed yet.[16]

Like rap, hip-hop, and rock 'n' roll, ragtime became a genre name directly from its shape, form, and sound; it was the syncopated sum of its component parts.

Defining a musical genre, and the consumer's ultimate acceptance of that genre, does not impart universal objectivity, appreciation, or respect. In December 1900, *Billboard* magazine ran a story titled "Decadence of 'Rag-Time' Music." Michael Brand, whom Billboard described as a man with

> a world-wide reputation, not only as a performer, but as an orchestral and band director ... has always refused to lower the standard of his concerts at the dictation [sic] of those who follow fads and are not impressed by music of good quality. Mr. Brand has been a persistent and consistent foe to so-called rag-time music....
> "The rag-time craze was an epidemic, and the evil influence resulting therefrom is just as disastrous to the divine art of music as the wreckage after a storm, or casualties after a battle. It came as a scourge, and like a scourge, it inflicted its debasing character upon all

alike. The very air was filled with its poisonous contagion, and nowhere could one take himself to get rid of its harshly juggled syncopation."[17]

With that impassioned start ("epidemic," "evil") Mr. Brand was just getting warmed up. He further assured the reader that ragtime produced musical "crimes and criminals," was "vulgar," "crude," and "depraved," and the world would not be safe until "the Avenging Angel ... empties the [vials] of his wrath upon the would-be defamers of the divine art of music...."[18] Brand's invective, unfortunately, did not target latent or conscious racism contained in the lyrics of some of the music. Instead it was focused on the apparent temerity of ragtime's practitioners—calling for divine intervention to save music from this new scourge.

Perhaps within a single compact package a ragtime melody represented the intellectual or emotional escape of black musicians (or by extension, black Americans in general) into a freewheeling alternate reality—even if just for the duration of the song or the performance. The syncopated rhythms, the driving physicality, and the emotions all jump out of the piano and, in the process, transfer from the performer to the listener. One can almost feel the musician pushing the keyboards to the limits of physical punishment in an effort to achieve an emotional release.

Despite the criticisms of Michael Brand and his ilk, ragtime survived and evolved. In a more historical view, the music may have signaled freedom of the spirit, but ironically, it probably reinforced one or more stereotypes of blacks in America by virtue of the imitation that it would inspire. In effect it created a musical paradox. "Although it was a part of the underground black subculture long before it appeared in print, ragtime was not published until 1896."[19] Variations on the theme preceded ragtime. Coon songs (music with lyrics) and cakewalks (instrumental performances) were historically, musically, and socially connected, and they were accompanied by racist attitudes from post-Reconstruction America, embodied in an entertainment style known as the minstrel show. The instrumental cakewalks,[20] "that dance of plantation origin had been taken up by minstrels and given a special place in their shows, sometimes as a feature entitled 'walking for that cake'...."[21] Without patently offensive lyrics, racism was minimized in cakewalks, and rhythm was key.

As the public accepted, supported, or otherwise affirmed the popularity of musical styles like minstrel songs, recording companies would be ready and willing to exploit these newly identified avenues of sales. After all, "in the almost thirty years between 1885 and the First World War, the modern American popular song began to emerge. The rhythms of minstrelsy continued to percolate into the mainstream; the cakewalk demanded something that the waltzes, polkas and marches of European music could not supply."[22] In addition to their popularity on the live-performance circuit, minstrel recordings would find their way into the catalogs of the early record companies. Even with this expansion of the genre there is a dose of reality to consider. Although cakewalks and so-called coon songs were extremely popular, a popularity that lasted for decades, that popularity should not be viewed as a springboard for musicians of color. During the early recording era most early recording artists, as will be discussed in detail in chapters 16 and 17, were white.

To put the success of these recorded songs in context, one needs to consider the social climate in America. First, there was a history of minstrel shows featuring song and dance numbers not infrequently performed (co-opted) by whites. These shows, and many of these songs and basic melody lines, predated the American Civil War. Consequently, the style — whether performed by blacks or whites — was already familiar to audiences. Second, for many listeners, music and performance from the slave experience were simply entertainment, with no particular political implications. Third, "racist segregation laws of the South were given federal legitimacy in 1896 with the Supreme Court decision on the *Plessy v. Ferguson* case. The court upheld a state law separating races on railroads and, by extension, elsewhere."[23] A court-affirmed separation of the races reinforced racial stereotypes. No one should be surprised, then, that near the turn of the century American recording companies devoted part of their catalogs to recordings that fostered stereotypes. After all, mainstream American culture saw no controversy inherent in the recordings, and the repertoire was well known, the performers modestly paid for their time in the studio, and the musical instruments adaptable to the early recording process. For the recording industry, the songs were just business.

Like Jazz its blood-relative descendant, Ragtime is an important American musical genre. It isn't just about rhythm, although its rhythm speaks to the listener. It isn't just about syncopation, yet syncopation is a defining element. It isn't just about society and its social issues, yet its conception is traced to one of the bloodiest chapters in American history — the American Civil War with its resultant 600,000 deaths. Ragtime's birth is entwined with events leading up to and through the so-called "Gay Nineties," and into the twentieth century. Writing about E. L. Doctorow's novel *Ragtime*, Berndt Ostendorf declared that the ragtime era "set a new agenda in popular music and ushered in a social revolution."[24] The ragtime musical genre and its root name were well represented in record titles during the first thirty years of recording.

Song	Performer	Record	Release Year
St. Louis Rag	Arthur Pryor's Band	Victor 2783	1904
Buffalo Rag	Vess Ossman	Victor 4628	1906
Maple Leaf Rag	Vess Ossman	Columbia 3626	1907
The Old Time Rag	Arthur Collins	Edison 9956	1908
That Lovin' Rag	Nora Bayes	Victor 60023	1910
Red Rose Rag	Dolly Connolly	Columbia 1028	1911
The Skeleton Rag	American Quartet	Victor 17041	1912
Alexander's Ragtime Band	Victor Military Band	Victor 17006	1912
Waiting for the Robert E. Lee	Dolly Connolly	Columbia 1197	1912
Florida Rag	Fred Van Eps	Victor 17308	1913
That International Rag	Prince's Orchestra	Columbia 5532	1914
That Moaning Saxophone Rag	Six Brown Brothers	Victor 17677	1915
Tiger Rag	Orig. Dixieland Jazz Band	Victor 18472	1918

Production

Production songs were often created using three of the previously described musical types: ballads, romantic themes, and novelty songs. In general, the styles were unified to create content for musical theater, "specifically for each scene to introduce its theme and to frame solo specialty numbers or songs. Many [but not all] production songs gained popularity on their own, among them ... 'A Pretty Girl Is Like a Melody'"[25] from the *Ziegfeld Follies of 1919*. The number of shows opening on Broadway during the first thirty years of recording continued to multiply, and the available material to record grew exponentially. For example, there were more than 150 shows playing just during the 1909–1910 season, many of them musicals, some by significant lyricists and composers. A selection of popular shows of the era include Gilbert and Sullivan's *The Gondoliers and The King of Barataria* (1890), *The Mikado* (1910), and *H.M.S. Pinafore* (1915), Koven and Smith's *Robin Hood* (1891), Brandl and Frost's *The Merry Countess* (1895), Victor Herbert's *The Serenade* (1900), George M. Cohan's *Little Johnny Jones* (1905) and *Forty-five Minutes from Broadway* (1906), and *Cohan and Harris Minstrels* (1908). Songs from these and other musicals included:

Song	Performer	Record	Release Year
Toyland	Corrine Morgan	Victor 2721	1904
Because	Haydn Quartet	GramOPhon 105	1900
Yankee Doodle Boy	Billy Murray	Columbia 3051	1905
Give My Regards to Broadway	S. H. Dudley	Victor 4385	1905
Harrigan	Edward Meeker	Edison 9616	1907
I Wonder Who's Kissing Her Now	Henry Burr	Columbia 707	1909
Tramp, Tramp, Tramp	Byron Harlan/ Frank Stanley	Victor 16531	1910
By the Light of the Silvery Moon	Haydn Quartet	Victor 16460	1910
Life's a Funny Proposition After All	George M. Cohan	Victor 10042	1911

Song	Performer	Record	Release Year
March of the Toys	Victor Herbert & Orchestra	Victor 70048	1911
Peg o' My Heart	Charles Harrison	Victor 17412	1913
Hello Frisco	Elida Morris	Columbia 1801	1915
I'm Always Chasing Rainbows	Charles Harrison	Victor 18496	1918
Hail! Hail! The Gang's All Here	Irving Kaufman	Columbia 2443	1918

Dance

Recordings today are about more than simply listening. One person may choose to play an instrument to accompany the recording, a second might acquire a digital sample for a different purpose, and still another may simply dance to the music. Things were not that different a century ago (although there was the absence of digital recording technology) when then, as now, recordings were not all created with the idea of an audience passively enjoying the melodies. As with production numbers, "exhibition ballroom dancing grew so in popularity that by 1913 it was a required feature of vaudeville, revues, cabarets, and musical shows."[26] Such live shows were all sources of demonstrating or determining the popularity of music which might subsequently be recorded, and with luck, become a hit record.

It is a given that the popularity of a particular song or series of songs can influence recorded music consumers to embrace a new style of music or choose to begin learning a new type of dance. One only has to think back to Arthur Gibbs & His Gang's "Charleston" (1924), Chubby Checker's "Twist" (1960), or Los Del Rio's "Macarena" (1992) to appreciate the impact one record can have on a musical audience willing to step out on the dance floor. In the early years of recording

> publishers, their writers, and song-pluggers were first bewildered, then enchanted by a national mania for dancing. Up to 1910 the waltz had been supreme in the ballroom, for the slow ballads that were popular music's main fare lent themselves easily to three-quarter tempo. But suddenly people stopped rotating and started to glide, hop, and dip.[27]

In some cases the songwriters, record companies, or performers likely assigned names to dance styles, regardless of whether or not the names were organic (as part of the creative process) or inorganic (indiscriminately labeled or appropriated based on observations rather than the underlying music). The rag, reel, waltz, aeroplane waltz (and various other waltzes), tango, cakewalk, old zip coon quadrille, fox-trot, turkey-trot (and numerous "trot" variations), rumba, kangaroo dip/hop, polka, fish walk, bunny hug, one-step, two-step, glide, shimmy, grizzly bear, etc., were all visible (and audible) during recording's first thirty years.[28] Dance styles may come and go, but regardless of one style's duration as a popular entity the impact may enjoy only a lingering moment in the public's consciousness. For example, Cohen-Stratyner lists five dance songs—four in 1914, one in 1919—as having been created by or for the dance team of Vernon and Irene Castle, including their signature dance, the "Castle Walk,"[29] while the Charleston lived on past the Roaring 20s due in no small part to the impact of radio and films with sound.

While people have always been able to dance to music in general (adapting their steps to the tempo and rhythm of the music being played), songs have regularly been written to create, promote, or simply capitalize on a dance, dance-idea or dance-craze. Therefore the list of representative songs for this section will exclude recordings that would qualify rhythmically, but have no specific reference in the title to a type of dance. Dance recordings from the early years:

Song	Performer	Record	Release Year
Turkey in the Straw (Zip Coon)	Billy Golden	Columbia	1891
Hiawatha Two-Step	Sousa's Band	Victor 2443	1903
Blue Danube Waltz	Sousa's Band	Victor 31450	1905
The St. Louis Rag	Arthur Pryor's Band	Victor 2783	1904
Waltz Me Around Again, Willie	Billy Murray	Victor 4738	1906
Maple Leaf Rag	Vess Ossman	Columbia 3626	1907
The Cubanola Glide	Billy Murray	Victor 5769	1910
Oh That Beautiful Rag	Arthur Collins	Columbia 853	1910
The Honeymoon Glide	Arthur Collins/ Byron Harlan	Indestructable 1437	1910
Red Rose Rag	Dolly Connolly	Columbia 1028	1911
The Mississippi Dippy-Dip	Arthur Collins/ Byron Harlan	Victor 16870	1911
Chicken Reel	Frank Stanley	Victor 16897	1911
That Aeroplane Glide	Peerless Quartet	Victor 17113	1912
In Ragtime Land	Arthur Collins	Victor 17126	1912
Fo' de Lawd's Sake, Play Waltz	Elsie Janis	Victor 60091	1913
When I Waltz with You	Helen Clark	Victor 17298	1913
Turkey-Trot Dance Medley, II	Prince's Orchestra	Columbia 5459	1913
The Castle Walk	Jim Europe Society Orch.	Victor 17553	1914
Castle's Half and Half	Prince's Band	Columbia A 5562	1914
Everybody Rag with Me	George O'Connor	Columbia 1706	1915
My Tango Girl	Albert & Monroe Jockers	Columbia 5683	1915
That Moanin' Saxophone Rag	Six Brown Brothers	Victor 17677	1915
That Hula Hula	Elizabeth Brice	Columbia 2226	1916
Missouri Waltz	Jaudas' Society Orchestra	Edison Amberol 2950	1916
The Darktown Strutter's Ball	Six Brown Brothers	Victor 18376	1917
Castle Valse Classique	Earl Fuller's Novelty Orch.	Columbia 5989	1917
Waltz of the Hours	Cincinnati Symphony	Columbia 5943	1917
Tiger Rag	Original Dixieland Jazz Band	Victor 18472	1918

Patriotic, Military, Marches

Patriotic recordings and the previously mentioned military themes were represented in a variety of musical tempos and styles beyond the ballad. In fact, most people's introduction to any of the industry's earliest recordings is patriotic songs, many of them military-style marches. The best known examples were made by conductor-composer John Philip Sousa, or performances by one of the numerous military (or pseudo-military) performing bands. Names like Voss' 1st Regiment Band, the United States Marine Band, and of course Sousa's Band were recording military-themed songs including "The Stars and Stripes Forever." But why would military music and marches connect with consumers?

> The marching band of brass instruments was commonplace in nine-teenth-century America. During the Civil War more military music was heard because many new bands were formed. When the war was over, band music was the popular music of America. [. . .] It could be found in streets, parks, and factory yards. It was played in concert halls, music theaters, ballrooms, and circuses.[30]

Once again, as with ragtime, a predisposition among potential cylinder or disc purchasers made the decision to record military marches and marching bands an easy one for the early recording companies. The fact that the obvious (and dominant) brass instruments did not have all of the previously described recording problems associated with string instruments aided the proliferation of brass-instrument recordings. These marches were joined by other patriotic-oriented songs composed by Cohan, Sousa, and numerous others.

There were other song styles that can be discussed with the patriotic and military genres. Much like the rise and fall of public opinion in the support for war and other American military adventures overseas were the sentiments of the public as expressed through popular music. Many fifty-to-sixty year-old members of the baby-boom generation can recall the timing of two polar-opposite popular hits from the Vietnam War years: 1965's "Eve of Destruction" by Barry McGuire and 1966's "The Ballad of the Green Berets" by U.S. Army Staff Sergeant Barry Sadler. Both recordings reached #1 in *Billboard*. The lines between patriotism, support for the military, and jingoism could be blurred, and of course they might also be contradicted by those opposing American military involvement in one way or another. Pacifist and other anti-military themes will be discussed a little later; with a few exceptions the recordings cited here are primarily positive and supportive of the military:

Song	Performer	Record	Release Year
Semper Fidelis	U.S. Marine Band	Columbia -	1890
Volunteers' March	Gilmore's Band	New York -	1892
The Star Spangled Banner	Gilmore's Band	New Jersey -	1892
Yankee Doodle	Vess Ossman	North American 905	1894
Lincoln's Speech at Gettysburg	Russell Hunting	Edison 3821	1897
Columbia the Gem of the Ocean	Frank Stanley	Edison 5000	1898
America Forever March	71st Regmntl. Band	Edison 7283	1898
The Stars and Stripes Forever	Sousa's Band	Gram-o-Phone 306	1901
Your Dad Gave His Life for His Country	Franklyn Wallace	Zonophone-5793	1903
Battle Cry of Freedom	Harlan & Stanley	Edison 8805	1894
Soldier Boy	Byron G. Harlan	Columbia 3067	1905
I'm a Yankee Doodle Dandy	Billy Murray	Columbia 298	1905
The Good Old USA	Byron G. Harlan	Columbia 3463	1906
You're a Grand Old Flag	Arthur Pryor's Band	Victor 31539	1906
It's Great to Be a Soldier Man	Byron G. Harlan	Edison 9600	1907
ABC's of the U.S.A.	A. Jones & B. Murray	Edison 9903	1908
Yankee Doodle's Come to Town	Haydn Quartet	Victor 5504	1908
U.S. Army Bugle Calls	N.Y. Military Band	Edison (4) 1069	1912
Spirit of Independence March	Conway's Band	Victor 18559	1912
Keep the Home Fires Burning	James F. Harrison	Victor 17881	1915
The Star Spangled Banner	M. Woodrow Wilson	Columbia 1685	1915
I Didn't Raise My Boy to Be a Soldier	Morton Harvey	Victor 17650	1915
America, I Love You	Sam Ash	Columbia 1842	1916
Wake Up America	James F. Harrison	Victor 17984	1916
Battle Hymn of the Republic	Columbia Mixed Qt.	Columbia 2012	1916
Goodbye Broadway, Hello France	Peerless Quartet	Columbia 2333	1917
America	Louis Gravieure	Columbia 5449	1917
For Your Country and My Country	Francis Alda	Victor 64689	1917
We're Going Over	Peerless Quartet	Columbia 2399	1917
Say a Prayer for the Boys Out There	Peerless Quartet	Victor 18411	1918
Au Revoir but Not Goodbye, Soldier Boy	Peerless Quartet	Victor 18438	1918
Just Like Washington Crossed the Delaware, Pershing Will Cross the Rhine	Arthur Fields	Columbia 2545	1918
Life in a Trench in Belgium	Rice & Burr	Columbia 2410	1918
Hello Central Give Me No Man's Land	Al Jolson	Columbia 2542	1918
I'm Going to Follow The Boys	Elizabeth Spencer	Victor 18433	1918
If He Can Fight Like He Can Love	Farber Sisters	Columbia 2556	1918
When Uncle Joe Steps into France	Collins & Harlan	Victor 18492	1918
How Ya Gonna Keep 'Em Down on the Farm, After They've Seen Paree	Nora Bayes	Columbia 2687	1918
Pack Up Your Troubles in Your Old Kit Bag (and Smile, Smile, Smile)	Columbia Stellar Qt.	Columbia 6028	1918
The Navy Took Them Over, the Navy Will Bring Them Back	Royal Dadmun	Okeh 466	1918
You Keep Sending 'Em Over	Arthur Fields	Columbia-2636	1918
Would You Rather Be a Colonel with an Eagle on Your Shoulder or a Private with a Chicken on Your Knee	Arthur Fields	Columbia 2669	1918
Liberty Loan March	Sousa's Band	Victor 18430	1918
The Yanks Are at It Again	Arthur Fields	Columbia 2620	1918
Somewhere in France Is the Lily	Nora Bayes	Columbia 2408	1918
Over There	Enrico Caruso	Victor 87294	1918
You'll Find Old Dixieland in France	Deiro Pietro's Band	Victor 18547A	1919
When the Boys Come Home	Louis Gravieure	Columbia 2709	1919

Political, Religious, Promotional, Social

Separate and apart from military or patriotic music were songs of a political, social, religious, or promotional nature. Between 1900 and 1919 there were campaign songs for or against the political parties, as well as songs targeted at specific politicians and events such as William McKinley, Woodrow Wilson, Theodore Roosevelt, Tammany Hall, the suffrage movement, temperance, unions, and labor movements.[31] One example of an event song is "I'll Carry the Flag to Mexico, but I'll Leave My Heart with You." This would have fallen under the blended category of march/ballad. Some music we view today as a traditional American folk song (or country music) had its origins— at least in terms of popular acclaim — during these years. "Will the Circle Be Unbroken" remains a familiar song, generally associated with gospel music. Pacifism was found in songs like "I Didn't Raise My Boy to Be a Soldier"; politics— in this case presidential politics— was personified by titles like "Will Taft, We're Looking for You" (in support of President William Taft). Optimism might be inferred from the oratory of William Jennings Bryan; social issues— like socialism or women's suffrage were described in songs like "Workers of the World Awaken" (1916) and "Woman's Right Is Woman's Duty" (1911). It's not terribly hard to find religious songs, of which "Ave Maria" was a popular recording choice. Advertising was found in popular music with songs like "In My Merry Oldsmobile," extolling the praises of one Detroit automobile brand.

Song	Performer	Record	Release Year
Abide with Me	Frank Stanley	Edison 5019	1898
Asleep in the Deep	Hooley	Edison 7295	1899
Ave Maria	Guarini	Edison 7287	1899
The Rosary	Henry Burr	Columbia 1354	1903
Tammany	S. H. Dudley	Victor 4297	1905
In My Merry Oldsmobile	A. Collins/B. Harlan	Zonophone 290	1905
Break Up the Solid South	William H. Taft	Columbia 1012	1908
Foreign Missions	William H. Taft	Columbia 1013	1908
Immortality	William Jennings Bryan	Columbia 1014	1908
Ideal Republic	William Jennings Bryan	Columbia 1016	1908
Imperialism	William Jennings Bryan	Columbia 1016	1908
Christ the Lord Is Risen Today	Edison Concert Band	Edison 10099	1909
Swing Low, Sweet Chariot	Fisk Univ. Jubilee Qt.	Victor 16453	1910
Silent Night, Hallowed Night	Elsie Baker	Victor 17164	1912
Progressive Covenant with the People	Theodore Roosevelt	Edison(4) 1146	1912
Social and Industrial Justice	Theodore Roosevelt	Edison(4) 1149	1912
Jesus Lover of My Soul	Louise Homer	Victor 87200	1915
I Didn't Raise My Boy to Be a Soldier	Morton Harvey	Victor 17716	1915
You Don't Need Wine to Have a Wonderful Time	Eddie Cantor	Pathe 22163	1919

16

Immigration and Recordings

The preceding chapter looked at most of the recorded music genres. It is now time to take a more detailed look at ethnic recordings. This genre is unique within the early period. Although the songs are categorized as ethnic, the genre remains a type of popular music, and its contribution to the first thirty years of recording is no less important than the purely American recordings already discussed. That importance, however, must be placed within the larger context (and examination) of popular recordings, as we explore the ethnic music and spoken-word performances recorded in the United States from 1889 to 1919. In this chapter you will find ethnic recordings in all of their diversity, identified, defined, and contextualized within the significantly East Coast, American recording industry. One should take note that in most cases, ethnic recordings made in other countries and imported into the United States will not be included, nor will the majority of European classical repertoire, regardless of country of origin.

Foreign recordings, even those produced outside the United States by American companies (or their affiliates), were readily available in countries around the world. "Victor had issued nearly 6,000 ethnic records by 1920, offering records in Lithuanian, Ukrainian, Dutch, Serbian, Croatian, Yiddish, Rumanian, Slovak, Finnish, Hawaiian, Armenian, Syrian, Portuguese, Slovenian, [and] Arabic…. Victor and Columbia were also making records in various oriental tongues…."[1] The sheer number of individual recordings—Victor alone accounted for 6,000—is significant, but the quantity of each recording that was manufactured was usually small, in many cases just a few hundred copies. The fact that these were recorded and manufactured outside of the United States limited any domestic availability; consequently their impact on the growing American music industry was minimal.

The introduction to this book looked at the question of viewing European-classical music as a part of, or in contrast to, popular music in general, and whether or not to address such an inclusion or specific contrasts within this text. (The answer to the first question was, essentially, minimally.) In evaluations of Euro-classical music as ethnic music, some might argue that recordings of opera, e.g., *Aida* by Giuseppe Verdi (1813–1901), are ethnic due to the European heritage of many of the creators—in Verdi's case the Parma region of Italy; or a similar case might be made for inclusion of Euro-classical as ethnic because of the use of a non-English language, e.g., Italian or German, in the libretto. However, classical repertoire then and now is in a class by itself, related to, but apart from other musical styles. This is consistent with the generally accepted definition of popular music, which is the larger focus of this book. Context is an important factor in considering ethnic recordings in the early music business, and choosing not to explore most classical repertoire is logical.

There are other reasons justifying the minimalization of Euro-classical recordings within this genre. Elie Siegmeister explains that "to the great classic masters, composing was a way of functioning as well as expressing oneself."[2] The great works—i.e. the expression contained within Johann Sebastian Bach's (1685–1750) *Brandenberg Concerti*, Georg Friedrich Handel's (1685–1759) *Messiah*, and Wolfgang Amadeus Mozart's (1756–1791) *Marriage of Figaro*—would not constitute ethnic recordings for the purposes of this section; nor would, for example, Ludwig von Beethoven's (1770–1827) *Eroica*, even though Beethoven's agenda was, in part, a political statement motivated by the composer's personal disappointment.[3]

The bulk of what we commonly refer to as "classical music," particularly by these composers and their contemporaries, was written during the eighteenth and nineteenth centuries, without regard to (or the visionary anticipation of) specific ethnic realities of the 1889–1919 period. Therefore any exceptions found within this chapter and/or its various sub-sections are related to the ethnicity of performers, e.g., Enrico Caruso, and not to the compositions of the great European masters or their birth language.

You may recall that some of the background for classical repertoire was addressed in the concept of a jukebox phenomenon. Classical repertoire was a serious and often topically relevant creation at the time of the composer's inspiration (as in the case of Beethoven's *Eroica*). However, its accepted position as fine art with the dawning of the era of recorded music provides another credible rationale for separating classical music from the period's popular music, including its ethnic genre. Regardless of the importance, sincerity, inspiration, desire, larger purpose, or popularity seen in its original creation, most Euro-classical music does not fall within the category of popular music today, nor did it fall within the popular category during the first thirty years of recording.[4]

Validating ethnic recordings and connections to New York City between 1889 and 1919 fits within the basic arguments for this chapter's research:

- the late nineteenth- and early twentieth-century immigration waves helped make up the character of New York City; immigrants (including internal migrants) of all colors and nationalities defined the city's character;
- the recorded music industry was born in the region in 1889 under the vision of Edison and Berliner;
- the waves of immigrants entering America—via New York City in the vast majority of cases—constituted an ebb and flow of ethnic influence: arrivals introduced or bolstered one ethnic group, while internal or reverse migration diminished another. For example, Germans were the dominant immigrant group in the city in 1900 (see Table 1 and Table 4) when more than 300,000 people counted and identified as foreign-born arrived from Germany. Ten years later, Russian-born and Italian-born communities each had a greater representation in New York City than did the German-born;
- the center of the American population remained decidedly east of the Mississippi River. Therefore, the developing recording industry could, to a large extent, see who their potential customers were, including ethnicity;[5]
- musical-variety theater was launched in 1865 in New York City and vaudeville, in general, was on a roll. Some of the early recording artists were successful singers, comics, and musicians from vaudeville,[6] particularly those performing in theaters in New York;
- Finally, songwriting and the music publishing business was centered in Manhattan, along a section of 28th Street known as Tin Pan Alley.

TABLE 1. COMPARISON OF FOREIGN-BORN
POPULATION IN NEW YORK CITY AND
SHIFTING ETHNIC NUMBERS: 1900, 1910

Census Year 1900 New York City (immigrant's country)	no. of foreign-born	% of foreign-born	Census Year 1910 New York City (immigrant's country)	no. of foreign-born	% of foreign-born	% Black or foreign-of total*
Germany	324,224	24.4%	Russia	484,193	23.8%	10.2%
Ireland	275,102	20.7%	Italy	340,770	16.7%	7.1%
Russia	180,432	13.6%	Germany	278,137	13.7%	5.8%
Italy	145,433	10.9%	Ireland	252,672	12.4%	5.3%

Census Year 1900 New York City (immigrant's country)	no. of foreign- born	% of foreign- born	Census Year 1910 New York City (immigrant's country)	no. of foreign- born	% of foreign- born	% Black or foreign- of total*
Austria	90,477	6.8%	Austria	190,246	9.3%	4.0%

Source: U.S. Department of Commerce, Bureau of the Census, Historical Statistics of the United States: Colonial Times to 1970, Part 1 (Washington, D.C.: GPO, 1975), Table 16.

Immigrant Groups, Language, and Music's Global Village

It should be clear now that helping drive the demand for new ideas in repertoire was America's growing ethnic population, i.e., those within the foreign-born population and their descendants. The first generation immigrants, plus their children and grandchildren, became the potential source of, and a viable market for, ethnic repertoire. One might think about the steps in the process of creating a consumer market for ethnic recordings: Europe was the primary source of new consumers, getting to America was their goal, Ellis Island was the funnel, and New York City became the immediate destination. As ships brought more and more immigrants, those immigrants and their progeny swelled the city's ethnic numbers. One part of an ethnic consumer-market was arriving on those same ships, while another was simultaneously being born in New York.

The late twentieth-century view of most Americans is that today's destination of choice for many immigrants seeking a better life is the United States. While that may be true, most of those arriving after World War II (and continuing today) are simply retracing routes taken by their familial ancestors, others from their country, or immigrants from dozens of other countries. The United States has been that primary destination for more than two hundred years, giving cities like New York a uniquely rich heritage. New York's diversity — and the richness derived from it — is a product of generations of immigration.

Some have generalized about the immigrants arriving in America during the late nineteenth and early twentieth centuries. Was one immigrant group stronger or better than another? Beyond appearances, customs, or language, how did various members of immigrant America view themselves? In Coming to America Roger Daniels describes the composition of the old and new immigrants and some subjective views:

> The classic description of the differences between the two groups runs something like this. The old immigrants, persons from the British Isles

and northwestern Europe who came before the 1880s, were of very much like the settlers of the colonies and were relatively easy to assimilate. The new immigrants, persons from southern and eastern Europe, who came after the 1880s, were of very different ethnicity ... who spoke strange languages and worshipped strange gods—that is, they were not Protestant.[7]

When one thinks of the diverse origins of those immigrants remaining in New York City — and the contribution they made to the city's vitality, one will usually focus on European arrivals, and with good reason.

This European influx can be illustrated by analyzing the numbers contained within the U.S. census. For example, among the foreign-born population in the whole of the United States in 1900 were 2.8 million from Germany and 484,000 from Italy. The number of Italian immigrants almost tripled in the decade after 1900. In 1910, 1.3 million Italian-born immigrants called America home, with 340,000 of them living in New York City.[8] In 1900 one state, New York, had a foreign-born population of almost 2 million; by 1910 there were that many foreign-born residents in New York City alone. One must keep in mind that these are numbers of foreign-born. The children and grandchildren of these immigrants, born in the United States yet retaining their familial ethnicity, increased these numbers and their corresponding ethnic representation significantly.

To many nineteenth-century observers on both sides of the Atlantic, it must have seemed as if all of Europe was headed to America. In fact, in the century from 1821 to 1920 more than 30 million immigrants arrived

CHART 1. FOREIGH-BORN POPULATION OF UNITED STATES, BY COUNTRY/REGION, 1850–1920

	1850	1860	1870	1880	1890	1900	1910	1920
Ger/Aus/Sca/Swi	617,000	1,427,000	2,078,000	2,620,000	4,064,000	4,283,000	4,533,000	3,560,000
Ireland/U K	1,342,000	2,200,000	2,626,000	2,772,000	3,123,000	2,784,000	2,573,000	2,173,000
Poland/Russia	1,000	10,000	19,000	85,000	330,000	807,000	2,122,000	2,540,000
France/Benelux	65,000	147,000	176,000	180,000	219,000	231,000	289,000	361,000
Italy	4,000	12,000	17,000	44,000	183,000	484,000	1,343,000	1,610,000

TABLE 2. U.S. CENSUS DATA FOR ALL IMMIGRATION
TO THE UNITED STATES, 1821–1920

	1820–1890	1891–1900	1901–1910	1911–1920	1820–1920
All Countries	15,436,042	3,687,564	8,795,386	5,735,811	33,654,803
Europe	13,724,737	3,555,352	8,056,040	4,321,887	29,658,016
Caribbean	92,532	33,066	107,548	123,424	356,570
Canada	1,047,964	3,311	179,226	742,185	1,972,686
Mexico	27,032	971	49,642	219,004	296,649
Central America	1,624	549	8,192	17,159	27,524
South America	11,030	1,075	17,280	41,899	71,284
Asia	300,631	74,862	323,543	247,236	946,272
Africa	1,863	350	7,368	8,443	18,024
all other	228,629	18,028	46,547	14,574	307,778

Source: David M. Brownstone and Irene M. Franck, Facts About American Immigration *(New York: H.W. Wilson Company, 2001), Table 1.9 and Table 5.3. (These figures have been adjusted due to an error found in Brownstone and Franck's calculations. The numbers for Mexico contained in Table 1.9 for years 1891–1970 are identical to those in years 1820–1890. The error was confirmed by cross-checking the numbers with Table 5.3. The corrected numbers were used in the above table.)*

in the United States (see Table 2). The journey for the overwhelming majority (88%) of these travelers began in Europe, and those journeys were not unique to Germans and Italians. England, Ireland, Scandinavia, Austria-Hungary, Russia, and other nations saw their sons and daughters choose to start their lives anew in America. Non-European immigrants came from China, Japan, and diverse parts of Asia and Oceania. Immigrants traveled north from Mexico, Central and South America; some English and French-speaking Canadians moved south; and it was not uncommon to find immigrants arriving from Africa and the Caribbean. The United States, particularly New York City, was the destination.

In addition to this documented European, Asian, Latin American, and African-Caribbean immigrant diversity arriving at the turn of the twentieth century, there was still another ethnic group present: blacks had already been living in the Northeast for two hundred years, although their numbers were dwarfed by the population of blacks in the American South. In the late eighteenth century,

> only ten percent of the slave population lived north of Maryland.... Slaves were spread thinly throughout the north; their highest concentration in that region was in New York City, where they may have formed as much as 17 percent of the population.... Slaves in the north worked side by side with white field servants in the country-side and as laborers in the towns. They mingled with the poorest elements among the whites, formed stable families, and even managed to accumulate small sums on the side when they were "hired out" by their

masters to work for others. These northern blacks—field hands, town laborers and factory workers— were mostly native-born Americans....[9]

By the end of the nineteenth century, New York City had blacks who had been free all of their lives, were former slaves, or were the sons and daughters of former slaves.

There is room for interpretation when one considers the census of American blacks who were *counted* compared to the number of foreign-born blacks. The census documented the black/Negro population in both 1900 and 1910. Those blacks who were counted cannot all be considered immigrants when looking at those identified as "foreign-born," nor can one assume that they were all "indigenous," i.e., living in the area since 1800 or earlier. As the following analysis shows, this black/Negro ethnic group was a combination of immigrants and internal migrants, whether their history was free or slave.

This difference between newly arrived blacks and indigenous blacks can be clarified (and quantified) by comparing census populations. In 1900, 60,000 persons living in New York city were categorized as Black/Negro, even though the most likely arrivals to be counted as black or Negro within those designated as foreign-born — those from the Caribbean and Africa — totaled only 28,000 (47%). Ten years later (according to the 1910 census), 91,000 persons in the city had been categorized as black/Negro, of which 52,000 (57%) were considered foreign-born.[10] Therefore the most generous estimates supporting the numbers of blacks/Negroes through immigration would be based on two unlikely assumptions: first, all of the black/Negro residents of New York City were counted during each decennial census; second, all of the foreign-born residents of the city arriving from Africa and the Caribbean were black/Negro. Neither assumption can be accepted as accurate. Logic dictates, and one can easily conclude — based on lingering post-Civil War and post-Reconstruction biases— that the black/Negro census data was less than accurate, at least when compared to the data for the white population.

TABLE 3: ESTIMATE OF FOREIGN-BORN BLACK/
NEGRO VERSUS NATIVE BLACK/NEGRO POPULATION

New York City Census Year	1900	1910
Documented arrivals from Africa and the Caribbean	28,000	52,000
Census of those classified as Black/Negro	60,000	91,000
Total (% "native black")	32,000 (53%)	39,000 (47%)

Source: Thirteenth Census of the United States, taken in the year 1910: Abstract of the Census. Table 19.

TABLE 4. FOREIGN BORN AND BLACK POPULATION OF NEW YORK CITY: 1900 AND 1910

Census Year 1900 immigrant country or Black im/migrant	no. Black or foreign-born	% Black or foreign-born	Census Year 1910 immigrant country or Black im/migrant	no. Black or foreign-born	% Black or foreign-born	% Black or foreign-of total*
Germany	324,224	24.4%	Russia	484,193	23.8%	10.2%
Ireland	275,102	20.7%	Italy	340,770	16.7%	7.1%
Russia	180,432	13.6%	Germany	278,137	13.7%	5.8%
Italy	145,433	10.9%	Ireland	252,672	12.4%	5.3%
Austria	90,477	6.8%	Austria	190,246	9.3%	4.0%
England	68,836	5.2%	Black#	91,709	4.5%	1.9%
Black#	60,666	4.6%	England	78,483	3.9%	1.6%
Hungary	31,516	2.4%	Hungary	76,627	3.8%	1.6%
Sweden	28,320	2.1%	Sweden	34,952	1.7%	0.7%
Canada French & English	21,926	1.6%	Romania	33,586	1.6%	0.7%
Scotland	19,836	1.5%	Canada French & English	26,320	1.3%	0.6%
France	14,755	1.1%	Scotland	23,123	1.1%	0.5%
Norway	11,387	0.9%	Norway	22,281	1.1%	0.5%
Romania	10,499	0.8%	France	18,293	0.9%	0.4%
Switzerland	8,371	0.6%	Cuba/West Indies	16,415	0.8%	0.3%
All Other	7,079	0.5%	Switzerland	10,452	0.5%	0.2%
China	6,080	0.5%	Turkey	9,855	0.5%	0.2%
Cuba/West Indies	5,867	0.4%	Greece	8,038	0.4%	0.2%
Denmark	5,621	0.4%	Denmark	7,997	0.4%	0.2%
Finland	3,733	0.3%	Finland	7,410	0.4%	0.2%
The Netherlands	2,608	0.2%	All Other	6,626	0.3%	0.1%
Wales	1,686	0.1%	The Netherlands	4,193	0.2%	0.1%
Spain	1,491	0.1%	China	3,936	0.2%	0.1%
Turkey	1,401	0.1%	Spain	3,359	0.2%	0.1%
Greece	1,309	0.1%	Belgium	2,260	0.1%	0.0%
Belgium	1,221	0.1%	Wales	1,779	0.1%	0.0%
Japan	311	0.0%	Japan	957	0.0%	0.0%
Mexico	282	0.0%	Bulgaria, Serbia, Monenegro	540	0.0%	0.0%
Portugal	277	0.0%	Portugal	431	0.0%	0.0%
Bulgaria, Serbia,	0	0.0%	Mexico	426	0.0%	0.0%
black/foreign-born total:	1,330,746	100.0%	total:	2,036,066	100.0%	42.7%

*1910 NYC Population: 4,766,883

#Assumes that at least one-half of Blacks (Negroes) were internal migration due to the "official" number of African and Caribbean documented foreign-born immigrants included in the 1820–1920 census statistics (18,024).

Like many immigrants arriving in America today, black immigrants of the early 1900s may have had an inherent mistrust of government officials asking questions, and such mistrust suggests that the nonwhite census counts were somewhat flawed, skewed, or misrepresented. In *Coming to America* Daniels states that by the late nineteenth century, many of the "best and the brightest" minds in America had become convinced that of all the many "races" (we should say "ethnic groups") of Europe one alone — variously called Anglo-Saxon, Aryan, Teutonic, or Nordic — had superior innate characteristics.... The census of 1890, which as the historian Frederick Jackson Turner (1861–1932) announced, signaled the end of the frontier in America, demonstrated to these elite leaders that immigration was ... changing for the worse, the composition of the country.[11]

One might safely conclude (as Table 3 attempts to show) that approximately one-half of the black/Negro population in America during the two census periods was not made up of recent immigrants, but rather was comprised of either long-term residents or internal migrants arriving primarily from rural America.[12] Blacks, then, were not much different from other ethnic groups; some were first generation, some second, some third, and so on. Like their European counterparts, black immigrants' ethnicity, nationality, language, and skin-color were important factors in defining groups and neighborhoods within New York City.

Language and the Local Village

Turning again to early statistics, the new century's first census, completed in 1910, found that 4.8 million people called New York City home, almost 2 million of whom were foreign-born or black.[13] The three largest ethnic groups—totaling 1 million foreign-born — were from Germany, Italy, and Russia (see Appendix 1). Ireland's expatriates, the city's fourth largest foreign-born population, totaled more than 250,000. In all, more than thirty countries had emigrants living in New York City in 1910. After completing the journey safely, the new arrivals looked up acquaintances, relatives, and friends; they sought out those with similar ethnic and socio-economic histories, common language, and religious backgrounds who had already settled in this part of America. The easiest assimilation would belong to those immigrants with the greatest number of contacts or family members already living in New York. In New York City, as elsewhere, neighborhoods of people were transformed into ethnic enclaves for moral, social, and economic support. These urbanized, ethnic, mini-villages also provided a cultural taste of the old country even if, for example, the "old country" had been a black's prior existence in rural America, or an Irishman's life on a poor Irish-country farm.

One of the most significant aspects of immigrant culture was language. In 1888, New York's polyglot Lower East Side had numerous enclaves: German immigrants had Kleindeutschland, the Chinese had Mott Street, and "one had only to turn into Bayard Street and walk one block westward to be on 'Boulevard des Italiens'— Mulberry Street...."[14] Determining the language of the immigrants was not as simple as walking through the neighborhoods or looking at each person's declared country of origin. A diverse list of languages is found within documentation of the foreign-born counted in the 1910 census (see Table 5).[15] More than fifteen languages were spoken just among the immigrants arriving from Germany; in fact, of the 2.5 million "white persons born in Germany" recorded in the census, more than 200,000 had a first language other than German (and presumably other than English).[16] The British Isles brought the English language, but also Gaelic and Welsh; those from Switzerland might speak Italian, German, or French; Belgians might speak French, Dutch, or Flemish. When one looks through the languages that were catalogued as part of the early census process, a list of mother tongues develops that is both extensive and somewhat surprising.

Language, therefore, could not be discounted as an important cultural ingredient in the creation of New York City's ethnic villages. Consider the reaction of an average American traveler today hearing English (particularly American-English) being spoken among the crowds in Cairo's Khan El Khahili bazaar. In a sea of people speaking primarily Arabic, a note of familiarity is heard; for that American, hearing English signals community in otherwise unfamiliar territory. Similarly, for new immigrants in New York, particularly non-English speakers, economic and social support, and ultimate assimilation into their new life in America required kinship or at least the other necessary elements of social interaction found in ethnic neighborhoods. These islands of commerce, tradition, social integration, and religion facilitated an immigrant's ability to settle into a new life. Little, if any, of this would have been accomplished without cultural support, and language was the key to gain access to the support found in these enclaves. As Robert Ezra Park states, "Among immigrant people mother-tongue, rather than country of birth, is the basis of association and organization."[17]

TABLE 5. LANGUAGES OF IMMIGRANTS
TO THE UNITED STATES, 1910.

Continental Europe

Bohemian	Finnish	Hebrew	Polish	Slovak
Croatian	Flemish	Italian	Portuguese	Slovenian
Danish	French	Lettish	Rumanian	Spanish
Dutch	Frisian	Lithuanian	Russian	Swedish
English	German	Magyar	Ruthenian	Yiddish
	Greek	Moravian	Serbian	

British Isles

| English | Welsh | Gaelic | | |

Middle East

| Arabic | Turkish | Hebrew | Farsi | |

Far East

| Japanese | Filipino | Chinese | Hindi | Korean |

Latin America

| Spanish | Portuguese | | | |

Canada

| English | French | | | |

Source: U.S. Department of Commerce and Labor, Bureau of the Census, Thirteenth Census of the United States, taken in the Year 1910: Abstract of the Census (Washington, D.C.: GPO, 1913), 192–3.

The Language of Music

Language, commerce, social organizations, religion, and food were all cultural elements existing within the nineteenth-century ethnic neighborhood. Culture, predictably, was found in the arts as well, and the art of music brought a soothing bit of familiarity. Live music was found in abundance from neighborhood to neighborhood, emanating from homes, taverns, meeting halls, churches, parks, and other public spaces. Familiarity was more than just a song in the background at a tavern on Saturday night or the music heard in church on Sunday morning. As the old century disappeared into the new, music could also be heard coming from a new form of public and home entertainment: the phonograph.

The phonograph changed the nature of entertainment, particularly at home. In the 1890s, cylinders and discs were sold containing what has been described as generic popular music — music appealing to the general population, with themes that were anything but controversial. There were relatively simple songs of love, patriotism, family, and religious piety. Leftover musical styles from the American Civil War were common, including brass band, marches, and minstrelsy. Apart from these basic themes, however, there were also recordings that one might gently describe as culturally-centered. This latter description could be further broken down into two specific fields of repertoire, which have already been briefly mentioned: ethnic and pseudo-ethnic recordings.[18]

The first field, ethnic recordings, are those recordings made by transplanted members (or identifiable descendants) of an ethnic group, usually for their own population. The second field, pseudo-ethnic recordings, are at best a caricature of an immigrant's cultural markers, and often worse. Pseudo-ethnic are those recordings made by performers from outside an ethnic group. All of these recordings could include traditional or modern dance music (modern, at least for the 1890s and early 1900s), folk songs, political songs, humorous themes, or songs with religious overtones. To put the ethnic and pseudo-ethnic labels in context, one might recall the two performers cited earlier: John McCormack and Arthur Collins.

McCormack's recording of "When Irish Eyes Are Smiling" is ethnic and a classic of the genre. Sigmund Spaeth states that "this eternally popular song belongs with *Mother Machree* and … *My Wild Irish Rose* in the top trio of modern Irish balladry."[19] Collins' recording of "Nigger Loves His Possum" is pseudo-ethnic and would not stand the gentle test of time enjoyed by McCormack's choice of material. "When Irish Eyes Are Smiling" describes an Irish-American wistfully reminiscing about the culture of his birth — those Irish eyes are idyllic. Collins' recording is exploitative, for it plays into negative black stereotypes of the time in its vocalization as well as its title and lyric content. Ethnic recordings can be complimentary or at least neutral. Pseudo-ethnic recordings often contain lyrics or vocalized accents not necessarily connected to the performer's nationality. Therefore, while ethnic recordings from recording's first thirty years often presented a reflective or introspective look at the members of one's own group, pseudo-ethnic recordings were likely to be about another ethnic group entirely. The *pseudo-ethnic* recordings were sometimes humorous by design or by accident but, in fact, they could often incorporate ethnic stereotypes or derision, often hurtful, racist, and xenophobic.

Separating Recording and Manufacturing

To separate, or draw a distinction between the recording process and the manufacturing process, it's useful to place the recordings made during these early years into two groups: artist/song titles recorded by the various companies, and consumer units manufactured by the companies. "Artist/song titles" refers to the A&R efforts of the companies; that is to say that the A&R staff organized the individual recording sessions, which then produced a series of separate and distinct tracks (or sides) recorded by the companies. For example, if during three separate recording sessions — sessions "A," "B," and "C"— the Columbia label recorded three separate singers performing three separate versions of "When Irish Eyes Are Smiling," those sessions would have produced three artist/song titles. On the other hand, "consumer units" refers to the number of copies of any single title manufactured by any one label. Again, using the Columbia label as an example, the manufacturing of 5,000 copies of any one of the three artist/song titles for sale to consumers— e.g., the session "B" version of "When Irish Eyes Are Smiling"— represents 5,000 consumer units.

TABLE 6. ESTIMATED RECORDINGS PRODUCED
AND RELEASED BY AMERICAN COMPANIES
BETWEEN 1889 AND 1919, BY SOURCE.[20]

Recording Company	Number of Titles
Edison Speaking Phonograph Co.	6,200
Victor Talking Machine Company	6,000
Columbia Phonograph Company	5,100
Berliner Gramophone Company	600
Okeh Phonograph Corporation	500
American Recording Company	300
Vocalion Record Company	100
assumption for missing labels (25%)	4,700
Total Individual Recordings (est)	23,500

Looking through a variety of sources one might estimate that at least 23,500 *artist/song titles* (separate recordings), were made in the United States during the first thirty years (see Table 6). From these same sources, more than 1,700 recordings were identified as *ethnic* or *pseudo-ethnic*.

Before the introduction of radio (1919) and sound in films (1927) there was no outside influence — except for live performance — to drive consumer demand for recordings and shape the public's musical taste; exposure of recorded music was limited. The earliest buyers listened to new music at record, phonograph and gramophone stores. In some cases they may have been influenced by recordings owned and recommended by friends.

Record stores and recommendations from friends also helped determine the popularity of recordings. Without accurate sales figures, it is difficult to establish the weight of these titles within the context of the total recorded music business. Popularity charts of the day were of limited use. "No company files tell us precise numbers; trade journals never systematically ranked records... ; record catalogs contain no information about sales.... [Besides,] a chart of hits means little for an era when records of many popular titles were made in the hundreds, not thousands or millions."[21] What can be determined is that ethnic and pseudo-ethnic recordings represent approximately 8% of the estimated 23,500 total recordings issued between 1889 and 1919. An attempt will now be made to understand the various ethnic and pseudo-ethnic recordings as each ethnic group is addressed.

The Recordings, an Overview

A wide variety of ethnic groups were depicted in the early recordings released by the predominantly East Coast-based American companies. Each had some aspect of their nationality, culture, language, self-image, skin color, intelligence, or beauty addressed in one or more recordings, some aspects seemingly ascribed, others imputed. (Samuel Johnson suggested, "We usually ascribe good, but impute evil.") In many cases, the performers were looking at their own culture and finding delight in its beauty, or humor in its exaggerations. In other recordings, the performers were speaking or singing as outsiders, sometimes seeing the beauty, but often quite the opposite. Beyond the identified ethnic groups and nationalities, I chose to create a composite group designated as *exotic*, which will also be explored. This group represents foreign elements that many in the West have from time to time deemed strange, different, and mysterious; American songwriters, performers, and consumers often found continents, countries, cities, and peoples something to desire or at least fantasize about through lyrics and melodies.[22] Places and people Americans had rarely seen first-hand became fodder for the companies. Faraway lands could be reinvented by songwriters who, judging by their lyrics, knew little of the land or the people that each wrote about. One by one each of the ethnic groups will be explored.

Included within many of these ethnic groups will be the comedy and novelty recordings created by these ethnic performers or targeted at another ethnic or immigrant group. Before moving on to an examination of the various ethnic groups, this idea of recordings with a humorous edge needs some specific consideration. Ethnic humor, like ethnic recordings in general, has at least two sides to it: the first looks inward at one's own cultural, religious, racial, color, or national group; the second looks at members of any other cultural, religious, racial, color, or national group. Therefore, one person's attempt at humor may be received by another person as either good humor or as an insult.

The topicality and humor of late-twentieth century comedians Chris Rock, Don Rickles, Richard Pryor, and Lenny Bruce has at one time or another been lauded by one person or group and simultaneously decried by another. Looking at turn-of-last century recordings, examples already existed of both innocuous humor and sarcastic or derisive comedy. In considering ethnicity, who you are and what you are can be characteristics worn with pride or they can be targets of ethnic humor. Ann Charters wrote in *Nobody: The Story of Bert Williams*, her biography of the early black stage and recording star, that "to some extent every immigrant group found its background ridiculed on the music hall stage...."[23] It should come as no surprise that many early comedy and novelty records had racist, xenophobic, or insulting words, lyrics, and dialects, using immigrants as easy targets.

TABLE 7. THE TEN LARGEST ETHNIC/
PSEUDO-ETHNIC RECORDING GROUPS,
1889–1919, FROM THE RECORDINGS SURVEYED

Ethnic	Recordings		# Ethnic	# Pseudo-Ethnic	% Ethnic	% Pseudo-Ethnic
	no. of	Share of				
Black/Negro*	363	21.4%	2	361	0.6%	99.4%
Hawaii	286	16.8%	185	101	64.7%	35.3%
Ireland	270	15.9%	163	107	60.4%	39.6%
Germany	172	10.1%	98	74	57.0%	43.0%
Exotic*	90	5.3%	0	90	0.0%	100.0%
Italy	90	5.3%	40	50	44.4%	55.6%
Jewish/Yiddish	81	4.8%	72	9	88.9%	11.1%
China*	56	3.3%	0	56	0.0%	100.0%
Poland	47	2.8%	10	37	21.3%	78.7%
Native American*	30	1.8%	0	30	0.0%	100.0%
All Other	215	12.6%	61	154	28.4%	71.6%
Total	1700		631	1069	37.1%	62.9%

* identifies ethnic groups which were 100% (or virtually 100%) *pseudo-ethnic.*
Sources: Koenigsberg, *Edison Cylinder Records* and *The Online Discographical Project.*

In contrast to the popular genres of recordings already discussed, which included a separate genre-category for comedy and novelty, we must follow a different road when it comes to evaluations of ethnic and pseudo-ethnic comedy and novelty recordings. Instead of a separate categorization, comedy and novelty will be explored in the following chapters alongside the various forms of popular music within each larger ethnic genre. The reason for this arrangement is that the various ethnic groups themselves became topics or targets of these comedy and novelty recordings—a fact that is, once again, attributable at least in part to the numbers of people emigrating to or already observed in the United States between 1890 and 1910.

The newly arrived immigrants—Swedes, Italians, Irish, Jews, and some French, Germans and Chinese as well—portrayed themselves in novelty songs or heard their own ethnic group portrayed by others. For most consumers it didn't matter whether the name was Blatz, Blitz, Calligan,

Casey, Chong, Clancy, Cohen, Flanagan, Frenchie, Haley, Harrigan, Heine, Kelly, Levinsky, Machree, Pedro, Reilly, Schneider, or Billy Magee. The idea might be self-deprecating or targeted to another. Most consumers were clearly aware of divisions of culture, lines drawn implicitly between ethnic groups— neighborhoods with political and cultural boundaries, or hierarchical opinions held by one group in regard to another. Some individuals or groups have been more easily offended by ethnic or racial slurs than others, but the decision to record them was nevertheless a business decision made by the record companies. Finally, these portrayals were not just about the lyrics sung or the words that were spoken. Part of the "successful" delivery required the use of a suitable dialect. Many of these songs used "Hebrew, Italian, Irish, Oriental, Swedish, or Black dialects, some to humorous ends, others to insult the group."[24] Many labels released records that reinforced America's stereotypical social identities and perhaps, knowingly or not, suggested its unofficial caste system.

17

Culture Swing —
The Ethnic Recordings

When surveying the recordings for this book, I identified thirty-two ethnic groups (plus exotic) within the songs included for this chapter. To simplify the analysis, it made sense to remove the bottom twenty-three groups from further detailed evaluation, as each had, on average, less than 10 total recordings assigned to their particular ethnic group (see Appendix 2).[1]

The remaining ten ethnic groups contain between 30 and 363 recordings each. I divided this now smaller group again into six groups with a recognizable mix, or split, of ethnic and pseudo-ethnic recordings (see Table 7: "% Ethnic," "% Pseudo-ethnic") and four groups with no realistic mix (indicated "*"). The most lopsided ethnic group within the (revised, smaller) mixed group is Poland (21%/79%), while the most balanced mix belongs to Italy (44%/56%). Three of the four groups marked "*" have no *ethnic* mix/split at all, i.e. the recordings of these three groups were 100% pseudo-ethnic; the fourth has more than 99% pseudo-ethnic.

Each of the ten groups will now be examined, and a list of all 1,700 recordings will be included at the end of this book.

The Black/Negro Recordings

Black/Negro recordings constitute the largest group within the genre: 363 recordings out of the 1,700 selected, representing 21.4% of the ethnic total. Assuming my estimate of 23,500 titles (Table 6) is reasonably complete, the 1,700 ethnic recordings is hard to ignore, and the one-fifth share belonging to the Black/Negro group is equally significant. By reading through the Irish, Italian, and Hawaiian performers and titles, I inferred that a large number of performers from within each ethnic group helped create the body of recordings. However, the almost complete absence of blacks as recording artists performing these mostly pseudo-ethnic songs speaks volumes about the character of much of the black/Negro repertoire.

When one considers the music that was heard during the post–Civil War years, four musical types stand out: the brass band performances, minstrelsy, comic performances, and general popular music. Brass band music was music for public spaces. "It could be found in streets, parks, and factory yards. In cities such as New Orleans and Chicago, band music was an important part of everyday life, and it could be heard in schools, factories, fraternal organizations, and even orphans' homes."[2] It was present in the musical recordings of Sousa and others. Generic, yet nostalgic marches continued to evoke some positive, uplifting continuity with the past. The marches were mostly instrumental recordings and will not be addressed here.

Comic themes (or attempts at humor) and generally popular styles—love songs, sentimental ballads, etc.—can be found in some of the recordings from the black/Negro category. However minstrelsy, ragtime, and the related coon songs and cakewalks were evocative styles finding an audience.

The genres of minstrelsy and ragtime are connected to each other both directly and through the demi-genres of the coon song and the cakewalk. That common link has a less-than-benign history. Francis Davis' superb book *The History of the Blues: The Roots, the Music, the People from Charley Patton to Robert Cray* looks at these root genres including their connections to some musical instruments—in one specific case, the banjo:

> The banjo was introduced to America by black slaves. It crossed over to the white culture via blackface minstrel shows, musical reviews in which white performers wearing burnt cork on their face would spoof blacks sometimes affectionately, sometimes viciously. By no means exclusive to the South, minstrel shows started about two or three decades before the civil war. On a musical level, minstrelsy was the sincerest form of flattery. Minstrel shows provided scores of white Americans with their first taste of black music, no matter that it was second hand and often presented as travesty.[3]

The two demi-genres have no less interesting (if only slightly less offensive) histories. Both coon songs and cakewalks are tied to minstrelsy and by association to ragtime as well, and both can be described and defined independently with specific characteristics.

When evaluating the first of the demi-genres, the coon song, one might search for a benign or affectionate use for the term *coon*, but in reality it is more likely to be a condescending, or racially biased epithet. While there may be some wiggle room in defining *coon* at the turn of the century, its context in the lyrics of songs and in the covers of the sheet music published in the late nineteenth century forces one to conclude otherwise. Even if, and that is a large *if*, the term was used at some distant moment as a benign label, it became anything but benign. "By the time [coon songs] had reached their height in popularity around 1897, the term [*coon*] had become a degrading stereotypical appellation.... There were literally thousands of 'coon songs' written based on nothing but minstrel-show images of the black man as lazy, dishonest, cowardly, immoral, gluttonous, and stupid."[4]

That other demi-genre, the cakewalk, evokes at least some contemporary recognition. After all, it was not uncommon in the late twentieth century to hear someone describe a task or responsibility as a cakewalk, meaning that the task or responsibility can be easily accomplished. Its origins and its relation to music, as Terry Waldo described it, are more complex and go back much further than twentieth century America.

> It was a vigorous and exciting dance, and as a musical form ... [it] transcended the racial stereotypes that surrounded it. The dance itself is said to have originated as early as 1840 with slaves who dressed up in "high fashion" and mimicked the formal dances of their masters.... By the time the ragtime era began in 1896, the cakewalk was being performed by blacks imitating whites who were imitating blacks who were imitating whites.[5]

Hopefully it is now reasonably clear that ragtime, minstrelsy, coon songs, and cakewalks were, in some ways, related, derivative, and connected musical forms. It is also obvious that first there continued to be musical instances of whites mimicking blacks into the twentieth century, and second, there was an effect — the genuine influence of black musicians— on white musicians who have seriously pursued traditionally black genres of American music, the foremost of which is jazz. For example, the later mimics might include those recording artists who attempted a blatant (and perfectly legal) cover of original, successful recordings made popular by blacks, e.g., Pat Boone's covers of hits by Fats Domino ("Ain't That a Shame") and Little Richard ("Tutti Frutti"). The less-obvious but no less influenced recordings of Elvis Presley (Arthur Crudup's "My Baby

Left Me"), Bill Haley (Joe Turner's "Shake, Rattle, and Roll"), or Michael Bolton (Percy Sledge's "When a Man Loves a Woman") can arguably be placed in this first category. In some cases the covers were released while the originals were still selling, as was the case with Pat Boone's cover of "Tutti Frutti." In others, like Michael Bolton's cover of Percy Sledge, the cover versions were released years after the original.[6] In the second category, a significant number of nonblack musicians have followed the greats of jazz and blues, whether through adaptation, adoption, influence, or inspiration, and have done justice to the genre.

The style and themes of minstrelsy were somewhat schizophrenic. Minstrelsy came from the post–Civil War era, but to some, much of its allure was likely to be a reinforcement of things some people yearned for (and others chose not to see). For many its connection was to the pre-war American South, and some must have let their minds drift back to the "good old days of slavery." For others it was an occasionally subtle, often usually clear reinforcement of the American caste system. Both groups of people were unfortunately tied to a society which would not begin to shake off these dusty concepts until the 1950s, and the legacy lingers in American society today.

The genres were not tied to the evolution of recording or vaudeville, nor were they recent; Eileen Southern adds detail to the musical styles described earlier by Terry Waldo:

> Blackface minstrelsy was a form of theatrical performance that emerged during the 1820s and reached its zenith during the years 1850–1870. Essentially it consisted of an exploitation of the slave's style of music and dancing by white men, who blackened their faces with burnt cork and went on the stage to sing "Negro songs" (also called "Ethiopian songs"), to perform dances derived from those of slaves, and to tell jokes based on slave life. One in caricature of the plantation slave with its ragged clothes and thick dialect; the other portraying the city slave, the dandy dressed in the latest fashion, who boasted of his exploits among the ladies. The former was referred to as Jim Crow and the latter, as Zip Coon.[7]

Beyond performance, coon songs became a popular genre for the early A&R directors. Recording company catalogs, including those of the Big Three, contained lists or entire sections of coon songs. Much like the musical subsets created for the chapter on genres, many of the then-current, larger musical genres could be broken down into specific musical styles. "The great number of coon songs in catalogues led the companies to subdivide this genre into 'Negro' songs, Negro love songs and lullabies, 'pickaninny' songs, 'old man Negro' songs … and Negro songs and dances."[8]

TABLE 8. BLACK/NEGRO RECORDINGS, BROKEN
DOWN BY THEMATIC SUBSETS (RANKED BY RECORDINGS).

Black/Negro Subsets	No. of Recordings	No. of Songs
Coon Songs	24.3%	20.6%
Novelty	21.1%	24.8%
Sentimental	19.0%	20.6%
Traditional	9.9%	8.0%
Dance	8.6%	10.1%
Love / Serenade Song	7.8%	7.6%
Old Negro	4.3%	2.1%
Religious / Gospel	3.2%	4.2%
March / Military	1.9%	2.1%

Note: "No. of Recordings" is the total number of recordings in each subset of the 1700 sample; "No. of Songs" is the total number of identifiable songs within each subset (some songs were recorded multiple times).

Due to the overwhelming majority of whites performing the repertoire, the Black/Negro ethnic group is almost exclusively pseudo-ethnic (99.4%). By creating the nine subsets (see Table 8) it also became clear that more than 45% of all Black/Negro songs and recordings fell into two categories: Coon Songs and Novelty. In both cases, the lyric content was overtly stereotypical, often condescending, and far too often simply racist. Consider a sample of titles from the two categories (see Table 9). Looking at the lyrics and phonetics of one of the songs, "Little Alabama Coon," one can see that even a seemingly gentle subject takes on the familiar attributes or contradictions of pseudo-ethnic recordings:

> *I's a little Alabama Coon, and I hasn't been born very long,*
> *I 'member seein' a great big round moon, I 'member hearin' one sweet song!*
> *When dey tote me down to de cotton field, Dar I roll and I tumble in de sun,*
> *While my daddy pick de cotton, mammy watch me grow.*

Note the dichotomy of the gentle, child-thought qualities within the lyric compared to the reality of an obviously difficult life. Another of the coon songs, "'All Coons Look Alike to Me,' ... contributed to a tremendous vogue for syncopated coon songs, from which both black and white songwriters profited. Published in 1896, the song was an immediate hit...."[9] Songwriters exploited the coon style, and the recording artists were usually white.

Eileen Southern has placed minstrel songs "into three categories: Ballads, comic songs, and specialties."[10] In an effort to clarify some of the documented recordings within this chapter's black/Negro category, recordings, including minstrel, were placed in a larger group of subsets as found in Table 8: Coon Songs, Love/Serenade, March/Military, Traditional, Religious/Gospel, Old Negro, Dance, Novelty, and Sentimental. In some cases one has to liberally apply the category names to accommodate the recordings. Consider the section "Love/Serenade." It contains songs with titles like "Ain't Dat Lovin'," "Doan Ye Cry, Mah Honey," "Down de Lover's Lane," "I'll Make Dat Black Girl Mine," "Ma Pretty Chloe from Tennessee," "My Charcoal Charmer," "My Coal Black Lady," and "All I Want Is My Black Baby Back." In the late twentieth century it may be hard to appreciate this categorization for these titles. Is "All I Want Is My Black Baby Back" (1898) a love song, lament, or serenade in the same vein as many generally popular songs? If it is, can it be compared thematically with the familiar sincerity of Paul McCartney's "Yesterday" (1965) or Jimmy Webb's "By The Time I Get to Phoenix" (1967)?

> *"All I Want Is My Black Baby Back" by Gus Edwards and Tom Daly*
>
> *A Darktown bell and her yeller man had a terrible fuss*
> *Because she called this big black coon a lazy cuss*
> *He got right mad and left the house without a word to say*
> *And she's been hunting 'round the town for him 'most every day*
> *He says he's done with her and won't come back no more*
> *He's goin' back to his other gal in Baltimore*
> *The wench is crazy and pines for him most every day*
> *And every one she meets these words she'll say*
> *All I want is my black baby back, He's the sweetest man and that's a fac'*
> *You can have all of my money, If you'll only find my honey*
> *All I want is my black baby back.*

One can probably safely conclude that the lyrics of the Edwards-Daly song carry a similar theme, even if the answer is qualified due to the sixty-plus years of change in popular music reflected in "Yesterday" or "By The Time I Get to Phoenix."

Stephen Foster (1826–1864), the nineteenth century American songwriter, has 200 songs credited to him. Most observers believe that the original songs of black Americans influenced Foster, an influence felt during his youth in Pittsburgh and later when he worked along the Ohio River in Cincinnati. Perhaps it is accurate to point to "the minstrel shows and their songs, the singing of Negroes on the wharves of the Ohio River, and the sentimental songs that were carried through the country by the so-called 'singing families'" as *the* powerful influence on Foster.[11] His writing may have also created a vicarious rural, southern life for him. "Camptown Races," "Oh! Susanna," "My Old Kentucky Home," and "Massa's in de Cold Cold Ground" are representative of both minstrelsy and of Stephen Foster.

As has been shown, white performers imitated black faces on stage with burnt cork, and they imitated black voices by recording the songs in the perceived dialect of blacks. (One must keep in mind that the songwriters in many cases were white too.) The necessary framing of the song's lyric into a cultural dialect was a creation of the songwriter, with phonetic spelling for the lyrics of sheet music as a guide for the singer. For example, "dat," "dis," "de," "dare," and "dey," replaced "that," "this," "the," "there," and "they." Stephen Foster incorporated this phonetic

TABLE 9. SAMPLE LIST OF COON SONGS AND NOVELTY SONGS

Coon Songs	Novelty
All Coons Look Alike to Me	Bake Dat Chicken Pie
Coon Coon Coon	Dar's a Watermelon Spoilin' at Johnson's
Hush My Little Coon	Give That Nigger a Ham
I Don't Allow No Coon to Hurt My Feelings	Nigger Fever
	Nigger in the Barnyard
If the Man in the Moon Were a Coon	Nigger Love a Watermelon
Little Alabama Coon	Run Nigger Run
Stuttering Coon	Tar Baby
The Hottest Coon in Town	You May Be a Hawaiian on Broadway, but You're Just Another Nigger to Me
You May Be a Hawaiian on Broadway, but You're Just Another Nigger to Me	

approach to the words of some of his songs, which are visible in the sheet music for his 1852 composition "Massa's in de Cold Cold Ground":

> *Round de meadows am a ringing*
> *De darkeys' mournful song,*
> *While de mockingbird am singing,*
> *Happy as de day am long.*
> *Where de ivy am a creeping*
> *O'er de grassy mound,*
> *Dare old massa am a sleeping,*
> *Sleeping in de cold, cold ground.*[12]

This lyric shows Foster's phonetic approach, converting a phrase like "There, old master is sleeping" to "Dare old massa am a sleeping."

The sentimental subset also contained a large number of recordings (19%) and songs (20.6%). While somewhat less harsh on the surface than the coon or novelty songs, the titles in this group—many of them centered on "mammy"—often signaled (and sometimes belied) the stereotypical content: "Daddy's Pickanniny Boy," "Darkies Dream," "Mammy's Little Choc'late Cullud Chile," "Mammy's Little Coal Black Rose,"

"Mammy's Little Pumpkin Colored Coons," "Mammy's Pickaninny Don't You Cry," and "Pickaninny Lullaby." The lyrics of "Pickaninny Lullaby"— much like those in "Little Alabama Coon" earlier — paint an outsider's view of being black in America's nineteenth-century South:

> I see a gray coon in de corn, Sleep little baby sleep,
> I hear de mastah blow his horn, Sleep little baby sleep,
> I see a niggah at the gray coon shoot,
> I heah de echo of de old horn's toot,
> An' I hear an owl in de wildwood hoot.

Once again, the idealized gentle life painted in this song ignores the reality of living black in the share-cropping, postslavery American south.

The balance of the recordings in the black/Negro group are generally less blind to the lyrical reality of their subject matter, as many of the songs travel a sometimes traditional, sometimes folk, sometimes popular road. Stephen Foster's 1860 composition "Old Black Joe" was recorded no less than twelve times during the period. "De Gospel Train Am Coming" and "Oh Dem Golden Slippers" followed the religious thread that was found in most nineteenth-century southern black lives. "On Emancipation Day" and many plantation songs appeared to have more introspective roots than most of the songs described earlier.

Perhaps the most famous song of the early black/Negro recordings is "The Darktown Strutters' Ball." Shelton Brooks' 1915 composition was remarkable for a number of things. This dance song was music for the times, i.e., a fox trot. There were at least five documented recorded versions of this song before 1920, including one by Arthur Collins and another by the Original Dixieland Jazz Band. The song had staying power during the twentieth century. Its lyrics were less racist, although no less descriptive of American society. The difference here is that these lyrics were about taking a piece of the night life, which was uptown, or downtown depending on your city, but always *that* part of town that might be referred to as *Darktown*:

> I've got some good news, honey,
> An Invitation to the Darktown Ball
> It's a very swell affair, all the high browns will be there
> I'll wear my high silk hat and a frocktail coat
> You wear your Paris gown and your new silk shawl,
> There ain't no doubt about it, babe,
> We'll be the best dressed in the hall
> (Chorus)
> I'll be down to get you in taxi, honey,

> *You better be ready about half past eight*
> *Now dearie don't be late,*
> *I want to be there when the band starts playing*
> *Remember when we get there, honey,*
> *The Two-steps, I'm goin' to have 'em all*
> *Goin' to dance out both my shoes,*
> *When they play the "Jelly Roll Blues"*
> *Tomorrow night at the Darktown Strutters' Ball.*[13]

The phrase "high browns" was a reference to bourgeois, light-skinned, or otherwise acceptable blacks. Many have written about shades of color as creating a hierarchical affect within American society:

> In post-World War I America, color differences and their meaning for Afro-Americans were a popular subject in magazines and journals.... The authors generally believed that lighter-skinned Negroes were more acceptable to whites and therefore had a more advantageous position in the black community.... Even in Social life, various authors presented evidence of color snobbery among Afro-Americans; lighter-skinned blacks frequently congregated in their own churches and social clubs.... Because many Afro-Americans seem to have internalized white values and standards of appearance, they regarded African skin color, hair, and facial features as "bad." In contrast, European features, hair texture, and light skin were felt to be "good." The light-skinned Negroes even had such value-laden titles as "high-brown," "fair brown," or "bronze."[14]

Brooks' view was not unique, nor short-lived. Irving Berlin, in 1927, included this idea in his song made famous by a 1930 film. "'Puttin' on the Ritz' was originally about Manhattan whites going uptown, and it too spoke of 'high browns.'"[15] Unlike Berlin, Shelton Brooks was black, and "The Darktown Strutters' Ball" was the song that "placed him permanently among the masters of ragtime. This rhythmically irresistible song was inspired by an actual social gathering attended by the composer in San Francisco at the time of the [Pan Pacific] Exposition."[16] And Brook's "Darktown" theme was not ignored by other writers of the time, as no less than seven different songs (and recordings) contained the *Darktown* reference during the 1910s: "Darktown Barbeque," "Darktown Belle's March," "Darktown Colored Band," "A Darktown Courtship," "Darktown Is Out Tonight," "Darktown Poets," and of course "The Darktown Strutters' Ball."

Serious recordings made by members of the black/Negro ethnic group, and made for that group, were not the norm. Most historians and researchers of the early music industry are familiar with the success of George W. Johnson's 1890s recordings of "The Laughing Song." As discussed in Chapter 9, before the development of mass production, quantities of inventory were made in a series of original takes with the performer in a room with a dozen or more cylinder phonographs. Some people have estimated that Johnson sang "The Laughing Song" thousands of times to create enough cylinders to sell. "The Laughing Song" made Mr. Johnson the first black recording artist and a durable one at that. Most date his first recording to 1891. The most famous of the early black recording artists was probably Bert Williams. Some of his repertoire was straight popular songs, and some was drawn "from black musicals of the period. Victor also recorded bluesman Gus Canon singing a blues to his own banjo accompaniment, but no proof of it is extant."[17] Instrumental recordings by black performers, particularly musician-instrumentalists are documented between 1903 and 1919, although most of these recordings would not qualify as ethnic for this study due to their lack of lyrics.

The recordings of the black/Negro group were made by mostly white performers—who churned out a significant volume of recordings, while the group's white and black composers captured the times with their lyrics, melodies, and rhythms. The early whispers of jazz were formed from the inspiration of black musicians and black styles of music. Contributing types included ragtime, blues, brass band and marches, and some of the dance music of the period. Elements within these genres—rhythm, syncopation, innovation—were also factors. As we know from looking back on the origins of rock 'n' roll, rap or hip-hop, a genre can emerge by incorporating ingredients from other styles or genres, and jazz is no exception. Jazz came from just such a fusion. James T. Maher wrote that "the straight line from plantation music to the earliest recorded jazz (1917) runs through ragtime: the impact of Negro syncopation is the major force in the Americanization of popular music."[18]

Recording of any significant repertoire by black performers was minimal during the first thirty years of recording. A few black recording artists would set the stage for many other black performers during the thirty years, into the 1920s, and beyond. Until then, a small circle of black singers and musicians like Bert Williams, the Dinwiddie Colored Quartet, the Fisk Jubilee Singers, and C. Carroll Clark would make some traditional recordings, while the overwhelming number of recordings in the black/Negro category were performed by whites.

The Hawaiian Recordings

The Hawaiian group contains almost 300 recordings. The songs of this group, the second largest surveyed, had an ethnic/pseudo-ethnic ratio of almost 2:1 (185 ethnic, 101 pseudo-ethnic). Three questions come to mind when looking at the Hawaiian repertoire. First, what is the repertoire? Second, who is performing it? Third, what accounts for such a significant representation of recorded Hawaiian music when compared to such a small, genuinely ethnic Hawaiian population — both those living in the islands and those who moved to the U.S. mainland long before statehood arrived in Hawaii?

One factor may have been the isolation of the islands. Compared to the air travel afforded by the pre-World War II Pan Am Clipper stopovers and the post–1960 explosion of commercial airline trips to Hawaii from the postwar mainland, in 1898 the islands were decidedly not a major crossroads.[19] Musically, however, the islands may have already experienced the influx of outside musical influences, or as some might describe it cultural pollution. "In 1898, the Islands already had a hybrid popular music that combined native and Euro-American elements."[20] Consistent with the alliances, associations, and partnerships that the early music industry developed around the world, by 1900 recording was already taking place in Hawaii. Regardless of the influence outsiders exerted on Hawaiian music, it appears that the early recordings were regularly made for, and continued to appeal to, consumers on the islands as well as for record buyers in mainland America.

There was the Berliner company whose catalog listed two recordings made in 1898 and 1900. In 1905 the American Record Company suddenly issued twenty-seven recordings, all of which have a recording date of September 1905. However, in spite of this relatively early recorded music, most of the Hawaiian recordings made during the period (84%) were produced between 1913 and 1919. Documents and lists show that more than one hundred recordings were issued on the Columbia label between 1914 and 1919 (one recording was dated 1910). Victor also lists more than one hundred releases between 1913 and 1919. Still other companies, such as the Okeh and Hawaiian labels, offered Hawaiian repertoire.

Ethnic Hawaiian recordings are generally easy to identify. With some exceptions, those with ethnic artists and ethnic repertoire appear with names like the Royal Hawaiian Troubadours and titles like "Beautiful Keala." The pseudo-ethnic artists are more likely to be singers like Albert Campbell or groups like Prince's Band, with titles like "Down Honolulu Way" or "I Can Hear the Ukeleles Calling Me." There are a number of titles that show a clear naiveté on the part of the songwriters, but there is only one example on the list of ethnic recordings of what one might describe as an overtly racist song. This latter is a title that can be readily classified under both black/Negro and Hawaiian ethnic headings: "You May Be a Hawaiian on Broadway, but You're Just Another Nigger to Me." While the intent of this song and its inclusion of the infamous racial epithet "nigger" is obviously condescending to blacks, its juxtaposition with Hawaiians attempts to position whites as superior to both. That example aside, the ethnic/pseudo-ethnic breakdown is about repertoire chosen for the recordings, but it is also clearly about the ethnic authenticity of the performers.

Tim Gracyk gives much credit for the Hawaiian influence in early American recordings to a few key ethnic Hawaiian performers. Some exhibited a traditional approach to the music, while others combined their ethnicity with some mainland-style promotion and production. Frank Ferera, the Royal Hawaiian Troubadours, the Royal Hawaiian Quartette, Pale K. Lua, David Kaili, the Irene West Royal Hawaiians, and the Toots Paka Hawaiian Troupe dominate the list of recording artists. All of these, and some others, have more immediate ethnic credibility with Hawaiian repertoire than do performers like Al Jolson, the Sterling Trio, Prince's Band, Anna Chandler, and Dan Quinn.

In addition to artists and repertoire, the style of music was a key element in identifying Hawaii as a unique culture. "The Hawaiians ... used a steel bar held in the left hand to produce the distinctive sliding sound characteristic of Hawaiian guitar playing, using a technique possibly learned from Indian farm labourers. They began playing the old hula tunes, European waltzes and new ragtime numbers in this way."[21] The Hawaiian steel guitar is a signature sound in music today, but one can readily imagine the non-Hawaiian ears that were caught-off-guard when listening to these early recordings in the early 1900s. A predecessor to the ukelele was also introduced and subsequently embraced by local Hawaiians. It may have been as early as 1879 "when a Portuguese ship brought a small, four-stringed guitar called a braguinha to the islands. That instrument quickly gained popularity in Hawaii and became known as the ukulele (islanders pronounce it oo-koo-le-le, which means "jumping flea").[22]

First among the ethnic recording artists was Frank Ferera who "introduced steel guitar and slide guitar playing [to a worldwide audience.] ... He was not the first Hawaiian guitarist to record. That was probably Joseph Kekuku, the steel guitar's reputed inventor ... who performed with Toots Paka's Hawaiian troupe on Edison cylinders...."[23] Based on the catalog of songs from the various labels, Ferera and his wife, Helen Louise, became the most prolific recording artists to come out of the Hawaiian Islands. The couple is represented on the ethnic list with fifty-two recordings for four different labels from 1913 to 1919. Ferera and Louise, when combined with the next four ethnic Hawaiian artists, accounted for 77% (143) of the 185 ethnic recordings.

Most of the ethnic titles appear consistent with titles that most likely represent authentic Hawaiian Island music: "Kohala March," "Kamehameha," "Hilo Hawaiian March," "Kauaihau Waltz," and "Pua Carnation." In some cases, titles were so popular that they were recorded numerous times. "Aloha Oe" (twelve versions on the list) was the most recorded, but others were popular too. "Kauaiihau Waltz" was recorded at least four times during the period, and a dozen songs, e.g., "Kai Malino," were recorded more than once. The pseudo-ethnic titles offered, predictably, mainland-centric points of view: "Back to my Sunny Honoloo," "Down Honolulu Way," "Hawaiian Nights," "Hello Hawaii, How are You," "Honolulu, America Loves You," "Honolulu Hicki Boola Boo," "I'm Down in Honolulu Looking Them Over," "They're Wearing 'Em Higher in Hawaii," and an Irish cross-cultural gem titled "O'Brien Is Learning to Talk Hawaiian." These pseudo-ethnic compositions were simplistic, sophomoric, juvenile yet still in keeping with much of the faddish writing coming out of Tin Pan Alley.

Having dispensed with the first two questions, the nature of Hawaiian repertoire and its performers, consideration must turn to the second question, why? History provides the first part of the answer, and geopolitics—not music—is central. One of America's most famous orators, Daniel Webster, advised President John Tyler of Hawaii's strategic importance. Tyler, in turn, told Congress in 1842 that the "United States would not approve of any [foreign] power trying to take control of the [Hawaiian] islands."[24] Events during the next fifty years moved Hawaii from being little known or understood by the American public, to being annexed outright by the U.S. government. According to Arthur Schlesinger events unfolded this way:

• 1843: President Tyler sent a diplomatic mission to Hawaii. Tyler's diplomat, George Brown, ignored a suggestion from Britain and France that the United States recognize the Hawaiian kingdom as an independent state.
• 1849: Hawaii and the United States signed a friendship and trade agreement.
• 1881: Outgoing Secretary of State James Blaine extended the Monroe Doctrine to include Hawaii.
• 1893: America's Ambassador to Hawaii, John Stevens, in concert with businessmen/developers like Sanford Dole, overthrew Queen Liliuokalani. The Ambassador officially recognized the new probusiness government, and the United States Marines helped solidify control (all without the knowledge of the State Department). The American flag now

flew over Hawaii, and Stevens "declared Hawaii a United States protec-
torate."[25] One month after the coup, Stevens submitted an annexation
treaty to Washington. It did not succeed, and President Grover Cleveland chose not to resubmit the treaty.

• 1897: Annexation was resubmitted to Washington.
• 1898: Annexation was approved, the timing of which coincided with the
  Spanish-American War, reinforcing the perception of Hawaii's strategic
  value. President McKinley signed the annexation.

One must also keep in mind that the postannexation approach to mainland information about Hawaiian culture was likely to be Caucasian-cen-
tric. Aside from strategic concerns, the white, Euro-American, mainland
view was that the Hawaiian Islands offered a safe opportunity to experience the exotic in the company of an idealized native population, a population painted with a gentle, acceptable hue:

> A century ago this ideal image emerged amid the same social and
> political conditions that fostered the birth of tourism as an organized
> industry: imperial expansion combined with bourgeois desires for
> contact with the rejuvenating "primitive." But despite a generalized
> Anglo-Saxon longing for "primitives," not just any primitive would
> do. Hawaiians — and especially Hawaiian women — occupied a special
> position in the Caucasian imagination. Native Hawaiians were seen as
> attractive, warm, welcoming, unthreatening, generous hosts. Impor-
> tantly, Euramericans perceived them as "brown," not "black," "red," or
> "yellow," in the colorist terminologies of … the day. For elite, white
> mainlanders Hawaiians seemed to offer an alluring encounter with
> paradisiacal exoticism, a nonthreatening soft primitivism — primitive,
> yes, but delightfully so.[26]

The combination of Euro-American-centric views and mainland American politics are step one in explaining why.

Those twenty-seven original 1905 American Record Company recordings described earlier and a subsequent tour by the Royal Hawaiian Troubadours were both promoted by the label as having been made for
"educational purposes." Whether the Royal Hawaiian Troubadours were
educating anyone or not, performances and other appearances on the
mainland in the years shortly after annexation must have had some impact
on non-Hawaiian consumers, at least due to the exotic nature of this
music. Although they were one of the early indigenous recording acts, the
Royal Hawaiian Troubadours were not alone in bringing this unique music
to a new audience. "Hawaiian musicians traveled across the United States
to its remotest corners, taking in review theaters and circus companies

along the way, leaving waves of young beginners in their wake. The mail-order shops of New York did a brisk business in Hawaiian guitars and text-books."[27] Country music performers began incorporating the steel guitar into their own repertoire. Touring musicians, early recordings, and the unique Hawaiian sound represented the second step in the rise of Hawaiian music.

The final step in answering the why question is centered around two events at the turn of the twentieth century—one theatrical and the other international: the debut of a new Broadway production and the opening of the Panama-Pacific Exposition in San Francisco. Thousands of miles east of Hawaii in New York City, Richard Walton Tully's play *Bird of Paradise* ran on Broadway for 112 performances, with an impact that was felt well beyond Broadway. Ethnic Hawaiian music, including "Kaua i ka huahuai" (popularized in the twentieth century as "The Hawaiian War Chant") "Ku'u Home," and "Tomi Tomi" represent some of the authentic Hawaiian compositions included in the incidental music to Tully's play. *Bird of Paradise*, which opened on Broadway in January 1912, introduced audiences on the American East Coast to what the *New York Times* described as the "weirdly sensuous music" of Hawaii.[28]

Three thousand miles west, the theme of the Panama-Pacific Exposition in San Francisco was to commemorate the completion of the Panama Canal (1914) and the resulting connection of the two great oceans. (The exposition also signaled San Francisco's rising from the ashes of the 1906 earthquake.) Although actual ticket sales or turnstile-counts seem elusive, it appears that between 150,000 and 300,000 people attended the exposition's opening day. President Woodrow Wilson opened the exposition on February 20, 1915, and total attendance for the run (which ended December 4, 1915) was in the millions. Those millions were directly exposed to Hawaiian culture:

> The hugely popular Hawaii pavilion at the Panama Pacific Exposition of 1915 showcased Hawaiian music and hula dancing.... After the expo, Tin Pan Alley and jazz writers and musicians took interest in the [ukelele.] Songs such as "Ukulele Lady" and "Oh, How She Could Yacki Hacki Wicki Wacki Woo (That's Love in Honolulu)" were published in sheet-music format.[29]

Millions of visitors from around the world (twenty-four countries created exhibits for the exposition) were given a front-row seat to experience Hawaiian music. These events in New York and San Francisco were step three.

For Hawaiian music, these three steps enabled the genre to reach a wide audience in the early years of recording. First, geopolitics placed the Hawaiian Islands within the bounds of the Monroe Doctrine and created a national awareness of this island kingdom. Added to the politics was a combination of promotion and tourism laced with the exotic, aimed at a mainland audience. Second, recordings and tours brought the sound of the islands into the homes of that mainland audience with sounds that in their own way were exotic: the ukelele, steel guitar, and original Hawaiian music and dance. The third and final step was attention brought to Hawaii by two separate events of the 1910s, occurring a continent apart: Tully's play (1912) and the Pan-Pacific Expo (1915).

The Irish Recordings

Unlike the sequence of events that came together to explain the large number of Hawaiian-themed recordings, repertoire from or about the Emerald Isle needed no such serendipity. Irish-Americans have been a noticeable ethnic group for most of the last one hundred and fifty years. One need look no further than the immigration numbers to begin to see why. In the nineteenth century, Irish began to leave their homes for North America. "Altogether, about 4.5 million Irish immigrated to the United States between 1820 and 1930...."[30] There seemed to be separate Irish waves of immigration to America: significant numbers prior to 1840, a surge during the famine decades of 1840–1860, and continued postfamine immigration through the 1920s. Daniels writes that "nothing so deflates the notion that most Irish are descended somehow from famine immigrants than a look at post-famine migration figures.... More than 2.6 million Irish came in the decades after 1860, an absolute majority of all Irish immigrants."[31]

Irish arriving after 1860 found assimilation into America — although not necessarily into American society — uncomplicated, given the numbers of Irish already settled. "The new Irish tended to settle where Irish pioneers had established sizeable urban enclaves, which contributed to their relative invisibility."[32] Irish immigrants included a significant number of women. Jobs for women, even menial jobs in America, were still an improvement over conditions in Ireland. Men found work in construction, local government, streetcars, police, and fire departments. (The stock character of the Irish cop was a staple in American films of the 1940s and 1950s that is ingrained in most Americans' psyche. Political names like Mayor Richard Daley, President John Kennedy, and New York Senator Daniel Patrick Moynahan reinforce the real or perceived image of the Irish-American presence.

America's preoccupation with the movement from one socio-economic level to the next impacted each Irish-American social class, often based only on timing. Who came first often determined who came second:

> Although it may be difficult to believe, the Irish had once occupied a place in American estimation that was as low as or lower than that of the Negro. In the pre-Civil War South, Irish laborers were employed in construction work in places considered too diseased and deadly to use black slave labor. In the tumult of the "Dorr War" and the effort to revise the franchise in Rhode Island in 1841–1842, the vote was extended to blacks but not to foreign-born whites—most of whom were Irish. New England was filled with signs which read: "No Irish Need Apply."[33]

Many, if not most immigrant groups found themselves at one time or another on the bottom of the American economic and social ladder looking up.

The high-profile of Irish immigrants—in legend, in the reality of high visibility jobs, and in their political clout—was echoed in the work of some of the early musical performers, musicians, and songwriters. One of the most famous of these was George M. Cohan ("Give My Regards to Broadway," "Harrigan"). He and many others were proud to display their Irish names or adopt an Irish stage name. In the songs I researched for this book I found a variety of recording artists who have Irish names: Campbell, Casey, Collins, Donovan, Harlan, Harrison, McCormack, Murray, Scanlan (Walter van Brunt became Walter Scanlan), and the Shannon Four. Wilfred Glenn, who organized this latter foursome said that "he chose the name Shannon Four because in 1917 anything Irish seemed to be popular, especially Irish songs and singers."[34] By any name Irish-born immigrants and their descendants had a significant impact on American society and on American music.

The music designated as Irish—both ethnic and pseudo-ethnic—was the third largest group in numbers of recordings, behind Hawaiian and black/Negro. It differs from the other two in that its influence and its staying-power with the mainstream American audience continues to be visible today. A list of standards, that is songs that have repeatedly been recorded and performed throughout the twentieth century, contains a number of songs written by early Irish songwriters—"Give My Regards to Broadway," "Over There"—and songs filled with themes pulled from the Emerald Isle: "My Wild Irish Rose," "Goodnight Irene." Another thematic song from the period, "Danny Boy," has made various popular music charts through hits like Conway Twitty's 1959 version and by black-American rhythm & blues singer Jackie Wilson in 1965.

While the majority of the recordings categorized as Irish are ethnic (60% versus 40% pseudo-ethnic), the split could easily be moved in either direction based on the application of the label (see Table 7). Perhaps that is because the repertoire represents a mix of recordings that, lacking a more scientific label, might be thought of as either gentle or self-depre-cating. The vast majority of the recordings probably received a sympa-thetic hearing, even when the title indicated a nonmusical and stereotypical theme, as with "Flanagan at the Doctor" or "The Irish Washerwoman." In my breakdown of Irish repertoire, those recordings categorized as pseudo-ethnic were, more often than not, given that label due to the ethnicity of the performer, not because of the content, and rarely due to overtly neg-ative or racist content.

To many American ears the Irish accent is immediately disarming. We hear the charm but have not witnessed the five centuries that made it charming. The conflict between English speakers and Irish or Gaelic speak-ers in the British Isles (ignoring Wales and Scotland, for the moment) has a long history. This chapter is not about to tackle the science, politics, cul-ture, or ethnography that created the lyrical quality of an Irishman's brogue. However, that vocalization, to some an encapsulation of Ireland itself, is an unmistakable calling card; at times it has been an entre to a larger society. Song titles reinforce the lyric quality of the Irish. Each one seems to flow over the lips as a clear brook moves effortlessly downstream. The names can be found in a Dublin telephone directory, and the song ref-erences on a map of the Emerald Isle. (See Table 11).

Aside from the accent, both the songs and the musical styles must also be categorized. This might be most easily accomplished by beginning with the styles. Mick Moloney, in "Irish Ethnic Recordings and the Irish Imag-ination," uses four categories to identify ethnic Irish performers and recordings, paraphrased below:

1. nineteenth-century Anglo-Irish songwriters and performers, who usually had been trained in classical traditions;
2. the Stage Irish, known for an exaggerated, theatrical approach to Irish music, including the brogue, mannerisms, characterizations;
3. traditional dance music often played on traditional instruments: fiddle, uillean pipes, concertina, etc.;
4. an Irish hybrid of 1–3 above, along with some American influ-ence.[35]

The most famous musical name in recordings during the 1889–1919 period was John McCormack. Born in Ireland, he eventually moved to the

United States, became a citizen, and a household name. McCormack was classically trained, but his repertoire was anything but exclusively classical. Much of what he recorded had a connection to the folk tradition or the church, and some songs contained samples of people and place names listed earlier. Consider some selections of his pre-1920 body of work (see Table 10). In all, McCormack had fifty recordings identified by Joel Whitburn as being successful before 1920, another twenty-three after 1920.[36] There is nothing in McCormack's repertoire that one would categorize as pseudo-ethnic, including his recording of "The Star-Spangled Banner." McCormack can be placed in Moloney's first and fourth categories.

TABLE 10. SELECT JOHN MCCORMACK RECORDINGS, 1910–1919.

Classical/Religious	Folk/Traditional	People	Places
Carmen	Drink to Me Only	Annie Laurie	Killarney
The Rosary	with Thine Eyes	Mother Machree	Come Back to
Ave Maria	Danny Boy	Kathleen	Erin
Aida	A Little Bit	Mavourneen	Where the River
	of Heaven	My Wild Irish	Shannon Flows
		Rose	

The Stage Irish category is found throughout the list of recordings. Titles like "I'll Not Go Out with Reilly Anymore," "McGinty at the Living Pictures," "Casey As Umpire at a Ball Game," "St. Patrick's Day at Clancy's," "Flanagan's Ocean Voyage," "Mrs. Reilly's Trouble with the Dumb Waiter," "Pat O'Brien's Automobile," and "Evening at Mrs. Clancy's Boarding House" are easily representative of Moloney's more detailed definition. Each includes some level of exaggeration. There is a theatrical approach to music and to performance, including the brogue, mannerisms, characterizations, jokes, blunders, drinking, staying out late, or any combination of these. Moloney tells how the Stage Irishman was described as "bestial" in appearance, and makes use of stereotypical attire:

> His hair is fiery red; he is rosey-cheeked, massive, and whiskey loving … [He has] a tall felt hat … cutty-clay pipe … an open shirt collar, three-caped coat, knee breeches, worsted stockings … and cockaded brogue shoes…." [Furthermore, he] "has an atrocious Irish brogue, perpetually jokes, blunders and bulls in speaking, and never fails to utter some … wild speech.[37]

Since the exaggerated Irishman had been "incorporated into the burgeoning New York stage and music halls" in the nineteenth century, the characterizations could be seen in the mind's eye when one listened to some of these recordings.

The remaining category is that of traditional dance music which was often performed on traditional instruments. The list of Irish recordings includes a sampling of these, including jigs and reels. Examples are far more numerous than those included on this list, but only a few have been included due to the instrumental nature of most of them.

The songs were usually comfortable extensions of the Irish image. There are names of pretty girls and strong men, beautiful places, and connections to the dominant Roman Catholic faith. Consider a sampling of proper names in titles related to gender and geography: Kathleen, Eileen, Irene, Erin, Katie, Nora, and Mother Machree; Patrick, Billy, Casey, Flanagan, and Clancy; Richmond Hill, Killarney, County Mayo, Inniscara, Dublin, and County Derry. Of course there have always been songs of a religious nature, often associated with the Roman Catholic Church: "Father O'Flynn," "The Bells of Saint Mary's," and "There's Another Angel Now in Killarney."

Thinking about the song titles listed throughout this section, one does not have to be Irish to visualize the character known as Harrigan, see Casey wagging his finger at the batter, observe a group of boarders at Mrs. Clancy's boarding house, or assume what Reilly must have done to make someone opt to "not go out with him anymore." Had non-Irish performers conjured up all of these performances, many would easily be seen as pseudo-ethnic and, in fact, that is how many of these exaggerations have been categorized. Most, however, are self-deprecating approaches to being Irish, and while they might be better categorized as self-inflicted wounds, it is up to an Irishman to determine the true nature, the "pseudoness" of each. Some Irish did object to the portrayals, and some of them resisted the stereotyping. Moloney documents "a seventy-one-year-old accordion player from County Kilkenny [explaining] how he used to take part in vigilante-style activities to stop *Stage Irish* productions, causing loud disruptions in theaters where they took place."[38]

TABLE 11. SELECTED SONG TITLES AND NAMES OF
PERFORMERS FROM IRISH ETHNIC AND PSEUDO-ETHNIC LISTS.

Sample Titles	Stage and Family Names
Along the Rocky Road to Dublin	Campbell, Albert
The Bells of Saint Mary's	Casey, Michael
Bonnie Jean	Clarke, Herbert
Danny Boy	Collins, Arthur
Fields of Ballyclare	Donovan, Hugh
Ireland Must Be Heaven	Harlan, Byron
Kathleen Mavourneen	Harrison, Charles
Killarney	MacDonough, Harry
Loch Lomond	McAuliffe, James C.

Sample Titles	Stage and Family Names
Mother Machree	McClaskey, Harry
My Wild Irish Rose	McCormack, John
Twas Only an Irishman's Dream	Murray, Billy
There's Something in the Name of Ireland	O'Connell, Margaret
There's Nothing Too Good for the Irish	Quinn, Dan
When Irish Eyes Are Smiling	Scanlan, Pat

Note: song titles and the names of performers in this table are not necessarily linked.

The Irish were synonymous with the American experience during the years explored here. They were visible in ways that the public found acceptable, often reassuring in the blue-collar trades and the two most important service trades: police and fire departments. They were powerful in ways that the public may have at different times—for better or worse—accepted as America's political norm: from William Marcy "Boss" Tweed (1823–1878) to the "Daley Machine" and the Kennedy family political dynasty of the mid-to-late-twentieth century. The religion recognized by so many Irish immigrants was able to carve a niche and coexist in the previously mostly Protestant United States. The Irish survived brute characterizations, epitomized in the Stage Irish described earlier and amplified by the press. (Nineteenth century cartoonist-journalist Thomas Nast who, working against Tweed, "popularized one of the great ethnic slurs of American Journalism, the depiction of the Irishman as a stupid brute with simian characteristics"[39]). The lyrics contained in the recordings of the period allowed the Irish to laugh at themselves, think wistfully of the land they or their parents or grandparents left behind, and join together in an ethnic community. That community moved beyond stereotypes, overcame stereotypes, but assimilation into America never meant that their heritage too had become assimilated or lost. The music helped keep the ethnicity alive.

The German Recordings

German-language recordings were not an after-thought or simply an extension of the American recorded-music business. One can recall the German-born inventor Emile Berliner who helped transform the American cylinder recording business into the disc recording business, a standard that continues to exist today,[40] almost eighty years after the last cylinders were released. Technology transcended borders.

Edison had a separate cylinder company in London as early as 1898, which along with his American company would divide worldwide business between the two operations. "By 1907, Edison's National Phonograph Company had offices in New York, London, Paris, Berlin, Brussels, Mexico City, Sydney and Buenos Aires."[41] The National Gramophone Company, which controlled the disc-oriented patents developed by Berliner, was also in London, trying to create a partnership. "In May 1898 the Gramophone Company was formed with [sufficient] working capital ... and the exclusive right to sell gramophone merchandise throughout Europe."[42] Within two years Gramophone had a few thousand titles in its catalog, many in German. Columbia operated internationally, and successful independent companies were found elsewhere, including France (Pathé) and Germany (Beka and Lindstrom, which would acquire numerous firms and become the giant Deutsche Grammophon Gesellschaft, DGG).[43] Recordings in a variety of languages were fast becoming the norm. However, in most cases, recordings were made on location. These were not simply field recordings of native peoples, but rather they were recordings made for local domestic consumption that were nevertheless represented in the larger company's catalogs. "By 1905 the [Gramophone] Company had already made recordings in most European and Asian countries, including Helsinki, Tiflis, and Rangoon.... Iceland had 78,000 inhabitants in 1900; yet beginning in 1910, the Gramophone Company took pains to record Icelandic artists fairly regularly, first in Copenhagen and later in Reykjavik."[44] A worldwide business established a market for recordings in multiple languages, at least for domestic consumption.

German immigrants, like other immigrant populations, wanted a new life in America, but wherever possible they also wanted to retain and renew memories of their original culture. Books, theater, newspapers, and musical performance were all available in the German language for those who had come to America. "Seventy-four daily newspapers had a circulation of three hundred thousand.... The nearly four hundred weeklies had a combined circulation of more than a million [not including estimates for multiple-readers]...."[45] Ironically, by the end of World War I, anti-German sentiment was so strong that it likely accelerated the English-language assimilation of German immigrant families. Before the war, German immigrant families became consumers of German-language cylinders and discs. The larger population would see another aspect of German ethnic recordings.

Many of the German recordings on the list were truly ethnic. There were familiar songs, often in German, occasionally in English; and of course there were also pseudo-ethnic recordings. Like the black/Negro group, recordings were made of and by native, white American performers of both non-German and German ancestry. Some recordings poked fun at German-English phonetics, while others—like those found in the earlier groups, were taking aim at German (and German-American) social and political life. German recordings took on a new function as sentiment against things German rose with the advent of World War I. Songs like "In diesen heiligen Hallen" (ethnic) or "On the Banks of the Rhine with a Stein" (pseudo-ethnic) were accompanied or replaced by anti-German lyrics, as found in "When Uncle Joe Steps into Heinie Land" and "The Beast of Berlin: We're Going to Get Him" (see Table 12.)

Of all of the recordings I identified as German ethnic or pseudo-ethnic (172), documents confirm that more than half of those with exact recording dates (56%, 96 recordings) were released between 1898 and 1913, while 45% were released during the war years. There is an additional group of recordings (39) which have no exact dates to confirm their release. However, judging by the titles and presumed content of those I have not listened to, it seems reasonable to assume that all but one were released prior to the start of World War I (1914), or at least prior to the United States entering the war (1917). Adding these undated titles to the prewar/postwar analysis changes the numbers significantly: 78% prewar, 22% during World War I or postwar.

TABLE 12. GERMAN ETHNIC AND PSEUDO-ETHNIC
TITLES (INCLUDING ANTI-GERMAN: WORLD WAR I)

Ethnic Titles	Pseudo-Ethnic Titles	Anti-Germany (WWI)
Zauberlied	Moonlight on the Rhine	When Uncle Joe Steps
Christkind Kommt	Oh How That German Could	into Heinie Land
In diesen heiligen	Love	The Beast of Berlin:
Hallen	Music Vots Music Must Come	We're Going to
Vater, Musser,	from Berlin	Get Him
Schwester, Brudder	On the Banks of the Rhine with	We Don't Want the
Deutschland über	a Stein	Bacon (What We
Alles	Hilda Loses Her Job	Want Is a Piece of
	Krausmeyer and His Dog	the Rhine)
	Schneider	
	Heine at College	

America's interest in German ethnic and pseudo-ethnic recordings by both German and non-German residents declined with the war. Prior to the conflict, however, consistencies with previously discussed ethnic recordings are clear. Recordings existed about the German immigrants, and for and by the German immigrants. Humorous recordings ("Blitz and Blatz in an Aeroplane") sat side-by-side with other repertoire, including serious ("Prince of Pilsen March"), religious ("Stille Nacht, Heilige Nacht"), and Americanized popular songs with a German flavor ("My Little German Home across the Sea"). With the onset of war, romance and sentimentality seemed to disappear.

The Italian Recordings

The Italian group has some commonality with the German group (and the Irish for that matter), yet they had distinctive elements in terms of both their immigration and their recorded repertoire. In sheer numbers, Italians rivaled any of the other European immigrant groups migrating in the period. Their arrivals began later than the Germans or Irish, but the speed with which their numbers in America grew (see Chart 1) quickly equaled (and in some cases surpassed) those groups whose immigration had begun much earlier. Roger Daniels states that "no other ethnic group in American history sent so many immigrants in such a short time...."[46] The census numbers confirm the arrivals and the foreign-born Italians remaining (after any return migration to Italy.) Daniels goes on to state that "some 97 percent of Italians [arriving] in the four and a half decades after 1880 migrated through the port of New York, and vast numbers stayed there."[47]

TABLE 13. ITALIAN IMMIGRANT ARRIVALS
AND ITALIAN-BORN RESIDENTS

Census Years	Italian Arrivals	Italian-born residents
1900	650,000	484,000
1910	2,045,000	1,343,000
1920	1,110,000	1,610,000

Note: Italian immigrants had a significant rate of return migration, which Daniels estimates ran as high as 30–50%. Therefore, numbers of foreign-born counted during census would not necessarily be equal to number of arrivals.

The ninety examples of ethnic Italian recorded music appear relatively evenly split between ethnic (44%) and pseudo-ethnic (56%). In some cases European classical music is appropriate for inclusion within the ethnic recordings of a particular group, and Italians are such a group: e.g., recordings of Giuseppe Verdi ("Celeste Aida") or Ruggiero Leoncavallo ("Vesti la giubba" from I Pagliacci). Staples from the Roman Catholic Church moved from the sanctuary to recordings for the home ("Ave Maria," "The Rosary"). The Italians brought their national anthem to American recordings. "Inno di guerra dei cacciatori della Alpi" ("Battle Hymn of the Alpine Huntsmen") became the "Garibaldi Hymn" following Garibaldi's successful military campaign in 1860. "From then on the song was known as 'Inno di Garibaldi.'"[48] I found seven versions of the popular "Funiculi, Funicula," and I cataloged the numerous recordings by Enrico Caruso (with three exceptions) as ethnic. The exceptions include "For You Alone," which was Caruso's first recording in English.[49]

Pseudo-ethnic recordings were primarily those made by American (non-Italian) performers, names that should be recognizable by now: Albert Campbell, Henry Burr, Byron Harlan, Charles Harrison, and Billy Murray. Two somewhat surprising entries were recordings by Hawaiians Helen Louise and Frank Ferera ("O Solo Mio") and Pali Lua and David Kaili ("The Rosary"). Other pseudo-ethnic songs recorded were "Good-Bye Mister Caruso," "I'll Take You Back to Italy," "Nighttime in Little Italy," "On the Shore of Italy," "Wop Blues," and "Pedro the Hand Organ Man." This last recording is a somewhat derogatory look at the stereotypical Italian street-corner man and his monkey.

The Jewish/Yiddish Recordings

Jewish immigration to America was minimal in the early nineteenth century, with populations increasing as Jews within national ethnic groups began arriving in larger numbers. "At the outbreak of the Civil War, Jewish communities once confined to the coastal littoral had spread across the continent in more than 150 places, however the East Coast continued to attract most Jewish immigrants and their descendants.... There were an estimated 40,000 [in New York] by 1860."[50]

Once again, community was apparent. Community for Jewish immigrants was community within community. That is the large community, New York City, containing a large Jewish population, could be broken down into smaller ethnic populations, based on national origin: Germany, Russia, Romania, Hungary, England, Canada. For many Jewish immigrants, some commonality was found beyond Judaism in the use of Yiddish for communication and in their mutual preference for the city versus the country. For example, urban settlement and association marked German Jewish immigrants, which was in contrast to many non-Jews from Germany. Given what we know today and given statistics from writers like Daniels one can conclude that agriculture was an occupation of last resort for many, if not most, German Jews. New York City (and other urban centers) would retain many of these immigrants. Still, by the late 1800s their numbers totaled less than 300,000, although Daniels states that Jewish numbers in America may have reached 4 million before the implementation of the Immigration Act of 1924.[51] It should not be surprising, therefore, that the East Coast-based American recording companies created recordings about, for, and by Jews. "It has been estimated that a quarter of American Jews lived in New York in 1860, about a third lived there in 1880, and close to half in 1920.... In 1910 more than five hundred thousand Jews were wedged into tenements in the 1.5 square miles of New York's Lower East Side."[52]

The Jewish/Yiddish recordings I found were primarily ethnic in nature (see Table 7). I gave them the ethnic designation in many cases due to the combination of the performer and Jewish/Yiddish repertoire. Many recordings were religious, such as performances of "Eli Eli" by Cantor Joseph Rosenblatt or "Rezei" ("Accept Our Prayers") by Cantor G. Sirota. A large number of the documented recordings were comedic, apparently by Jewish performers. The Jewish character of "Cohen" was "worked over" regularly in the recording studio: e.g., "Cohen at the Real Estate Office," "Cohen Gets Married," "Cohen on the Telephone," "Cohen on his Honeymoon," "Cohen Owes Me 97 Dollars," "Cohen Telephones the Health Department." "Cohen" was not the only target, although some of these other recordings may have been less satirical—but that determination must be made by the listener: "Goldstein Goes into the Railroad Business," "Levinsky at the Wedding," "My Yiddish Matinee Girl," "Nathan, For What You Waiting," and "At the Yiddish Wedding Jubilee."

Some songs from popular genres found their way into Jewish ethnic recordings. There was a series of Hebrew vaudeville recordings, usually centered around a familiar song: "In the Good Old Summer Time," "On a Sunday Afternoon," and "In the Shade of the Old Apple Tree" were all recorded by Julian Rose. Rose also recorded a coon song titled "Ain't Dat a Shame." A small group of performers identified as non-Jewish made up the bulk of the pseudo-ethnic recordings. "Cohen" was reworked by George Thompson in "Cohen Phones the Garage." Ralph Bingham recorded "Goldstein Behind Bars," Edward Meeker declared "I'm a Yiddish Cowboy," and Maurice Burkhardt sang of the "Yiddisha Nightingale."

The Chinese Recordings

Given the small number of immigrants from China, the Chinese could easily have been a group that I lumped into "all other" or "exotic." However, like the Hawaiian group, recordings that I categorized as Chinese were represented far in excess of their proportional population. The number of foreign-born Chinese in New York City in 1900 was 6,080; in 1910 that population had dropped by one-third to 3,936. In the nineteenth century, most Chinese immigrants lived in the American West: 99% in 1870, 72% in 1910. Even if one adjusts the figures for a possible under-count due to lack of cooperation or to allow for agricultural migration, the United States' Chinese numbers in total will stay relatively modest compared to the larger population, particularly in the eastern United States.

There was no significant population for these New York-based companies to cater to or to draw repertoire from. The recordings I categorized as Chinese are all pseudo-ethnic. These recordings are anything but authentic or ethnic as four examples will illustrate:

(1) "Chinatown My Chinatown," written by William Jerome and Jean Schwartz (1910), was included in a Broadway show titled *Up and Down Broadway* (1910) and was recorded by American Quartet (1914);

(2) "Chinese Lullaby," written by Robert Bowers (1919), was the theme for the Broadway play *East Is West* (1919), and was recorded by Columbia Orchestra (1919);

(3) "Chin Chin Chinaman" (1896), written by Harry Greenbank and Sidney Jones for the Broadway show *The Geisha* (1896), was recorded by Dan Quinn (1896);

(4) "Wedding of the Chinee and the Coon," written by Bob Cole and Billy Johnson (1897), was recorded by Dan Quinn (1897).[53]

Non-Chinese songwriters created a collection of songs for Broadway and popular consumption that at best romanticized a Chinese society— whether observed locally, in America's numerous *Chinatowns*, or out of a naive fantasy of life in China itself. "From Here to Shanghai," "My Dreamy Little Lotus Flower," "In Blinky Winky Chinky Chinatown," and "Uncle Josh in a Chinese Laundry" all are westernized views. In "Chong, He Come from Old Hong Kong," phonetic instructions— much like those created by Stephen Foster — were given to singers to allow for the "Chinese dialect lyrics attached to [this] dance music."[54] For example, consider the sheet music lyrics for Robert Bowers' "Chinese Lullaby":

> *Sing song, sing song, so hop toy*
> *Al-lee same like China-boy*
> *But he sel-Lee girl with joy*
> *Pity poor Ming-Toy*

Songwriters, producers, performers, and record companies all clearly ignored the real lives of the Chinese people who came to the United States, only to be victimized by anti-Chinese legislation in 1870 and 1882. "The first [the Naturalization Act of 1870] which limited naturalization to 'white persons and persons of African descent,' meant that Chinese immigrants were in a separate class: They were aliens ineligible for citizenship.... The second [the Chinese Exclusion Act of 1882] ... made the Chinese, for a time, the only ethnic group in the world that could not freely immigrate to the United States."[55] The fifty-six songs I have placed in the Chinese ethnic group are 100% pseudo-ethnic. Obviously.

The Polish Recordings

Polish immigrants to America, like many of their European brethren, arrived at Ellis Island. Unlike so many of the other Euro-immigrants, the Poles often moved through New York and on to other destinations. While New York had many Polish immigrants and second generation Poles, during the first decades of the century Chicago had more. Milwaukee, Pittsburgh, Detroit, and Buffalo had a combined ethnic-Polish population twice as large as New York. One might suggest that the Poles came for bread and, to get that bread, worked at the bottom of the employment food chain. Working in the worst jobs, these immigrants still found time to induce others to come. Judging by the size of the urban communities, and seeing the surrounding support from organizations like the Polish Roman Catholic Union under the Protection of the Sacred Heart of Jesus (organized 1873)[56] and the Zwiazek Narodowy Polski (the Polish National Alliance) (organized 1880),[57] Poland's emigrants coming to America could reassure immigration officials, should they ask, that they had family, friends, and other support in their new country. This connection to their former life was apparent in their religion and politics in America as well. Catholicism — reflected in houses of worship and social organizations— was brought with them, and supported in their new country. Was it, however, *their* new country? "Nationalism also was the crucial issue among Polish secular organizations which were long oriented more to Polish politics than American."[58]

Polish recordings show less interest in Americanized music beyond one significant exception: the polka. Its origins in Bohemia or Poland aside, the polka on its own can be separated into ethnic and pseudo-ethnic polkas if only on the basis of the performer. Banda Rossa recorded the "Celebrity Polka"; Columbia Band the "Gem Polka"; Edison Grand Concert Band the "Nutmeg Polka"; Sousa's Band the "Little Coquette Polka"; only five recordings that I found did not have the word *polka* in the title. If the early recordings were anything, they were consistent. "By 1910 ... Edison and Columbia cylinders, and Columbia and Victor flat discs all were available with increasing quantities of Polish music on them...."[59] Chopin was available, as were folk songs and traditional dance recordings, but many of them were produced locally, near the previously-cited centers of Polish population and Polish repertoire. Nationally, the genres available were much more limited, and polka recordings were the dominant musical form.

The Native American Recordings

Obviously we do not have immigration numbers for Native American Indians. The history of their population reduction since contact with Europeans began five centuries ago is well documented. The recording of ethnic American Indian music is less apparent than the pseudo-ethnic songs created in Tin Pan Alley. "The first commercial recordings by a Native American were made for Berliner records in the 1890s. In 1904 Ho-Nu-Ses recorded Iroquois songs for the Victor Talking Machine Company."[60] Other recordings would be made during the century, but only sporadically, and most after the advent of electric recording in the 1920s.

The Tin Pan Alley pseudo-ethnic recordings deserve little space, as they generally comprise that fantasized view discussed earlier (see Hawaii, China). The artists arc almost all from the rosters of the Big Three companies: Arthur Collins, Byron Harlan, Columbia Band, Edison Military Band, Harry MacDonough. The song titles were predictable: "Hiawatha," "Honest Injun," "Navajo Two-Step," "Oh That Navajo Rag," and "Who Played Poker with Pocahontas."

The Exotic Recordings

I created the exotic group to accommodate a large group of recordings that were otherwise inappropriate for inclusion elsewhere, or that I would not have considered due to the small group each would have represented. Each of these recordings embraced diverse themes clearly associated with otherness. These songs contained references to places that often sounded familiar, but were obviously foreign or fiction. An important ingredient in this category is the fact that none of the cities, countries, or other geographic references were European. Familiarity in America was minimal at best.

The history, literature, and phonetics of the names Cairo, Constantinople, Bombay, Singapore, Siam, Mandalay, Zanzibar, Arabia, and Borneo all lent themselves to a curious interest in America. Americans may have known the names due the colonial history of the European nations and by association the colonial history of American immigrants themselves. "On the Road to Mandalay" (1907) was based on "[Rudyard] Kipling's 'Barrack Room Ballads', [and] became a favorite for male vocalists…" [while another song, "Dardanella" (1919) was] "a Fox-trot billed as 'an echo from the East'…."[61] The same held true for the people of this group — Sultans, Gungha Din, Bedouins, Arabs, Fakirs, Cleopatra — which were all thematic material for the recordings, as for example in "Egypt, My Cleopatra" (1904), a ballad made exotic by its subjects. One can imagine a listener seeing the locales, noticing the faces, and appreciating the costumes. The mind's eye, aided by the themes, built the image of the exotic.

The Other Countries

There were a number of countries that were represented in such small quantities that no real analysis was required. I found sixteen recordings with an Argentinean theme, most of them related to the dance known as the tango. I found ten recordings connected to Austria. Five songs had a Belgian theme. Four were Brazilian; fifteen Canadian (three of which were the anthem "Oh Canada"); four Cuban; one Chilean; one Danish; twenty-one from England (five were versions of "It's a Long Way to Tipperary"; six recordings had *king and country* themes); twenty were French, eight of which were recordings of "La Marseillaise"; three were Guatemalan; five Hungarian; twelve Japanese; sixteen were Mexican; one from Norway; six from the Netherlands; two were Panamanian; one of the Philippines; seven Russian; twenty-five Scottish; twenty-seven Spanish; two Swedish; and three were Swiss.

The Recordings, by Ethnic Group: A Conclusion

As one considers the original questions posed by this chapter, it appears that the influence of immigrants on authentic ethnic music is as significant as the influence of that music on the immigrants. The members of the period's ethnic communities benefited from the availability of native-language recordings as a reminder of both their birth language and their birth countries. To the degree that this kept the communities vital, recordings played an important cultural role. Some recordings created an awareness of an ethnicity when no awareness, or very little, existed. I found few examples of political solicitude. For example, I identified some patriotic language as heard in national anthems as political statements, such as opposition to sides in war. There is no immediate evidence that the recordings brought any two groups together through improved understanding. A more likely outcome was solidification of already-held views of about those outside the immigrant's groups, whether good, bad, or indifferent.

The most positive images are presented in two groups of ethnic recordings: Irish and Polish; the worst were presented in the groups labeled Chinese, Native American, and black/Negro. The former have a significant majority of repertoire fostering a positive theme, or at least, an absence of xenophobia. In contrast, the latter group, with virtually all of the repertoire labeled pseudo, presents these immigrant groups in (at least) a naive, condescending, or patronizing way, and sometimes in terms that are clearly racist. Some songs created during the period incorporated Tin Pan Alley's politically unsophisticated view of foreigners; the lyrics of some songs may simply have been poor judgment (regardless of the popularity or acceptability to a large American audience), reinforcing the worst existing ethnic stereotypes of these groups. One does not have to give a great deal of thought to the inauthentic, stereotypical, and racist songs to recognize them for what they were; in most cases titles said it all:

> "All Coons Look Alike to Me"
> "Chong, He Come from Old Hong Kong"
> "Who Played Poker with Pocahontas"

Two categories of ethnic music, the exotic and the Jewish/Yiddish, have repertoire that, while not always presenting what a critic might consider thoughtful songwriting, at least managed to avoid the most objectionable lyric content. Where the two groups differ is the ethnicity of the performers— most of the Jewish/Yiddish group's performers appear to be Jewish, while the performers in the exotic group appear to be anything but exotic:

> Exotic
> "Bedouin Love Song" (John Myers)
> "Yukaloo, My Pretty South Sea Island Lady" (Sterling Trio)
> "Under the Yellow Arabian Moon" (Billy Murray and Irving Kaufman)
>
> Jewish/Yiddish
> "Levinsky at a Wedding" (Julian Rose)
> "V'Hakohanim" (Yoselle Rosenblat)
> "Kol Nidrei" (Leo Schultz)

The remaining groups have repertoire and/or performers that touch both worlds, as a sampling of the recordings, both patronizing (*pseudo*) and authentic (*ethnic*) in the list of 1,700 titles illustrates:

> Hawaii
> "They're Wearing 'Em Higher in Hawaii"
> "Kanilehua (I Love You)"
>
> Italy
> "Funiculi, Funicula"
> "Pedro the Hand Organ Man"

The difficulties (and in some cases miseries) experienced by the immigrants were rarely assuaged by the presence of ethnic music, and a passing desire to return to their birth country was not transformed into action based on that music. The simplest view is that ethnic music was what the record companies were eager to provide — entertainment — even if their vision of what constituted ethnic was often blurred. John McCormack's recordings and those of Enrico Caruso and Cantor Joseph Rosenblatt were welcomed by their primary audiences (respectively, Irish, Italian, and Jewish). In the case of McCormack and Caruso, a larger audience was found as music lovers from outside the core groups often found these recordings regularly worth listening to, worth purchasing, worth collecting. Predictably, while some non-Jews may have enjoyed the humor of "Levinsky at the Wedding" or "Cohen on the Telephone," the focused nature of "Eli Eli" or "Kol Nidrei" did not reach out to, nor was it expected to find, a waiting audience among non-Jews. However, whether self-deprecating or not, three separate "Cohen" recordings of ethnic humor found a wider audience.[62] Given the Jewish/Yiddish accents generally used on these recordings, and in some cases the issue of money (as in the Irving Berlin composition "Cohen Owes Me 97 Dollars"), one can look back and conclude that stereotypes were inevitably reinforced.

Two non-musical aspects of recordings during the period showed a relationship beyond entertainment: class consciousness and politics. Class consciousness could be seen in a significant number of the recordings. Lyrics suggesting or articulating in a straightforward manner a superiority of white-America were easy to find in the 1,700 recordings surveyed, particularly in the black/Negro, Chinese, and Native American groups. A very small number of the ethnic recordings of the period demonstrated any relationship with issues of the period. Politics were apparent in the German group, when lyric content shifted from appearing benign to becoming anti-German ("The Beast of Berlin: We're Going to Get Him"). The recording of national hymns and anthems of various countries also demonstrates some political representation (Russia, Panama, Italy, United States, and others).

Hawaiian tourism, not the minimal Hawaiian community outside of the Islands, was the beneficiary of mainland interest. Touring musicians appeared on the mainland, a Broadway show featured Hawaiian music, and Tin Pan Alley songwriters picked up the fad and began spewing out pseudo-ethnic titles like "Oh, How She Could Yacki Hacki Wicki Wacki Woo (That's Love in Honolulu)." The bulk of Hawaiian repertoire after 1905 clearly points to a mainland consumer, with a fascination for the "ideal native" (as Jane Desmond stated in her essay). Frank Ferera, Toots Paka, and others brought some authenticity to the mainland audience; Harry MacDonough, Billy Murray, and Margaret O'Connell used the Tin Pan Alley repertoire to codify a new understanding of Hawaiian music — the pseudo-ethnic. No benefit (tourism or otherwise) came to China. American race relations did not improve as a result of ethnic recordings. The first likely reaction by modern listeners to the majority of pseudo-ethnic recordings is that they are more than American-centric, or Euro-centric, or to borrow Jane Desmond's term "Euramerican"-centric. They are white-European-American-mainland-centric. If ethnic recordings reflect the immigration waves, the pseudo-ethnic recordings reflect the biases of the period created by these waves.

Perhaps the essence of the pseudo-ethnic recordings can also be seen in one particular song. While the first recorded versions of this song do not appear until 1920 (one year out from the targeted years of this book), the weight of these lyrics more than sums up the idea of a pseudo-ethnic song. Nativism, xenophobia, and stereotyping — aimed at the wave of immigrants from Eastern and Southern Europe — come through loud and clear. This song may represent the totality of the period's ethnic recordings. Our American form of pluralism does not always stand as a pure beacon to others. Consider "The Argentines, the Portuguese and the Greeks":

> *Columbus discovered America in fourteen ninety-two,*
> *Then came the English, and the Dutch, the Frenchman and the Jew*
> *Then came the Swede and Irishman who helped our country grow,*
> *Still they keep a'coming and now everywhere you go, there's*
> *The Argentines and the Portuguese, the Armenians and the Greeks,*
> *One sells you papers, one shines your shoes,*
> *Another shaves the whiskers off your cheeks,*
> *When you ride again in a subway train notice who has all the seats, and*
> *You'll find they're held by the Argentines, the Portuguese, and the Greeks*[63]

Historian Pekka Gronow, as capably as anyone, has articulated the essence of ethnic and pseudo-ethnic recordings in the early years of the record business:

The record industry did not set out to change musical traditions. It recorded whatever it thought could be sold, seeking its artists from opera houses as well as the music halls. In the United States that meant both the Metropolitan Opera, and the beer gardens....[64]

The importance of ethnic recordings from the early labels might best be summed up by paraphrasing Shakespeare. Within the evolving ethnic communities, familiar music was "the food of life."

18

Images, Music, and the Inevitable Transition

Most long-playing (LP) records, extended-play (EP) records, and some 7-inch and 12-inch singles released since the introduction of vinyl discs (1948) have featured artist-specific packaging. The front and back covers of those packages might have a photograph or illustration of the musician or singer, or a conceptual artwork (illustration, photograph, photographic montage, or painting) that may or may not suggest the musical content. In most cases these would also include text information, which might simply list the song titles (usually in order of sequence) the names of the songwriters and music publishers, or the running times. The text may also contain the artist's biography, discography, or other relevant information. Whether purchasing vinyl records or compact discs, the consumer today generally expects to have some type of graphic art and text incorporated into the package. This was not always the case.

During the first thirty years of recording, the artist — whether performer or sideman, musician, or vocalist — was secondary, at least in terms of packaging, to the company or the founder. Much like Lee Iacocca's image as the spokesman for Chrysler during the 1980s, or Colonel Sanders' role selling Kentucky Fried Chicken, Thomas Edison's image, name, and credibility were selling points for the early cylinder packages, perhaps to the chagrin of some of his recording artists.

Consider a typical release from Thomas Edison's National Phonograph Company, circa 1907. A cylinder would be sold in a tube-shaped paperboard package from the "Edison Gold Moulded Record" [sic] series. This type of package would have space for graphics around the outside and on the enclosing top and bottom caps, as well as a photograph of the inventor, a list of patents received from the government, and a detailing of legal restrictions (including copyright ownership.) The artist's image, the artist's name, and the song title were not featured on the printable exterior of the tube package components. Instead, just a selection number was printed on the top cap. For example, one cylinder I examined has the song title "Will There Be Any Stars in My Crown" printed or molded into the edge, as well as a reference to the type of performance contained on this particular cylinder, in this case a duet. There is also Thomas Edison's graphically reproduced signature along with the selection number; in this case the selection number is 9491. Except for information available at the retail store carrying the Edison cylinders, the performer might remain unknown at least until the cylinder was played.

Similarly, 78-rpm discs were usually sold in plain, often brown sleeves. The exterior surfaces of the paper sleeve, if they carried printing, advertised or promoted the company, not the artists. At the turn of the nineteenth century the manufacture of small quantities of numerous recordings— short runs of hundreds or a few thousand —could make custom sleeves for each artist cost-prohibitive. Therefore, a die-cut circular hole in the center of the record sleeve enabled the consumer to read artist and song information from the record disc's label. The label-specific tan or brown sleeve became standard issue. Familiarity with prior cylinder recordings by that performer could enlighten or remind the listener of the performer's identity. Emphasis was placed on the company, not the performer.

What is popular one minute is passé the next. Today's hit gift item, a pet rock or hula hoop, is tomorrow's anthropological footnote. Similarly, a hit song and the artist that recorded that song may rise and fall on the basis of just one recording. Consider the 1963 recording of "Dominique" by the Singing Nun (Philips 40152), or 1997's "Barbie Girl" by Denmark's pop group Aqua (MCA 55392). One can easily find hundreds or thousands of other such examples. In terms of quantitative success there is no question of the respective popularity of these songs in 1963 or 1997. Their unrelated success appeared thirty-four years apart. "Dominique" spoke to an American Roman Catholic constituency hearing an infectious French folk song sung by one of the faithful in the heyday of the Kennedy presidency. "Barbie Girl," on the other hand, was an irreverent parody of an American icon, which triggered an American lawsuit (between Mattel, the owner of the "Barbie Doll" franchise, and MCA Records, the American record company that released the offending Aqua recording). Today each recording exists as the equivalent of a radio footnote, heard on radio stations programming oldies and in the case of "Barbie Girl" as a campy video seen occasionally on MTV.

This is not to say that classic songs are not being written today. However, the application of the term *classic* to a song or recording requires time. The Beatles ("Yesterday," 1965 and "Something," 1969) along with their contemporaries— Janis Ian ("At Seventeen," 1975), Billy Joel ("New York State of Mind," 1976), and Stephen Sondheim ("Send in the Clowns," 1973)—have created these and other pieces of music that many already consider classics. It always falls to future generations to evaluate the staying power and popularity of music and musical performances.

A look through a list of songs (see Appendix 1) from the first thirty years of recorded music reveals compositions that remain familiar today:

- "The Stars and Stripes Forever" (1897)
- "I Love You Truly" (1901)
- "Bill Bailey Won't You Please Come Home" (1902)
- "The Entertainer" (1902)
- "Give My Regards to Broadway" (1904)
- "Will You Love in September as You Do in May?" (1905)
- "Take Me Out to the Ball Game" (1908)
- "Aloha Oe" (1908)
- "By the Light of the Silvery Moon" (1909)
- "My Melancholy Baby" (1912)
- "Saint Louis Blues" (1914)
- "Memories " (1915)
- "Jelly Roll Blues" (1915)
- "I Ain't Got Nobody" (1916)
- "For Me and My Gal" (1917)
- "Hail, Hail the Gang's All Here" (1917)
- "Over There" (1917)
- "Rock A Bye Your Baby" (1918)
- "Somebody Stole My Gal" (1918)
- "Till We Meet Again" (1918)
- "I'm Always Chasing Rainbows" (1918)
- "Swanee" (1919)

There was discussion earlier of the difference between popularity and critical acclaim — quantitative versus qualitative evaluations. Labels can generally be applied to specific compositions written between 1889 and 1919. As one reads through the above list of several popular song titles it is impossible to ignore those that are easily recognized a century after having been written. One must also recognize those that moved beyond mere recognition to a respect or admiration of their quality. Many of these songs transcend the almost superficial labels such as good or very good. Many of the popular songs of the period must be elevated to the status of classics.

Separate and apart from the songs is a consideration of the recordings. The original decision-making process of the recording companies was based on simple criteria, which included the owner's taste, A&R diligence, and any discernible public demand. While the taste of the owners and their A&R people was not a guarantee of success, the recording industry had access to some nonscientific popularity charts reflecting the popularity of recorded music and the public's taste. Success with the public was reported beginning in 1896 with *Phonoscope*, in 1904 with the *Talking Machine News*, and in 1913 with *Billboard*. *Phonoscope* published for only four years. *Talking Machine News* was published in London (and *Talking Machine World* in the United States) until 1929. *Billboard* continues to publish on a weekly basis.

Phonoscope began listing popular songs in its first issue. That first chart (November 1896) was broken down into four types of music: "Descriptive Songs and Ballads," "Comic," "Coon," and "Waltzes." Given the specific song-types already available, it is almost surprising to find the additional catch-all category of "Miscellaneous." Early in 1897 two charts were listed side-by-side: "The Latest Popular Songs" and "New Records for Talking Machines." This seemed to be the norm through the balance of the four years of *Phonoscope*'s published issues.

The early issues of *Talking Machine News* featured advertisements from recording companies and cylinder and disc distributors. By 1905 it was also reviewing new releases. An advertisement in the January 1906 issue featured releases by the Gramophone Records label. The ad included military marches, comic and novelty, and concert music. Columbia Records, also in this issue, was advertising a release featuring General Booth, the Commander-in-Chief of the Salvation Army; the ad was a de facto (and preferential) review:

> In short, forceful sentences, delivered with splendid oratorical effect, he paints a graphic picture of the misery of the "submerged tenth." The address is practical Christianity in a Nutshell." [The magazine also reviewed the General's recording, paying some attention to the message but also providing detail to the characteristics:] "volume good and the enunciation decidedly above average.... Indeed if one did not know that the leader of the Salvation Army was nearing his eightieth year one would never suspect it from this record...."[1]

Billboard must have wrestled with the type of popularity chart that it would feature in its early magazine. "*Billboard*'s earliest music charts were sheet music listings in 1913."[2] Subsequent featured charts were based on sales of recorded music or performances in vaudeville, the latter starting with New York stages only, but later adding Chicago and San Francisco. A song might be too new to be recorded and to secure sufficient sales to be in *Billboard's* Top Ten. However, the music publishers of Tin Pan Alley might be able to place a song with one of the many vaudeville song and dance acts. If the audience response to the song was enthusiastic, it might stay in their routine and get noticed by the music business people.

In these early publications, particularly in the 1890s, emphasis was placed squarely on two selling fronts. The first was the type of music being sold: ballads, marches, spoken word, etc. The second was the name of the company: Columbia, Edison, Clarion, Pathé, Gramophone, and so on. Consumers were not yet sufficiently empowered to significantly influence the demand-side of the supply-and-demand paradigm. Choice was being controlled by the suppliers, and, much as with the case during the 1980s launch of compact disc players in the United States, those consumers that could afford the phonographs wanted or needed something to play.

In one of its first chart issues (July 19, 1913) *Billboard* listed "Last Week's Ten Best Sellers Among the Popular Songs."[3] As important as which songs or records were in *Billboard's* Top Ten was the magazine's brief description of how the ten were determined:

> Reports received from one hundred and twelve music retailers and department stores in different parts of the country carefully analyzed and averaged indicate that the ten best-selling popular songs last week were as follows....[4]

The magazine then printed its chart. This clearly indicated that a shift was underway from a supplier driven representation of popularity to an analytical chart theoretically based on sales data. This is not to suggest that the chart was scientific. It is merely to show that the determination of popularity was shifting away from record labels and phonograph makers, and that consumers were taking control and determining popularity by using their wallets. With that control, consumers became the real arbiters of popularity.

The style of the popular recordings of the day mirrored the styles of the popular songs of the day and the theater performances. Edison, his contemporaries, and those who followed could see that the public was increasingly choosing music over spoken word. "When the public demanded music he gave them vaudeville ditties."[5] Each of the Big Three companies was vertically integrated, in that each produced the recordings, sold the recordings, and of course sold the instrument on which one would play the recording. As the competition to sell phonographs began to increase, so too did the competition to sell music for those machines. When price or the reputation of the company began to deteriorate as a marketing edge, the response was obvious: it was time to begin making serious recordings; it was time for the entrance of Enrico Caruso.

19

The Caruso Effect

It needs to be stated at the outset that Enrico Caruso (1873–1921) was not the first great vocalist or musician from the European classical tradition to record, nor were his the first American recordings of European classical music. Prior to Caruso's April 1902 sessions, others had recorded music from the European tradition and had them released by American companies. One such artist was French baritone Bernard Bégué, who in 1898 recorded Bizet's "Toreador Song" from *Carmen* for Columbia. Edward Banta's Popular Orchestra recorded Giuseppe Verdi's (1813–1901) "Anvil Chorus" from *Il Trovatore* in the mid 1890s; and the "Grand March" from *Tannhäuser* by Richard Wagner (1813–1883) was recorded by the Edison Grand Concert Band in 1899.

It must also be noted that other entrepreneurs—beyond Edison and Berliner—were exploring great music. Italian-born New Yorker Gianni Bettini (1860–1938) made his own contributions to the early phonograph and its repertoire. Roland Gelatt quotes an article from an 1896 edition of *Phonoscope* that helps establish Bettini's roots in early classical recordings. Among the artists Bettini recorded were "Victor Maurel, the well-known baritone singer [and] Tomaso Salvini, who rolled out a grand passage from 'Othello' in the Italian translation."[1]

In the decade prior to Caruso, the classical offerings from American labels may have been extremely slim, and although there were classical music releases, on the whole the greatest of the performers were not venturing into the recording studio. After 1900 both the Victor and Columbia companies had "gradually brought to the market more highbrow music, opera and classical, while Edison stuck with the old chestnuts, marching songs, and ballads of yore."[2] Even if companies wanted to release classical records, getting the highest quality performers and performances was a difficult proposition.

As described earlier, not every artist was enthusiastic about his or her

voice being recorded on these relatively new machines. It was not a matter of the early recordings seeming or feeling cold. It was a more direct
problem: the greater the stature of the performer, the less inclined they
seemed to be about lending their talent to the new phonograph. The early
machines were not always sympathetic to the great vocalists, and they
reproduced a performance that was often lost under a mountain of surface noise. "The great stars refused to sing into the horn of the phonograph because they knew that it could not do justice to their voices."[3]
Listening today to cylinder recordings of the 1890s or hearing the surface
noise of a very scratched shellac 78-rpm disc provides an understanding
of the reticence of those great early performers. (For those who have never
listened to a cylinder recording, it is fair to say that if 78-rpm recordings
sound noisy in this digital age, cylinders sound almost calamitous.) Not
everyone was nervous about immortalizing his voice, and Enrico Caruso
became, serendipitously or strategically, the focal point of Victor's creative search for a star.[4]

Caruso probably had little difficulty deciding to begin his recording
career when opportunity came calling, even though his March 1902 performance of Alberto Franchetti's (1860–1942) *Germania* at the Teatro Alla
Scala[5] was not an unqualified success with the critics. "In the judgment of
the reviewer of the [newspaper] *Corriere della Sera* ... 'Caruso did not
appear suited to deliver efficiently his role, which calls for outbursts and
pause of voice.'"[6] The opinion of the general audience was another matter. According to Enrico Caruso, Jr., it was his father's "delivery of the role
that prompted [Gramophone Company representative] Fred Gaisberg to
offer him a contract to record ten selections. The recording venture turned
out to be an immediate success."[7]

Events leading up to the March 1902 opening at Teatro Alla Scala
clarify the singer's ultimate decision to venture where other classical artists
had chosen not to go. Enrico Caruso may not have been thinking about
records that evening, and he may not have become a recording artist in
the spring of 1902 strictly for the money. On the other hand, he was already
aware of his growing stature as a stage performer, and that recognition does
not suggest that he had forgotten about his leaner days as a singer, particularly before 1895. In his book *Caruso*, Howard Greenfield presents a
portrait of the young tenor in Naples. To help his family, Enrico Caruso
took on factory work in 1889 at the age of sixteen. The factory was his job,
but singing is what he desired. In Naples there was

> an immensely popular form of entertainment known as the café-chan-
> tant — the sunny café. Neapolitan songs were sung throughout the city
> ... but nowhere more powerful than in the cafés that lined the city's

colorful harbor…. Caruso joined friends in singing at public baths, baptisms, weddings, and birthday celebrations, and continued to take part in church festivities.[8]

In 1894 — at the age of twenty-one — he was called to serve in the army, a service that for Caruso was happily short. After the military months he also worked as a bookkeeper and continued to sing at small cafes and public baths.

Singing was paramount to Caruso even though income from singing was small and, at times, nonexistent. "'Come here and sing' the owner of the baths had said. 'What my patrons give to you you may keep.'"[9] Pierre V. R. Key included, in his biography of the tenor, a handwritten January 1895 note from the singer to a performance benefactor. In the note Caruso clearly points to the small amount of money being offered for the proposed appearance, nevertheless agreeing to perform for the "fee of L. 15 and the railroad fares. I make this [special] price only for you … otherwise [I should be paid] 28 Lire."[10] There is no need to recalculate the value of the Italian lire in 1895, or the exchange rate with the United States dollar. This payday — whether 15 lire or 28 — was a modest payment.

A detailed appearance chronology for Caruso suggests he was paid for just one performance in 1894. Perhaps his January 1895 decision to accept only 15 lire was a good omen as he finished the year with fifty-seven performances. Between 1894 and 1901 (the eight years before his first Victor recordings in 1902) Caruso averaged forty-six performance per year. Between 1902 and 1909 (also eight years) Caruso averaged eighty-nine performances per year.[11] As the number of performances increased, so too, one can surmise, did Caruso's income. Enrico Caruso, Jr., wrote that "Father was a one-man mint. There was a well-known cartoon showing him singing with sheet music in his hand, as the notes floating from his open mouth turned into a cascade of gold coins."[12]

The early 1900s marked a significant change from Caruso's days singing in the Italian baths and cafes for tips from patrons. His tours took him beyond Europe and the United Kingdom, to South America and finally, on November 23, 1903, to the United States and New York's Metropolitan Opera. The next day the *New York Times* paid little attention to the work—*Rigoletto*—but offered tribute to the Met's refurbished performance space ("resplendent in new decorations"), administration, and philanthropic benefactors ("under a new manager, with every promise of a public support such as has never before been given to opera in New York"), and new talent, i.e., Enrico Caruso. In essence, the critic cared less about which opera was performed, instead presenting an overall critique of the night itself:

> The opera did not greatly matter. Its performance was in every way
> superb. It signaled the first appearance of one of the most important of
> [the Met administration's] new artists, one upon whom much will
> depend during this coming season — Enrico Caruso, who took the part
> of the Duke. He made a highly favorable impression, and he went far
> to substantiate the reputation that had preceded him to this country.[13]

For his efforts during that premier 1903–1904 season at the Metropolitan,
Caruso "received $960 a performance. This amount was raised to $1,440
by 1906–1907, and jumped to $2,000 in the following year.... Father's high-
est single year of earnings at the Metropolitan was 1907–1908, when he
received $140,000 [$2.8 million IADs] for sixty-eight opera performances
and two concerts."[14]

Bear in mind that with respect to the tenor's personal finances, Caruso,
Jr. is describing his father's income from New York's Metropolitan Opera
alone. During the 1903–1904 season, Caruso made twenty-five appearances for the Metropolitan, approximately 20% of his American commitments. In subsequent years, his commitment to the Metropolitan could
total 60% or more of the total performances he gave in any one year. Individual concerts and private performances brought even more income to
Caruso, "some of which rose as high as $15,000 a performance, paid in
gold."[15] The days of singing for tips in cafes and the public baths were long
past. Having enjoyed a steady increase in the number of live performances
and performance income, did the great tenor need to dive into the murky
waters of the relatively new recording industry?

The transformation of Caruso from performer to recording artist
began with Fred Gaisberg's evening at the opera in Milan in the spring of
1902. It was the tenor's second turn at Teatro Alla Scala (he gave thirty-
five performances in Milan between December 1900 and March 1901).[16]
Much like a local twenty-first century record person touting a talented
discovery for the A&R department of his company, Gaisberg had been
encouraged to see and hear the talent in Milan for himself. Rising star-
tenors Enrico Caruso and Alessandro Bonci (1870–1940) "were causing a
sensation at La Scala, and ... either or both of them should be immediately engaged.... Though he failed to get tickets for the premier of *Germania*, Gaisberg managed to find seats for the second performance [and
was] overwhelmed by the power and beauty of Caruso's voice...."[17] Details
of the deal vary between Gaisberg's recollection and Caruso's numerous
biographies. Most accounts agree that Caruso requested or demanded to
be paid £100 ($487 in 1902, $10,100 in 2004 IADs), a price which Gaisberg's superiors believed to be too high, which they emphatically stated in
a telegram to Gaisberg:

"FEE EXORBITANT FORBID YOU TO RECORD."[18]

Gaisberg opted to make the recordings anyway, in which case the company was obligated to pay. Ultimately it was to become a happy obligation. Caruso, Jr. makes an easy case for the profitability of the deal: "I heard 15,000 [British] Pounds net profit mentioned as a result of the [Milan recordings]. At the prevailing [1902] exchange rate of about six dollars to the English pound, this totals about $90,000 — not a bad return for a one hundred pound investment and a two hour recording session."[19]

When one looks at the history of that pivotal recording session, the tenor's quick success might have been predicted by paying attention to both the personal and the practical. His mettle was evident in the style he put forth that momentous day. Contrary to the *prima donna-esque* manner he might have seriously presented, the afternoon appeared to be one of "light-hearted professionalism." Stanley Jackson relates the recording event of that afternoon:

> Caruso looked "debonair and fresh," according to Gaisberg, when he arrived at their suite in the Grand Hotel.... It was a sunny and very warm afternoon and he complained ruefully of having to delay his lunch, but otherwise he seemed to be treating the whole affair as an amusing outing. Accompanied by a pianist perched on a packing case, he sang for two hours into a bell-shaped tin horn hanging five feet from the floor. The programme [was] effortlessly delivered.... He then pocketed his cheque, shook hands with the Gaisbergs, embraced the accompanist and hurried off, whistling cheerfully, to join [his wife] Ada for a late lunch.[20]

It could easily be said that anyone who received a payment of £100 in 1902 ($10,100 in IADs) for two hours work better be "debonair and fresh" and that they should be "whistling cheerfully" as they left for lunch, even if they were a little late. Having pocketed a quick $10,100[21] wouldn't we all cheerfully go out for some lunch?

Caruso got paid this large sum for far more than his charm or wit, his mettle, or the trajectory of his live performances (which were already positioning him for a long career on the stage). Enrico Caruso was paid because he could deliver as a recording artist. In addition to his professionalism and his obvious vocal talent, it could be said that Caruso's voice and the machine were made for each other:

> [Caruso's] voice was perfectly suited to the talking machine; it emerged from the horn with such clarity and power that it seemed to fill the room with music. Unlike sopranos and bass voices [some of

whom declined an early opportunity to record based on the machine's idiosyncrasies] the full range of the tenor fell within the narrow band of sound frequencies picked up by the recording horn.[22]

The company's money was well invested in Caruso because, as his son later wrote, "immediately after the records hit the market, sales exceeded all expectations."[23] Here was an early (and good) example of the marriage of man and machine. A second recording session was held in November 1902, and ten new recordings were made for a fee to the artist of £200/$974 (£20/$97.40 per song), doubling the original fee of £100/$487. Looking once again at the exchange rates and the value of that payment today, we can see that Caruso was paid the equivalent of $20,000 in 2004 IADs to record ten songs.[24]

Then there was the contract. In the contemporary music business, an artist who achieves success and is not bound to a label by an ironclad, long-term contract is sought after by any and all competitors. Caruso's success did not go unnoticed by his label, the Victor Talking Machine Company (or their affiliate, the Gramophone & Typewriter Company, Ltd. of London). Victor was quickly recognizing the costs, sales, and profits that it earned. Such success could also have been estimated by outsiders, and was very likely determined by Victor's competition. Correspondence between New York and London, between Victor and the Gramophone Company, indicates a diligent effort to conclude a binding agreement with Caruso in 1904, especially, as Eldridge Johnson wrote on behalf of Victor, since "the Columbia people were after Caruso and were willing to pay him more money than we [Victor] paid him."[25]

Even if those competitive estimates were off the mark by one-half to two-thirds, the profit was still significant, and Caruso would likely find himself in play.[26] The original profits were impressive but the potential profits for Victor signaled a valuable artist worth trying to protect contractually. Caruso too, could calculate that potential and attempt to extract a favorable agreement from the label. The first detailed contract between Caruso and the Victor/Gramophone companies was concluded in 1904, and tells much of Caruso's bargaining leverage:

> The contract stipulated a fifty cents royalty per record and a sizeable advance against royalties. It also called for $2,000 to be paid on January 28 "of each year for five years so that he will not sing for another talking machine company or party for the purpose of making Talking Machine records ... for the period of five years, to wit, from January 28, 1904, to January 28, 1909."...
>
> When the first contract expired, a new contract was drawn up, this time to run for a twenty-five year period, from 1 January 1909 to 1 January 1934.[27]

Enrico Caruso, Jr.'s biography makes it clear that his father's royalties, advances, and perks were, if not unique, unusual for the early record labels.

Caruso had approval rights during the sessions in case any recordings did not meet his high standards (such recordings would be rejected). Instead of a flat recording fee, he was to receive an advance against royalties. He was reimbursed $2,000 if he traveled to New York for recording sessions or other Victor business. His royalty was specified as 25¢ for 10" 78-rpm records, 50¢ for the larger (and longer playing) 12" records. Provided he made at least three recordings, he was guaranteed a minimum of $10,000 in royalty payments annually. The royalty payments were to succeed Caruso. That is, his estate or his heirs (as documented by the contract and a legal representative of his estate) would continue to receive royalties after Caruso's death. These deal points were further sweetened by a contract revision in 1919. Instead of receiving a flat 25¢ for 10" records and 50¢ for 12" records, Caruso would be paid "10 percent of the catalog price ... and Victor guaranteed him an annual minimum payment of $100,000."[28] And the deal was exclusive to Victor. With the signing of the tenor to a contract to sing for Victor, the dynamics of recording agreements changed forever. Caruso, although young, was talented and his star — already rising in Italy — began an ascent in America. The Caruso recordings had multiple impacts on the world of recorded music, some of which are in evidence today.

First, Caruso's success established him as the new star of recording and of opera. He was paid a flat fee, less than $500 to record ten songs in 1902, which seems like a bargain today, even as shown earlier in 2004 dollars (IADs).[29] Those initial recordings were done quickly and inexpensively by recording them one after another into the horn in the space of two hours.

Second, it established Victor's place, at least for the moment, in the competition with Columbia and Edison. A few years after the original recordings were completed, one print advertisement for the Victor company read, "The Victor Record of Caruso's voice is just as truly Caruso as Caruso himself.... When you hear Caruso on the Victrola in your own home, you hear him just as truly as if you were listening to him in the Metropolitan Opera House."

Third, it brought other respected artists to the recording machine. Most of the established stars of opera had kept their distance from the talking machine, but that distance might ultimately be bridged if a credible, talented star could make the successful transition to recording artist. After Caruso, a list of opera stars began to sign on, although some of the most famous chose to hold out until either lingering doubts about the talking machine were erased or the money offered for a recording contract proved irresistible. In addition to Caruso's gramophone debut, recordings were made by Mario Sammarco (1867–1930), Antonio Scotti (1866–1936), Pol Plançon (1851–1914), Nellie Melba (1861–1931), and Maurice Renaud (1861–1933). Others, like Adelina Patti, took their time. "Although in past years [pre-1905] representatives of various talking machine companies had tried to persuade Patti to record, she had resisted all advances, considering the gramophone a toy."[30] Patti would relent in November 1905. The talking machine was no longer a "toy."

Fourth, it helped bolster Victor's bottom line. Caruso's son later recalled that his father's records enjoyed long success, in fact producing "a small fortune" for the Carusos and "a large fortune for Victor."[31] Could anyone have truly foreseen that the almost simple, original idea of Gaisberg's to record the tenor in a hotel room in Milan would help generate nearly $5 million for Caruso over the next twenty years? Could anyone, including Gaisberg or Caruso, have envisioned that the 1902 "Milan sessions" would launch sales that could generate twice what the recorded music industry had previously known? That "large fortune" Victor earned seems obvious when one considers that Caruso was to be paid either 25–50¢ per disc or a 10 percent royalty, and a one-sided disc of Caruso's on RCA's Red Seal Label "could cost [the consumer] as much as seven dollars which in 1906 could get you a full suit of clothes."[32]

Fifth, the evolution of a contract relationship between an artist and a recording company was clearly in motion. No more Caruso recordings based on a flat fee. What would be described today as a work-for-hire arrangement with the artist disappeared. In its place was the prototype of today's contract. Advance payments to the artist, royalty payments to the artist after recoupment based on unit sales, royalties calculated on a percentage of the company's revenue for each record sold, artistic control (in the event Caruso believed a recording was flawed), travel expense reimbursement, minimum guaranteed payments, an exclusive agreement to keep Caruso from recording with any other label, assignment of the contract should the company be sold, and payments to Caruso's heirs in the event of his death. When Adelina Patti negotiated a contract, she used Caruso's contract as a guide. She insisted that her recordings be sold "at the same price as [Caruso, Melba, and Tetrazzini] have agreed to ... and that the royalty payable shall be at the same rate as that paid by the company to the above-mentioned artistes [sic], namely 10% of the retail selling price of each record sold."[33]

Finally, the ability to create a market for recorded music can be traced to Caruso, Melba, and Patti, and it can be further credited to their recordings and to recordings by other stars of the day. No longer content to simply take just anything home to fill their talking machines and phonographs, American consumers could express their taste with a trip to the Victor dealer. "Victor's Red Seal recordings of Enrico Caruso and other stars of the Metropolitan Opera became must-haves for every self-respecting American middle-class home."[34] As the price of discs came down, income was no longer an impediment to the arts. As the advertisement cited earlier stated, when one heard Caruso in their own home, they heard him "just as truly as if [they] were listening to him in the Metropolitan Opera House."

To understand the impact of Enrico Caruso, one can also look strictly at the recordings and their lasting impact. Caruso's success did not translate into a series of number one chart listings. Early popularity lists and success rankings were highly subjective and not an accurate reflection of "best sellers." However, the lists do provide insight into the success of Caruso, much as the importance of a contractual relationship between the great tenor and his record company signals Caruso's high value in the music marketplace. Considering all of the information available, one can come to a realistic and enthusiastic evaluation with some level of confidence.

Joel Whitburn lists forty-five releases by Caruso in his book *Pop Memories: 1890–1954 — The History of American Popular Music*. All of them reached his Top Ten, and most reached his Top Five. All but three were released in America between 1904 and 1921. A search of Caruso among the offerings of the Internet company Amazon.com lists more than two hundred Caruso-related recordings. Of these more than one hundred are currently available, including a boxed set titled *The Complete Caruso*, which retails for more than $100. The impact of Caruso's voice, his recordings, his contract, his use by Victor as a marketing tool, his ability to draw other top stars to the new medium — in short, his mass appeal coming at the same time that mass-production techniques were coming on line changed everything. The days of music hall stars like Billy Murray dominating the popularity charts were over. Murray, Ada Jones, Henry Burr, Byron G. Harlan, and others would continue to record and achieve a level of success. However, from this moment on, stars like Caruso and Al Jolson would lead the way to a different music business.

20

Enter Marconi

When Edison created the practical phonograph there were no radios, televisions, or motion pictures with sound. Nintendo, Play-Station, cable television, and the Internet did not exist. There was little entertainment competition for consumers to ponder. During this quiet period amidst the noise of the late nineteenth-century industrialization, individuals like Edison, Berliner, and Johnson and companies like Columbia and Victor were attempting to turn sound into a commodity. The quest was for personal honor, fame, fortune, and corporate profits. In the end, the recording devices were created, refined, and exploited. Fortunes were made and bankruptcies were numerous. Trial and error with equal measures of luck, perseverance, and intuition created a business. While larger, more competitive, and arguably less entrepreneurial than at anytime in its history, the recording industry still exists today. In those first thirty years, however, the industry was inventing itself, and the only competition for the creators was that which they created within their new recording business. Consumers were song driven. They purchased songs (not artists) at first, and that allowed for multiple companies to have success with proprietary recordings of repertoire that duplicated the output of other recording companies. Four different versions of "Over There" and three versions of "Till We Meet Again" reached #1 from 1916 to 1918.

If Caruso can be seen as the first significant example of the internal music industry competition to come, the first sounds of true external competition were sounded in 1901. On a December evening, a twenty-seven-year-old man sat at a table wondering if his idea would work. Much like Edison twenty-four years earlier, this man was about to get an answer to a question: Was it possible to take the idea of Bell's telephone or Morse's telegraph, and communicate without the wire? Outside the building a kite was flying a few hundred feet above the roof, with a wire trailing down to a device on the table. On the table sat a box containing his brainchild. At a predetermined hour, another man at a table two thousand miles away in England began to tap three dots— Morse code for "S"— into a telegraph key.[1] Guglielmo Marconi sat at the table in Newfoundland, Canada, and heard the dots. His assistant listened and confirmed the reception. At that moment, though the recording business could not have known it, a form of competition was on its way to America and the world.

It would take years of experiments before radio began to be a significant factor in the United States. Marconi's invention did provide an opportunity for perhaps the first documented radio broadcast of classical music. "In the early 1900s, [early radio pioneer] Lee De Forest broadcast from the stage of the Manhattan Opera House, via Marconi air waves, an aria from *Carmen* sung by Mariette Nazarin."[2] It was in 1919, however, that the first formal, licensed radio station signed on the air: KDKA in Pittsburgh. By the mid-1920s almost eight hundred stations were broadcasting to America. Networks were forming. Crystal-sets gave way to table and console radios.

Franklin Roosevelt helped solidify radio as the centerpiece of the American home with his Fireside Chats. When war came to Europe in 1939, more than fourteen hundred radio stations were licensed to broadcast in the United States. "Today ten thousand stations in this country reach 99 percent of all households, and less than 1 percent have fewer than five receivers."[3] Radio would draw record buyers to its programs, its voices, and its music. Many listeners wondered why they should buy music when the radio gave it to them for free? While that notion gave many in the recording industry a reason to reconsider their investment, records and radio have consistently figured out how to coexist. If radio killed anything in particular, it was probably one of the reasons for the demise of vaudeville, which was declared dead with the closing of the Palace Theater in 1932.

Returning to the record industry, one might say that during those first thirty years of recording, the music consumers and the record companies danced with each other. At times the industry would lead, and at times the consumers would take charge. With Caruso the star was created, and artists began to insert themselves into the equation, taking home a larger share of the income and choosing which repertoire they would record.

As the year 2004 began, multi-national corporations and Internet-based companies were still acquiring or merging with other record companies. There is something about the creative work of the artists and the ability of the consumer to take that art home that continues to drive recorded music. Radio changed music in the 1920s by creating its own stars, or taking stars from records and giving them their own radio shows. It changed the music business by changing the demand. Radio influenced the buying decisions of music consumers by virtue of its growing listening audience and the music that it sent out to homes for free. The record business responded by selling anything and everything that radio was willing to program. But before radio, people like Edison, Berliner, Gaisberg, and Caruso were in charge. They were the tastemakers. It may be only a footnote in the history of records and radio, but Caruso began to change recorded music as Marconi was waiting to hear those three dots, and the great tenor died in 1921 as radio began to work its way into the American consciousness.

Songwriter Charles K. Harris attempted to define popular music when he wrote

> The word "popular" ... has been employed expressly to designate the various classes of songs which are written, published and sung, whistled and hummed by the great American "unmusical" public, as distinguished from the more highly cultivated musical class which often decries and scoffs at the tantalizing and ear-haunting melodies that are heard from ocean to ocean in every shape and form. Argument in favor of their merit is undoubtedly proven beyond question by their enormous sale; and many a sad and weary heart has been made glad by the strains of these "popular" songs.[4]

Ignoring, for a moment, his biased position as a popular songwriter, the fact is that there (was then and) is now a "more highly cultivated musical class" which truly listens to the music of the great masters in an appreciative way. These listeners have enthusiasm for the work, enjoyment of the performance, and reverence for the composer or musician's place in musical history.

That being said, the closing comment of Harris speaks as well to the place of popular musical performance and popular songwriting of the twenty-first century as it did when he wrote his comment in 1906. One might expand on his thoughts and realize that all music — Chopin and Caruso, or Madonna, Garth Brooks, or Eminem — that is loved by audiences large and small is, in fact, popular music. One's mood or emotions can be transformed by music. An individual's love, respect, praise, and admiration of country, friend, lover, or self can be altered temporarily, permanently, or to any degree in between by the right composition or performance. Who does Aaron Copland speak to in "Fanfare for the Common Man," or Elvis Presley in "Love Me Tender"? Does Leonard Bernstein lift us out of, or deposit us into, a tough urban neighborhood by virtue of songs like "Maria" or "Tonight"? Perhaps it is both, and it is our preference at the moment of listening that determines the direction we are taken. Consider who should be designated that greatest composer of songs during the first one hundred years of recorded music? Was it Irving Berlin, Cole Porter, Johnny Mercer, John Lennon, Paul McCartney, or Dianne Warren? Clearly this is a subjective exercise.

To the extent that any of these people (or all of them and others) change us—even if only for the duration of the song—then for that moment, each takes his or her place on our personal list as one of the greatest. For two or three minutes, for an hour or more, we can be transformed. Regardless of the rules of respectability in songwriting and musical performance, there is no need to debate Harris's assertion that "many a sad and weary heart has been made glad by the strains of these 'popular' songs."[5] We have all had our weary hearts made glad, even if it was only for a moment. Perhaps that, is what Edison envisioned in the first place.

Appendix 1

Recordings in Popular Non-Ethnic Genres, 1889–1919

The recordings in this table are representative of the various non-ethnic, i.e., generally popular recorded music genres of the years 1889–1919. Those categories and their shortened category IDs are:

Ballad/Romance/Parlor	BALRP
Comedy/Novelty	COMN
Dance	DANC
Patriotic/Military/March	PMIL
Political/Religious/Social/Promotional	PRSP
Production	PROD
Ragtime	RAGT
Regional	REGL

The table shows (title, performer, record label, selection number, year of release, and category). The recordings have been sorted by category and then by year of release.

Song Title	Name of Artist(s)	Label Sel#	Year	Categ.
The Picture Turned Toward the Wall	Manhansett Quartette	North American	1892	BALRP
The Fatal Wedding	George Gaskin	New Jersey	1893	BALRP
Sweet Marie [sic]	George Gaskin	New Jersey	1894	BALRP
When You Were Sweet Sixteen	Jere Mahoney	Edison 7410	1900	BALRP
To the End of the World	Reed Miller	Victor 17026	1901	BALRP
Hello Central Give Me Heaven	Byron Harlan	Edison 7852	1901	BALRP
In the Good Old Summer Time	Haydn Quartet	Victor 16125	1903	BALRP

Song Title	Name of Artist(s)	Label Sel#	Year	Categ.
Oh Promise Me	Henry Burr	Edison 8929	1905	BALRP
Will You Love Me in December as You do in May?	Harry MacDonough	Edison 9198	1906	BALRP
Shine on Harvest Moon	Walton & MacDonough	Victor 16259	1908	BALRP
I Wonder Who's Kissing Her Now	Henry Burr	Columbia 707	1909	BALRP
By the Light of the Silvery Moon	Ada Jones	Edison 10362	1910	BALRP
It's Hard to Kiss Your Sweetheart When the Last Kiss Means Goodbye	Arthur C. Clough	Edison 10251	1910	BALRP
Down by the Old Mill Stream	Arthur C. Clough	Edison (4) 796	1911	BALRP
Drink to me Only with Thine Eyes	Frank Stanley	Edison (4) 615	1911	BALRP
I Want a Girl (Just Like the Girl That Married Dear Old Dad)	American Quartet	Victor 16962	1911	BALRP
Let Me Call You Sweetheart	Columbia Quartet	Columbia 1057	1911	BALRP
I Love You Truly	Elsie Baker	Victor 17121	1912	BALRP
Till the Sands of the Desert Grow Cold	Donald Chalmers	Edison 1043	1912	BALRP
Row, Row, Row	Arthur Collins	Columbia 1244	1912	BALRP
Moonlight Bay	Dolly Connolly	Columbia 1128	1912	BALRP
I'd Rather Be Kissed 'Neath the Mistletoe Than Spoon Under Any Old Tree	Campbell & Burr	Victor 17274	1913	BALRP
Your Eyes Have Told Me What I Did Not Know	Enrico Caruso	Victor 8719	1913	BALRP
When I Lost You	Manuel Romain	Columbia 1288	1913	BALRP
M-O-T-H-E-R (A Word That Means the World to Me)	George Wilton Ballard	Edison 50325	1916	BALRP
Till We Meet Again	James & Hart	Victor 18518	1919	BALRP
You're a Million Miles from Nowhere	Charles Harrison	Victor 18645B	1919	BALRP
Old Folks at Home	Columbia Stellar Quartet	Columbia 6082	1919	BALRP
The Laughing Song	George Johnson	Columbia (unk)	1891	COMN
Casey on the Bowery	Russell Hunting	Edison 3824	1897	COMN
Reuben Haskins from Skowhegan, Maine	Len Spencer	Columbia 31582	1901	COMN
Two Rubes in a Tavern	Frank Stanley	Columbia 938	1902	COMN
If Money Talks, It Ain't on Speaking Terms with Me	Arthur Collins	Victor 1631	1902	COMN
Uncle Josh on an Automobile	Cal Stewart	Columbia 1518	1903	COMN
Any Rags	Arthur Collins	Victor 2519	1903	COMN
Everybody Works but Father	Lew Dockstader	Columbia 3251	1905	COMN
Take Me Out to the Ball Game	Haydn Quartet	Victor 5570	1908	COMN
No News, or What Killed the Dog	Nat Wills	Victor 5612	1909	COMN
Casey Jones	Billy Murray	Edison (Amb) 450	1910	COMN
Cohen on the Telephone	Joe Hayman	Columbia 1516	1914	COMN
The Baseball Game	Weber & Fields	Columbia 2092	1917	COMN
I'm Forever Blowing Bubbles	George W. Ballard	Edison 3948	1919	COMN
Sneezing	Jay Laurier's			COMN
Turkey in the Straw (Zip Coon)	Billy Golden	Columbia	1891	DANC
Hiawatha Two-Step	Sousa's Band	Victor 2443	1903	DANC
The St. Louis Rag	Arthur Pryor's Band	Victor 2783	1904	DANC

Song Title	Name of Artist(s)	Label Sel#	Year	Categ.
Blue Danube Waltz	Sousa's Band	Victor 31450	1905	DANC
Waltz Me Around Again, Willie	Billy Murray	Victor 4738	1906	DANC
Maple Leaf Rag	Vess Ossman	Columbia 3626	1907	DANC
The Cubanola Glide	Billy Murray	Victor 5769	1910	DANC
Oh That Beautiful Rag	Arthur Collins	Columbia 853	1910	DANC
The Honeymoon Glide	Arthur Collins/ Byron Harlan	Indestructible 1437	1910	DANC
Red Rose Rag	Dolly Connolly	Columbia 1028	1911	DANC
The Mississippi Dippy-Dip	Arthur Collins/ Byron Harlan	Victor 16870	1911	DANC
Chicken Reel	Frank Stanley	Victor 16897	1911	DANC
That Aeroplane Glide	Peerless Quartet	Victor 17113	1912	DANC
In Ragtime Land	Arthur Collins	Victor 17126	1912	DANC
Fo' De Lawd's Sake, Play Waltz	Elsie Janis	Victor 60091	1913	DANC
When I Waltz with You	Helen Clark	Victor 17298	1913	DANC
Turkey-Trot Dance Medley, II	Prince's Orchestra	Columbia 5459	1913	DANC
The Castle Walk	Jim Europe Society Orch.	Victor 17553	1914	DANC
Castle's Half and Half	Prince's Band	Columbia A 5562	1914	DANC
Everybody Rag with Me	George O'Connor	Columbia 1706	1915	DANC
My Tango Girl	Albert & Monroe Jockers	Columbia 5683	1915	DANC
That Moanin' Saxophone Rag	Six Brown Brothers	Victor 17677	1915	DANC
That Hula Hula	Elizabeth Brice	Columbia 2226	1916	DANC
Missouri Waltz	Jaudas' Society orchestra	Edison Amb. 2950	1916	DANC
The Darktown Strutter's Ball	Six Brown Brothers	Victor 18376	1917	DANC
Castle Valse Classique	Earl Fuller's Novelty Orch.	Columbia 5989	1917	DANC
Waltz of the Hours	Cincinnati Symphony	Columbia 5943	1917	DANC
Tiger Rag	Original Dixieland Jazz Band	Victor 18472	1918	DANC
Semper Fidelis	U.S. Marine Band	Columbia (unk)	1890	PMIL
Volunteers' March	Gilmore's Band	New York (unk)	1892	PMIL
The Star Spangled Banner	Gilmore's Band	New Jersey (unk)	1892	PMIL
Yankee Doodle	Vess Ossman	North American 905	1894	PMIL
Battle Cry of Freedom	Harlan & Stanley	Edison 8805	1894	PMIL
Lincoln's Speech at Gettysburg	Russell Hunting	Edison 3821	1897	PMIL
Columbia the Gem of the Ocean	Frank Stanley	Edison 5000	1898	PMIL
America Forever March	71st Regmntl. Band	Edison 7283	1898	PMIL
The Stars and Stripes Forever	Sousa's Band	Gram-o-Phone 306	1901	PMIL
Your Dad Gave His Life for His Country	Franklyn Wallace	Zonophone-5793	1903	PMIL
Soldier Boy	Byron G. Harlan	Columbia 3067	1905	PMIL
I'm a Yankee Doodle Dandy	Billy Murray	Columbia 298	1905	PMIL
The Good Old USA	Byron G. Harlan	Columbia 3463	1906	PMIL
You're a Grand Old Flag	Arthur Pryor's Band	Victor 31539	1906	PMIL
It's Great to Be a Soldier Man	Byron G. Harlan	Edison 9600	1907	PMIL
ABC's of the U.S.A.	A. Jones & B. Murray	Edison 9903	1908	PMIL
Yankee Doodle's Come to Town	Haydn Quartet	Victor 5504	1908	PMIL

Song Title	Name of Artist(s)	Label Sel#	Year	Categ.
U.S. Army Bugle Calls	N.Y. Military Band	Edison (4) 1069	1912	PMIL
Spirit of Independence March	Conway's Band	Victor 18559	1912	PMIL
Keep the Home Fires Burning	James F. Harrison	Victor 17881	1915	PMIL
The Star Spangled Banner	M. Woodrow Wilson	Columbia 1685	1915	PMIL
I Didn't Raise My Boy to Be a Soldier	Morton Harvey	Victor 17650	1915	PMIL
America, I Love You	Sam Ash	Columbia 1842	1916	PMIL
Wake Up America	James F. Harrison	Victor 17984	1916	PMIL
Battle Hymn of the Republic	Columbia Mixed Qt.	Columbia 2012	1916	PMIL
Goodbye Broadway, Hello France	Peerless Quartet	Columbia 2333	1917	PMIL
America	Louis Gravieure	Columbia 5449	1917	PMIL
For Your Country and My Country	Francis Alda	Victor 64689	1917	PMIL
We're Going Over	Peerless Quartet	Columbia 2399	1917	PMIL
Say a Prayer for the Boys Out There	Peerless Quartet	Victor 18411	1918	PMIL
Au Revoir but Not Goodbye, Soldier Boy	Peerless Quartet	Victor 18438	1918	PMIL
Just Like Washington Crossed the Delaware, Pershing Will Cross the Rhine	Arthur Fields	Columbia 2545	1918	PMIL
Life in a Trench in Belgium	Rice & Burr	Columbia 2410	1918	PMIL
Hello Central Give Me No Man's Land	Al Jolson	Columbia 2542	1918	PMIL
I'm Going to Follow the Boys	Elizabeth Spencer	Victor 18433	1918	PMIL
If He Can Fight Like He Can Love	Farber Sisters	Columbia 2556	1918	PMIL
When Uncle Joe Steps Into France	Collins & Harlan	Victor 18492	1918	PMIL
How Ya Gonna Keep 'Em Down on the Farm, After They've Seen Paree	Nora Bayes	Columbia 2687	1918	PMIL
Pack Up Your Troubles in Your Old Kit Bag (and Smile, Smile, Smile)	Columbia Stellar Qt.	Columbia 6028	1918	PMIL
The Navy Took Them Over, the Navy Will Bring Them Back	Royal Dadmun	Okeh-466	1918	PMIL
You Keep Sending 'Em Over	Arthur Fields	Columbia-2636	1918	PMIL
Liberty Loan March	Sousa's Band	Victor 18430	1918	PMIL
The Yanks Are at It Again	Arthur Fields	Columbia 2620	1918	PMIL
Somewhere in France Is the Lily	Nora Bayes	Columbia 2408	1918	PMIL
Over There	Enrico Caruso	Victor 87294	1918	PMIL
You'll Find Old Dixieland in France	Deiro Pietro's Band	Victor-18547A	1919	PMIL
When the Boys Come Home	Louis Gravieure	Columbia 2709	1919	PMIL
Abide with Me	Frank Stanley	Edison 5019	1898	PRSP
Asleep in the Deep	Hooley	Edison 7295	1899	PRSP
Ave Maria	Guarini	Edison 7287	1899	PRSP
The Rosary	Henry Burr	Columbia 1354	1903	PRSP
Tammany	S. H. Dudley	Victor 4297	1905	PRSP
In My Merry Oldsmobile	A. Collins/B. Harlan	Zonophone 290	1905	PRSP
Break Up the Solid South	William H Taft	Columbia 1012	1908	PRSP
Foreign Missions	William H Taft	Columbia 1013	1908	PRSP
Immortality	William Jennings Bryan	Columbia 1014	1908	
Ideal Republic	William Jennings Bryan	Columbia 1016	1908	PRSP
Imperialism	William Jennings Bryan	Columbia 1016	1908	PRSP
Christ the Lord Is Risen Today	Edison Concert Band	Edison 10099	1909	PRSP
Swing Low, Sweet Chariot	Fisk Univ. Jubilee Qt.	Victor 16453	1910	PRSP

Song Title	Name of Artist(s)	Label Sel#	Year	Categ.
Silent Night, Hallowed Night	Elsie Baker	Victor 17164	1912	PRSP
Progressive Covenant with the People	Theodore Roosevelt	Edison(4) 1146	1912	PRSP
Social and Industrial Justice	Theodore Roosevelt	Edison(4) 1149	1912	PRSP
Jesus Lover of My Soul	Louise Homer	Victor 87200	1915	PRSP
I Didn't Raise My Boy to Be a Soldier	Morton Harvey	Victor 17716	1915	PRSP
Would You Rather Be a Colonel….	Arthur Fields	Columbia 2669	1918	PRSP
You Don't Need Wine to Have a Wonderful Time	Eddie Cantor	Pathe 22163	1919	PRSP
Because	Haydn Quartet	Gramophone 105	1900	PROD
Toyland	Corrine Morgan	Victor 2721	1904	PROD
Give My Regards to Broadway	S. H. Dudley	Victor 4385	1905	PROD
Yankee Doodle Boy	Billy Murray	Columbia 3051	1905	PROD
Harrigan	Edward Meeker	Edison 9616	1907	PROD
I Wonder Who's Kissing Her Now	Henry Burr	Columbia 707	1909	PROD
Tramp, Tramp, Tramp	Byron Harlan/ Frank Stanley	Victor 16531	1910	PROD
By the Light of the Silvery Moon	Haydn Quartet	Victor 16460	1910	PROD
Life's a Funny Proposition After All	George M. Cohan	Victor 10042	1911	PROD
March of the Toys	Victor Herbert & Orchestra	Victor 70048	1911	PROD
Peg o' My Heart	Charles Harrison	Victor 17412	1913	PROD
Hello Frisco	Elida Morris	Columbia 1801	1915	PROD
I'm Always Chasing Rainbows	Charles Harrison	Victor 18496	1918	PROD
Hail! Hail! The Gang's All Here	Irving Kaufman	Columbia 2443	1918	PROD
St. Louis Rag	Arthur Pryor's Band	Victor 2783	1904	RAGT
Buffalo Rag	Vess Ossman	Victor 4628	1906	RAGT
Maple Leaf Rag	Vess Ossman	Columbia 3626	1907	RAGT
The Old Time Rag	Arthur Collins	Edison 9956	1908	RAGT
That Lovin' Rag	Nora Bayes	Victor 60023	1910	RAGT
Red Rose Rag	Dolly Connolly	Columbia 1028	1911	RAGT
The Skeleton Rag	American Quartet	Victor 17041	1912	RAGT
Alexander's Ragtime Band	Victor Military Band	Victor 17006	1912	RAGT
Waiting for the Robert E. Lee	Dolly Connolly	Columbia 1197	1912	RAGT
Florida Rag	Fred Van Eps	Victor 17308	1913	RAGT
That International Rag	Prince's Orchestra	Columbia 5532	1914	RAGT
That Moaning Saxophone Rag	Six Brown Brothers	Victor 17677	1915	RAGT
Tiger Rag	Orig. Dixieland Jazz Band	Victor 18472	1918	RAGT
Carry Me Back to Old Virginny	Edison Male Quartette	Edison 2237	1896	REGL
My Old New Hampshire Home	George Gaskin	Berliner 068	1898	REGL
The Girl I Loved in Sunny Tennessee	Albert Campbell	Edison 5718	1899	REGL
Dixie	Edison Grand Concert Band	Edison 8133	1902	REGL
O Susanna	Unknown Tenor w/Chorus		1904	REGL
Meet Me in Saint Louis, Louis	S. H. Dudley	Victor 2807	1904	REGL
Old Folks at Home	Louise Homer	Victor 81077	1905	REGL
My Old Kentucky Home	Geraldine Farrar	Edison 2223	1910	REGL
Below the Mason Dixon Line	Arthur Collins	Edison (4) 698	1911	REGL
On the New York, New Haven, & Hartford	Edward Meeker	Edison (4) 882	1912	REGL

Song Title	Name of Artist(s)	Label Sel#	Year	Categ.
Sailing Down the Chesapeake Bay	Henry Burr & A. Campbell	Columbia 1378	1913	REGL
Hello Frisco	Sam Ash	Columbia 1801	1915	REGL
For Dixie and Uncle Sam	Nora Bayes	Victor 45100	1916	REGL
Beale Street Blues	Earl Fuller's Novelty Orch.	Victor 18369	1917	REGL
Rock-a-Bye Your Baby with a Dixie Melody	Al Jolson	Columbia 2560	1918	REGL
Beautiful Ohio	Sam Ash	Emerson 9132	1919	REGL

Ballad/Romance/Parlor	BALRP
Comedy/novelty	COMN
Dance	DANC
Patriotic/Military/March	PMIL
Political/Religious/Social/Promotional	PRSP
Production	PROD
Ragtime	RAGT
Regional	REGL

Appendix 2

Ethnic Recordings,
1889–1919

The recordings in this table are representative of the various ethnic recorded music genres of the years 1889–1919. Like Appendix 1, this appendix lists title, performer, record label, selection number, year of release, and the ethnicity or ethnic theme, with an additional column indicating whether, in the opinion of the author, the recording is *ethnic* (E) or *pseudo-ethnic* (P). Recordings labeled as ethnic were usually made by persons sharing a distinctive racial, national, religious, linguistic, or cultural heritage. Pseudo-ethnic recordings have an ethnic flavor but were made by performers outside the ethnic group — for example, a white performer recording a minstrel song. The recordings have been sorted by ethnicity/theme and by song title.

Song Title	Name of Artist(s)	Label and Selec. No.	Year Rec.	Ethnicity/ Theme	
Aeroplane Tango	Prince's Band	Columbia 1541	-	Argentina	P
The Aeroplane	Municipal Band of Buenos Aires	Columbia 1464	-	Argentina	E
Argentine Dance	Moskowitz, Joseph	Victor 18155	1916	Argentina	P
Argentine Tango	Prince's Band	Columbia 5513	1913	Argentina	P
Argentines, Portuguese, and Greeks	Bayes, Nora	Columbia 2980	1919	Argentina	P
Auxillo Tango	Municipal Band of Buenos Aires	Columbia 1466	-	Argentina	E
Bregeiro Tango	Conrad's Society Orchestra	Victor 17607	1914	Argentina	P
El Chicon	Municipal Band of Buenos Aires	Columbia 1466	-	Argentina	E
El Ladiao Tango	Municipal Band of Buenos Aires	Columbia 1465	-	Argentina	E
El Sanduchero	Municipal Band of Buenos Aires	Columbia 1467	-	Argentina	E
Himno Nacional Argintino	Banda Militare	Berliner 252	1899	Argentina	E
My Rose of Argentine	Peerless Quartet	Columbia 1758	1915	Argentina	P
Pasate el Paine Tango	Municipal Band of Buenos Aires	Columbia 1465	-	Argentina	E
Tango Bonita	Bernard, Mike	Columbia 1590	1913	Argentina	P
Tango South America	Prince's Band	Columbia 1429	-	Argentina	P
To My Manis Tango	Municipal Band of Buenos Aires	Columbia 1467	-	Argentina	E
Belgium Forever	Wiederhold, Albert	Columbia 1766	1915	Belgium	E
Fun in Flanders	Rice, Gladys / Burr, Henry	Victor 18405	1917	Belgium	P
La Brabancomme	Victor Military Band	Victor 17668	1914	Belgium	P
My Belgian Rose	Shaw, Elliott / Hart, Charles	Victor 18479	-	Belgium	P
There's a Green Hill in Flanders	Campbell, Albert/Roberts, Bob	Columbia 2471	1917	Belgium	P
Ain't Dat a Shame	Collins, Arthur	Harvard 378	-	Black/Negro	P
Ain't Dat a Shame	Denny, Will	Edison 7875	1901	Black/Negro	P

Song Title	Name of Artist(s)	Label and Selec. No.	Year Rec.	Ethnicity/ Theme	
Ain't Dat a Shame	Dulcimer	Edison 8021	1902	Black/Negro	P
Ain't Dat Lovin'	Collins, Arthur	Edison 7916	1901	Black/Negro	P
All Coons Look Alike to Me	Collins, Arthur	Edison 7317	1899	Black/Negro	P
All Coons Look Alike to Me	Haley's Concert Band	Berliner 63	1897	Black/Negro	P
All Coons Look Alike to Me	Quinn, Dan	Edison 1001	1896	Black/Negro	P
All Coons Look Alike to Me	Victor Minstrels	Victor 30293	-	Black/Negro	P
All I Want Is My Black Baby Back	Collins, Arthur	Berliner 756	1899	Black/Negro	P
All I Want Is My Black Baby Back	Quinn, Dan	Edison 6902	1899	Black/Negro	P
American Cake Walk	accordion	Edison 9341	1906	Black/Negro	P
At Mammy's Fireside	Jolson, Al	-	1913	Black/Negro	P
At the Darktown Strutter's Ball	Six Brown Brothers	Victor 18376	1917	Black/Negro	P
At the Minstrel Show	Edison Military Band	Edison 9275	1906	Black/Negro	P
Bake Dat Chicken Pie	Collins / Harlan	Columbia 486	1907	Black/Negro	P
Bake Dat Chicken Pie	Collins, Arthur / Harlan, Byron	Edison 9499	1907	Black/Negro	P
Bake Dat Chicken Pie	Collins, Arthur / Harlan, Byron	Columbia 2290	1917	Black/Negro	P
Bake Dat Chicken Pie	Coon duet	Edison 50082	-	Black/Negro	P
Black America Two Step	Edison Symphony Orchestra	Edison 509	1896	Black/Negro	P
Black Jim	Columbia Male Quartet	Columbia 423	1907	Black/Negro	P
Black Man Dwelling in the Western World	String Orchestra	Edison	-	Black/Negro	P
Brown Skin	Victor Military Band	Victor 18203	1916	Black/Negro	P
Bullfrog and the Coon	Six Brown Brothers	Columbia 1041	1911	Black/Negro	P
Bullfrog and the Coon (medley)	American Saxophone Band	Columbia 1041	-	Black/Negro	P
The Bullfrog and the Coon	Jones, Ada	Victor 4873	-	Black/Negro	P
Carolina Mammy	Dalhart, Vernon	Emerson 10643	-	Black/Negro	P
Carve Dat Possum	Browne, H.C.	Columbia 2590	1917	Black/Negro	P
Characteristic Negro Melody	Columbia Male Quartet	Columbia 352	1902	Black/Negro	P
Chocolate Soldier: My Hero	Barbour, Inez	Columbia 843	1910	Black/Negro	P
Climb Up Ye	Rambler Minstrels	Columbia 5138	-	Black/Negro	P
Climb Up Ye Chillin'	Browne, H.C.	Columbia 2590	1917	Black/Negro	P
The Coleville Coon Cadet	American Quartet	-	-	Black/Negro	P
Colored Major March	Ossman, Vess	Edison 1904	-	Black/Negro	P
The Colored Major	Ossman, Vess	Columbia 232	1901	Black/Negro	P
Colored Preacher	Graham, George	Berliner 620z	1896	Black/Negro	P
The Colored Recruit	Golden & Hughes	Okeh 1024	1918	Black/Negro	P
Congo Love Song	Collins, Arthur	Zonophone 5659	-	Black/Negro	P
Congo Love Song	-	-	-	Black/Negro	P
A Coon 'Possum Hunt	Collins, Arthur	Edison 17221	-	Black/Negro	P
Coon Band Contest	banjo	Edison 7561	1900	Black/Negro	P
Coon Band Contest	Levi, Maurice Band	Edison 10128	1909	Black/Negro	P
A Coon Band Contest	Arthur Pryor's Band	Victor 4069	-	Black/Negro	P
A Coon Band Contest	Fuller, Earl Famous Jazz Band	Victor 18394	1917	Black/Negro	P
A Coon Band Contest	Ossman, Vess	Columbia 231	1901	Black/Negro	P
A Coon Band Contest	Ossman, Vess	Victor 154	-	Black/Negro	P
A Coon Band Contest	Sousa's Band	Berliner 1170	1900	Black/Negro	P
Coon Coon Coon	Collins & Natus	Edison 7750	1901	Black/Negro	P
Coon Courtship	Jones, Ada / Spencer, Len	Edison 9695	1907	Black/Negro	P
The Coon Mariners	Golden / Marlowe	Perfect 11200	-	Black/Negro	P
Coon Medley	Haydn Quartet	Berliner 4272	-	Black/Negro	P
Coon Song Medley	banjo	Edison 2638	1897	Black/Negro	P
Coon Songs Medley	Edison Male Quartet	Edison 2228	1897	Black/Negro	P
Coon Songs Medley	Golden & Collins	Edison 4006	1899	Black/Negro	P
Coon Songs Medley	Golden, Billy	Edison 4006	1899	Black/Negro	P
Coon Songs Medley	Golden, Billy	Edison 8491	1903	Black/Negro	P
The Coon That Got the Shake	baritone (-)	Berliner 169	-	Black/Negro	P
Coon Vanderville Sketch Henry	Jones, Ada / Spencer, Len	Zonophone 772	-	Black/Negro	P
The Coon Waiters	Knight, Harlan E.	Edison 50532	-	Black/Negro	P
Coon Wedding in Southern Georgia	Peerless Quartet	Edison 10348	1910	Black/Negro	P
A Coon Wedding in Southern Georgia	Columbia Male Quartet	Columbia 370	1901	Black/Negro	P
A Coon Wedding in Southern Georgia	-	Little Wonder 338-		Black/Negro	P

Song Title	Name of Artist(s)	Label and Selec. No.	Year Rec.	Ethnicity/ Theme	
Coon's Attempted Suicide	Golden, Billy / Marlowe, Jim	Columbia 5752	1915	Black/Negro	P
A Coon's Attempted Suicide	Marlowe, Jim	Columbia 5752	-	Black/Negro	P
Coon's Birthday	Arthur Pryor's Band	Victor 16435	-	Black/Negro	P
A Coon's Love Song (Negro characteristic)	Morton, Eddie	Victor 16650	-	Black/Negro	P
Coon, Coon, Coon	Victor Mixed Chorus	Victor 26546	-	Black/Negro	P
Coontown Capers	Metropolitan Orchestra	Berliner 1704	-	Black/Negro	P
Coonville Cullad Band	Collins, Arthur	Columbia 450	1904	Black/Negro	P
Coonville's Colored Band	Collins, Arthur	Edison	-	Black/Negro	P
Coonville's Cullad Band	Collins, Arthur	Edison 8610	1904	Black/Negro	P
Daddy's Pickanniny Boy	Carroll, Clark	Columbia 748	1909	Black/Negro	P
Dar's a Watermelon Spoilin' Down at Johnson's	Collins, Arthur	Edison 5447	1898	Black/Negro	P
Darkey Tickle	banjo	Edison 2608	1897	Black/Negro	P
Darkey Volunteers	banjo	Edison 7113	1899	Black/Negro	P
Darkey's Dream	Columbia Orchestra	Columbia 157	1902	Black/Negro	P
Darkey's Tickle — Plantation Medley	Columbia Orchestra	Columbia 160	1902	Black/Negro	P
Darkeys Patrol	Ossman, Vess	Columbia 221	1902	Black/Negro	P
Darkie Awakening	Ossman, Vess	Columbia 233	1904	Black/Negro	P
Darkie's Serenade	Collins, Arthur / Harlan, Byron	Columbia 1769	1915	Black/Negro	P
Darkies Awakening	banjo	Edison 2607	1897	Black/Negro	P
Darkies Awakening	Ossman, Vess	Lakeside 70235	-	Black/Negro	P
Darkies Dream	banjo	Edison 2605	1897	Black/Negro	P
Darkies Dream	Edison Military Band	Edison 8878	1906	Black/Negro	P
Darkies Dream	Edison Military Band	Edison 8878	-	Black/Negro	P
Darkies Dream	Peerless Orchestra	Edison 703	1896	Black/Negro	P
Darkies Jubilee	piccolo	Edison 2802	1897	Black/Negro	P
Darkies Patrol	banjo	Edison 2606	1897	Black/Negro	P
Darktown Barbeque	-	-	1904	Black/Negro	P
Darktown Belle's March	Edison Symphony Orchestra	Edison 654	1896	Black/Negro	P
Darktown Colored Band	Collins, Arthur	Edison 5403	1898	Black/Negro	P
A Darktown Courtship	Jones, Ada / Spencer, Len	Columbia 288	1906	Black/Negro	P
Darktown Is Out Tonight	Quinn, Dan	Edison 6905	1899	Black/Negro	P
Darktown Poets	Golden / Hughes	Columbia 1085	1911	Black/Negro	P
Darktown Strutter's Ball	Collins, Arthur / Harlan, Byron	Columbia 2478	1918	Black/Negro	P
Darktown Strutters Ball	Collins, A. / Harlan, B.	Columbia 2478	1917	Black/Negro	P
Darktown Strutters Ball	Original Dixieland Jazz Band	Columbia 2297	1917	Black/Negro	P
Darktown Strutters Ball	Sweatman's, Wilbur Jazz Band	Columbia 2596	1918	Black/Negro	P
Darktown Strutters Ball	J. R. Europe's Hell Fighters	Pathe	1917	Black/Negro	P
Darky Oration on Women	Golden & Marlowe	Columbia 2235	1919	Black/Negro	P
Darky Song	Victor Minstrels	Victor 35095	-	Black/Negro	P
Darky Stories — Two Coon Stories	Wills, Nat M.	Victor 17768	1915	Black/Negro	P
Dat Possum Rag	-	-	1910	Black/Negro	P
Dat's de Way to Spell Chicken	Collins, Arthur	Edison 8301	1903	Black/Negro	P
De Cakewalk in the Sky	Newton, Marguerite	Edison 7143	1899	Black/Negro	P
De Coonville Grand Cake Walk	Quinn, Dan	Edison 1121	1896	Black/Negro	P
De Goblin's Glide	-	-	1911	Black/Negro	P
De Gospel Train Am Coming	Browne, H.C.	Columbia 2255	1917	Black/Negro	P
De Little Pickaninny's Gone to Sleep	-	-	1910	Black/Negro	P
De Pickaninny's Dream	Newton, Marguerite	Edison 7129	1899	Black/Negro	P
De Possum Chase	Collins, Arthur	Edison 7318	1899	Black/Negro	P
De Pullman Porter's Ball	Quinn, Dan	Edison 7965	1901	Black/Negro	P
De Trumpet in de Cornfield	Gaskin, George	Berliner 943	1896	Black/Negro	P
De Wedding Ober de Hill	Golden, Billy	Berliner 730	1896	Black/Negro	P
Deed I Do (Coon Love Song)	-	Standard 270	-	Black/Negro	P
Dese Bones Shall Rise Again	Spencer, Len/Porter, Steve	-	1901	Black/Negro	P
Dixie	Pryor, Arthur	Victor 16819	-	Black/Negro	P
Dixie Medley	Van Epps, Fred	-	1908	Black/Negro	P
Dixie Medley*	-	-	-	Black/Negro	P
Dixieland Memories No. 1	Orpheus Male Quartet	Edison	-	Black/Negro	P
Doan Ye Cry, Mah Honey	Rycroft & Haydn Quartet	Berliner 1304	1900	Black/Negro	P
Doan You Cry Ma Honey	Clark, Carroll	Columbia 627	1909	Black/Negro	P

Song Title	Name of Artist(s)	Label and Selec. No.	Year Rec.	Ethnicity/ Theme	
Don't Leave Me Mammy	Dalhart, Vernon	Emerson 10511	-	Black/Negro	P
Don't Leave Me Mammy	Imperial Marimba Band	Edison 50915	-	Black/Negro	P
Down Among the Sugar Cane	Collins, Arthur/Harlan	Indestructable 1015	-	Black/Negro	P
Down de Lover's Lane	-	-	1900	Black/Negro	P
Down on the Old Plantation	Edison Symphony Orchestra	Edison	1904	Black/Negro	P
Down Where the	Rambler Minstrels	Columbia 5138	-	Black/Negro	P
Drowsy Dempsey (a coon shuffle)	Stehl, George	Columbia 601	1908	Black/Negro	P
Every Nigger Has a Lady but Me	Leachman, Silas	Victor 1131	-	Black/Negro	P
Every Race Has a Flag but a Coon	Collins, Arthur	Edison 7580	1900	Black/Negro	P
For Lawdy Sakes Feed My Dog	Collins, Arthur	Edison 1904	1904	Black/Negro	P
The Ghost of the Banjo Coon	Golden / Hughes	Victor 17011	-	Black/Negro	P
Gimme de Leavins	-	-1904	1904	Black/Negro	P
Give That Nigger a Ham	-	-	-	Black/Negro	P
Go to Sleep My Little Pickaninny (Alabama Coon)	Bartlett, Jane	Playtime 217A	-	Black/Negro	P
Granny You're My Mammy's Mammy	Homestead Trio	Edison 50915	-	Black/Negro	P
Green's, Eli Cake Walk	banjo	Edison 7116	1899	Black/Negro	P
Green's, Eli Cake Walk	Edison Brass Quartet	Edison 3406	1898	Black/Negro	P
Hear the Pickaninny Band	Van Brunt, Walter	Edison 10568	1912	Black/Negro	P
Hear the Picksnniny Band	Columbia Quartet	Columbia 1136	-	Black/Negro	P
Hot Corn Coon Song	Collins, Arthur	Columbia 493	1907	Black/Negro	P
The Hottest Coon in Town	Spencer, Len	Berliner 9	1899	Black/Negro	P
The Humming Coon	Collins, Arthur	Columbia 5138	-	Black/Negro	P
The Humming Coon	Collins, Arthur	Columbia 5138	-	Black/Negro	P
Hush My Little Coon — Yodel	Lamaire, Peter	Columbia 571	1905	Black/Negro	P
I Don't Allow No Coon to Hurt My Feelings	Collins, Arthur	Edison 5458	1898	Black/Negro	P
I Don't Allow No Coon to Hurt My Feelings	Collins, Arthur	Berliner 887	1900	Black/Negro	P
I Don't Care If You Nebber Come Home	Quinn, Dan	Edison 1040	1896	Black/Negro	P
I Love the Land of Old Black Joe	American Quartet	Vocalian 14080	-	Black/Negro	P
I Want Dem Presents Back	Terrell, John	Berliner 1626	-	Black/Negro	P
I'd Love to Fall Asleep and Wake Up in My Mammy's Arms	Jones, Reese	Edison 50698	-	Black/Negro	P
I'll Make Dat Black Girl Mine	Harding, Roger	Edison 2024	1897	Black/Negro	P
I'll Make That Black Girl Mine	Quinn, Dan	Edison 1044	1896	Black/Negro	P
I's Getting Up a Watermelon Party	Quinn, Dan	Edison 7203	1899	Black/Negro	P
I'se Gwine Back to Dixie	Brilliant Quartet	Berliner 658	1899	Black/Negro	P
I'se Gwine Back to Dixie	Columbia Male Quartet	Columbia 376	1902	Black/Negro	P
I'se Gwine Back to Dixie	Edison Male Quartet	Edison 2222	1897	Black/Negro	P
I'se Gwine back to Dixie	Peerless Quartet	Columbia 1881	1915	Black/Negro	P
I'se Gwine Back to Dixie	Seagle, Oscar	Columbia 1570	1914	Black/Negro	P
I've Got a White Man Workin' for Me	Collins, Arthur	Edison 7779	1901	Black/Negro	P
I've Got a White Man Working for Me	Collins, Arthur	-	-	Black/Negro	P
If the Man in the Moon Were a Coon	Jones, Ada	Columbia 502	1906	Black/Negro	P
If the Man in the Moon Were a Coon	Jones, Ada	Edison 9372	1906	Black/Negro	P
Ise Gwine Back to Dixie	MacDonough, Harry	-	1902	Black/Negro	P
Ise Gwine Back to Dixie	Zonophone Minstrels	Zonophone 1903	-	Black/Negro	P
Jolly Darkies	banjo	Edison 2618	1897	Black/Negro	P
Jordan Am a Hard Road to Travel	Browne, H.C.	Columbia 2255	1916	Black/Negro	P
King Cotton	Sousa's Band	Berliner 143ZZ	1896	Black/Negro	P
Koontown Kaffee Klatch	Ossman, Vess	Columbia 218	1906	Black/Negro	P
Koonville Koonlets	banjo	Edison 8026	1902	Black/Negro	P
Little Alabama Coon	Burr, Henry	Columbia 1837	1913	Black/Negro	P
Little Alabama Coon	Edison Male Quartet	Edison 2221	1897	Black/Negro	P
Little Alabama Coon	Garrison, Mabel	Victor 64697	-	Black/Negro	P
Little Alabama Coon	Gaskin, George	Edison 1523	1896	Black/Negro	P
Little Alabama Coon	Gaskin, George	Berliner 69	1897	Black/Negro	P
Little Alabama Coon	Gaskin, George	Columbia 297	1902	Black/Negro	P
Little Alabama Coon	Haydn Quartet	Berliner 870Z	1898	Black/Negro	P
Little Alabama Coon	Middleton, Arthur	Edison 82562	-	Black/Negro	P

Song Title	Name of Artist(s)	Label and Selec. No.	Year Rec.	Ethnicity/ Theme	
Little Alabama Coon	Ponselle, Rosa and Male Quartet	Columbia 33003	–	Black/Negro	P
Little Alabama Coon	Shannon Quartet	Victor 19343	–	Black/Negro	P
Little Black Lamb	Carroll, Clark	Columbia 805	1909	Black/Negro	P
Little Black Me	Campbell, Albert	Edison 7416	1900	Black/Negro	P
Little Black Me	Harlan & Madeira	Edison 7823	1901	Black/Negro	P
Little Black Me	Natus, Joseph	Edison 7585	1900	Black/Negro	P
Little Pickaninnies	banjo	Edison 7162	1899	Black/Negro	P
Looking for a Coon Like Me	Gaskin, George	Edison 1524	1896	Black/Negro	P
Looking for a Coon Like Me	Parlophone Quartet with Orchestra	Parlophone 5896	–	Black/Negro	P
A Lovesick Coon	Golden / Marlowe	Perfect 11200	–	Black/Negro	P
Ma Pickanniny	Murray, Billy / Oakland, Will	Victor 17819	1914	Black/Negro	P
Ma Pretty Chloe from Tennessee	Columbia Male Quartet	Columbia 579	1905	Black/Negro	P
Mamma's Black Baby Boy	Edison Male Quartet	Edison 2211	1897	Black/Negro	P
Mammie Come Kiss Your Honey Boy	baritone (-)	Berliner 170	–	Black/Negro	P
Mammy Blossom's Possum Party	Collins, Arthur / Harlan, Byron	Victor 18354	1917	Black/Negro	P
Mammy Jinny's Jubilee	Deiro, Guido	Columbia 1428	–	Black/Negro	P
Mammy Jinny's Jubilee Medley	Prince's Orchestra	Columbia 5502	–	Black/Negro	P
Mammy Lou	Criterion Quartet	Edison 50915	–	Black/Negro	P
Mammy o' Mine	Rowland, Adele	Victor 18560	1919	Black/Negro	P
Mammy o' Mine	Sterling Trio	Columbia 2718	1919	Black/Negro	P
Mammy of Mine	Smith, Joseph & His Orchestra	Victor 18615	1919	Black/Negro	P
Mammy of Mine	Sterling Trio	Okeh 1197	1919	Black/Negro	P
Mammy's Chocolate Soldier	Harris, Marion	Victor 18493	1918	Black/Negro	P
Mammy's Chocolate Soldier Boy	Harris, Marion	Victor 18493	1918	Black/Negro	P
Mammy's Chocolate Soldier Boy	Hindermeyer, Harvey	Okeh 1076	1918	Black/Negro	P
Mammy's Good-Night Lullaby	Crescent Trio	Edison 50698	–	Black/Negro	P
Mammy's Little Choc'late Cullud Chile	Sissle, Noble / Blake, Eubie	Pathe	1917	Black/Negro	P
Mammy's Little Coal Black Rose	Broadway Quartet	Columbia 2114	1916	Black/Negro	P
Mammy's Little Coal Black Rose	Orpheus Quartet	Victor 18183	1916	Black/Negro	P
Mammy's Little Coal Black Rose	Romain, Manuel	Edison 50465	1916	Black/Negro	P
Mammy's Little Dinah	Quinn, Dan	Edison 6927	1899	Black/Negro	P
Mammy's Little Pansy	Harrison, Charles	Columbia 2543	1918	Black/Negro	P
Mammy's Little Pumpkin Colored Coons	Sousa's Band	Berliner 8013	–	Black/Negro	P
Mammy's Little Punkin' Colored Coon	Collins, Arthur	Edison 5414	1898	Black/Negro	P
Mammy's Lullaby	Okeh Dance Orchestra	Okeh 1250	1919	Black/Negro	P
Mammy's Lullaby	Smith, Joseph & His Orchestra	Victor 18531	1919	Black/Negro	P
Mammy's Pickaninny Don't You Cry	Bayes, Nora	Columbia 2771	–	Black/Negro	P
Mammy's Shufflin' Dance	Murray, Billy	Edison 10574	1912	Black/Negro	P
Mammy's Shufflin' Dance	-	-	-	Black/Negro	P
Man in the Moon Is a Coon	Quinn, Dan	Edison 1063	1896	Black/Negro	P
Massa's in de Cold Cold Ground	Carroll, Clark	Columbia 852	1910	Black/Negro	P
Massa's in de Cold Cold Ground	chimes	Edison 3240	1898	Black/Negro	P
Massa's in de Cold Cold Ground	clarinet	Edison 3607	1898	Black/Negro	P
Massa's in de Cold Cold Ground	Conway's Band	Victor 18519	1918	Black/Negro	P
Massa's in de Cold Cold Ground	cornet	Edison 2422	1897	Black/Negro	P
Massa's in de Cold Cold Ground	Gaskin, George	Berliner 168X	1897	Black/Negro	P
Massa's in de Cold Cold Ground	Gates, Lucy	Columbia 6015	1917	Black/Negro	P
Massa's in de Cold Cold Ground	Haydn Quartet	Berliner 4253	–	Black/Negro	P
Massa's in de Cold Cold Ground	Haydn Quartet & Dudley, S.H.	Berliner 413	1899	Black/Negro	P
Massa's in de Cold Cold Ground	Taylor Trio	Columbia 1934	1915	Black/Negro	P
Me an de Minstrel Ban'	Murray, Billy	Edison 9037	1905	Black/Negro	P
Medley of Coon Songs	Seigel, Sam	Victor 449	–	Black/Negro	P
Medley of Plantation Songs	Columbia Male Quartet	Columbia 958	1910	Black/Negro	P
Minstrel Boy	Alexander, George	Columbia 455	1906	Black/Negro	P
The Minstrel Boy	Hart, Charles	Okeh 1191	1919	Black/Negro	P
The Minstrel Boy	White, Malachy	Columbia 2348	1917	Black/Negro	P
Minstrel Show Up Dere in de Sky	Graham / Terrell	Berliner 6010	1898	Black/Negro	P
Minstrels 6: Cake Walk in Coontown	MacDonough, Harry	-	–	Black/Negro	P
Minstrels 8: Scene at the Levee	MacDonough, Harry	-	–	Black/Negro	P

Song Title	Name of Artist(s)	Label and Selec. No.	Year Rec.	Ethnicity/ Theme	
Mr. Black Man	Edison Military Band	Edison 8669	1904	Black/Negro	P
My Charcoal Charmer	Big Four Quartet	Edison 7765	1901	Black/Negro	P
My Charcoal Charmer	Peerless Orchestra	Edison 7761	1901	Black/Negro	P
My Coal Black Lady	Eldridge, Press	Edison 5205	1898	Black/Negro	P
My Coal Black Lady	Imperial Minstrels	Berliner 6021	-	Black/Negro	P
My Coal Black Lady	Knoll / McNeil	Berliner 3647	-	Black/Negro	P
My Creole Sue	Columbia Male Quartet	Columbia 366	1902	Black/Negro	P
My Creole Sue	Shannon Quartet	Victor 19343	-	Black/Negro	P
My Creole Sunshine Sue	Columbia Male Quartet	Columbia 866	1902	Black/Negro	P
My Louisiana Coon Song	Columbia Quartet	Columbia 499	1901	Black/Negro	P
My Mammy	Crescent Trio	Path 22495	-	Black/Negro	P
My Sugar Coated Chocolate Boy	Campbell, A. / Burr, H.	Columbia 2755	1919	Black/Negro	P
Negro Laughing Song	Johnson, George W.	Columbia 297	-	Black/Negro	P
Negro Oddity	Golden, Billy	Berliner 732	1897	Black/Negro	P
Negro Recollections	Collins, Arthur	Edison 7665	1901	Black/Negro	P
New Parson at the Darktown Church	Columbia Quartet	Columbia 490	1907	Black/Negro	P
Nigger & the Bee	Golden / Hughes	Columbia 2974	-	Black/Negro	P
Nigger & the Bee	-	Victor 2995	-	Black/Negro	P
Nigger Blues	Bernard, Al	Edison 50542	-	Black/Negro	P
Nigger Blues	Jolson, Al	Columbia 2064	-	Black/Negro	P
Nigger Blues	O'Connor, George	Columbia 2064	1916	Black/Negro	P
Nigger Blues	Prince's Band	Columbia 5854	1916	Black/Negro	P
Nigger Blues	Victor Military Band	Victor 18174	1916	Black/Negro	P
Nigger Fever	piccolo	Edison 2809	1897	Black/Negro	P
Nigger Fever	Schweinfest, George	Columbia 214	1901	Black/Negro	P
Nigger in a Fit	banjo	Edison 2625	1897	Black/Negro	P
Nigger in the Barnyard	Edison Military Band	Edison 9856	1908	Black/Negro	P
Nigger in the Barnyard	Prince's Orchestra	Columbia 1784	-	Black/Negro	P
Nigger Love a Watermelon	Browne, H.C.	Columbia 1999	-	Black/Negro	P
Nigger Loves His 'Possum	Collins, Arthur / Harlan, Byron	Edison 9160	1905	Black/Negro	P
Nigger Loves His Possum	Collins & Harlin	American 31245	-	Black/Negro	P
Nigger Loves His Possum	Collins, Arthur	Edison 9160	1905	Black/Negro	P
Nigger Loves His Watermelon	Collins, Arthur	Victor 17256	-	Black/Negro	P
Nigger Stew	Invincible Quartet	Edison 8537	1903	Black/Negro	P
Nigger Town	-	-	-	Black/Negro	P
Nigger, Nigger Neber Die	Collins, Arthur	Edison 5448	1898	Black/Negro	P
Nobody Is Lookin' but de Owl and de Moon	Morgan / Stanley	Columbia 394	1904	Black/Negro	P
Oh Dem Golden Slippers	Browne, H.C.	Columbia 2116	1916	Black/Negro	P
Oh Dem Golden Slippers	Collins, Arthur & Minstrels	Columbia 5309	1911	Black/Negro	P
Oh Lawdy Something's Got Between Ebeneezer & Me	Williams, Bert	Columbia 2710	1919	Black/Negro	P
Oh You Coon	Jones, Ada / Murray, Billy	Zonophone 5163	-	Black/Negro	P
Oh, You Coon	Jones, Ada / Murray, Billy	Edison 10075	1909	Black/Negro	P
Old Black Joe	Arndt, Felix	Victor 17674	1914	Black/Negro	P
Old Black Joe	Arthur Pryor's Band	Victor 16819	-	Black/Negro	P
Old Black Joe	Banda Rossa	Berliner 116	1898	Black/Negro	P
Old Black Joe	Collins, Arthur	Edison 7484	1900	Black/Negro	P
Old Black Joe	Columbia Quartet	Columbia 5032	1906	Black/Negro	P
Old Black Joe	Edison Male Quartet	Edison 8823	1904	Black/Negro	P
Old Black Joe	Graveure, Louis	Columbia 5959	1917	Black/Negro	P
Old Black Joe	Haydn Quartet	Berliner 4294	-	Black/Negro	P
Old Black Joe	Holt, Mrs. Stewart	Columbia 5175	1910	Black/Negro	P
Old Black Joe	Lowe, Charles	Berliner 3263	-	Black/Negro	P
Old Black Joe	Paulist Choristers of Chicago	Columbia 2468	1917	Black/Negro	P
Old Black Joe	Peerless Quartet	Victor 16531	-	Black/Negro	P
Old Zip Coon	Richardson, Don	Columbia 2140	1916	Black/Negro	P
Old Zip Coon	Victor Band	Victor 18356	1917	Black/Negro	P
Olds Zip Coon	Arthur Pryor's Band	Victor 16819	-	Black/Negro	P
On Emancipation Day	Collins, Arthur	Edison 8097	1902	Black/Negro	P
On Emancipation Day	Spencer & Hunter	30622	-	Black/Negro	P
Patriotic Coon	Eldridge, Press	Edison 5206	1898	Black/Negro	P

Song Title	Name of Artist(s)	Label and Selec. No.	Year Rec.	Ethnicity/ Theme	
Piccaninny Lullaby	Imperial Quartet	Victor 18158	1916	Black/Negro	P
Pickaninnies	Collins, Arthur	Edison 5466	1898	Black/Negro	P
Pickaninnies Paradise	Sterling Trio	Columbia 2623	1918	Black/Negro	P
Pickaninny Dreams	Okeh Dance Orchestra	Okeh 1249	1919	Black/Negro	P
Pickaninny Paradise	Sterling Trio	Okeh 1095	1918	Black/Negro	P
Pickaninny Paradise	Sterling Trio	Victor 18512	1918	Black/Negro	P
Pickaninny Polka	xylophone	Edison 7683	1901	Black/Negro	P
Pickaninny's Dance	banjo	Edison 7408	1900	Black/Negro	P
Pickaninny's Lullaby	Baker, Elsie	Edison 10552	1912	Black/Negro	P
Pickaninny's Lullaby	Collins, Arthur	Edison 5443	1898	Black/Negro	P
Pickaninny's Serenade	piccolo	Edison 7636	1901	Black/Negro	P
Pickanniny Polka	Lowe, Charles	Columbia 201	1902	Black/Negro	P
Plantation Songs Medley	Columbia Quartet	Columbia 869	1902	Black/Negro	P
Poo Bah of Blackville Town	Collins, Arthur	Edison 8354	1903	Black/Negro	P
Possum Pie	Collins, Arthur / Harlan, Byron	Edison 8697	1904	Black/Negro	P
Possum Supper at Darktown Church	Stewart, Cal	Columbia 5098	1909	Black/Negro	P
The Preacher and the Bear	Collins, Arthur	Edison 17221	1912	Black/Negro	P
The Preacher and the Bear	Collins, Arthur	Columbia 2290	1917	Black/Negro	P
Push Dem Clouds Away	Browne, H.C.	Columbia 2502	1917	Black/Negro	P
Ragtime Medley of Coon Songs	banjo	Edison 2628	1897	Black/Negro	P
Rastus Take Me Back	Dressler, Marie	Edison 2001	1909	Black/Negro	P
Run Brudder Possum Run	Collins, Arthur / Harlan, Byron	Columbia 745	1909	Black/Negro	P
Run Nigger Run	Shipp, K. & C.	AAFS 20	-	Black/Negro	P
Sambo and Dinah	Nelson & Stanley	Edison 9043	1905	Black/Negro	P
Sambo at the Cake Walk	Peerless Orchestra	Edison 683	1896	Black/Negro	P
Sammy Darktown Poker Club	Williams, Bert	Columbia 1504	1914	Black/Negro	P
Saxophone Sam	Six Brown Brothers	Victor 18309	1917	Black/Negro	P
Selection from Chocolate Soldier	Prince's Orchestra	Columbia 781	1909	Black/Negro	P
Shanghai Laying for a Coon	Collins, Arthur	Edison 5427	1898	Black/Negro	P
Shuffling Coon	Edison Symphony Orchestra	Edison 585	1896	Black/Negro	P
Sim and Sam, the Musical Coons	Spencer, Len / Mozarto	Edison 9929	1908	Black/Negro	P
Sissereta's Visit to the North (Negro Shout)	Golden, Billy	Columbia 508	1906	Black/Negro	P
Slavery Days	Edison Male Quintette	Edison 8710	1904	Black/Negro	P
Sleep Time Mah Honey	Carroll, Clark	Columbia 748	-	Black/Negro	P
Stuttering Coon	Quinn, Dan	Edison 6947	1899	Black/Negro	P
Swinging in de Sky	Collins, Arthur / Harlan, Byron	Columbia 896	1910	Black/Negro	P
Taint de Kind o' Grub I've Been Gettin' Down Home	Roberts, Bob	Edison 8983	1905	Black/Negro	P
Tar Baby	Humphrey, Harry	Victor 17996	1916	Black/Negro	P
The Imperial Minstrels	Spencer, Len/Porter, Steve	-	1901	Black/Negro	P
The Preacher and the Bear	Collins, Arthur	Edison 50520	1912	Black/Negro	P
They'll Be Proud in Dixie of Old Black Joe	Campbell, A. / Burr, H.	Columbia 2641	1918	Black/Negro	P
Three Pickaninnies	Collins, Arthur / Harlan, Byron	Okeh 1022	1918	Black/Negro	P
Two Darky Stories	Wills, Nat	Columbia 1765	1915	Black/Negro	P
Uncle Tom One Step	Kopp, Howard	Columbia 2058	1916	Black/Negro	P
Uncle Tom Two Step	Blue & White Marimba Band	Columbia 2136	1916	Black/Negro	P
Victor Minstrels #10	Victor Minstrels	Victor	1908	Black/Negro	P
Virginia Humming Coon	Rambler Minstrels	Columbia 5138	1909	Black/Negro	P
Watermelon Whispers	Green, George Hamilton	Edison 50488	-	Black/Negro	P
Watermelon Whispers	Xylophone & Rega's Novelty	Okeh 1041	1918	Black/Negro	P
Watermillon Song	Bangs, David	Berliner 186	1895	Black/Negro	P
When de Big Bell Rings	Mystic Quartet	Berliner 852	1896	Black/Negro	P
When de Moon Comes up Behind de Hill	Dudley, S. H.	Edison 7879	1901	Black/Negro	P
Whistling Coon	Dudley, Murray	Victor 16821	-	Black/Negro	P
Whistling Coon	Johnson, George	Berliner 196	1896	Black/Negro	P
Whistling Coon	Johnson, George	Edison 4012	1899	Black/Negro	P
Whistling Coon	Murray, Billy	Columbia 292	-	Black/Negro	P
The Whistling Coon	Johnson, George	Berliner 196	1896	Black/Negro	P
Whistling Minstrels	Prince's Band	Columbia 57	1906	Black/Negro	P

Song Title	Name of Artist(s)	Label and Selec. No.	Year Rec.	Ethnicity/ Theme	
Who dar Cakewalk	mandolin	Edison 7245	1899	Black/Negro	P
Who Dat Say Chicken in Dis Crowd	Sousa's Band	Berliner 1208	1900	Black/Negro	P
Who dat say Chicken in Dis Crowd?	Collins, Arthur	Edison 5475	1898	Black/Negro	P
Who's Dat Callin' So Sweet	Knoll / McNeil	Berliner 3643	-	Black/Negro	P
You're Just Too Sweet to Live	Coon duet	Edison 50082	-	Black/Negro	P
Brazilian Dreams	Prince's Band	Columbia 5579	1914	Brazil	P
Childhood Days—The Girl from Brazil	Rice, Gladys	Edison 50385	-	Brazil	P
Come Back Sweet Dream — The Girl from Brazil	Rice, Gladys	Edison 50385	-	Brazil	P
Rolling Down to Rio	Jell, George	Columbia 828	1909	Brazil	P
By the Saskatchewan	Sarto, Andrea	Columbia 1024	1911	Canada	P
By the Saskatchewan	Werrenrath, Reinald	Victor	1910	Canada	P
Canada	Victor Band	Victor 17593	1915	Canada	P
Canadian Airs	Prince's Military Band	Columbia 973	1910	Canada	P
Canadian March Medley	Sousa's Band	Berliner 142	1898	Canada	P
Canadian Melody	Victor Band	Victor 17653	1916	Canada	P
In Old Quebec	Victor Military Band	Victor 17998	1916	Canada	P
In Old Quebec : Vive la Canadienne	Victor Military Band	Victor	1916	Canada	P
Land of the Maple Leaf Maple Leaf Forever	Prince's Military Band	Columbia 974	1910	Canada	P
Maple Leaf Forever	Victor Band	Victor 17593	1915	Canada	P
Maple Leaf Forever	Victor Military Band	Victor 17999	1915	Canada	P
O Canada (1916)	Victor Military Band	-	1916	Canada	P
Oh Canada	Columbia Mixed Quartet	Columbia 1369	-	Canada	P
Oh Canada	Victor Military Band	Victor 17999	1915	Canada	P
Song of Canada	Sarto, Andre	Columbia 1369	-	Canada	P
Cubanolo Glide	Prince's Orchestra	Columbia 811	1909	Cuba	P
Cubanolo Glide	Southe, Paul	Columbia 800	1910	Cuba	P
Hello People: Havana 1909	Stanley, Frank	Columbia 708	1909	Cuba	P
I'll See You in C-U-B-A	Palace Trio	Victor	1920	Cuba	P
Santiago Waltz	Columbia Orchestra	Columbia 152	1902	Chile	P
All Aboard for Chinatown	American Quartet	Victor 17993	1916	China	P
All Aboard for Chinatown	Collins, Arthur / Harlan, Byron	Columbia 1954	1916	China	P
Chin Chin Chinaman	Prince's Band	Columbia 6008	1917	China	P
Chin Chin Chinaman	Quinn, Dan	Edison 1011	1896	China	P
Chin Chin Chinaman	Quinn, Dan	Berliner 525	1898	China	P
Chin Chin Love Moon	Kline, Olive & Lyric Quartet	Victor 17665	1914	China	P
Chin Chin Medley	Prince's Band	Columbia 5757	1916	China	P
Chin Chin Open Your Heart	Six Brown Brothers	Victor 18149	1916	China	P
Chin Chin Vocal Gems	Columbia Light Opera Company	Columbia 5639	1914	China	P
Chin Chin Waltz	Prince's Band	Columbia 5634	1914	China	P
Chin Chin: Love Moon	Wells, John	Columbia 1661	1914	China	P
China We Owe a Lot to You	Watson Sisters	Columbia 2375	1917	China	P
Chinatown My Chinatown	American Quartet	Victor 17684	1914	China	P
Chinatown My Chinatown	Prince's Orchestra	Columbia 5674	1915	China	P
Chinatown, My Chinatown	Wells, John / Kerns, Grace	Columbia 1624	1914	China	P
Chinee Sojer Man	Dudley, Murray	Edison 7733	1901	China	P
Chinese Blues	Kaufman, Irving	Victor 17919	1915	China	P
Chinese Honeymoon Selection	Peerless Orchestra	Edison 8080	1903	China	P
Chinese Lullaby	Columbia Orchestra	Columbia 2777	1919	China	P
Chinese March	Ellery Band	Columbia 1367	-	China	P
Chinese March	Peerless Orchestra	Edison 670	1896	China	P
Chinese March — Kwang Hsu	Edison Concert Band	Edison 10140	1909	China	P
Chinese Picnic	banjo	Edison 2603	1897	China	P
Chinese Picnic	Van eps Trio	Victor 17601	1914	China	P
Chinese Wedding Procession	Prince's Orchestra	Columbia 5684	1915	China	P
Ching Chang	xylophone	Edison 9253	1906	China	P
Ching Chong	Prince's Band	Columbia 5986	1917	China	P
Ching Chong	Van Epps, Fred Trio	Victor 18404	1917	China	P
Chong	Van Epps, Fred	Okeh 1199	1919	China	P
Chong He Come from Hong Kong	Kaufman, Irving	Okeh 1206	1919	China	P

Song Title	Name of Artist(s)	Label and Selec. No.	Year Rec.	Ethnicity/ Theme	
Chong, He Come from Old Hong Kong	Columbia Saxophone Sextet	Columbia 2730	1919	China	P
Chong, He Come from Old Hong Kong	Kaufman, Irving	Columbia 2714	1919	China	P
Chu Chin Chow	Orpheus Quartet	Victor 18336	1917	China	P
From Here to Shanghai	Greene, Gene Quartet	Victor 18242	1917	China	P
From Here to Shanghai	Jolson, Al	Columbia 2224	1916	China	P
From Here to Shanghai	Victor Band	Victor 18267	1917	China	P
Hong Kong	Deiro, Guido	Columbia 2316	1917	China	P
Hong Kong	King, Charles / Brice, Elizabeth	Columbia 2232	1917	China	P
Hong Kong	Peerless Quartet	Victor 18295	1917	China	P
Hong Kong Cakewalk	Prince's Band	Columbia 776	1909	China	P
Hong Kong Jass Step	Prince's Band	Columbia 5967	1917	China	P
Hong Kong Romance	Tally, Harry	Columbia 1892	1915	China	P
In Blinky Winky Chinky Chinatown	Peerless Quartet	Victor 17875	1915	China	P
My Dreamy China Lady	Lyric Quartet	Victor 18034	1916	China	P
My Dreamy China Lady	Nash, Grace / Burr, Henry	Columbia 2002	1916	China	P
My Dreamy Little Lotus Flower	Lyric Dance Orchestra	Lyrophone 4161	-	China	P
My Dreamy Little Lotus Flower	Van eps Trio	Victor 18640	-	China	P
My Little China Doll	Deiro, Guido	Columbia 2316	1917	China	P
Old Black Joe	Nielsen, Alice	Columbia 5678	1915	China	P
Oriental Echoes	Band	Berliner 40	1896	China	P
Orientalische Motive 2	Zehngut, Oscar	Victor	-	China	P
Ting Ling Toy	Columbia Saxophone Sextet	Columbia 2760	1919	China	P
Trip to Chinatown Lancers	Edison Symphony Orchestra	Edison 627	1896	China	P
Uncle Josh in a Chinese Laundry	Stewart, Cal	Columbia 289	1903	China	P
Under the China Moon	Campbell, A. / Burr, H.	Victor 18365	1917	China	P
Wedding of the Chinee and the Coon	Quinn, Dan	Edison 1115	1896	China	P
Danish Dance	Victor Band	Victor 17821	1914	Denmark	P
Ach Wie Ist Moglish	Classen, Julia	Columbia 5719	1915	Germany	E
Am Rhein und Beim Wein	Muench, Emil	Columbia 517	1903	Germany	E
Amojze in Gewashen	Littman, Frank	Columbia 549	1907	Germany	E
Annchen von Taurau	Jorn, Karl	Columbia 1862	1915	Germany	E
Aud der Jugendzeit	Muench, Emil	Columbia 523	1903	Germany	E
Auf der Alm da gibst K Sun	Jorn, Karl	Columbia 1794	1915	Germany	E
Auf Wiedersehn	Kerns, Grace / Williamson, Hardy	Columbia 1819	1915	Germany	E
Auf Wiedersehn Waltz	Green & MacDonough	Victor 17858	1915	Germany	P
The Beast of Berlin: We're Going to Get Him	Hall, Arthur	Columbia 2602	1918	Germany	P
Bienenhaus Marsch	Ziehrer, Orchestra	Berliner 7111	-	Germany	P
Bismarck March	Edison Grand Concert Band	Edison 8117	1902	Germany	P
Blitz and Blatz in an Aeroplane	Duprez, Fred / Roberts, Bob	Columbia 758	1909	Germany	P
Bring Back the Kaiser	American Quartet	Victor 18414	1917	Germany	P
Christkind Kommt	Kinerchoir	Victor	1911	Germany	E
Cradle Song (in German)	Fremstad, Olive	Columbia 1488	-	Germany	E
Dachstein Marsch	Renoth / Huber	Columbia 513	1903	Germany	E
Das Edelweiss	Muench, Emil	Columbia 515	1903	Germany	E
Das Heidenroselein	Muench, Emil	Columbia 511	1903	Germany	E
Das Herz	New York German Liederkranz	Columbia 5392	1911	Germany	E
Das Herz am Rhein	Jorn, Karl	Columbia 1776	1915	Germany	E
Das Mutterherz	Muench, Emil	Columbia 514	1902	Germany	E
Der Faderland for Mine	-	-	1906	Germany	E
Der Rattenfenger	Leonhardt, Robert	Columbia 518	1903	Germany	E
Der Rattenfenger	Muench, Emil	Columbia 516	1903	Germany	E
Der Steirerbauer	Renoth / Huber	Columbia 512	1903	Germany	E
Der Waffenshcmied	Braun, Carl	Columbia 5865	1916	Germany	E
Der Zifferblatt von Chokmes Nuschem	Seiden, Frank	Columbia 559	1903	Germany	E
Deutsche Mutter	Muench, Emil	Victor 17788	1915	Germany	E
Deutschland Uber Alles	Schliegel, Carl	Victor 17670	1914	Germany	E
Deutschland, Deutschland	Muench, Emil	Columbia 524	1900	Germany	E
Die Beiden Grasmuechen	Columbia Orchestra	Columbia 184	1910	Germany	P

Song Title	Name of Artist(s)	Label and Selec. No.	Year Rec.	Ethnicity/ Theme	
Die Beiden Kleinen Finken	Columbia Orchestra	Columbia 178	1908	Germany	P
Die Deutchmeister	-	Victor 77362	-	Germany	E
Die Heimath	German vocal	Columbia 891	1903	Germany	E
Die Heimath	Renoth / Huber	Columbia 512	1903	Germany	E
Die Kappelle	quartet (-)	Berliner 807	-	Germany	E
Die Lorelei	New York German Liederkranz	Columbia 5361	1911	Germany	E
Die Nachtigall	Eidner, Frau	Berliner 388	1898	Germany	E
Die Wacht am Rhein	Columbia Band	Columbia 60	1901	Germany	P
Die Wacht am Rhein	Muench, Emil	Columbia 5030	1906	Germany	E
Die Wacht am Rhein	Schliegel, Carl	Victor 17670	1914	Germany	E
Die Wacht am Rhein	Sousa's Band	Victor 17669	1911	Germany	E
Die Wacht am Rhein	Muench, Emil	Columbia 570	1907	Germany	E
Die Wide	Goldin Quartet	Columbia 551	1905	Germany	E
Die Zigeuner Baron: Schatz	Columbia Orchestra	Columbia 753	-	Germany	P
Die Zwei Daires	Suchow, M.	Columbia 561	1905	Germany	E
Du Liegst mir im Herzen	Jorn, Karl	Columbia 1778	1915	Germany	E
Emmet's German Yodel	Watson, George P.	Columbia -	1901	Germany	P
Emmett's German Yodel	Lamar, Peter	Columbia 575	1902	Germany	P
Fehrberliner Reiter Marsch	Emperor's Guard Band	Columbia 76	1903	Germany	P
Freiheit die ich Meine	Muench, Emil	Columbia 519	1903	Germany	P
Freischuetz — Prayer & Air	Hoyle, Jennie	Berliner 480	-	Germany	P
Freut Euch das Lebens	Jorn, Karl	Columbia 1778	1915	Germany	E
(Let Us Be Joyous)					
Fritz and Louisa	Spencer, Len/Jones, Ada	American 31303	-	Germany	P
German Army March	Columbia Orchestra	Columbia 153	-	Germany	P
German Fidelity March	-	Victor 17577	-	Germany	P
German Folk Potpurri	Wormser	Victor 17862	1913	Germany	E
German Patriotic Air:	Sousa's Band	-	-	Germany	P
Die Wacht Am Rhein					
Grad aus dem Wirthshaus	Muench, Emil	Columbia 513	1900	Germany	E
Gretchen	Collins, A. / Harlan, B.	Columbia 273	1905	Germany	P
Gut Nacht Fahr Wohl	Muench, Emil	Columbia 520	1903	Germany	E
Hans and Gretchyn	Spencer, Len/Jones, Ada	Victor 31567	-	Germany	P
Hans und Liese	Heineman, Alex	Columbia 982	1911	Germany	E
Happy German Twins	Spencer / Watson	Columbia 460	1906	Germany	P
Happy Heine	Columbia Band	Columbia 106	1905	Germany	P
Happy Heine	Regimental Band of the Republic	American 31234	-	Germany	E
Happy Heine	Yerkes, Harry	Columbia 196	1905	Germany	P
Happy Heine March	Lua, Pali / Kaili, David	Victor 17859	1914	Germany	E
Heidelberg Stein	Columbia Stellar Quartet	Columbia 1853	1915	Germany	P
Heidelberg Stein	Orpheus Quartet	Victor 17899	1915	Germany	P
Heidelberg Stein Song	Criterion Quartet	Columbia 380	1905	Germany	P
Heine	Spencer, Len/Jones, Ada	Victor 4150	-	Germany	P
Heine at College	Weber, Grace & Fields, Arthur	Columbia 1168	-	Germany	P
Heine at College	Weber/Fields	Columbia 1168	-	Germany	P
Heinie	Jones, Ada / Spencer, Len	Columbia 287	1905	Germany	P
Herz am Rhein	Muench, Emil	Victor 17788	1915	Germany	E
Hilda Loses Her Job	Sadler, J	Victor 16783	-	Germany	P
Hilda Loses Her Job	Sadler, Josie	Victor 16783	-	Germany	P
How Can I Leave Thee (in German)	Fremstad, Olive	Columbia 1488	-	Germany	E
Hushabye Baby	yodel song	Columbia 571	1902	Germany	P
Ich Hatte ein Schones Vaterland	Wormser	Victor 17860	1913	Germany	E
Ich Liebe Dich	-	Victor	1995	Germany	P
Ich Liebe dich	-	Victor	1995	Germany	P
Ich Weiss Nicht Was	Muench, Emil	Columbia 517	1900	Germany	E
Seight es Bedeuten					
Im Hotel zur grunen weise	-	Victor 77362	-	Germany	P
In diesen heiligen Hallen	Knupfer, Paul	Berliner 42194	1898	Germany	E
In Dunkler Nacht	Muench, Emil	Columbia 515	1900	Germany	E
In Einem Kuhlen Grunde	New York German Liederkranz	Columbia 5392	1911	Germany	E
Jagerleben (Hunter's Life)	Jorn, Karl	Columbia 1841	1915	Germany	E
Kaernthner Liedermarsch	Columbia Orchestra	Columbia 162	1903	Germany	E

Song Title	Name of Artist(s)	Label and Selec. No.	Year Rec.	Ethnicity/ Theme	
Kaernthner Liedermarsch	Emperor's Guard Band	Columbia 60	1903	Germany	E
The Kaiser and the Girl	Clark, Miriam	Columbia 979	1910	Germany	P
Kaiser Friedrich March	New York Military Band	Edison 50319	-	Germany	P
Kaiser Friedrich March	United States Marine Band	Edison 10296	1910	Germany	P
Kaiser Jaeger March	Columbia Orchestra	Columbia 154	1909	Germany	P
The Kaiser March	Banda Rossa	Berliner 98	1898	Germany	E
Krausmeyer and His Dog Schneider	Spencer, Len	Columbia 386	1905	Germany	P
Krausmeyer Taking the Census	Jones, Ada / Spencer, Len	Edison 10422	1910	Germany	P
Krausmeyer's Birthday Party	Spencer, Len & Mozarto	Edison 9853	1907	Germany	P
Kuessen ist Keine Suend	Horsten, Hans	Columbia 523	1906	Germany	E
Lena from Germany	Sadler, Josie	Edison 10198	1909	Germany	E
Lied an den Abendstern	Berger, Rudolf	-	1904	Germany	E
Listen to the German Band	-	Victor 24090	-	Germany	P
Listen to the German Band	-	Vocalion 3338	-	Germany	P
A Little German Trouble	Sadler, Josie	Columbia 596	1908	Germany	P
Lorelei	Jorn, Karl	Columbia 1862	1915	Germany	E
Maedchen mit dem Rotten Mundchen	Muench, Emil	Columbia 521	1903	Germany	E
Medley of Berlin Songs	Bernard, Mike	Columbia 1386	-	Germany	P
Medley of Emmet's Yodels	Lamar, Peter	Columbia 573	1902	Germany	P
Mein Gluck	Muench, Emil	Columbia 520	1905	Germany	E
Mister Dinkelspiel	Roberts, Bob	Indestructable 877	-	Germany	P
Moonlight on the Rhine	Ash, Sam	Columbia 1758	1915	Germany	P
Moonlight on the Rhine	Campbell, A. / Burr, H.	Victor 17779	1915	Germany	P
Morgen Hymne	Jorn, Karl	Columbia 1840	1915	Germany	E
Music Vots Music Must Come from Berlin	Burkhart, Maurice	Columbia 1176	-	Germany	P
My Little German Home Across the Sea	-	Edison 51909	-	Germany	P
Nacht Lichter Gruss	Muench, Emil	Columbia 514	1902	Germany	E
O Schoene Zeit	Muench, Emil	Columbia 518	1903	Germany	E
O Schone Zeit	Leonheart, Robert	Columbia 2053	1916	Germany	P
Och Muder ich will en ding	Heineman, Alex	Columbia 982	1911	Germany	E
Oh How That German Could Love	Berlin, Irving	Columbia 804	1910	Germany	E
Old Berlin March	Columbia Orchestra	Columbia 145	1908	Germany	P
Old Berlin March	United States Marine Band	Edison 10486	1911	Germany	P
On Guard (Auf de Wacht)	Columbia Orchestra	Columbia 124	1906	Germany	P
On the Banks of the Rhein with a Stein	Collins, Arthur / Harlan, Byron	Edison 9124	1906	Germany	P
On the Banks of the Rhine with a Stein	Collins & Harlin	American 31246	-	Germany	P
Prince of Pilsen Medley March	Columbia Orchestra	Columbia 135	1902	Germany	P
Rhine Song (Rhinelied)	Jorn, Karl	Columbia 1776	1915	Germany	E
Schlafe mein susse kind	-	Victor	1995	Germany	P
Schlittschulaufer (the skaters)	Columbia Orchestra	Columbia 142	1909	Germany	P
Schlummer Liedchen	Jorn, Karl	Columbia 1840	1915	Germany	E
Schmaltzes German Band	Peerless Quartet	Columbia 1918	1915	Germany	P
Schneider's Hollenfahrt	Muench, Emil	Columbia 516	1903	Germany	E
Schneidige Truppe	Emperor's Guard Band	Columbia 91	1903	Germany	E
Scholem Elechem	Littman, Pepi	Columbia 562	1904	Germany	E
Schwanlied aus Lohengrin	Kraus, Ernst	-	1904	Germany	E
Spielmann's Leben	Goritz, Otto	Columbia 2066	1916	Germany	E
Spielmannslied	Leonhardt, Robert	Berliner 42335	-	Germany	E
Stille Nacht, Heilge Nacht	Dunlap, Marguerite/ Victor Orchestra	Victor 17187	1912	Germany	P
Stille Nacht, Heilge Nacht	Matzenaur, Margaret	Columbia 5641	1914	Germany	E
Stille Nacht, Heilge Nacht	Stehl — Lufsky — Ointo Trio	Columbia 5083	1908	Germany	E
Stille Nacht, Heilge Nacht	Stehl — Lufsky — Prince	Columbia 7501	1908	Germany	E
Stille Nacht, Heilge Nacht	Arndt, Felix	Victor 17842	1914	Germany	E
Tegnerseer Landler	Strassmeier Dachauer Bauernkapelle	Columbia -	-	Germany	E
Teufels Lied	Hebrew vocal	Columbia 558	1902	Germany	P

Song Title	Name of Artist(s)	Label and Selec. No.	Year Rec.	Ethnicity/ Theme	
That Little German Band	Jolson, Al	Columbia 1356	-	Germany	P
Traumerei	Columbia Band	Columbia 88	1902	Germany	P
Traumerei	Falk, Jules	Columbia 1110	-	Germany	E
Traumerei	violin solo	American 31266	-	Germany	P
Two German Lieder Singers	-	Gramophone Shop 1007	-	Germany	P
U Buchferl Zant Schiaben	Alpinia Gangergefellfchaft	Okeh	1919	Germany	E
Uber den Sternen Ist Ruh	Muench, Emil	Columbia 519	1903	Germany	E
Uber den Sternen Ist Ruh	Deusing, W.C.	Edison 7151	1899	Germany	E
Under Prussian Banners	Columbia Orchestra	Columbia 133	1909	Germany	P
Ungeduld (Impatience)	Jorn, Karl	Columbia 1777	1915	Germany	E
Unter dem Siegesbanner	Emperor's Guard Band	Columbia 87	1909	Germany	E
Vater, Musser, Schwester, Brudder	Muench, Emil	Columbia 521	1902	Germany	E
Verlassen	Classen, Julia	Columbia 5361	1911	Germany	E
Verschwender Hobelied — (Carpenter's Place)	Jorn, Karl	Columbia 1795	1915	Germany	E
Wald Andacht	Weil, Herman	Columbia 5864	1916	Germany	E
We Don't Want the Bacon (What We Want Is a Piece of the Rhine)	Peerless Quartet	Gramophone 18505	-	Germany	P
Wei mag es Gekommen Sein	Muench, Emil	Columbia 524	1903	Germany	E
Wein Bleibt Wein	Prince's Band	Columbia 1256	-	Germany	P
Weisusu von Achschweirosh	Seiden, Frank	Columbia 556	1904	Germany	E
Wenn Schwalben Heimats Zie	Jorn, Karl	Columbia 1841	1915	Germany	E
Weseuref	Goldin Quartet	Columbia 569	1905	Germany	P
When Uncle Joe Steps Into Heinie Land	Collins, Arthur / Harlan, Byron	Victor 18492	1918	Germany	P
Wohlauf noch Getrunken	Bennhan, Carl	Berliner 634	1899	Germany	E
Yodel Marsch	Graus Choir	Berliner 3192	1898	Germany	E
Zauberlied	Alma, Marian	Berliner 42317	-	Germany	E
Zeigeuner Weisen	Falk, Jules	Columbia 1518	1914	Germany	E
Zwei Auglein Braun	Muench, Emil	Columbia 522	1902	Germany	E
British Grenadiers	Fife & Drum Corps	Columbia 1654	1914	England	E
Christmas Time in Merry England	-	Edison	1906	England	E
For King and Country	Hamilton, Edward	Victor 17711	1914	England	E
God Save the King	Columbia Band	Columbia 65	1901	England	P
God Save the King	New York Military Band	Edison	1911	England	P
God Save the Queen	Sousa's Band	Berliner 148	1898	England	P
Imperial Edward Coronation	Columbia Band	Columbia 65	1902	England	P
It's a Long Way to Tipperary	American Quartet	Victor 17639	1914	England	P
It's a Long Way to Tipperary	Bispham, David	Columbia 5629	1914	England	E
It's a Long Way to Tipperary	Kirby, Stanley	Columbia 1608	1913	England	E
It's a Long Way to Tipperary	Prince's Band	Columbia 1620	1914	England	P
It's a Long Way to Tipperary	Victor Band	Victor 17673	1914	England	P
Little English Girl March	Ellery Band	Columbia 5391	1911	England	E
Rule Britannia	Columbia Band	Columbia 974	1910	England	P
Rule Britannia	New York Military Band	Edison 50186	-	England	P
The Further It Is from Tipperary	Murray, Billy	Edison	-	England	P
Twickenham Ferry	Miller, Reed	Columbia 5276	1910	England	P
Wake Up England March	Band of HM Coldstream Guards	Victor 17759	1915	England	E
Where the Oceans Meet in Panama	Kaufman, Irving	Victor 17699	1914	England	P
While London Sleeps	Foster, Charles	Berliner 2677	1899	England	E
Your King and Your Country Want You	Baker, Elsie	Victor 17711	1914	England	P
Allah Give Me Mine	McClaskey, Harry	Victor 17977	1915	Exotic	P
Allah's Holiday	Jausas' Society Orchestra	Edison 50424	-	Exotic	P
Allah's Holiday	Prince's Band	Columbia 5945	1917	Exotic	P
Allah's Holiday	Smith, Joseph & His Orchestra	Victor 18246	1917	Exotic	P
Along the Way to Damascus	Hickman, Art & His Orchestra	Columbia 2917	1919	Exotic	P
Arab Love Song	Jones, Ada	Edison 10078	1909	Exotic	P
Arab Love Song	MacDonough, Harry	Victor 16803	-	Exotic	P
Arab Love Song	Murray, Billy	Columbia 628	1909	Exotic	P
Arab Love Song	Prince's Band	Columbia 5094	1908	Exotic	P

Song Title	Name of Artist(s)	Label and Selec. No.	Year Rec.	Ethnicity/ Theme	
Arabian Dreams	Louise, Helen / Ferera, Frank	Columbia 2574	1918	Exotic	P
Arabian Nights	Schwab, Charles Orchestra	Okeh 1238	1919	Exotic	P
Arabian Nights	Sharock Trio	Okeh 1225	1919	Exotic	P
Arabian Nights	Waldorf Astoria Orchestra	Victor 18536	1918	Exotic	P
Arabian Serenade	Prince's Orchestra	Columbia 2501	1917	Exotic	P
Araby	MacDonough, Harry	Victor 17889	1915	Exotic	P
Araby/Medley	Conway,	Victor 35496	-	Exotic	P
Bedouin Love Song	Hooley, William	Edison 4903	1899	Exotic	P
Bedouin Love Song	Myers, John	Berliner 965	1896	Exotic	P
Bedouin Love Song	Myers, John	Edison 7839	1901	Exotic	P
Bedouin Love Song	Stanley, Frank	Columbia 427	1907	Exotic	P
Burmah Moon	Ash, Sam	Okeh 1205	1919	Exotic	P
Burmese Bells	Hickman, Art & His Orchestra	Columbia 2841	1919	Exotic	P
Cairo One Step	Hickman, Art & His Orchestra	Columbia 2858	1919	Exotic	P
Cleopatra Had a Jazz Band	Ash, Sam	Columbia -	1917	Exotic	P
Cleopatra Had a Jazz Band	Carus, Emma	-	1917	Exotic	P
Cleopatra Had a Jazz Band	Prince's Band	Columbia -	1917	Exotic	P
Cleopatra Had a Jazz Band	Tucker, Sophie	-	1917	Exotic	P
Constantinople	Wheaton, Anna	Columbia 2295	1917	Exotic	P
Dardanella	Murray, Billy	Victor	1919	Exotic	P
Down in Bom Bombay	Collins, Arthur / Harlan, Byron	Victor 17841	1915	Exotic	P
Down in Hindustan	Fuller's, Earl Novelty Orchestra	Columbia 2595	1918	Exotic	P
Egyptland	Fuller's, Earl Novelty Orchestra	Columbia 2722	1919	Exotic	P
Egyptland	Six Brown Brothers	Victor 18562	1919	Exotic	P
Ethiopian Mardi Gras	Ossman, Vess	Berliner 867	1900	Exotic	P
Fakir Selling Corn Cure	Graham, George	Berliner 639Y	1897	Exotic	P
Ginger Bread Man — Jap Doll	Kline, Olive	Victor 18015	1916	Exotic	P
Gunga Din	Humphrey, Harry	Columbia 6033	1916	Exotic	P
Hindustan	All Star Trio	Edison 50447	-	Exotic	P
Hindustan	Burr, Henry	-	1918	Exotic	P
Hindustan	Campbell, A. / Burr, H.	Columbia 2661	1918	Exotic	P
Hindustan	Jockers Brothers	Columbia -	1918	Exotic	P
Hindustan	Smith, Joseph & His Orchestra	Victor 18507	1918	Exotic	P
I Was Born in Turkey	Farkoa, Maurice	Berliner 2701	1899	Exotic	P
I'll Sing Thee Songs of Araby	Burr, Henry	Columbia 5028	1906	Exotic	P
I'll Sing Thee Songs of Araby	Chalmers, Thomas	Edison 10065	1909	Exotic	P
I'll Sing Thee Songs of Araby	Turner, Alan	Columbia 659	1908	Exotic	P
I'm on My Way to Mandalay	Campbell, A. / Burr, H.	Victor 17503	1913	Exotic	P
In My Harem	Van Brunt, Walter	Columbia 1302	-	Exotic	P
Katinka: Allah's Holiday	Columbia Saxophone Sextet	Columbia 2203	1917	Exotic	P
Lovely Daughter of Allah	-	-	-	Exotic	P
Maori — Samoan Rag	Bernard, Mike	Columbia 1427	-	Exotic	P
My Cairo Love	Allstar Trio	Victor 18602	1919	Exotic	P
My Cairo Love	Knecht's Joseph Waldorf orchestra	Columbia 2764	1919	Exotic	P
My Maid form Hindustan	Collins, Arthur	Edison 8232	1902	Exotic	P
Not So Very Far from Zanzibar	Sterling Trio	Columbia 2083	1916	Exotic	P
Old Time Street Fakir	Porter, Steve / Harlan, Byron	Columbia 1036	1911	Exotic	P
On the Bosporous	Prince's Orchestra	Columbia 841	1910	Exotic	P
On the Road to Mandalay	Broderick, George	Edison 7648	1901	Exotic	P
On the Road to Mandalay	Humphrey, Harry	Columbia 6033	1917	Exotic	P
On the Road to Mandalay	Phillips, Joe	Okeh 1191	1919	Exotic	P
On the Road to Mandalay	Quinn, Dan	Edison 6935	1899	Exotic	P
On the Streets of Cairo	Hickman, Art & His Orchestra	Columbia 2811	1919	Exotic	P
Rose of Mandalay	Hickman, Art & His Orchestra	Columbia 2917	1919	Exotic	P
Sahara	Walker, Esther	Victor 18613	1919	Exotic	P
Salute to the Sultan	Remington Typewriter Band	Columbia 1433	-	Exotic	P
Siam	American Quartet	Victor 17993	1916	Exotic	P
Siam Fox Trot	Prince's Band	Columbia 5827	1916	Exotic	P
Siamese National Hymn	Prince's Band	Columbia 39	1905	Exotic	P
Siamese Patrol	Columbia Band	Columbia 1657	1914	Exotic	P
Siamese Patrol	Edison Military Band	Edison 9661	1907	Exotic	P
Singapore	Fields, Barney	Victor 18529	1919	Exotic	P

Song Title	Name of Artist(s)	Label and Selec. No.	Year Rec.	Ethnicity/ Theme	
Singapore	Green Brothers	Okeh 1199	1919	Exotic	P
Singapore Medley	Fuller's, Earl Novelty Orchestra	Columbia 2686	1918	Exotic	P
Sounds from Africa	banjo	Edison 2631	1897	Exotic	P
Sreets of Cairo	Quinn, Dan	Berliner 171Z	1895	Exotic	P
Street Fakir	Graham, George	Berliner 638Y	1896	Exotic	P
Sunny South Medley	Pryor, Arthur	Victor 16819	-	Exotic	P
Sweet Siamese	Frantzen's Orchestra	Victor 18546	1919	Exotic	P
Sweet Siamese	Fuller's, Earl Novelty Orchestra	Columbia 2712	1919	Exotic	P
Sweet Siamese	Green Brothers	Okeh 1196	1919	Exotic	P
There's Egypt in Your Dreamy Eyes	Dixon, Raymond	Victor 18238	1917	Exotic	P
There's Egypt in Your Dreamy Eyes	Wilson, George	Columbia 2168	1916	Exotic	P
Turkestan	American Quartet	Columbia -	1919	Exotic	P
Turkestan	Premier American Quartet	Okeh 1205	1919	Exotic	P
Turkish March	Creatore Band	Columbia 5363	1911	Exotic	P
Turkish Patrol	Columbia Band	Columbia 72	1902	Exotic	P
Under the Yellow Arabian Moon	Murray, Billy / Kaufman, Irving	Victor 17923	1915	Exotic	P
War of the Worlds— In Siam	Burr, Henry	Columbia 1630	1914	Exotic	P
Way Down in Borneo	Collins, Arthur / Harlan, Byron	Columbia 2004	1916	Exotic	P
Wondrous Eyes of Araby	Hindermeyer, Harvey	Okeh 1097	1918	Exotic	P
Yukaloo— My Pretty South Sea Island Lady	Sterling Trio	Victor 18227	1917	Exotic	P
A La Bien Aimee	Eisler, Paul	Okeh 1247	1919	France	P
Don't Cry Frenchy Don't Cry	Hart, Charles / Shaw, Elliott	Victor 18538	1919	France	P
Frenchie Come to Yankee Land	Kaufman, Irving	Okeh 1228	1919	France	P
Frenchy Come to Yankee Land	Fields, Arthur	Columbia 2727	1919	France	P
Goodbye Frenchy	Peerless Quartet	Victor 18514	1918	France	P
La Marsellaise	Sousa's Band	Berliner 117	1898	France	P
La Marsellaise	Columbia Band	Columbia 81	1901	France	P
La Marsellaise	Edison Grand Concert Band	Edison 40	1896	France	P
La Marsellaise	Giannini, Ferrussio	Berliner 901	1896	France	P
La Marsellaise	Occellier, Victor	Columbia 5030	1906	France	E
La Marsellaise	Rothier, Leon	Columbia 5823	1916	France	P
La Marsellaise	Sousa's Band	Berliner 117y	1898	France	P
Laughing Song (in French)	Farkoa, Maurice	Berliner 1302	1896	France	E
Le Fou Rire	Farkoa, Maurice	Berliner 2125	1898	France	E
Le Renard et la Petite Poule	Clement, Margaret	Columbia 7542	-	France	E
Les Blondes	Farkoa, Maurice	Berliner 2129	1898	France	E
Loin du Bal	Columbia Band	Columbia 90	1901	France	P
Lorraine, My Beautiful Alsace	Burr, Henry	Columbia 2490	1917	France	P
Mamselle	Gilman, Mabel	-	1900	France	P
The Marseillaise	Hamilton, Edward	Victor 18338	1917	France	P
Marsellaise	Sousa's Band	Victor 17668	1909	France	P
Oh Frenchy	Gordon, Elaine	Okeh 1061	1918	France	P
Oh Frenchy	Smith, Joseph & His Orchestra	Victor 18511	1918	France	P
On the Road to Calais	Jolson, Al	Columbia 2690	1918	France	P
Oui, Oui, Marie	Fields, Arthur	Gramophone 18505	-	France	P
Over There**	Caruso, Enrico	Victor 87294	-	France	P
Parisienne March	Banda Rossa	Berliner 118	1898	France	P
When Its Night Time Down in Burgundy	Prince's Band	Columbia 5607	1914	France	P
Flag of Guatemala	Royal Marimba Band	Columbia 1936	1915	Guatemala	P
Guatemala Panama March	Hurtado Brothers Marimba Orchestra	Victor 18040	1916	Guatemala	E
Guatemalan Girls March	Royal Marimba Band	Columbia 1880	1915	Guatemala	E
Across the Sea	Leite, June Ululani	Hawaiian	1919	Hawaii	E
Ahi Ahi Poakolu	Paka, Toots Hawaiian Company	Columbia 1588	1914	Hawaii	E
Aiaihea	Hawaiian Troupe	Victor 18578	1913	Hawaii	E
Ainahau	Lua, Pali / Kaili, David	Victor 17864	1914	Hawaii	E
Akahi Elua Akolu (One, Two, Three)	Royal Hawaiian Troubadors	American 30940	1905	Hawaii	E
Akahi Hoi	Hawaiian Troupe	Victor 18575	1913	Hawaii	E

Song Title	Name of Artist(s)	Label and Selec. No.	Year Rec.	Ethnicity/ Theme	
Akahi Hoi	Paka, Toots Hawaiian Company	Victor 18585	1914	Hawaii	E
Akahi Hoi (Only One)	Royal Hawaiian Troubadors	American 30964	1905	Hawaii	E
Aloha Land	Louise, Helen / Ferera, Frank	Columbia 2362	1917	Hawaii	E
Aloha Land	Louise, Helen / Ferera, Frank	Victor 18380	1917	Hawaii	E
Aloha Oe	Columbia Stellar Quartet	Columbia 5960	1916	Hawaii	P
Aloha Oe	Gluck, Alma	Victor 74534	1916	Hawaii	P
Aloha Oe	Hawaiian Troupe	Victor 18577	1913	Hawaii	E
Aloha Oe	Henton, Benne H. / Conway's Band	Victor 18344	1917	Hawaii	E
Aloha Oe	Hilo Hawaiian Band (Pryor)	Victor 18579	1913	Hawaii	E
Aloha Oe	Lua, Pali / Kaili, David	Victor 17803	1915	Hawaii	E
Aloha Oe	orchestra (-)	Berliner 515	1898	Hawaii	E
Aloha Oe	Paka, Toots Hawaiian Company	Columbia 1616	1914	Hawaii	E
Aloha Oe	Prince's Orchestra	Columbia 1667	1914	Hawaii	E
Aloha Oe	Rose, E. K.	Victor 35622	1917	Hawaii	P
Aloha Oe	Royal Hawaiian Troubadors	American 30936	1905	Hawaii	E
Aloha Oe	Sterling Trio	Okeh 1046	1918	Hawaii	P
Aloha Oe Waltz	Blue & White Marimba Band	Columbia 2136	1916	Hawaii	P
Along the Waikiki Way	Louise, Helen / Ferera, Frank	Columbia 2362	1917	Hawaii	E
Along the Way	Louise, Helen / Ferera, Frank	Okeh 4192	-	Hawaii	E
Along the Way to Waikiki	Peerless Quartet	Victor 18326	1917	Hawaii	P
Aole Wau E Poina Laoe (I Will Never Forget You)	Royal Hawaiian Troubadors	American 30942	1905	Hawaii	E
Back to My Sunny Honoloo	Reed, James / Harrison, Charles	Columbia 2060	1916	Hawaii	P
Beautiful Keala (mountain)	Royal Hawaiian Troubadors	American 30669	1905	Hawaii	E
By the Sad Luana Shore	Brunt, Walter van	Edison 50378	-	Hawaii	P
By the Sad Luana Shore	Campbell, Albert / Burr, Henry	Columbia 2038	1916	Hawaii	P
By the Sad Luana Shore	Farrell, Margaret	Victor 18105	1916	Hawaii	P
Dear Old Honolulu	Wright, Horace / Dietrich, Rene	Columbia 2257	-	Hawaii	P
Down Honolulu Way	Green, Alice / Dixon, Bob	Victor 18114	1916	Hawaii	P
Down Honolulu Way	Peerless Quartet	Columbia 2060	1916	Hawaii	P
Everybody Hula	Louise, Helen / Ferera, Frank	Columbia 2253	1917	Hawaii	P
Fair Hawaii	Broadway Quartet	Columbia 2109	1916	Hawaii	P
Fair Hawaii	Brown, Edna / Reed, James	Victor 18032	1916	Hawaii	P
Fair Hawaii	Brunt, Walter van	Edison 50373	-	Hawaii	P
Far Away in Honolulu	Van & Schenk	Victor 18269	1917	Hawaii	P
Ghost of the Ukelele	King, Charles / Brice, Elizabeth	Columbia 2257	1917	Hawaii	P
Ghost of the Ukelele	Peerless Quartet	Victor 18254	1917	Hawaii	P
Halona	Paka, Toots Hawaiian Company	Victor 18586	1914	Hawaii	E
Hapa Haole Hula Girl	Louise, Helen / Ferera, Frank	Columbia 1935	1915	Hawaii	E
Hapa Haole Hula Girl	Louise, Helen / Ferera, Frank	Edison 50392	-	Hawaii	E
Hawaii and You	Reed, James / Harrison, Charles	Columbia 2168	1916	Hawaii	P
Hawaii I'm Lonesome for You	Louise, Helen / Ferera, Frank	Victor 18380	1917	Hawaii	E
Hawaii Ponoi	Kiawea, S. Hawaiian Troupe	Victor 18576	1913	Hawaii	E
Hawaiian Blues	Prince's Band	Columbia 5971	1917	Hawaii	P
Hawaiian Breezes	Louise, Helen / Ferera, Frank	Columbia 2673	1918	Hawaii	E
Hawaiian Butterfly	King, Charles / Brice, Elizabeth	Columbia 2226	1917	Hawaii	P
Hawaiian Butterfly	Prince's Band	Columbia 5967	1917	Hawaii	P
Hawaiian Butterfly	Sterling Trio	Victor 18272	1917	Hawaii	P
Hawaiian Butterfly Medley	Jausas_ Society Orchestra	Edison 50424	-	Hawaii	P
Hawaiian Dreams	Louise, Helen / Ferera, Frank	Columbia 2311	1917	Hawaii	P
Hawaiian Echoes	Louise, Helen / Ferera, Frank	Victor 18147	1916	Hawaii	E
Hawaiian Echoes Medley	Louise, Helen / Ferera, Frank	Columbia 2368	1917	Hawaii	E
Hawaiian Hotel	Lua, Pali / Kaili, David	Columbia 1874	1915	Hawaii	E
Hawaiian Hours with You	Seville, Carl / Geddes, Jack	Columbia 2856	1919	Hawaii	P
Hawaiian Hula Medley	Louise, Helen / Ferera, Frank	Victor 18069	1916	Hawaii	E
Hawaiian Hula Medley	Louise, Helen / Ferera, Frank	Okeh 1029	1918	Hawaii	E
Hawaiian Love Song	Barton, Ward / Carroll, Frank	Victor 17965	1915	Hawaii	P
Hawaiian Lullaby	Campbell, A. / Burr, H.	Columbia 2781	1919	Hawaii	P
Hawaiian Lullaby	Hart, Charles / Shaw, Elliott	Victor 18597	1919	Hawaii	P
Hawaiian Medley	Paka, July	Columbia 1747	1915	Hawaii	E
Hawaiian Medley	Paka, Toots Hawaiian Company	Columbia 1616	1914	Hawaii	E

Song Title	Name of Artist(s)	Label and Selec. No.	Year Rec.	Ethnicity/ Theme	
Hawaiian Medley	Victor Military Band	Victor 17733	1915	Hawaii	P
Hawaiian Medley — Fox Trot	Hawaiian Troupe	Okeh 1172	1919	Hawaii	E
Hawaiian Medley Kamehameha	Louise, Helen / Ferera, Frank	Columbia 2158	1916	Hawaii	E
Hawaiian Medley of Hulas	Kalaluhi's, George Orchestra	Columbia 2077	1916	Hawaii	E
Hawaiian Medley One Step	Prince's Band	Columbia 5787	1916	Hawaii	P
Hawaiian Medley Two-Step	Louise, Helen / Ferera, Frank	Columbia 2016	1916	Hawaii	E
Hawaiian Medley Waltz	Hawaiian Troupe	Okeh 1244	1919	Hawaii	E
Hawaiian Medley Waltz	Prince's Orchestra	Columbia 5673	1915	Hawaii	P
Hawaiian Medley: Moana Lua Hulas	Louise, Helen / Ferera, Frank	Columbia 2457	1916	Hawaii	E
Hawaiian Melodies	Louise, Helen / Ferera, Frank	Victor 18570	1913	Hawaii	E
Hawaiian Nights	Ferera, Frank / Franchini, Frank	Columbia 2918	1918	Hawaii	E
Hawaiian Nights	Prince's Band	Columbia 5974	1917	Hawaii	P
Hawaiian Portuguese Song	Louise, Helen / Ferera, Frank	Columbia 2119	1916	Hawaii	E
Hawaiian Smiles	Yerkes Happy Six	Columbia 2760	1919	Hawaii	P
Hawaiian Waltz Medley	Lua, Pali / Kaili, David	Victor 17701	1914	Hawaii	E
Hdureu Polish Mazurka	Prince's Band	Columbia 27	-	Hawaii	P
He Lei No Kaiulani	Louise, Helen / Ferera, Frank	Columbia 2253	1917	Hawaii	E
He Lei No Kaiulani	Paka, Toots Hawaiian Company	Victor 18583	1914	Hawaii	E
Hello Aloha Hello	Campbell, Albert/Roberts, Bob	Columbia 2413	1917	Hawaii	E
Hello Aloha Hello	Prince's Band	Columbia 5996	1917	Hawaii	E
Hello Aloha Hello	Shannon Four	Victor 18401	1917	Hawaii	E
Hello Hawaii How Are You?	Chandler, Anna	Columbia 1939	1915	Hawaii	E
Hello Hawaii How Are You?	Murray, Billy	Victor 17944	1916	Hawaii	E
Hello Hawaii How Are You?	Pietro, Deiro Band	Victor 18118	1916	Hawaii	E
Hello Hawaii How Are You	Prince's Band	Columbia 5780	1916	Hawaii	E
Hiilawe (The Cascade)	Royal Hawaiian Troubadors	American 30977	1905	Hawaii	E
Hilo Hawaiian March	West, Irene Royal Hawaiian Orchestra	Victor 17767	1914	Hawaii	E
Hilo Hawaiian March	West, Irene Royal Hawaiian Troupe	Columbia 1812	1915	Hawaii	E
Hilo March	Louise, Helen / Ferera, Frank	Edison 50354	-	Hawaii	E
Ho'o Mau	Paka, Toots Hawaiian Troupe	Victor 17907	1914	Hawaii	E
Honolulu America Loves You	American Quartet	Victor 18192	1916	Hawaii	P
Honolulu America Loves You	Columbia Quartet	Columbia 2148	1916	Hawaii	P
Honolulu Blues	Peerless Quartet	Columbia 2000	1916	Hawaii	P
Honolulu Blues	Peerless Quartet	Victor 18068	1916	Hawaii	P
Honolulu Hicki Boola Boo	American Quartet	Victor 18235	1917	Hawaii	P
Honolulu Hicki Boola Boo	Knickerbocker Quartet	Columbia 2160	1916	Hawaii	P
Honolulu March	Lua, Pali / Kaili, David	Victor 17710	1914	Hawaii	E
Honolulu Rag	Lua, Pali / Kaili, David	Columbia 1861	1915	Hawaii	E
Honolulu Tomboy	Hawaiian Troupe	Victor 18572	1913	Hawaii	E
Honolulu Town	Peerless Quartet	Victor 18101	1916	Hawaii	P
Hoo Mamao Oe	Paka, Toots Hawaiian Company	Victor 18584	1914	Hawaii	E
Hoo Mau	Paka, Toots Hawaiian Company	Victor 17907	1914	Hawaii	E
Hula Hula Cake Walk	Sousa's Band	Berliner 1201	1900	Hawaii	P
Hula Medley	Lua, Pali / Kaili, David	Victor 17774	1914	Hawaii	E
I Can Hear the Ukeleles Calling Me	Reed, James / Harrison, Charles	Columbia 2259	1917	Hawaii	P
I Can Hear the Ukeleles Calling Me	Orpheus Quartet	Victor 18282	1917	Hawaii	P
I Left Her on the Beach in Honolulu	MacDonough, Harry	Victor 18104	1916	Hawaii	P
I Left Her on the Beach at Honolulu	Brunt, Walter van	Edison 50378	-	Hawaii	P
I Lost My Heart in Honolulu	Prince's Band	Columbia 5862	1916	Hawaii	P
I Lost My Heart in Honolulu	Sterling Trio	Columbia 2045	1916	Hawaii	P
I Lost My Heart in Honolulu	Stuart / Harrison	Victor 18114	1916	Hawaii	P
I Love You Honolulu	Wilson, George / Lewis, Robert	Columbia 2300	1917	Hawaii	P
I'm Down in Honolulu Looking Them Over	Jolson, Al	Columbia 2143	1916	Hawaii	P
Isles of Aloha	Wright, Horace / Deutsch, Rene	Victor 18347	1917	Hawaii	P
Kai Maia Oka Maoli	Louise, Helen / Ferera, Frank	Victor 18157	1916	Hawaii	E
Kai Malino	Paka, Toots Hawaiian Company	Victor 18584	1914	Hawaii	E
Kai Malino	Paka, Toots Hawaiian Company	Columbia 1879	1915	Hawaii	E
Kaiwi Waltz	Lua, Pali / Kaili, David	Columbia 1861	1915	Hawaii	E

Song Title	Name of Artist(s)	Label and Selec. No.	Year Rec.	Ethnicity/ Theme	
Kalua O Pua	Paka, Toots Hawaiian Company	Victor 18585	1914	Hawaii	E
Kamawe	Paka, Toots Hawaiian Company	Victor 18581	1914	Hawaii	E
Kamawee Hula — Move Your Feet	Paka, Toots Hawaiian Company	Columbia 1588	1914	Hawaii	E
Kamehameha	Louise, Helen / Ferera, Frank	Victor 18090	1916	Hawaii	E
Kanilehua (I Love You)	Royal Hawaiian Troubadors	American 30946	1905	Hawaii	E
Kaowe Ake Kai	Paka, Toots Hawaiian Company	Victor 18580	1914	Hawaii	E
Kaowe Ake Kai (Roaring Sea)	Paka, Toots Hawaiian Company	Columbia 1571	1914	Hawaii	E
Kaua I Ka Huahuai	Hawaiian Quintette	Victor 18568	1913	Hawaii	E
Kauai Kahio Medley	Biltmore Kalaluhi Hawaiian Orchestra	Columbia 2200	1916	Hawaii	E
Kauaika Huahuai	Hawaiian Troupe	Victor 18568	1913	Hawaii	E
Kawaihau Waltz	Louise, Helen / Ferera, Frank	Victor 17892	1915	Hawaii	E
Kawaihau Waltz	Louise, Helen / Ferera, Frank	Columbia 2673	1918	Hawaii	E
Kawaihau Waltz	Lua, Pali / Kaili, David	Victor 17863	1914	Hawaii	E
Kawaiihau Waltz	Paka, July	Columbia 1747	1915	Hawaii	E
Kawiliwiliwai	Aeko, W. Hawaiian Troupe	Victor 18567	1913	Hawaii	E
Ke Kaupu (The Seagull)	Royal Hawaiian Troubadors	American 30972	1905	Hawaii	E
Kilima Waltz	Lua, Pali / Kaili, David	Victor 17701	1914	Hawaii	E
Kilima Waltz	Lua, Pali / Kaili, David	Columbia 1874	1915	Hawaii	E
Ko Maka Palupalu	Paka, Toots Hawaiian Company	Victor 17867	1914	Hawaii	E
Kohala March	Hawaiian Troupe	Okeh 1244	1919	Hawaii	E
Kohala March	Lua, Pali / Kaili, David	Victor 17710	1914	Hawaii	E
Kohala March	Lua, Pali / Kaili, David	Columbia 1812	1915	Hawaii	E
Kokohi (Native Hawaiian Song)	Waiaiole, Ben	Victor 18576	1913	Hawaii	E
Ku'u Home (My Home, aka Old Plantation)	Kaiawe, S. M. with Hawaiian Quintette	Victor 18577	1913	Hawaii	E
Kumukahi	Hawaiian Troupe	Victor 18578	1913	Hawaii	E
Kuu Home	Hawaiian Troupe	Victor 18577	1913	Hawaii	E
La Paloma	Louise, Helen / Ferera, Frank	Columbia 2405	1917	Hawaii	P
Laika Wai Mapuna	Paka, Toots Hawaiian Company	Victor 17907	1914	Hawaii	E
Lanihuli	Paka, Toots Hawaiian Company	Victor 18586	1914	Hawaii	E
Lei Aloha	Wright, Horace / Deutsch, Rene	Victor 18228	1916	Hawaii	P
Lei Awapuhi (The Ginger Wreath)	Royal Hawaiian Troubadors	American 30943	1905	Hawaii	E
Lei Ia Aloha	Paka, Toots Hawaiian Company	Victor 18583	1914	Hawaii	E
Lei Poni Moi (Wreath of carnations)	Rose, E. R. Hawaiian Quintet	Victor 18571	1913	Hawaii	E
Lei Rose o Kawika	Paka, Toots Hawaiian Company	Victor 18580	1914	Hawaii	E
Lelia — Pasillo Waltz	Louise, Helen / Ferera, Frank	Columbia 2311	1917	Hawaii	E
Lia Ika Wai Mapuna	Paka, Toots Hawaiian Company	Columbia 1571	1914	Hawaii	E
Little Honolulu Lou	Harrison, Charles	Victor 17883	1915	Hawaii	P
Luana Lou	Peerless Quartet	Victor 17992	1916	Hawaii	P
Mahina Malamalama	Kalani, Pete and Kalei	Columbia 2457	1916	Hawaii	E
Mahina Malamalama	Kalani, Pete Octet	Columbia 1985	1916	Hawaii	E
Mai Poina Oe Iau	Hawaiian Troupe	Victor 18569	1913	Hawaii	E
Maid of Honolulu	Kiawea, S. Hawaiian Troupe	Victor 18567	1913	Hawaii	E
Maid of Honolulu	Lua, Pali / Kaili, David	Victor 17859	1915	Hawaii	E
Malanai	Royal Hawaiian Troubadors	American 30965	1905	Hawaii	E
Malanai Anu Ka Makani	Louise, Helen / Ferera, Frank	Columbia 2918	1918	Hawaii	E
Malu Iki Au (Always Ahead)	Royal Hawaiian Troubadors	American 30975	1905	Hawaii	E
Maui Aloha	Louise, Helen / Ferera, Frank	Victor 18087	1916	Hawaii	E
Maui Girl	Hawaiian Quintet	Victor 18579	1913	Hawaii	E
Maui Girl	Paka, Toots Hawaiian Company	Columbia 1879	1915	Hawaii	E
Maui Girl	Royal Hawaiian Troubadors	American 30945	1905	Hawaii	E
Mauna Kea	Kiawea, S. Hawaiian Troupe	Victor 18574	1913	Hawaii	E
Mauna Kea	Louise, Helen / Ferera, Frank	Columbia 2033	1915	Hawaii	E
Mauna Loa (Hawaiian Two-Step)	Royal Hawaiian Troubadors	American 30937	1905	Hawaii	E
Maunakea	Clark, Henry	Columbia 1967	1916	Hawaii	E
Medley of Hawaiian Melodies: Haloma Lee Mamo	Biltmore Kalaluhi Hawaiian Orchestra	Columbia 2200	1916	Hawaii	E
Medley of Hawaiian Waltzes	Louise, Helen / Ferera, Frank	Columbia 1814	1915	Hawaii	E
Medley of Hawaiian Airs — No. 1	Louise and Ferreia	Edison 50354	-	Hawaii	E
Medley of Hawaiian Airs — No. 2	Louise and Ferreia	Edison 50369	-	Hawaii	E
Mela Hula	Jocker Brothers	Columbia 2292	1917	Hawaii	P

Song Title	Name of Artist(s)	Label and Selec. No.	Year Rec.	Ethnicity/ Theme	
Meleana	Lua, Pali / Kaili, David	Victor 17864	1914	Hawaii	E
Mo-Ana-Hawaiian Waltz	Athenian Mandolin Quartet	Victor 18057	1916	Hawaii	P
Moana Hawaiian Waltz	Prince's Band	Columbia 5825	1916	Hawaii	P
Moana Lua (Two Oceans)	Royal Hawaiian Troubadors	American 30973	1905	Hawaii	E
Moana Lua Hawaiian Dance Song	Waiaiole, Ben	Victor 18570	1913	Hawaii	E
Moani Keala (Sweet Love)	Royal Hawaiian Troubadors	American 30950	1905	Hawaii	E
Moe Uhane Waltz	Louise, Helen / Ferera, Frank	Victor 17880	1915	Hawaii	E
The More I See Hawaii, the More I Like New York	O'Connell, Margaret	Columbia 2299	1917	Hawaii	P
My Bird of Paradise	Louise, Helen / Ferera, Frank	Victor 17892	1915	Hawaii	E
My Bird of Paradise	Prince's Band	Columbia 5688	1915	Hawaii	P
My Hawaii	Louise, Helen / Ferera, Frank	Columbia 2509	1918	Hawaii	E
My Hawaii You're Calling Me	Orpheus Quartet	Victor 18326	1917	Hawaii	P
My Hawaiian Medley	Wright, Horace / Deutsch, Rene	Victor 18228	1916	Hawaii	P
My Hawaiian Sunshine	Ash, Sam / Lewis, Robert	Columbia 2154	1916	Hawaii	P
My Hawaiian Sunshine	Campbell, A. / Burr, H.	Victor 18202	1916	Hawaii	P
My Hawaiian Sunshine	Ossman, Vess Banjo Orchestra	Columbia 5928	1916	Hawaii	P
My Hawaiian Sunshine	Prince's Band	Columbia 5951	1917	Hawaii	P
My Honolulu Hula Girl	Rose, E. R. Hawaiian Quintet	Victor 18573	1913	Hawaii	E
My Honolulu Hula Girl	Wright, Horace / Deutsch, Rene	Victor 18159	1916	Hawaii	P
My Honolulu Lady	Quinn, Dan	Edison 6930	1899	Hawaii	P
My Hula Hula Love	Metropolitan Quartet	Edison 10515	1911	Hawaii	P
My Hula Love	Lua, Pali / Kaili, David	Victor 17863	1915	Hawaii	E
My Hula Maid	Harrison, James / Reed, James	Victor 17812	1915	Hawaii	P
My Hula Maid	Reed, James / Harrison, Charles	Columbia 1789	1915	Hawaii	P
My Luau Girl	Wright, Horace / Deutsch, Rene	Victor 18132	1916	Hawaii	P
My Rose of Waikiki	Campbell, Albert/Roberts, Bob	Columbia 2413	1917	Hawaii	P
My Waikiki Ukelele Girl	Kaufman, Irving	Victor 18202	1916	Hawaii	P
Myona Hawaiian Waltz	Prince's Band	Columbia 5965	1917	Hawaii	P
Na Leio Hawaii	Holstein, Robert / Kalani, Pete	Columbia 1985	1916	Hawaii	E
Ninipo	Paka, Toots Hawaiian Company	Victor 18581	1914	Hawaii	E
Ninipo (Thinking of You)	Royal Hawaiian Troubadors	American 30935	1905	Hawaii	E
O'Brien Is Learning to Talk Hawaiian	Seagle, Oscar	Columbia 2166	1916	Hawaii	P
O'Brien Is Learning to Talk Hawaiian	Wright, Horace	Victor 18167	1916	Hawaii	P
Oh How She Could Yacki Wacki Woo	Collins, Arthur / Harlan, Byron	Victor 18110	1916	Hawaii	P
On Hoko Moko Isle	Collins, Arthur / Harlan, Byron	Columbia 1965	1916	Hawaii	P
On Hoko Moko Isle	Collins, Arthur / Harlan, Byron	Victor 17971	1916	Hawaii	P
On Honolulu Bay	Peerless Quartet	Victor 18212	1916	Hawaii	P
On the Beach at Waikiki	Kalahuli Hawaiians vi	Victor 17966	1916	Hawaii	E
On the Beach at Waikiki	Louise, Helen / Ferera, Frank	Columbia 1935	1915	Hawaii	E
On the Beach in Waikiki	Dietrick, Rene / Louise/Ferera	Victor 18132	1916	Hawaii	E
On the Beach in Waikiki	Louise, Helen / Ferera, Frank	Victor 17880	1915	Hawaii	E
On the Beach medley	Louise, Helen / Ferera, Frank	Edison 50369	-	Hawaii	E
On the Holo Moko Isle	Prince's Band	Columbia 5827	1916	Hawaii	P
One Two Three Four	Paka, Toots Hawaiian Company	Columbia 1702	1915	Hawaii	E
Ooe No Kai Ike (Ennui)	Royal Hawaiian Troubadors	American 30971	1905	Hawaii	E
Palakiko Blues	Louise, Helen / Ferera, Frank	Columbia 2214	1917	Hawaii	E
Papio Hula Medley	Lua, Pali / Kaili, David	Victor 17804	1914	Hawaii	E
Poli Pumehana	Paka, Toots Hawaiian Company	Victor 17867	1914	Hawaii	E
Pua Carnation	Louise, Helen / Ferera, Frank	Victor 18087	1916	Hawaii	E
Pua Carnation	Louise, Helen / Ferera, Frank	Columbia 2214	1917	Hawaii	E
Pua Mohala	Hawaiian Troupe	Victor 18575	1913	Hawaii	E
Pua Mohala	Wright, Horace / Deutsch, Rene	Victor 18347	1917	Hawaii	P
Pulupe (Apart)	Royal Hawaiian Troubadors	American 30948	1905	Hawaii	E
Puu O Hulu (I'll Be with You)	Royal Hawaiian Troubadors	American 30941	1905	Hawaii	E
Rain Tuahine	Paka, Toots Hawaiian Company	Victor 18582	1914	Hawaii	E
She Sang Aloha	Brunt, Walter van	Edison 50373	-	Hawaii	P
She Sang Aloha to Me	Broadway Quartet	Columbia 2109	1916	Hawaii	P
She Sang Aloha to Me	Orpheus Quartet / Dixon, Raymond	Victor 18032	1916	Hawaii	P
Since Mary Ann McCue Came Back from Honolulu	Chandler, Anna	Columbia 2105	1916	Hawaii	P

Song Title	Name of Artist(s)	Label and Selec. No.	Year Rec.	Ethnicity/ Theme	
Somewhere in Hawaii	Louise, Helen / Ferera, Frank	Columbia 2574	1918	Hawaii	E
Somewhere in Hawaii	Waikiki Hawaiian Orchestra	Edison 50498R	-	Hawaii	E
Song to Hawaii	Louise, Helen / Ferera, Frank	Victor 18069	1916	Hawaii	E
Song to Hawaii	Wright, Horace / Deutsch, Rene	Victor 18159	1916	Hawaii	P
Songs from Hawaii	Louise, Helen / Ferera, Frank	Columbia 2119	1915	Hawaii	E
Sweet Hawaiian Moonlight	Holt, Vivian / Rosedale, Lillian	Victor 18597	1919	Hawaii	E
Sweet Hawaiian Moonlight	Kalaluki Hawaiian orchestra	Columbia 2761	1919	Hawaii	E
Sweet Hawaiian Moonlight	Smith, Joseph & His Orchestra	Victor 18531	1919	Hawaii	E
Sweet Lei Lehua	Hawaiian Troupe	Okeh 1171	1919	Hawaii	E
Sweet Lei Lehua	Rose, E. R. Hawaiian Quintet	Victor 18572	1913	Hawaii	E
Sweet Leilehua (Sweet Flower)	Royal Hawaiian Troubadors	American 30966	1905	Hawaii	E
That Hula Hula	MacDonough, Harry	Victor 17930	1915	Hawaii	P
That Ukelele Band	Louise, Helen / Ferera, Frank	Columbia 2033	1916	Hawaii	E
They May Call you Hawaiian on Broadway	O'Connor, George	Columbia 2441	1917	Hawaii	P
They're Wearing 'Em Higher in Hawaii	Collins, Arthur / Harlan, Byron	Victor 18210	1917	Hawaii	P
They're Wearing 'Em Higher in Hawaii	Morton, Harvey	Columbia 2143	1916	Hawaii	P
They're Wearing 'Em Higher in Hawaii	Victor Band	Victor 18252	1917	Hawaii	P
Those Hawaiian Melodies	Peerless Quartet	Victor 18254	1917	Hawaii	P
Tomi Tomi	Hawaiian Quintette	Victor 16589	1913	Hawaii	E
Tomi Tomi	Hawaiian Troupe	Victor 18569	1913	Hawaii	E
Tomi Tomi (Hawaiian Hula Dance)	Royal Hawaiian Troubadors	American 30944	1905	Hawaii	E
Toots Paka Medley	Paka, Toots Hawaiian Company	Victor 18582	1914	Hawaii	E
Ua Like Noa Like	Lua, Pali / Kaili, David	Victor 17804	1914	Hawaii	E
Ua Like Noa Like (Sweet Constancy)	Royal Hawaiian Troubadors	American 30938	1905	Hawaii	E
Ua Like Noa Like	Hawaiian Troupe	Victor 18571	1913	Hawaii	E
Ua Like Noa Like	Paka, Toots Hawaiian Company	Columbia 1702	1915	Hawaii	E
Ua Pua Pila (The Well of Rain)	Royal Hawaiian Troubadors	American 30976	1905	Hawaii	F
Vahine (Flower)	Royal Hawaiian Troubadors	American 30667	1905	Hawaii	E
Waialae	Hawaiian Troupe	Victor 18574	1913	Hawaii	E
Waialae	Clark, Harry and the Kaai Glee Club	Columbia Y-30	1910	Hawaii	E
Waikiki Kamehameha (Hula Dance)	Royal Hawaiian Troubadors	American 30939	1905	Hawaii	E
Waikiki Mermaid	Louise, Helen / Ferera, Frank	Victor 18090	1916	Hawaii	E
Waikiki Mewrmaid Medley	Louise, Helen / Ferera, Frank	Columbia 2158	1916	Hawaii	E
Wailana (Still Waters)	Royal Hawaiian Troubadors	American 30947	1905	Hawaii	E
Wailana Waltz	Hawaiian Troupe	Victor 18568	1913	Hawaii	E
Wailana Waltz	Louise, Helen / Ferera, Frank	Columbia 2016	1916	Hawaii	E
Wailana Waltz	Louise, Helen / Ferera, Frank	Okeh 1029	1918	Hawaii	E
Waiu Luilululi	Louise, Helen / Ferera, Frank	Victor 18157	1916	Hawaii	E
Waiu Lulilui	Louise, Helen / Ferera, Frank	Columbia 2077	1916	Hawaii	E
Wiliwili Wai (Cascade)	Royal Hawaiian Troubadors	American 30668	1905	Hawaii	E
Yaaka Hula Hickey Dula	Collins, Arthur / Harlan, Byron	Victor 18014	1916	Hawaii	P
Yaaka Hula Hickey Dula	Jolson, Al	Columbia 1956	1916	Hawaii	P
Yaaka Hula Hickey Dula	Kopp, Howard	Columbia 2058	1916	Hawaii	P
Yock a Hilo Town	Ash, Sam	Columbia 2458	1917	Hawaii	P
A Harsfa Alatt	Berkes Hungarian Orchestra	Victor 17800	-	Hungary	E
Hungarian Czardas	Moskowitz, Joseph	Victor 17973	1916	Hungary	P
Hungarian Dance #6	Prince's Orchestra	Columbia 1095	1911	Hungary	P
Hungarian Lustspiel Overture	Edison Concert Band	Edison 50088	-	Hungary	P
Hungarian Rag	Prince's Band	Columbia 5541	1913	Hungary	P
All Erin's Calling Mavoureen	Harrison, Charles	Victor 18111	1916	Ireland	E
Along the Rocky Road to Dublin	American Quartet	Victor 17900	1915	Ireland	P
Along the Rocky Road to Dublin	Farrell, Margaret	Columbia 1920	1915	Ireland	E
Are You the O'Reilly	Columbia Stellar Quartet	Columbia 1783	1915	Ireland	P
As Long as the Shamrock Grows	Van Brunt, Walter	Columbia 1174	-	Ireland	P
Backyard Conversation Between Two Irish Women	Porter, Steve	Columbia 373	1901	Ireland	P
Bally Mooney and Billy Magee	Harrison, James	Columbia 1846	1915	Ireland	P

Song Title	Name of Artist(s)	Label and Selec. No.	Year Rec.	Ethnicity/ Theme	
Bally Mooney and Billy Magee	Murray, Billy	Victor 17885	1915	Ireland	P
Barney O'Hea	Nielsen, Alice	Columbia 5711	1915	Ireland	P
Because You're Irish	American Quartet	Victor 18279	1917	Ireland	P
Because You're Irish	Donovan, Hugh	Columbia 2263	1917	Ireland	E
Bells of Saint Mary's	Alda, Frances	Victor	1917	Ireland	P
Bells of Saint Mary's	Baker, Kenny	Victor	1917	Ireland	P
Bit o Blarney	Edison Grand Concert Band	Edison 8742	1904	Ireland	P
Bit o Blarney	Favor, Edward	Edison 8779	1904	Ireland	E
A Bit of Blarney	Columbia Band	Columbia 93	1904	Ireland	P
A Bit of Blarney	Ossman, Vess	American 30908	1905	Ireland	P
A Bit of Blarney	Sabel, Josephine	-	1904	Ireland	P
Black America	banjo	Edison 2602	1897	Ireland	P
Blarney	Bayes, Nora; Norworth, Jack	-	1909	Ireland	P
Bonnie Jean	Myers, John	Columbia 361	1906	Ireland	P
Bonnie Kate: Medley of Irish Reels	Kimmel, John	Victor 18998	1916	Ireland	P
Calligan — Call Again	Jose, R. J.	Victor	1900	Ireland	P
Calligan — Call Again	Natus, Joseph	Victor	1900	Ireland	P
Casey (12 add'l)	various	Edison 3800+	1898	Ireland	P
Casey and His Gang of Irish Laborers	White, James	Edison 7285	1899	Ireland	E
Casey and the Dude in a Street Car	Hunting, Russell	Edison 8360	1903	Ireland	E
Casey as Umpire at a Ball Game	Hunting, Russell	-	1898	Ireland	E
Casey at Home	Casey, Michael	Columbia 1972	1916	Ireland	E
Casey Courting His Girl	Kaiser, John	-	1905	Ireland	E
Casey Putting His Baby to Sleep	Huntin, Russell	Berliner 672	1897	Ireland	E
Casey Takes the Census	Casey, Michael	Columbia 1908	1915	Ireland	E
Christmas Morning at Clancy's	Porter, Steve	Victor	1911	Ireland	E
Clancy's Prize Waltz Contest	Spencer, Len	-	1904	Ireland	E
Cohan's Pet Names	Clarke, Herbert	Columbia 626	1908	Ireland	P
Cohan's Rag	Collins / Harlan	Columbia 583	1907	Ireland	P
Cohan's Rag Babe	Collins, Arthur	Edison 9934	1908	Ireland	E
Come Back to Erin	Columbia Stellar Quartet	Columbia 1751	1915	Ireland	P
Come Back to Erin	Harrison, Charles	Columbia 1144	-	Ireland	E
Come Back to Erin	McKee Trio	Victor 17995	1916	Ireland	E
Come Back to Erin	Myers, John	Columbia 445	1902	Ireland	P
Come Back to Erin Mona Darling	Harrison, James / Reed, James	Victor 17985	1916	Ireland	E
Come Back to Erin, Mona Darling	Reed, James / Harrison, Charles	Columbia 1968	1916	Ireland	E
Come Down McGinty (Irish Sketch)	Campbell, Albert/Roberts, Bob	-	1906	Ireland	E
Dancing 'Neath the Irish Moon	Peerless Quartet	Columbia 1773	1915	Ireland	P
Danny Boy	Schumann-Heink, Ernestine	Victor	1913	Ireland	P
Danny Boy	Steber, Eleanor	Victor	1913	Ireland	P
Daughter of Erin	Stuart, Herbert	Columbia 1676	1914	Ireland	E
Daughter of Rosie O'Grady	Victor Novelty Orchestra	Victor	1918	Ireland	P
Dear Little Shamrock	Ewing, Gerald	Columbia 784	1909	Ireland	E
Dear Old Fashioned Irish Songs	Burr, Henry	Columbia 1951	1915	Ireland	E
Dear Old Fashioned Irish Songs	Murray, Billy / Kaufman, Irving	Victor 18011	1915	Ireland	E
Dooley's Alibi	-	-	1902	Ireland	P
Dublin Bay	Columbia Quartet	Columbia 1148	-	Ireland	P
Dublin Daisies	Columbia Quartet	Columbia 731	1909	Ireland	P
Dublin Rag	Jones, Ada	Columbia 940	1910	Ireland	E
Eileen from old Killarney	Burr, Henry	Columbia 1829	1915	Ireland	E
Eileen: Ireland, My Ireland	Stiles, Vernon	Columbia 2247	1917	Ireland	E
Evening at Mrs. Clancy's Boarding House	Porter, Steve / Murray, Billy	Columbia 608	1906	Ireland	E
Every Tear Is a Smile in an Irishman's Heart	-	-	-	Ireland	E
Everybody Loves an Irish Song	American Quartet	Victor 18198	1916	Ireland	P
Everybody Loves an Irish Song	O'Connell, Margaret	Columbia 2129	1916	Ireland	P
Farewell Killarney	Edward's Newsboys	-	1906	Ireland	P
Father O'Flynnn	Wyper, Peter	Columbia 762	1909	Ireland	P
Faugh-a Ballagh	-	-	1917	Ireland	E
Fields of Ballyclare	Harrison, Charles	Columbia 2631	1918	Ireland	E
Finnegan's Flat	Porter, Steve	Columbia 585	1907	Ireland	E

Song Title	Name of Artist(s)	Label and Selec. No.	Year Rec.	Ethnicity/ Theme	
Flanagan (15)	various	Edison 9000+	1907	Ireland	P
Flanagan at the Barber's	Porter, Steve	Columbia 359	1907	Ireland	E
Flanagan at the Doctor's	Porter, Steve	Columbia 425	1907	Ireland	E
Flanagan at the Tailor's	Porter, Steve	Columbia 419	1907	Ireland	E
Flanagan on the Farm	Porter, Steve	Columbia 356	1907	Ireland	E
Flanagan's New Year Call	Porter, Steve	Columbia 380	1906	Ireland	E
Flanagan's Night Off	Porter, Steve	Columbia 383	1906	Ireland	E
Flanagan's Ocean Voyage	Porter / Kennedy	Columbia 626	1908	Ireland	E
Flannigan's Married Life	Porter, Steve	Edison 9575	-	Ireland	E
Flannigan's Troubles in a Restaurant	Porter, Steve	American 31435	1906	Ireland	E
For Freedom and Ireland	MacDonough, Harry	Victor	1900	Ireland	E
For Killarney and You	Burr, Henry	Columbia 1072	1911	Ireland	E
Girl with the Brogue	Jones, Ada	Columbia 829	1910	Ireland	P
Goodbye Mother Machree	Burr, Henry	Columbia 2604	1918	Ireland	E
Goodbye Mother Machree	McClaskey, Harry	Okeh 1094	1918	Ireland	E
Goodbye Mother Machree	Shannon Four / Macdonough, H.	Victor 18488	1918	Ireland	E
Goodbye, Mother Machree	Burr, Henry	Columbia -	1918	Ireland	E
Haley's Favorite Jigs	Kimmel, John	Victor 18727	1919	Ireland	E
Harrigan's Reel	Prince's Orchestra	Columbia 634	1909	Ireland	P
Has Anybody Here Seen Kelly?	Jones, Ada	Columbia 810	1909	Ireland	P
He's the Son of an Irishman	Farrell, Margaret	Columbia 1920	1915	Ireland	E
How Can You Tell Their Irish	Van & Schenk	Victor 18220	1916	Ireland	E
I Don't Like the Irish	Bonnell, Joe	Edison 7833	1901	Ireland	E
I Want to Go to County Mayo	O'Connell, Margaret	Columbia 2445	1917	Ireland	E
I'll Not Go Out with Reilly Anymore	Favor, Edward	Edison 7508	1900	Ireland	P
I'll Take You Home Again Kathleen	Seagle, Oscar	Columbia 5718	1915	Ireland	P
I'll Take You Home Again Kathleen	Thomas, William	Columbia 1435	-	Ireland	P
I'm on My Way to Dublin Bay	Prince's Orchestra	Columbia 5674	1915	Ireland	P
I'm on My Way to Dublin Bay	Stuart, Herbert / Burton, Billy	Columbia 1756	1915	Ireland	E
In the Good Old Irish Way	Van & Schenck	Columbia 2588	1918	Ireland	P
Ireland Must Be Heaven	Becker, Delos	Columbia 2068	1916	Ireland	P
Ireland Must Be Heaven	Harrison, Charles	Columbia 2123	1916	Ireland	E
Ireland Must Be Heaven	Harrison, Charles	Victor 18112	1916	Ireland	E
Irish Airs	Prince's Band	Columbia 1264	-	Ireland	P
Irish Airs Medley	Edison Symphony Orchestra	Edison 641	1896	Ireland	P
Irish Blood	Jones, Ada	Columbia 782	1909	Ireland	E
Irish Blood	Jones, Ada	Edison 10323	1910	Ireland	E
Irish Cake Walk	Collins, Arthur	Edison 5455	1898	Ireland	E
Irish Emigrant	McCormack, John	Victor 74237	-	Ireland	E
Irish Folk Song	Clark, Charles	Columbia 1470	-	Ireland	E
Irish Football Game	Quinn, Dan	Edison 1046	1896	Ireland	E
Irish Girl That I Love	Barrow, Edward	Edison 9140	1905	Ireland	P
The Irish Have a Great Day Tonight	Stiles, Vernon	Columbia 2247	1917	Ireland	E
Irish Hearts	van Epps, Fred	Columbia 1063	1911	Ireland	E
Irish Hearts March	Edison Military Band	Edison 9370	1906	Ireland	P
Irish Jigs Medley	accordion	Edison 9881	1907	Ireland	P
Irish King March	Columbia Band	Columbia 871	1905	Ireland	P
Irish Love Song	Barbour, Inez	Okeh 1049	1918	Ireland	P
Irish Love Song	Fugitt, Anne Grant	Columbia 5330	1911	Ireland	P
Irish Love Song	Kerns, Grace	Columbia 2139	1916	Ireland	E
Irish Love Song	White, Carolina	Columbia 5488	1913	Ireland	E
Irish Lullaby	Young, Beulah	Columbia 1103	-	Ireland	P
Irish Medley	Drum Corps	Berliner 701zz	1897	Ireland	P
Irish Medley	violin	Edison 6704	1899	Ireland	P
Irish on Parade	Steele, Will	Edison 7470	1900	Ireland	P
Irish Queen Schottische	Edison Symphony Orchestra	Edison 554	1896	Ireland	P
Irish Reel	piccolo	Edison 2806	1897	Ireland	P
Irish Reel	picolo solo	Columbia 887	1901	Ireland	P
Irish Reel	Schweinfest, George	-	1901	Ireland	P
Irish Reels	Kimmel, John	Victor 17849	1915	Ireland	E
Irish Reels Medley	accordion	Edison 10284	1910	Ireland	P
The Irish Shall March	Metropolitan Orchestra	Berliner 28B	1899	Ireland	P

Song Title	Name of Artist(s)	Label and Selec. No.	Year Rec.	Ethnicity/ Theme	
Irish Street Singer	Gaskin, George	Edison 1579	1896	Ireland	P
The Irish Tango	Peerless Quartet	Columbia 1515	1914	Ireland	P
Irish Tune from County Derry	Victor Concert Orchestra	Victor 17897	1915	Ireland	P
Irish Volunteers	Clarance, Edward	Edison 5503	1898	Ireland	P
Irish Waltz Medley	Prince's Orchestra	Columbia 5689	1915	Ireland	P
Irish Washerwoman	piccolo	Edison 7189	1899	Ireland	P
Irish Washerwoman	Prince's Orchestra	Columbia 1474	-	Ireland	P
Irish Washerwoman	Richardson, Don New York Orchestra	Okeh 1254	1919	Ireland	P
Irish Washerwoman Medley of Jigs	Scanlon, Pat	Edison 50500	-	Ireland	E
Irish Were Egyptians	Murray, Billy	Bluebird 10926	-	Ireland	E
Irish, the Irish	Favor, Edward	Edison 8686	1904	Ireland	P
Is Your Mother in Molly Malone	Murray, Billy	Columbia 307	1906	Ireland	E
Is Your Mother in Molly Malone	Trix, Helen	Edison 9365	1906	Ireland	P
Kathleen	Gaskin, George	Edison 1518	1896	Ireland	E
Kathleen	Regimental Band of the Republic	American 30589	1904	Ireland	P
Kathleen Mavourneen	Bispham, David	Columbia 5016	1906	Ireland	P
Kathleen Mavourneen	McKee Trio	Victor 18091	1916	Ireland	E
Katie O'Reilly	Harding, Roger	Edison 2004	1897	Ireland	E
Keep a Place in Your Heart for Ireland	Becker, Delos	Columbia 2039	1916	Ireland	P
Kilkenny	Harrison, Charles	Victor 17958	1916	Ireland	E
Killarney	Alexander, George	Columbia 444	1905	Ireland	E
Killarney	Alexander, George	Columbia 666	1905	Ireland	E
Killarney	Clarke, Herbert	Columbia 2553	1917	Ireland	E
Killarney	Columbia Band	Columbia 69	1901	Ireland	P
Killarney	Columbia Band	Columbia 610	1901	Ireland	P
Killarney	Gaskin, George	Edison 1567	1896	Ireland	E
Killarney	Harding, Roger	Edison 2025	1897	Ireland	E
Killarney	MacDonough, Harry	-	-	Ireland	P
Killarney	McKee Trio	Victor 18091	1916	Ireland	E
Killarney	Murdoch, MacKenzie	Columbia 1679	1914	Ireland	E
Killarney	Narelle, Marie	Edison 9081	1905	Ireland	E
Killarney	Nielsen, Alice	Columbia 5711	1915	Ireland	E
Killarney	Sarto, Andre	Columbia 1299	-	Ireland	P
Killarney	Sousa's Band	Berliner 556	1899	Ireland	P
Killarney	trombone	Edison 5602	1898	Ireland	P
Killarney	Vincent, Ruth	Columbia 5020	1908	Ireland	P
Killarney	xylophone	Edison 9165	1905	Ireland	P
Lament of the Irish Immigrant	McClaskey, Harry	Columbia 1230	-	Ireland	E
Lass from County Mayo	Oakland, Will	Columbia 1002	1911	Ireland	E
Lass from Glasgow Town	Williams, Billy	Columbia 1184	-	Ireland	E
Lass of Richmond Hill	Miller, Reed	Columbia 1198	-	Ireland	E
Lily of Killarney	Helder, Ruby	Columbia 5534	1913	Ireland	P
Little Bunch of Shamrocks	Burr, Henry & Stoddard, Edgar	Columbia 1315	-	Ireland	E
Little Irish Girl	Freeman, Betina	Columbia 856	1910	Ireland	P
Little Irish Girl	Furth, W. Francis	Columbia 1114	-	Ireland	E
Little Irish Girl	Miller, Reed	Columbia 2139	1916	Ireland	E
Loch Lomond	Alexander, George	Columbia 312	1905	Ireland	E
Maggie Clancy's New Piano	Jones, Ada / Spencer, Len	Edison 9311	1906	Ireland	E
Maggie O'Connor	MacDonough, Harry	Edison 7439	1900	Ireland	E
Mamie Reilly	orchestra (-)	Berliner 1469	1897	Ireland	P
Marty Maloney's Wake	Spencer, Len	Edison 8190	1902	Ireland	E
McCarthy He's a Frenchman	Watson, Fannie	Okeh 1228	1919	Ireland	E
McGinty at the Living Pictures	Favor, Edward M.	Columbia 303	1904	Ireland	E
McGinty at the Living Pictures	Favor, Edward M.	-	1906	Ireland	E
McGinty at the Living Pictures	Quinn, Dan	Edison 1066	1896	Ireland	E
Medley of Irish Airs	Sousa's Band	Berliner 8009	-	Ireland	P
Medley of Irish jigs	Fitzpatrick, Patrick	Edison 50616	-	Ireland	E
Medley of Irish Reels	Scanlon, Pat	Edison 50500	-	Ireland	E
Medley of Irish Reels	Touhey, Patrick	Victor 18727	1919	Ireland	E
Medley of Irish Reels #5	Kimmel, John	Victor	1917	Ireland	E
Meet Me Down at the Corner	Roberts, Bob	Harmony 449	1903	Ireland	P

Song Title	Name of Artist(s)	Label and Selec. No.	Year Rec.	Ethnicity/ Theme	
Mother Machree	Harrison, Charles	Victor 17780	1915	Ireland	E
Mother Machree	Harrison, Charles	Columbia 2170	1916	Ireland	E
Mother Machree	McCormack, John	Victor 64181	-	Ireland	E
Mother Machree	McKee Trio	Victor 17835	1915	Ireland	E
Mother Machree	Olcott, Chauncey	Columbia 1337	-	Ireland	E
Mother Machree	Taylor — Hackel-Berge Trio	Columbia 1735	1915	Ireland	E
Mrs. Casey: Bright Eyes	Jones, Ada	Columbia 830	1910	Ireland	E
Mrs. McCloud's Reel	McAuliffe, James C.	-	1899	Ireland	E
Mrs. Reilly's Trouble with the Dumb Waiter	Porter, Steve	Columbia 281	1906	Ireland	E
My Beautiful Irish	MacDonough, Harry	Victor 1617	-	Ireland	E
My Beautiful Irish Maid	Olcott, Chauncey	Columbia 1337	-	Ireland	E
My Father Was Born in Killarney	Williams, Billy	Edison 10562	1912	Ireland	E
My Gal Irene	Collins, Arthur/Harlan, Byron	Victor 5399	1908	Ireland	E
My Irish Molly O	Collins, Arthur	American 31155	1906	Ireland	E
My Irish Molly O	Hill, Hamilton	-	1906	Ireland	E
My Irish Molly O	Murray, Billy	Edison 9063	1905	Ireland	E
My Irish Molly O	Ossman, Vess	American 31254	1906	Ireland	E
My Irish Molly O	Tally, Harry	Columbia 308	1905	Ireland	E
My Irish Rosie	Jones, Ada	Edison 9484	1907	Ireland	E
My Irish Rosie	Myers, John	Columbia 470	1907	Ireland	E
My Irish Song of Songs	Harrison, Charles	Columbia 2631	1918	Ireland	E
My Little Irish Canary	Collins, Arthur / Harlan, Byron	Edison 8647	1904	Ireland	E
My Own Hometown in Ireland	Robbins, Will	Columbia 1846	-	Ireland	P
My Wild Irish Rose	Brunswig Quartet	Columbia 895	1910	Ireland	P
My Wild Irish Rose	Campbell, Albert	Edison 5720	1898	Ireland	E
My Wild Irish Rose	Campbell, Albert	Berliner 139	1899	Ireland	E
My Wild Irish Rose	Olcott, Chauncey	Columbia 1308	-	Ireland	E
My Yankee Irish Girl	Collins & Harlin	American 31200	-	Ireland	E
Nora Malone	Harlan, Byron	Columbia 831	1910	Ireland	E
O'Brien's Trials and Mishaps	Thompson, George	Okeh 1066	1918	Ireland	P
Olcott's Irish Serenade	Gaskin, George	Edison 1532	1896	Ireland	E
On the Rocky Road to Dublin	Edison Male Quartet	Edison 9457	1907	Ireland	P
On the Rocky Road to Dublin	Ossman, Vess	Columbia 226	1906	Ireland	P
Over in Erin	White, Malachy	Columbia 2445	1917	Ireland	P
Pat O'Brien's Automobile	Porter, Steve	Columbia 592	1908	Ireland	E
A Picture of Dear Old Ireland	Harrison, Charles	Victor 18234	1917	Ireland	E
Reminiscence of Ireland	Prince's Band	Columbia 1074	1911	Ireland	P
Rocky Road to Dublin	Herborn, Edward / Wheeler, James	Columbia 2217	1917	Ireland	P
Rose of Killarney	Redmond, William	Edison 8197	1902	Ireland	P
Royal Belfast Hornpipe	Wyper, Daniel	Columbia 652	1909	Ireland	P
Shamrock Belles	Campbell, Al & Burr, Henry	Columbia 1189	-	Ireland	E
Shamus O'Brien	Throckmorton, B. Russell	Edison 3860	1898	Ireland	P
The Shannon, the Shamrock, and You	Harrison, Charles	Columbia 2554	1918	Ireland	E
She's the Daughter of Mother Machree	Harrison, Charles	Victor 17948	1916	Ireland	E
She's the Daughter of Mother Machree	Romain, Manuel	Columbia 1951	1916	Ireland	P
The Singer Was Irish	Burr, Henry	Columbia 1349	-	Ireland	E
Soldiers of Erin	Scanlon, Pat	Emerson 10266	-	Ireland	E
Somewhere in Ireland	Harrison, Charles	Victor 18327	1917	Ireland	E
Somewhere in Ireland	Harvey, Morton	Columbia 2346	1917	Ireland	P
St. Patrick's Day at Clancy's	Invincible Quartet	American 30800	-	Ireland	P
Sweet Eileen	Ewing, Gerald	Columbia 784	1909	Ireland	E
Sweet Inniscara	Olcott, Chauncey	Columbia 1309	-	Ireland	E
That's the Meaning of Ireland	Burr, Henry	Columbia 1964	1916	Ireland	E
That's What Ireland Means to Me	Burr, Henry	Columbia 2365	1917	Ireland	E
That's Why I Love You and Call You Machree	White, Malachy	Columbia 2453	1917	Ireland	E
The Irish Have a Great Day Tonight	Weelsh, Scott	Victor 18285	1917	Ireland	E
There's Another Angel Now in Killarney	Ash, Sam	Columbia 2453	1917	Ireland	P
There's Nothing to Good for the Irish	O'Connell, Margaret	Victor 18364	1917	Ireland	E

Song Title	Name of Artist(s)	Label and Selec. No.	Year Rec.	Ethnicity/ Theme	
There's Something in the Name of Ireland	Donovan, Hugh	Columbia 2393	1917	Ireland	E
Tim Finnegan's Wake	Terrell, John	Berliner 1869	1898	Ireland	E
Tim Rooney's at the Fightin'	Reed, James / Harrison, Charles	Columbia 1968	1916	Ireland	E
Twas Only an Irishman's Dream	Burr, Henry	Victor 18198	1916	Ireland	E
Twas Only an Irishman's Dream	Empire Trio	Columbia 2151	1916	Ireland	P
Under the Irish Moon	Harlan, Byron	Columbia 727	1909	Ireland	E
Under the Irish Moon	Harlan, Byron	Edison 10181	1909	Ireland	E
Wearing of the Green	Myers, John	Columbia 328	1901	Ireland	E
Wearing of the Green	Thomas, William	Columbia 1676	1913	Ireland	E
The Wearing of the Green	Banda Rossa	Berliner 125	-	Ireland	E
The Wearing of the Green	Myers, John W.	Columbia 1174	-	Ireland	E
What an Irishman Means by Machree	McClaskey, Harry	Columbia 1860	1915	Ireland	E
When Ireland Comes Into Its Own	Oakland, Will	Okeh 1220	1919	Ireland	E
When Irish Eyes Are Smiling	McCormack, John	Victor 64631	1905	Ireland	E
When Irish Eyes Are Smiling	Olcott, Chauncey	Columbia 1310	-	Ireland	E
When It's Springtime in Killarney	Burr, Henry	Columbia 2005	1916	Ireland	E
Where the River Shannon Flows	Bradway Quartet	Columbia 1916	1915	Ireland	E
Where the River Shannon Flows	Burr, Henry	Columbia 815	1909	Ireland	E
Where the River Shannon Flows	McCormack, John	Victor 64311	1913	Ireland	E
Where the River Shannon Flows	McKee Trio	Victor 17898	1915	Ireland	E
Won't You Say a Word for Ireland?	Kaufman, Irving	Columbia 2313	1917	Ireland	P
You Brought Ireland Right Over to Me	Wilson, George	Columbia 2346	1917	Ireland	E
You Don't Have to Come from Ireland to Be Irish	O'Connell, Margaret	Columbia 2245	1917	Ireland	E
You Will Have to Sing an Irish Song	Jones, Ada	Columbia 1101	1911	Ireland	E
You've Got Me Going with Your Irish Eyes	Farrell, Margaret	Victor 18135	1916	Ireland	E
Aida: Celeste Aida (Verdi)	Caruso, Enrico	Victor	1904	Italy	E
Addio Mia Bella Napoli	DeBassini, A.	Columbia 525	1903	Italy	E
Amore, Amore	Parvis, Taurino	Columbia 529	1905	Italy	E
Ave Maria	Rappold, Marie	Edison 82536	-	Italy	P
Boccacio March	Band	Berliner 126	-	Italy	P
Cavallera Rusticana (drinking song)	Berti, Romeo	Columbia 531	-	Italy	E
Cavalleria rusticana, Siciliana (Mascagni)	Caruso, Enrico	Victor	1905	Italy	E
Cavalleria rusticana: Brindisi (Mascagni)	Caruso, Enrico	Victor	1905	Italy	E
Coplas de Bocaccio	Giannini, Sig F.	Berliner 294	1899	Italy	E
Day in Venice — Venetian Love Song	Prince's Orchestra	Columbia 1589	-	Italy	P
Deiro Rag	Deiro, Guido	Columbia 1229	-	Italy	P
Don Pasquale: Com gentil (Donizetti)	Caruso, Enrico	Victor	1905	Italy	E
Eco di Napoli	Prince's Orchestra	Columbia 5235	1910	Italy	P
El Seducion	Deiro, Guido	Columbia 1823	1913	Italy	E
Era La Notte Otello	Parvis, Taurino	Columbia 715	-	Italy	E
Funiculi, Funicula	Banda Rossa	Berliner 119	1898	Italy	E
Funiculi, Funicula	Cecil Orchestra	Berliner 509	1898	Italy	P
Funiculi, Funicula	Giannini, Signor	Columbia 528	1903	Italy	E
Funiculi, Funicula	Harrison, Charles Quartet	Columbia 1851	1915	Italy	P
Funiculi, Funicula	Louise, Helen / Ferera, Frank	Columbia 2614	1918	Italy	P
Funiculi, Funicula	Lyric Quartet	Victor 18968	1912	Italy	P
Funiculi, Funicula	Waldemar, Richard	Columbia 522	1908	Italy	P
Garibaldi Hymn	Banda Rossa	Berliner 95	1898	Italy	E
Garibaldi March	Banda Espanol	Columbia 5057	1907	Italy	E
Garibaldi March	Columbia Band	Columbia 66	1904	Italy	P
Gondoliers— Day in Venice	McClellan, John	Columbia 945	1910	Italy	P
Good-Bye Mister Caruso	-	-	1909	Italy	P
How Columbus Discovered America	Hill, Murray K.	Victor	1911	Italy	E
I Pagliacci: Vesti la giubba (Leoncavallo)	Caruso, Enrico	Victor 81032	1904	Italy	E
I Pagliacci: Vesti la giubba (Leoncavallo)	Caruso, Enrico	Victor 88061	1907	Italy	E

Song Title	Name of Artist(s)	Label and Selec. No.	Year Rec.	Ethnicity/ Theme	
I Pescatori di perle: Mi par dudir ancora	Caruso, Enrico	G&T 268i	1902	Italy	E
I'll Take You Back to Italy	Dalhart, Vernon	Edison 50473	-	Italy	P
I'll Take You Back to Italy	King, Charles / Brice, Elizabeth	Columbia 2459	1917	Italy	P
Il Trovatore: Mira D'Acerbe	Ciaparelli, Gina / Parvis, Taurino	Columbia 530	1906	Italy	E
Inno di Garibaldi	Guarini, M. A.	Edison 4285	1899	Italy	E
Italian Echoes	Cardenas Marimba Quartet	Columbia 1728	1911	Italy	E
Italian March	Royal Italian Band	Berliner 1071	1900	Italy	E
Italian National Hymn	Banda Rossa	Berliner 96	1898	Italy	E
Italian Suite	Place, William Mandolin Quartet	Columbia 1656	1914	Italy	P
Italians in Algeria Overture	American Symphony Orchestra	Edison	-	Italy	P
Italians in Algiers	Columbia Band	Columbia 96	1902	Italy	P
Lola — Italian Serenade	Conway's Band	Edison 50582	-	Italy	P
Mammi Mia Che Vo Sope	Daddi, Francesco	Columbia 5221	1910	Italy	E
Mattinata (Leoncavallo)	Caruso, Enrico	HMV	1904	Italy	E
Medley of Italian Airs	Street Piano	Victor 18328	1917	Italy	P
My Florence	Deiro, Guido	Columbia 2615	1912	Italy	E
Nightime in Little Italy	Collins, Arthur / Harlan, Byron	Victor 18262	1917	Italy	P
Nightime in Little Italy	Kopp, Howard	Columbia 2282	1917	Italy	P
Non e Ver	Giannini, Signor	Columbia 526	1904	Italy	E
O Castro Fior	Alessandroni, Cesare	American 31402	-	Italy	E
O Sole Mio	Louise, Helen / Ferera, Frank	Columbia 2509	1918	Italy	P
O Sole Mio	White, Caroline	Columbia 1330	-	Italy	P
Occhi di Fata	Parvis, Taurino	Columbia 527	1905	Italy	E
On the Shore of Italy	Burr, Henry	Columbia 1510	1914	Italy	P
On the Shores of Italy	Campbell, A. / Burr, H.	Victor 17602	1914	Italy	P
Organ Grinder's Troubles	Harlan & Porter	Victor	1912	Italy	P
Pedro the Hand Organ Man	Spencer, Len	Columbia 3620	-	Italy	P
Pedro, the Hand Organ Man	Spencer, Len	Columbia 454	1907	Italy	P
Pedro, the Hand Organ Man	Spencer, Len	Edison	1907	Italy	P
Pedro, the Hand Organ Man	Spencer, Len	Edison 9487	1907	Italy	P
Popular Italian Song	Banda Rossa	Berliner 99	1898	Italy	P
Prince of Piedmont March	Municipal Band of Milan	Columbia 1325	-	Italy	E
Prologo from Pagliacci	Scotti, Antonio	Victor 85071	1905	Italy	E
Rigoletto: Questa o quella (Verdi)	Caruso, Enrico	G&T	1902	Italy	E
Rigoletto: Questa o quella (Verdi)	Caruso, Enrico	Victor	1904	Italy	E
Rigoletto: Questa o quella (Verdi)	Caruso, Enrico	Victor 87017	1908	Italy	E
The Rosary	Lua, Pali / Kaili, David	Victor 17803	1914	Italy	P
Royal Italian March	Banda Espanol	Columbia 5047	1907	Italy	P
Royal Italian March	Edison Grand Concert Band	Edison 127	1896	Italy	P
Royal Italian March	Prince's Band	Columbia 2426	1917	Italy	P
Royal March of Italy	Italian Grenadiers Band	Columbia 2805	1918	Italy	E
Santa Lucia	Miller, Reed	Victor 18968	1911	Italy	P
Sei morta ne la vita mia (Costa)	Caruso, Enrico	Agsa	1918	Italy	E
Siciliana	Guarini, M.A.	Edison 4352	1899	Italy	E
Sicily	chimes	Edison 3221	1898	Italy	P
Stabat Mater: Through the Darkness	Pimazzoni, Giuseppi	Columbia 763	1909	Italy	E
Suoni in Tromba, e intrepido- I puritani	Parvis, Taurino	Edison	-	Italy	E
Sweet Italian Love	Murray, Billy	Edison 10427	1910	Italy	P
Sweet Italian Love Song	Harlan, Byron	Columbia 896	1910	Italy	P
That Italian Rag	Murray, Billy	Victor 16608	-	Italy	P
There's a Garden in Dear Old Italy	Campbell, Albert / Burr, Henry	Columbia 2000	1916	Italy	P
There's a Garden in Old Italy	Campbell, Albert / Burr, Henry	Victor 18066	1916	Italy	P
Urna fatale del mio destino— La Forza del destino	Niddleton, Arthur	Edison	-	Italy	P
Venetian Love Song	Herbert, Victor Orchestra	Edison 10297	1910	Italy	P
Viva La Francia	Italian Grenadiers Band	Columbia 2805	1918	Italy	E
When the Sun Goes Down in Romany	King, Charles / Brice, Elizabeth	Columbia 2059	1916	Italy	P
When You Kiss an Italian Girl	Burkhart, Maurice	Columbia 1046	1911	Italy	P
Wop Blues	Glantz, Nathan and His orchestra	Edison 51336	-	Italy	P

Song Title	Name of Artist(s)	Label and Selec. No.	Year Rec.	Ethnicity/ Theme	
Wop Blues	Johnson, Johnny	Lincoln 2158	-	Italy	P
Wop Blues	Musical Comrades	Muse 416	-	Italy	P
I Want to Go to Tokio	Lyric Quartet	Victor 17754	1915	Italy	P
I Want to Go to Tokio	Prince's Band	Columbia 5659	1915	Italy	P
I Want to Go to Tokio	Victor Military Band	Victor 17764	1915	Italy	P
Japanese National March	Prince's Band	Columbia 38	1905	Italy	P
Mikado Selections	Columbia Band	Columbia 43	1901	Italy	P
Poppy Time in Old Japan	Harrison, James / Reed, James	Victor 17924	1915	Italy	P
Poppy Time in Old Japan	Victor Military Band	Victor 18267	1917	Italy	P
Selections from Mayor of Tokio	banjo/mandolin/harp	Columbia 219	1906	Italy	P
Suki San	Wilson, George	Columbia 2302	1917	Italy	P
Underneath the Japanese Moon	Kaufman, Irving	Victor 17699	1914	Italy	P
Underneath the Japanese Moon	Prince's Band	Columbia 5623	1914	Italy	P
When It's Cherry Time in Tokio	Wilson, George	Columbia 2339	1917	Italy	P
A Weib	Hebrew vocal	Columbia 547	1901	Jewish/Yiddish	E
Adamoe Sechorany	Hebrew vocal	Columbia 565	1905	Jewish/Yiddish	E
Al Chatt	Hebrew vocal	Columbia 552	1905	Jewish/Yiddish	E
At the Yiddish Wedding Jubilee	Burkhardt, Maurice	Edison 50238	-	Jewish/Yiddish	E
At the Yiddish Wedding Jubilee	Tucker, Sophie	-1914	-	Jewish/Yiddish	E
Auf Jener Seit	Golden Quartet	Columbia 547	1905	Jewish/Yiddish	E
Awoide	Goldin Quartet	Columbia 554	1904	Jewish/Yiddish	E
Berchos Kohanim	Cantor G. Sirota	Victor 17771	-	Jewish/Yiddish	E
Ch Sidem	Hebrew vocal	Columbia 566	1902	Jewish/Yiddish	E
Chorben Kishineff	Seiden, Frank	Columbia 561	1903	Jewish/Yiddish	E
Cohen at the Picnic	Silver, Monroe	Victor 18608	1919	Jewish/Yiddish	E
Cohen at the Real Estate Office	Hayman, Joe	Columbia 2488	-	Jewish/Yiddish	E
Cohen Gets Married	Silver, Monroe	Victor 18501	1918	Jewish/Yiddish	E
Cohen on the Telephone	Silver, Monroe	Columbia 1516	-	Jewish/Yiddish	E
Cohen on His Honeymoon	Silver, Monroe	Victor 18501	1918	Jewish/Yiddish	E
Cohen on the Telephone	Bernard, Barney	Victor 18029	1916	Jewish/Yiddish	E
Cohen Owes Me 97 Dollars	Bernard, Rhoda	Victor 18023	1916	Jewish/Yiddish	E
Cohen Phones the Garage	Thompson, George	Okeh 1024	1918	Jewish/Yiddish	P
Cohen Telephones from Brighton	Hayman, Joe	Columbia 1885	1915	Jewish/Yiddish	E
Cohen Telephones from Brighton	Hayman, Joe	Columbia 2192	1915	Jewish/Yiddish	E
Cohen Telephones the Health Department	Hayman, Joe	Columbia 1863	1915	Jewish/Yiddish	E
Cohen Telephones the Health Department	Hayman, Joe	Columbia 2192	1915	Jewish/Yiddish	E
Das Beimele	Hebrew vocal	Columbia 566	1902	Jewish/Yiddish	E
Das Kriegele	Hebrew vocal	Columbia 564	1901	Jewish/Yiddish	E
Das Pekele	Hebrew vocal	Columbia 568	1901	Jewish/Yiddish	E
Der Pussik	Hebrew vocal	Columbia 549	1901	Jewish/Yiddish	E
Die Seder Nacht	Goldin Quartet	Columbia 555	1905	Jewish/Yiddish	E
Ein Gelechter	Hebrew vocal	Columbia 565	1902	Jewish/Yiddish	E
Eiz Chaim	Goldin Quartet	Columbia 556	1905	Jewish/Yiddish	E
Eli Eli	Rosenblatt, Cantor Joseph	Victor	1919	Jewish/Yiddish	E
Eli Eli	Victor Salon Orchestra	Victor	1919	Jewish/Yiddish	E
Emes	Goldin Quartet	Columbia 553	1905	Jewish/Yiddish	E
Fantasi Lied von Ben Hador	Seiden, Frank	Columbia 557	1903	Jewish/Yiddish	E
Goldstein Behind Bars	Bingham, Ralph	Victor 18231	1916	Jewish/Yiddish	P
Goldstein Goes Into the Railroad Business	Bernard, Barney	Victor 18029	1916	Jewish/Yiddish	P
Gott un Sein Misphet Is Gerecht	Seiden, Frank	Columbia 548	1905	Jewish/Yiddish	E
Habein Jakir Li	Cantor G. Sirota	Victor 17746	1914	Jewish/Yiddish	E
Hamavdel	Goldin Quartet	Columbia 557	1905	Jewish/Yiddish	E
Hashkivany	Goldin Quartet	Columbia 567	1905	Jewish/Yiddish	E
Hebrew Vaudeville Specialty: Ain't Dat a Shame	Rose, Julian	Edison 8498	1903	Jewish/Yiddish	E
Hebrew Vaudeville Specialty: In the Good Old Summer Time	Rose, Julian	Edison 8403	1903	Jewish/Yiddish	E
Hebrew Vaudeville Specialty: In the Shade of the Old Apple Tree	Rose, Julian	Edison 9176	1906	Jewish/Yiddish	E

Song Title	Name of Artist(s)	Label and Selec. No.	Year Rec.	Ethnicity/ Theme
Hebrew Vaudeville Specialty: On a Sunday Afternoon	Rose, Julian	Edison 8448	1903	Jewish/Yiddish E
Hebrew Vaudeville Specialty: Rip Van Winkle Was a Lucky Man	Rose, Julian	Edison 8383	1903	Jewish/Yiddish E
Hebrew Vaudeville Specialty: The I'd Be Satisfied with Life	Rose, Julian	Edison 9223	1906	Jewish/Yiddish E
Hebrew Vaudeville Specialty: When the Boys Go Marching By	Rose, Julian	Edison 8417	1903	Jewish/Yiddish E
Himoze Iopu	Cantor G. Sirota	Victor 17738	1912	Jewish/Yiddish E
I'm a Yiddish Cowboy	Meeker, Edward	Edison 9984	1908	Jewish/Yiddish P
Isrulik Kim a Heim	Goldin Quartet	Columbia 564	1905	Jewish/Yiddish E
Jaale — Let Our Prayer Ascend	Cantor G. Sirota	Victor 17739	1912	Jewish/Yiddish E
Kabet es Owichu von Bais Duwed	Seiden, Frank	Columbia 553	1905	Jewish/Yiddish E
Kadish	Goldin Quartet	Columbia 559	1905	Jewish/Yiddish E
Kadish fon Schwarten Yid	Goldin Quartet	Columbia 550	1905	Jewish/Yiddish E
Kevado	Golden, Max Quartet	Columbia 546	1905	Jewish/Yiddish E
King Lear	Hebrew vocal	Columbia 551	1902	Jewish/Yiddish E
Kol Nidrei	Casals, Pablo	Columbia 5722	1914	Jewish/Yiddish P
Kol Nidrei	Golden Quartet	Columbia 548	1905	Jewish/Yiddish E
Kol Nidrei	Schultz, Leo	Columbia 546	1905	Jewish/Yiddish E
Kol Nidrei	Schultz, Leo	Columbia 5638	1914	Jewish/Yiddish E
Koli Shama	Goldin Quartet	Columbia 567	1905	Jewish/Yiddish E
Levinsky at a Wedding	Rose, Julian	Columbia 2310	1917	Jewish/Yiddish E
Levinsky at a Wedding (4)	Rose, Julian	Columbia 2366	1917	Jewish/Yiddish E
Levinsky at the Wedding*	Rose, Julian	Columbia 2310	-	Jewish/Yiddish E
Lichajem	Seiden, Frank	Columbia 554	1904	Jewish/Yiddish E
Mamenu	Paskal, Simon	Columbia -	1909	Jewish/Yiddish E
My Yiddish Matinee Girl	Bernard, Rhoda	Victor 17994	1916	Jewish/Yiddish E
Nathan, for What You Waiting	Bernard, Rhoda	Victor 18023	1916	Jewish/Yiddish E
Original Cohens	Jones, Ada / Spencer, Len	Edison 9215	1906	Jewish/Yiddish P
Rezei — Accept Our Prayers	Cantor G. Sirota	Victor 17740	1912	Jewish/Yiddish E
Rip Van Winkle Was a Lucky Man	Rose, Julian	Edison 8383	1903	Jewish/Yiddish P
Roll Your Yiddish Eyes	Bernard, Rhoda	Victor 17994	1916	Jewish/Yiddish E
Schnieder, Does Your Mother Know You're Out	Watson, G. P.	American 31132	-	Jewish/Yiddish P
Somer bel nacht auf dechte	Seiden, Frank	Columbia 563	1905	Jewish/Yiddish E
Uwchain Jischadosh	Goldin Quartet	Columbia 569	1905	Jewish/Yiddish E
V'Hakohanim	Rosenblat, Yoselle		1916	Jewish/Yiddish E
Yehi Rozain	Goldin Quartet	Columbia 560	1905	Jewish/Yiddish P
Zadik Katomor	Cantor G. Sirota	Victor 17829	-	Jewish/Yiddish E
Zadik Kotomor	Goldin Quartet	Columbia 563	1905	Jewish/Yiddish E
Zim Blen	Corenfeld, Hyman	Columbia 562	1905	Jewish/Yiddish E
Zion's Techter	Hebrew vocal	Columbia 560	1901	Jewish/Yiddish E
Zur Israeil	Cantor G. Sirota	Victor 17832	-	Jewish/Yiddish E
Adios a Mexico	Adamini, Arturo	Edison 4222	1899	Mexico E
Ay Chiquita	Adamini, Arturo	Edison 4223	1899	Mexico E
Canto al Pueblo Marche	Banda Policia de Mexico	Columbia 636	1908	Mexico E
Dos Danzas un Adios Mas cu	Curti's Band	Columbia 53	1905	Mexico P
En Lan Montana	Banda Artillerie de Mexico	Columbia 808	1909	Mexico E
The Hot Tamale Man	Collins, Arthur	Indestructable 988	-	Mexico P
La Media Noche	United States Marine Band	Columbia -	1891	Mexico P
Manzanillo a Mexican Dance	Prince's Orchestra	Columbia -	1916	Mexico P
Mexican Kisses	Edison Concert Band	Edison 9924	1908	Mexico P
Mexican National Air	Edison Grand Concert Band	Edison 125	1896	Mexico P
Mexican National Hymn	Sousa's Band	Berliner 101	1898	Mexico P
Mexico	MacDonough, Harry	Edison 8936	1905	Mexico P
My Beautiful Mexican Rose	Top Notchers	Edison 51342	-	Mexico P
Primero de Montada	Banda Artillerie de Mexico	Columbia 808	1909	Mexico E
Rose of Mexico	Edison Symphony Orchestra	Edison 9885	1908	Mexico P
They're on Their Way back to Mexico	Halley, William	Columbia 1565	1914	Mexico P

Song Title	Name of Artist(s)	Label and Selec. No.	Year Rec.	Ethnicity/ Theme	
Big Chief Kill a Hun	Collins, Arthur / Harlan, Byron	Okeh 1113	-	Native American	P
Big Indian Chief	Myers, J. W.	Columbia -	1904	Native American	P
By Waters of Minnetonka	Prince Watawaso	Victor 18431	1917	Native American	P
From the Land of Sky Blue Waters	Maurel, Barbara	Columbia 2625	1918	Native American	P
Hiawatha	Edison Grand Concert Band	Edison 8347	1903	Native American	P
Hiawatha	MacDonough, Harry	Edison 8425	1903	Native American	P
Hiawatha	Soder's Band	Edison 50514	-	Native American	P
Hiawatha (parody)	Collins, Arthur / Harlan, Byron	Edison 8475	1903	Native American	P
Hiawatha March	Columbia Orchestra	Columbia 142	1903	Native American	P
Honest Injun	Collins, Arthur / Harlan, Byron	Columbia 2068	1916	Native American	P
Honest Injun	Collins, Arthur / Harlan, Byron	Victor 18128	1916	Native American	P
Indian War Dance	Edison Grand Concert Band	Edison 118	1896	Native American	P
Lost Arrow Indian Romance	Van Epps, Fred	Columbia 1821	1915	Native American	P
March of the Powhattan Guard	Prince's Band	Columbia 30	1907	Native American	P
Medley of Indian Songs	Prince's Orchestra	Columbia 5716	1915	Native American	P
Minnehaha Waltz Medley	Lua, Pali / Kaili, David	Victor 17807	1915	Native American	P
Navajo	MacDonough, Harry	Edison 8640	1904	Native American	P
Navajo Medley	Edison Military Band	Edison 8673	1904	Native American	P
Navajo Two-Step	Columbia Band	Columbia 62	1903	Native American	P
Oh That Navajo Rag	Connolly, Dolly	Columbia 1102	-	Native American	P
Papupooh — Deer Flower	Prince Watawaso	Victor 18444	1917	Native American	P
Penobscot Tribal Songs	Prince Watawaso	Victor 18444	1917	Native American	P
Pocahontas	Favor, Edward	Edison 9208	1906	Native American	P
Pocahontas	Premier	Edison 50754	-	Native American	P
Powhatan's Daughter March	Sousa's Band	Edison 10237	1910	Native American	P
Powhattan's Daughter march	Prince's Band	Columbia 19	1907	Native American	P
Reed Bird: Indian Bride	Myers, John	Columbia 505	1907	Native American	P
Song of Hiawatha	Kingston, Morgan	Columbia 5863	1916	Native American	P
Who Played Poker with Pocahontas	Jolson, Al	Columbia 2787	1919	Native American	P
Who Played Poker with Pocahontas	Watson, Fannie	Okeh 1193	1919	Native American	P
Norway the Land of the Midnight Sun	Campbell, A. / Burr, H.	Victor 17827	1915	Norway	P
It Was the Dutch	Collins, Arthur / Harlan, Byron	Edison 8509	1903	Netherlands	P

Song Title	Name of Artist(s)	Label and Selec. No.	Year Rec.	Ethnicity/ Theme	
It's Tulip Time in Holland	Prince's Band	Columbia 5724	1915	Netherlands	P
My Little Dutch Colleen	Murray, Billy	Columbia 804	1906	Netherlands	P
Netherland's National Hymn	Edison Grand Concert Band	Edison 129	1896	Netherlands	P
When It's Tulip Time in Holland	Grinderino, S.	Victor 17884	1915	Netherlands	P
When It's Tulip Time in Holland	MacDonough, Harry	Victor 17874	1915	Netherlands	P
Austrian Army March	United States Marine Band	Edison 10398	1910	Austria	P
Austrian National Hymn	Schliegel, Carl	Victor 17675	1914	Austria	P
Austrian National Hymn	Victor Military Band	Victor 17669	1914	Austria	E
Cillerthal — Tyrolean Yodel	Graus Choir	Berliner 3197	1897	Austria	E
Dorfschwalben aus Osterreich	Lanner Quartet	Victor 17757	-	Austria	E
Echos du Tyrol	Bergeret, M.	Columbia 570	-	Austria	E
Ein Morgen in Tyrol	Renoth / Huber	Columbia 511	1903	Austria	E
Oh Thou Mighty Austria	Columbia Orchestra	Columbia 125	1910	Austria	P
Prince Eugen of Austria	Schliegel, Carl	Victor 17675	1914	Austria	E
Tiroler und sein Kind	Jorn, Karl	Columbia 1794	1915	Austria	P
Himno Nacional de Panama	Prince's Band	Columbia 660	-	Panama	P
Through the Panama Canal	Prince's Band	Columbia 1528	1913	Panama	P
Hold dem Philippines	Collins, Arthur	Berliner 917	1900	Philippines	P
Amazonia Polka Bresilienne	National Promenade Band	Edison 50189L	-	Poland	P
Anvil Polka	Edison Concert Band	Edison 9593	1907	Poland	P
Bonnie Bouche Polka	Prince, Alexander	Columbia 2516	1914	Poland	P
Busby Polka	Wyper, Peter	Columbia 762	1909	Poland	P
Castle Polka	Victor Military Band	Victor 17644	1914	Poland	P
Celebrity Polka	Banda Rossa	Berliner 94	1898	Poland	E
Columbia Polka	Kryl, Bohumir	Columbia 226	1902	Poland	E
Deirina Polka	Deiro, Guido	Columbia 1351	-	Poland	P
Dinah Polka	Peerless Orchestra	Edison 692	1896	Poland	P
Elegant Polka	cornet (-)	Berliner 200	-	Poland	E
Fryksdal Polka	Victor Military Band	Victor 17510	1913	Poland	P
Gedenk Gedenk	Seiden, Frank	Columbia 555	1903	Poland	P
Gem Polka	Columbia Band	Columbia 197	1902	Poland	P
Glass in Hand Polka	Sousa's Band	Berliner 80Z	1898	Poland	P
Golden Robin Polka	Stengler & McNiece	Berliner 7747	-	Poland	P
Hornpipe Polka	Schweinfest, George	Berliner 626	1899	Poland	E
Ida and Dot Polka	Buono & Chiafferelli	Columbia 2806	1919	Poland	P
Ida and Dot Polka	Prince's Band	Columbia 225	1907	Poland	P
Invincible Polka	Edison Symphony Orchestra	Edison 553	1896	Poland	P
Josephine Polka	Oberammergauer Zither Trio	Edison 50299	-	Poland	E
Kyntnavs Polska	Finland Dance Orchestra	Victor 17963	1915	Poland	E
La Aurora Polka	Banda Rossa	Berliner 145	-	Poland	P
La Czarina	Victor Military Band	Victor 17980	1916	Poland	P
La Lansonet Polka	Schweinfest, George	Berliner 527	-	Poland	P
Le Secret Polka	cornet	Edison 8546	1903	Poland	P
Leonore Polka	Murillo, Emilio	Columbia 902	1910	Poland	P
Little Coquette Polka	Sousa's Band	Berliner 71	1897	Poland	P
Los Parrenderos Polka	Banda Espanol	Columbia 70	1906	Poland	P
Normandie (Polka)	Kopp, Howard	Columbia 1501	1914	Poland	P
Nutmeg Polka	Banda Rossa	Berliner 34	1896	Poland	P
Ostgota Polska	Victor Band	Victor 17777	1914	Poland	P
Parisian Polka	Victor Military Band	Victor 18600	1918	Poland	P
Pizzicato Polka	Kopp, Howard	Columbia 2305	1917	Poland	P
Polish Dance #1	Columbia Band	Columbia 95	1902	Poland	P
Polish National Dance	violin	Edison 7325	1899	Poland	P
Polka	Banda Rossa	Berliner 97	1898	Poland	P
Polka Caprice	Lufsky, Marshall	Columbia 16	-	Poland	E
Polka DeAngelis	Banda Rossa	Berliner 126	1898	Poland	P
Signal Polka	Pryor, Arthur	Berliner 3307	1897	Poland	P
Snow Flake Polka	Edison Grand Concert Band	Edison 90	1896	Poland	P
Sweet Birdie Polka	Lufsky, Marshall	Columbia 36	1906	Poland	E
Triplette Polka	cornet solo	Columbia 179	-	Poland	P
Twinkling Star Polka	Lufsky, Marsahll / Kopp, Howard	Columbia 1560	1914	Poland	E
Twinkling Star Polka	Wagner, W. / Hager, J.	Okeh 1036	1918	Poland	P

Song Title	Name of Artist(s)	Label and Selec. No.	Year Rec.	Ethnicity/ Theme	
Variety Polka	Deiro, Guido	Columbia 1003	1911	Poland	P
West Lawn Polka	Bacon, F. J.	Victor 17129	1912	Poland	E
Wren Polka	piccolo	Edison 2816	1897	Poland	P
Komarinskaja	Russian Symphony Orchestra	Columbia 5394	1911	Russia	E
Russian Carnival	Lufsky, Marshall	Columbia 841	1910	Russia	E
Russian College Yell	Balalaika, Arkaloff Orchestra	Columbia 1096	1911	Russia	E
Russian Hymn	Edison Grand Concert Band	Edison 63	1896	Russia	P
Russian National Hymn	Madeira, A. D.	Edison 7695	1901	Russia	P
Russian Rag	Fuller's, Earl Novelty Orchestra	Columbia 2649	1918	Russia	P
Russian Rag	Pietro, D. Orchestra	Victor 18743	1919	Russia	P
Blue Bells of Scotland	Chambers, W. Paris	Berliner 3405	1897	Scotland	P
Blue Bells of Scotland	Garden, Mary	Columbia 1191	-	Scotland	P
Blue Bells of Scotland	Haydn Quartet	-	-	Scotland	P
Blue Bells of Scotland	Keyes, Margaret	Columbia 5351	1911	Scotland	P
Blue Bells of Scotland	Kopp, Howard	Columbia 1687	1915	Scotland	P
Blue Bells of Scotland	Pryor, Arthur	Berliner 3312	1897	Scotland	P
Bonnie Dundee	Wiederhold, Albert	Columbia 1876	1915	Scotland	P
Bonnie Wee Thing	Burr, Henry	Columbia 1799	1915	Scotland	P
Every Laddie Loves a Lassie	Lauder, Harry?		1910	Scotland	P
Highland Mary Did the Highland Fling	Murray, Billy	Indestructable 899	-	Scotland	P
Highland Schottische	Wyper, Daniel	Columbia 716	1909	Scotland	P
Highlander's Fix Bayonets	Wiederhold, Albert	Columbia 1766	1915	Scotland	P
I Love a Lassie	Shaw, Sandy	Columbia 639	1908	Scotland	P
I've a Shooting Box in Scotland	Prince's Band	Columbia 5950	1917	Scotland	P
Lovely Maiden Schottische	Arriaga Instrumental Trio	Columbia 959	1910	Scotland	P
Medley of Scotch Airs	Columbia Band	Columbia 69	1902	Scotland	P
Moriah-Scotch	Montgomery-Stone	Victor 70044	-	Scotland	P
Scotch Bagpipe Medley	Lovat Bagpipes	Victor 17920	1915	Scotland	E
Scotland Burning	Kline, Olive / Dunlap, M. / Baker, E.	Victor 18277	1917	Scotland	P
Scots wa hae (Waiting at the Church)	Wiederhold, Albert	Columbia 1876	1915	Scotland	P
Scots Waa Hae Wi Wallace Bled	Burr, Henry	Columbia 458	1905	Scotland	P
Skotlandspojkar	Alexander Prince's band	Victor 17795	1915	Scotland	P
Songs of Scotland	Sousa's Band	Berliner 141	1898	Scotland	P
Within a Mile of Edinboro Town	Keyes, Margaret	Columbia 5290	1910	Scotland	E
Ye Banks and Braes of Bonnie Doon	Adams, Charles	Columbia 1689	1915	Scotland	E
Bolero	Ossman, Vess	Berliner 718F	1899	Spain	P
Cancion de Benedictina	Curti's Band	Columbia 47	1905	Spain	E
Caprice Espanol	Vessela's Italian Band	Victor 17908	1914	Spain	E
De Madrid a Paris	Curti's Band	Columbia 41	1905	Spain	E
El Capitan March	Columbia Band	Columbia 46	1901	Spain	P
El Capitan March	Sousa's Band	Berliner 42	1897	Spain	P
El Capitan March	Sousa's Band	Victor	1913	Spain	P
El Capitan March	Taft, Harry	Berliner 434	1898	Spain	P
El Chocio	National Promenade Band	Edison 50137	-	Spain	P
El Cuarro Poder	Banda Espanol	Columbia 105	1908	Spain	E
El Gorro Frigio	Caceres, Alberto	Columbia 509	1906	Spain	E
Emblema de la Paz	Banda Espanol	Columbia 73	1906	Spain	E
Fuentas March	Banda Espanol	Columbia 72	1906	Spain	E
Grenadiers of Saredinia Mar	Grenadiers Band	Columbia 2685	1918	Spain	P
In Old Madrid	Archibald, Vernon	Columbia 962	1910	Spain	P
Karama — Flamenco Gascon	Banda Flamenco	Columbia 636	1907	Spain	E
La Madre de Cordero	Banda Espanol	Columbia 53	-	Spain	E
La Mattchiche	Columbia Band	Columbia 53	1905	Spain	P
La Paloma	Wright, Rosa Linde	Columbia 509	1906	Spain	P
La Paolista	National Promenade Band	Edison 50147	-	Spain	P
La Tipica	Curti's Band	Columbia 54	1905	Spain	P
Los Toros Paso Doble	Banda Espanol	Columbia 62	1906	Spain	P
Minuto Paso Doble	Banda Espanol	Columbia 624	1906	Spain	E
Presidente Quintera March	Banda Espanol	Columbia 28	1906	Spain	E
Spanish Dance	Victor Orchestra	Victor 18445	1917	Spain	P

Song Title	Name of Artist(s)	Label and Selec. No.	Year Rec.	Ethnicity/ Theme	
Spanish Fandango	Edison Grand Concert Band	Edison 91	1896	Spain	P
Spanish Serenade	Prince's Orchestra	Columbia 5685	1915	Spain	P
Solveig's Song	Gates, Lucy	Columbia 5840	1916	Sweden	P
Solveig's Song	Leggett, Charles	Columbia 1175	-	Sweden	P
Lied von Suesse Maedel	Werber, Mia	Columbia 510	1903	Switzerland	E
Swiss Echo Song	Gates, Lucy	Columbia 5840	1916	Switzerland	P

Notes

Preface

1. Although unusual, examples categorized as both do exist. It might be *ethnic* due to the performers' ethnicity and *colloquial* based on the performance (due to the dialect or vernacular), but it could also be *racist* due to overtly negative stereotyping of the ethnic group (i.e., hateful and/or injurious lyrics).

2. Donald Clarke, *The Rise and Fall of Popular Music* (New York: St. Martin's Press, 1995), 62.

3. The earliest versions found are three in Edison's cylinder catalog: Edison Grand Concert Band, Arthur Collins, and Dan Quinn. All three were released between 1896 and 1899. Source: Allen Koenigsberg, ed., *Edison Cylinder Recordings, 1889–1912* (Brooklyn: APM Press, 1990).

4. Tim Gracyk, *Popular American Recording Pioneers* (Binghamton N.Y.: Haworth Press, 2000), 8.

5. See *Chapter 6: "A&R": Artists and Repertoire.*

Introduction

1. Kenneth Boulding, *The Meaning of the Twentieth Century: The Great Transition* (New York: Harper & Row, 1964), 7–8.

2. Alvin Toffler, *Future Shock* (New York: Bantam Books, 1990), 13.

3. Consumer preference for cassette players over turntables, and the cassette's compact size prompted A&M Records to pioneer the mass-market cassette single in 1987. Consumer acceptance resulted in the virtual extinction of the 7" 45-rpm single before the end of the twentieth century.

Sales of 7" singles dropped from 228 million units in 1973 to 15 million units in 1993, and less than 5 million by 2003. Source: Record Industry Association of America, http://www.riaa.com.

4. Bill Gates, *The Road Ahead* (New York: Viking Penguin, 1995), xiii.

5. John Horgan, "Bill Gates' Apocryphal History," *Scientific American*, February 1996, 32b.

6. AM radio station KDKA was granted the first commercial license by the Federal Communications Commission on October 27, 1920. Source: KDKA Radio.

7. United States Patent Number 200,521—Improvement in Phonograph or Speaking Machines—was filed on December 24, 1877, and granted on February 19, 1878. Source: Allen Koenigsberg, ed., *The Patent History of the Phonograph, 1877–1912* (Brooklyn: APM Press, 1990), 3.

8. Gracyk, *Recording Pioneers*, 25.

9. Jean de Léry, from *History of a Voyage to the Land of Brazil*, qtd. in Robin Blackburn, *The Making of New World Slavery: From the Baroque to the Modern 1492–1800* (New York: Verso, 1999), 165.

10. Ibid., 161.

11. Clarke, 18.

12. Barbara Cohen-Stratyner, ed., *Popular Music, 1900–1919: An Annotated Guide to American Popular Songs* (Bethesda: Gale Research, Inc., 1988), xv.

13. Sigmund Spaeth, *At Home with Music* (New York: Doubleday & Co., 1946), 6.

14. David Ritz, recording notes, *B. B. King's Greatest Hits*, MCA, compact disc.

Chapter 1

1. Alan Hall, "Shaping Sound," *Scientific American*, 21 December 1998, 2, http://www.sciam.com/article.cfm?articleID=00000454–7BF8-ICE2–95FB809EC588EF21&pageNumber=2&catID=4

2. R. Drew Griffith profiled Memnon in his article "The Origin of Memnon," published in *Classical Antiquity*: "Memnon is the main character of Arctinus' Aethiopis, a dithyramb of Simonides and an Aeschylean trilogy.... Son of the dawn-goddess Eos and the mortal Tithonus and king of the Ethiopians, Memnon helped Troy after the death of the pro-Trojan Amazon Penthesileia, summoned in one version, by Teutamus of Assyria. Very handsome like his father, he wore bronze armor made by Hephaestus. He killed Antilochus as the latter defended his own father, Nestor, whose chariot had been disabled by Paris' arrows and was in turn killed by Achilles. Eos begged Zeus to spare him, but a weighing of the fates during which the matres dolorosae Eos and Thetis flanked the scales, each pleading her son's case, determined that he must die. With Zeus' blessing, Eos made him immortal." R. Drew Grittifh, "The Origin of Memnon," *Classical Antiquity* 17.2 (1998): 213.

3. Ibid., 212–34.

4. Potes & Poets Press published Ray Dipalma's book of poetry titled *The Jukebox of Memnon* in 1989. No connection should be inferred.

5. Griffith, 220.

6. Oliver Read and Walter L. Welch. *From Tin Foil to Stereo: Evolution of the Phonograph* (Indianapolis: Howard W. Sams & Co., 1959), 1.

7. Donald Wright, *The World and a Very Small Place in Africa* (New York: M.E. Sharpe, Inc. , 1997), 12.

8. Horatio Alger, "Aunt Jane's Ear Trumpet," *Gleason's Literary Companion* 6, no. 14 (April 8, 1865), http://www.niulib.niu.edu/alger/auntjane.htm

9. NARAS® is the National Academy of Recording Arts and Sciences®, and its members vote for the Grammy Awards®. Grammy Awards® and NARAS® are registered trademarks of the National Academy of Recording Arts & Sciences, Inc. Source: http://naras.org/credits.aspx

10. Elie Siegmeister, ed., *The Music Lover's Handbook* (New York: William Morrow & Co., 1943), 322.

11. Ibid., 335.

Chapter 2

1. Read and Welch, 3.

2. Harry Geduld, *The Birth of the Talkies: From Edison to Jolson* (Bloomington: Indiana University Press, 1975), 4.

3. The name *phonautograph* was a derivative of the Greek words for "sound" and "(self) writer." F. B. Fenby later shortened the name to *phonograph*, and Edison would likewise choose that name for his invention.

4. *The Phonograph: Its History and Impact*, edited by David Mengel, 1 Oct 2002, http://www.nd.edu/~dmengel/hct/projects/phono/prehistory.html

5. Allen Koenigsberg, ed., *Edison Cylinder Recordings, 1889–1912* (Brooklyn: APM Press, 1987), xi.

6. Ibid., xi.

7. Roland Gelatt, *The Fabulous Phonograph: 1877–1977* (London: Cassell, 1977), 24.

Chapter 3

1. *A&M Secret*, Film director Chuck Beeson (Los Angeles: A&M Records, 1979).

2. The Beatles, *The Beatles Anthology* (San Francisco: Chronicle Books, 2000), 175.

3. Gelatt, 17–18.

4. The Morse code was developed by Samuel F. B. Morse (1791–1872) in 1844, enabling the transmission of messages in which letters of the alphabet and numbers are represented by specific sequences of dots and dashes, i.e., short and long signals. Most people are familiar with the Morse code designation of S-O-S as a distress signal.

5. Gelatt, 18.

6. Andre Millard, *America on Record: A History of Recorded Sound* (New York: Cambridge University Press, 1995), 24.

7. Koenigsberg, *Edison Cylinder Recordings*, xii.

8. Gelatt, 22.

9. "The Talking Phonograph," *Scientific American*, 22 December 1877, 384–385.

Chapter 4

1. Jason Camlot, "Early Talking Books: Spoken Recordings And Recitation Anthologies, 1880–1920," *Book History* 6 (2003), 153, http://80-muse.jhu.edu.libdb.fairfield.edu/journals/book_history/v006/6.1camlot.html
2. Archibald Henderson, *Contemporary Immortals* (Freeport: Books for Library Press, 1968), 55.
3. Koenigsberg, *Edison Cylinder Recordings*, xv.
4. Read and Welch, 26.
5. One should note, at least in passing, the uncanny (or diabolically brilliant) similarity between the name *phonograph* (Edison) and *graphophone* (Bell/Tainter)—only the "e" really marks a difference.
6. Read and Welch, 28.
7. Neil Baldwin, *Edison: Inventing the Century* (New York: Hyperion, 1995), 180.
8. Gelatt, 35.
9. Read and Welch, 119
10. Ibid., 36
11. Koenigsberg, *Edison Cylinder Recordings*, xix.
12. Read and Welch, 123

Chapter 5

1. Allen Koenigsberg, *Patent History*, xx.
2. Koenigsberg, *Edison Cylinder Recordings*, xvi.
3. Robert Conot, *A Streak of Luck* (New York: Seaview Books, 1979), 309.
4. Gelatt, 48.
5. Millard, 42.
6. Joel Whitburn, ed., *Pop Memories: 1890–1954 — The History of American Popular Music* (Menomonee Falls, Wisc.: Record Research, 1986), 12.
7. Berliner coined the name "gramophone," at least as early as his original patent application. It was granted — as patent number 372,786 — on November 8, 1887. Source: Allen Koenigsberg, *The Patent History of the Phonograph, 1877–1912* (Brooklyn: APM Press, 1990), xx.
8. Gelatt, 65.
9. Millard, 55–6.
10. Ibid., 125.

Chapter 6

1. Millard, 69.
2. Gracyk, *Recording Pioneers*, 18.
3. Leonard Feist, *An Introduction to Popular Music Publishing in America* (New York: National Music Publishers' Association, 1980), 33.
4. Millard, 82.
5. Conot, 309.
6. Charts of early record sales are useful in understanding the early recordings, but they may also be extremely unreliable. Actual counts were not always taken when stores were surveyed. No early version of the Recording Industry Association of America (RIAA) existed to give any credibility to sales figures. Tim Gracyk takes great issue with recreated or manufactured "charts" of the early recording industry. "Primary sources provide no basis for assigning chart numbers. No company files tell us precise numbers; trade journals never systematically ranked records... ; record catalogs contain no information about sales.... At no time in the acoustic era was enough information compiled or made available about sales for anyone today to create actual charts or rank best-sellers, and the further back in time we go, the more difficult we have in identifying hits.... A chart of hits means little for an era when records of many popular titles were made in the hundreds, not thousands or millions." Gracyk, *Recording Pioneers*, 11.
7. Whitburn, 332.
8. Koenigsberg, *Edison Cylinder Recordings*, 38.
9. Gracyk, *Recording Pioneers*, 250.
10. Joel Whitburn, ed., *Pop Memories*.
11. In the music industry there have been cover "versions" and cover "battles." A cover "version" is a re-recording of a song already made popular through an earlier recording. A cover "battle" is a recording of the same song by two (or more) artists recording for two (or more) record companies, and both versions are released within a short time frame, usually a few days, weeks or months. Example, *Cover versions*: Kim Weston released the first recording of "Take Me in Your Arms (Rock Me)" on Gordy records in 1965. The Isley Brothers made the charts with their version in 1968. Example, *Cover battle*: Does anyone remember Charity Brown's 1975 A&M Records release of "Take Me in Your Arms

(Rock Me)"? Her lack of success (the recording never made the *Billboard* charts) is directly proportional to the Doobie Brothers' successful version of the same title on Warner Brothers Records, a recording which peaked at #11 in May 1975.

12. Cohen-Stratyner, 32.

13. Evan Eisenberg, *The Recording Angel: Explorations in Phonography* (New York: McGraw-Hill, 1987), 14.

14. Ibid., 17–20.

15. Baldwin, 90.

Chapter 7

1. Ibid., 90.

2. The Consumer Price Index is one tool to estimate the value of the American dollar throughout history. During the next few chapters many of the prices listed will be expressed in various ways. (A) In most instances the first reference in the text will be in U.S. dollars. (B) The second reference will often be in "Inflation Adjusted (U.S.) Dollars" (or IADs), converted to prices today using the Consumer Price Index. Based on the CPI, a general "rule of thumb" for the years between 1878 and 1915 is that $1.00 equals $18–21.00 year-2004 dollars. After 1915 the multiple changes: 1916: $16.50; 1917: $14.00; 1918: $11.90; 1919: $10.30. (C) In some cases the U.S. dollars have been converted to a foreign currency, e.g., British pounds. Source: "How Much Is That," http://eh.net/hmit/ compare/

3. Gelatt, 70.

4. "This Is the Instrument," advertisement, *Atlantic Monthly Advertiser*, June 1899, 6.

5. Neil Maken's book, *Hand-Cranked Phonographs: It All Started with Edison*, offers some price perspective. "We all have a spare $7.50 which we would readily spend on a GEM, but in 1900 ... a pound of sugar [cost] 4¢, a dozen eggs 14¢ and a pound of butter 24¢...." Maken goes on to describe the cost of the *New York Times* (3¢), gentlemen's suits from $12–20, choice vaudeville concert tickets (15–35¢), a nine-day cruise to Bermuda for $37.50, and starting salaries as low as $20–30 per month. Neil Maken, *Hand-Cranked Phonographs: It All Started with Edison* (Huntington Beach: Promar Publishing, 1998).

6. Millard, 123

7. The 23 pages cited included only those companies advertising finished phonographs. Additional ads and pages featured motors, cabinets, parts, reproducers, needles, records, record sleeves, listening rooms, repairs, etc.

8. Aeolian Company Advertisement, *The Talking Machine World*, 15 Sept. 1916, 32–33.

9. To offer some perspective, why would a car buyer choose to spend $117,508 for a 2004 Hummer H1 and then complain about the high price of diesel fuel or the 10,300 pound (GVW) vehicle's relatively poor fuel economy? Source: Cars.com, http://www.cars.com/carsapp/national/?szc =06896&year=2004&srv=dealer&act=ncb- ssrch&sb=dst&sk=dst&so=asc&fs=&rd=10 0&ddrd=30&config=t&rt=quick_ncbs.tmp l&referrer=configurator&trf=homepage- new&mdnm=H1&mkid=363&=6148&zc= 06896

10. Russell Sanjek, *From Print to Plastic: Publishing and Promoting America's Popular Music (1900–1980)* (Brooklyn: Institute for Studies in American Music, 1983), 8.

11. Koenigsberg, *Edison Cylinder Recordings*, xvii.

12. Gracyk, Tim, ed., *Companion to the Encyclopedia of Popular American Recording Pioneers, 1895–1925: Rare items from the Recording Industry's Early Decades* (Granite Bay Calif.: Tim Gracyk, n.d.), 9–14.

13. The terms "juke" and "juke Joint" originated in America and were applied to what we might call today a diner. A juke-joint was a roadside cafe or restaurant serving inexpensive drinks and food and having music for dancing. The "box" inside the "jukejoint" provided the music for a nickel or a dime per song: a jukebox.

14. Read and Welch, 106.

15. A more detailed look at an actual recording session will be found in the next chapter.

16. Koenigsberg, *Edison Cylinder Recordings*, xvii-xviii.

17. Making an analog recording onto a blank cylinder or disc, using a prerecorded source — also analog — resulted in a loss of sound quality on the copy. Each subsequent copy, from a copy, resulted in more generational loss.

Chapter 8

1. Gelatt, 61

2. Gelatt, 61.

3. Both cylinders and discs benefited from evolving experiments in productivity and mass production, with stampers for discs and molds for cylinders.

4. Millard, 49

5. Eisenberg, 13.

6. Millard, 49.

Chapter 9

1. In 2003, the estimated dollar value of the American recording industry would be more than $11 billion. Source: Recording Industry Association of America.

2. Millard, 80

3. Gracyk, *Recording Pioneers*, 16.

4. "The Acoustic Process." *Southern Music in the 20th Century*, 1997–2003. Southern Music Network. 5 December 2004 http://www.southernmusic.net/acousticpro cess.htm

5. Koenigsberg, *Edison Cylinder Recordings*, 1–56.

6. "Stroh Violin 1904–1942," History Wired ©2004 National Museum of American History, Smithsonian Institution, 12 January 2005. http://historywired.si.edu/ object.cfm?id=46

7. *The Online Discographical Project*, edited by Steven Abrams, 2 Sep. 2003, http: //settlet.fateback.com/berliner.html

8. I write "apparently," as I have been unable to locate a specific reference to the recording described by Roland Gelatt in other texts, on the Internet, or at the Library of Congress. Whether or not this specific recording session took place — and it is likely that it did since Cappa's Band did exist — Gelatt's description is illustrative of the recording industry during the 1890s.

9. Gelatt, 47

10. Gelatt, 47

11. Based on Gelatt's description (pp. 47–48), one might assume the following: Ten machines x two minute sessions + four minutes for (a) machine-load/re-load, (b) announcements, and (c) simultaneous start = 6 minutes per session x 10 sessions per hour = 100 finished cylinders per hour.

12. Millard, 87.

13. Edison's company had two cylinder recordings of Lincoln's Gettysburg Address. Both were titled "Lincoln's Speech at Gettysburg." One was recorded by Russell Hunting and was released in 1897 (#3821), the other was recorded by Len Spencer and was released in 1901 (#8154). Other labels, including Victor, released Lincoln's speech.

14. *The Abraham Lincoln Papers at the Library of Congress Series 1. General Correspondence, 1833–1916.* "Edward Everett to Abraham Lincoln, November 20, 1863. Library of Congress, http://memory.loc. gov/cgi-bin/query/r?ammem/mal:@field (DOCID+@lit(d2813300))

Chapter 10

1. Dolby® is a registered trademark of Dolby Laboratories.

2. Michael Fink, *Inside the Music Industry: Creativity, Process, and Business* (New York: Schirmer books, 1996), 21.

3. Although few CDs continue to carry the code, it was regularly added to exterior packaging well into the first decade of compact disc releases— Def Leppard's *Hysteria* on Mercury (1987), for example. To digital purists, only a CD marked DDD is truly digital.

4. Catherine Moore, "Work and Recordings: The Impact of Commercialisation and Digitalisation," in *The Musical Work: Reality or Invention*, ed. Michael Talbot (Liverpool: Liverpool University Press, 2000), 92.

5. Maken, 57.

6. Robbie Lieberman, *My Song Is My Weapon: People's Songs, American Communism, and the Politics of Culture, 1930–1950* (Urbana: University of Illinois Press, 1995), 46.

7. David King Dunaway, *How Can I Keep from Singing: Pete Seeger* (New York: McGraw-Hill Publishers, 1981), 127.

8. Hughson F. Mooney, "Songs, Singers and Society, 1890–1954." *American Quarterly*, 6, no. 3. (Autumn, 1954): 223.

9. James West Davidson, et al., *Nation of Nations: A Concise Narrative of the American Republic, Volume Two — Since 1865* (New York: McGraw-Hill, 1996), 508.

10. Davidson, et al., 588.

11. Davidson, et al., 666.

12. Koenigsberg, *Edison Cylinder Recordings*, 110.

13. Millard, 56

Chapter 11

1. In the twenty-first century, con-

sumers might add computers, hard drives, CD-burners, DVD, the Internet, and iTunes as examples of hardware, software, and a blurring of the distinction. While this book will not be exploring MPEG-3 or the newer MPEG-4 Advanced Audio Coding (AAC) format, the born-again Napster, or other Napster-like file sharing services, they are not to be ignored as one considers the changing face of music technology.

2. Grammy Awards® is a registered trademark of the National Academy of Recording Arts & Sciences, Inc., http://naras.org/credits.aspx

3. Joel Whitburn, ed., *Top Pop Singles 1955–1990* (Menomonee Falls Wisc.: Record Research, 1991), 400.

4. The choice of three here is, to be obvious, arbitrary. Some number was needed, and three was the trigger based on the premise that almost anything can happen once, perhaps even twice, but three times begins to signal something more than luck.

5. Gracyk, *Recording Pioneers*, 11.

6. Early issues of *Billboard* magazine contained a regular feature called "The Billboard Song Chart" in which it listed "Songs Heard in Vaudeville Last Week." A 1915 issue listed more than thirty songs heard in New York vaudeville theaters (and a similar number listed for Chicago theaters). Among the songs listed for New York were "I Wonder Who's Kissing Her Now" and "It's a Long Long Way to Tipperary." *The Billboard*, 2 January 1915, 14.

7. "New York Vaudeville," Rev. of Fifth Avenue Theater performance, *The Billboard*, 8 January 1910, 7.

8. "Critical Song Reviews," Rev. "Sweetest Memory," *The Billboard*, 28 December 1912, 9.

9. *Billboard* magazine, in 2003, printed 23 genre charts (plus additional sub-genre charts) which encompassed Albums (14): Billboard 200 (overall popular), R&B/Hip-Hop, Country, Electronic, Latin, Bluegrass, Classical, Blues, Reggae, Jazz, Gospel/Christian, Childrens, New Age, and World Music; Singles (9): Billboard Hot 100, R&B/Hip-Hop, Country, Rap, Rock, Latin, Dance Music/Club, Adult Contemporary, Christian.

10. Geoff Mayfield, "Jackson Ends R&B Reign," *Billboard*, 30 August 2003, 55.

11. Alan Jackson and Norah Jones are representative of the idea expressed earlier in this chapter that some artists experience success beyond that associated with their core genre. In this case Jackson in *country* music and Jones in *jazz*. For both, topping the "Billboard 200" chart occurred *after* their original, genre-specific success.

12. Geoff Mayfield, "New POS Charts: Everything You Wanted To Know," *Billboard*, 11 January 1992, 1.

13. Occasionally the producer of a musical performance, instead of the performer, receives the name recognition in *Billboard* for the success of a recording, e.g., Cameron Macintosh for producing *Five Guys Named Moe*; ensemble soundtrack recordings are usually listed (as is the following example) by the generic term "soundtrack" followed by the title of the film: "Soundtrack, *Freaky Friday*," which was #19 the week of August 30, 2003. Source: *Billboard* magazine.

14. "That'll Do Thanks," *The Times of London*, 8 March 2000, http://80-web.lexis-nexis.com.libdb.fairfield.edu/universe/document?_m=6d1fc15938ec677731fcdbce3a6 8f64f&_docnum=19&wchp=dGLbVtz-zSkVA&_md5=4425bc89ea392bbfdbfb941 794a72fa6

15. The fact that it only reached #29, according to *Billboard*, was "not because consumers didn't want to buy the remake of Don MacLean's song; it's because the song [was] not commercially available [in the United States]." Fred Bronson, "Chart Beat: A Single As British As 'American Pie,'" *Billboard*, 18 March 2000.

16. "The Billboard Chart Key," *Billboard*, 10 April 2004. http://www.billboard.com/bb/biz/currentcharts/display_single.jsp?chart=THE%20BILLBOARD%20HOT%20100

Chapter 12

1. The first sides that Bryan Adams cut for A&M Records included a dance-oriented song he authored called (appropriately enough) "Let Me Take You Dancing," A&M Records SP-12014. His rock 'n' roll career would survive this recording. Worth noting is that his first single to chart on the *Billboard* "Hot 100" appeared in March 1982 and stayed on the charts only two weeks. For all intents and purposes, 1983 would be Adams' breakthrough year.

2. Cohen-Stratyner, xvi

Chapter 13

1. U.S. Department of Commerce and

Labor, Bureau of the Census, *Thirteenth Census of the United States, Taken in the Year 1910: Abstract of the Census* (Washington, D.C.: GPO, 1913), 82.

2. Julius Mattfield, ed., *Variety Music Cavalcade, 1620–1960. A Chronology of Vocal and Instrumental Music Popular in the United States* (New York: Prentice-Hall, 1952), 11.

3. The Internet Broadway Database. Used with permission. http://www.ibdb.com

4. Review of *I Pagliacci*. Grand Opera House, New York. *New York Times*, 15 June 1893, 4.

5. Gracyk, 18.

6. While it is reasonable to conclude that the creation of vaudeville helped clean up the sometimes bawdy image of variety theater, the descriptions offered — even during the transition phase to more respectable stages — maintain a certain maleness of the customer demographic. It fell to the songpluggers, whose job it was to get exposure for new material by theater performers, to achieve success for their employers, the music publishers. Meyer stated: "The songplugger covered a beat that made sissies out of reporters and policemen." Hazel Meyer, *The Gold in Tin Pan Alley* (Philadelphia: J. B. Lippincott Company, 1958), 46.

7. Ibid., 47–48.

8. Clarke, 44.

9. It may have been serendipity or coincidence, but the confluence of events that seemed to converge *creating* vaudeville also helped to *create* (or benefit) Tin Pan Alley. This area was the general location of theaters, publishing companies, booking agents, and entertainers. Hazel Meyer suggests that the decision by the music publishers to invest and ultimately dominate the area began in 1898 with the relocation of the House of Witmark publishing company to a "converted Brownstone on West Twenty-ninth Street" (Meyer, 35). In addition, *The New York Clipper*—an early entertainment industry trade paper — had its headquarters in the area. Tin Pan Alley would be a music-publishing/songwriting force through World War II.

10. Too many people appear to have offered their expert opinion as to who first applied the name *Tin Pan Ally* to the area, and why. Whether it was journalist/songwriter Monroe Rosenfeld, songwriter and music publisher Harry von Tilzer, author

O. Henry, or lyricist Stanley Murphy — all of whom are described in Meyer's book — the fact is that the street and the neighborhood were uniquely identified with songs, music publishing, and the theater.

11. "New York Songlines: Virtual Walking Tours of Manhattan Streets." 3 October 2003, http://home.nyc.rr.com/jkn/nysonglines/28st.htm

12. Meyer, 37.

13. Randy Poe, *Music Publishing: A Songwriter's Guide* (Cincinnati: Writer's Digest Books, 1997), 5.

14. Each song has been assigned a date referring to its earliest significantly recognized use in America. For example, (a) the song "Yankee Doodle" is assigned "1767," as available information suggests that this is the year that the song was Americanized, even though it was most likely brought from England much earlier; (b) the song "Auld Lang Syne" is assigned "18c" as no other specific document, beyond the lyrics attributed to Robert Burns, corresponds to a precise year of either the melody's original authorship or its first time published in the U.S.; (c) the first significance within the United States of "The Star Spangled Banner" is tied quite clearly to Francis Scott Key's lyrics having been authored in 1814; (d) the 1862 adaption of "Battle Hymn of the Republic" during the American Civil War. Most of the dates were found in *Handbook of Early American Sheet Music, 1768–1889* by Harry Dichter and Elliott Shapiro, and *A History of Popular Music* by Sigmund Spaeth. Other sheet music sources include: (a) University of Colorado Digital Sheet Music Collection; (b) Duke University, Rare Book, Manuscript, and Special Collections Library; (c) American Memory: Historical Collections for the National Digital Library. (See bibliography for complete information regarding the two texts and the sheet music online resources.) Additional information was referenced in other texts or was taken from original samples or copies of the early sheet music.

Chapter 14

1. Beyond their widely known pop success, the Eagles had three singles on the Top Country singles chart: "Lyin' Eyes" in 1975, "New Kid in Town" in 1977, and "Seven Bridges Road" in 1981.

2. These pre-1950 recordings were released with the following labels and selection numbers: (1) Victor 18626; (2) Black Swan 14127, (reissued (?) as Decca 7469); (3) Brunswick 4964; (4) Brunswick 6038; (5) Decca, 62738; (6) Bluebird 074058; (7) Bluebird 0725; (8) King 4210; (9) Imperial 5113, 1949; and (10) Gotham 188.

3. Nick Tosches, *Unsung Heroes of Rock 'n' Roll: The Birth of Rock in the Wild Years Before Elvis* (New York: Da Capo Press, 1999), 6.

4. John A. Jackson, *Big Beat Heat: Alan Freed and the Early Years of Rock & Roll* (New York: Schirmer Books, 1991), 83–84.

5. Eileen Southern, *The Music of Black Americans: A History* (New York: W.W. Norton & Co., 1997), 599.

6. Southern, 599.

7. K. Maurice Jones, *The Story of Rap Music* (Brookfield, Conn.: Millbrook Press, 1994), 46.

8. Nelson George, *Hip Hop America* (New York: Penguin Books, 1999), 57.

9. largo: very slow tempo; adagio: slow tempo; moderato: moderate tempo; andante: moderately slow tempo; allegro: quick, lively tempo; allegretto: moderately quick tempo; presto: very fast tempo; prestissimo: as fast a tempo as possible.

10. Ballad is derived from the Latin word *Ballare*: to dance.

11. Peter Herbst, *The Rolling Stone Interviews. Talking with the Legends of Rock & Roll: 1967–1980* (New York: St. Martin's Press, 1981), 78–9.

12. The peak chart (album) positions for the ten Dylan albums after *Nashville Skyline* were (in order) 5, 7, 16, 1, 3, 1, 1, 17, 11, 3. Source: *Billboard* magazine.

13. Two singles from Dylan's country flavored album made the Hot 100 singles chart including "Lay Lady Lay," which peaked at #7 (1969). (Dylan's singles did not appear on *Billboard*'s country music chart.)

Chapter 15

1. Cohen-Stratyner, xvi.
2. Clarke, 53.
3. Also recorded by songwriter Cochran and the group J. Frank Wilson & the Cavaliers in 1964.
4. Cohen-Stratyner, xvi.
5. Spaeth, 266.
6. Charles K. Harris, "Hello Central, Give Me Heaven." 1901. (Milwaukee: Chas. K. Harris, 1901.) Rare Book, Manuscript, and Special Collections Library, Duke University, http://scriptorium.lib.duke.edu:80/sheetmusic/n/n03/n0311/n0311–3–72dpi.html

7. George Evans, "In the Good Old Summer Time." 1912. (New York: Howley, Havilland, & Dresser, 1912.) Rare Book, Manuscript, and Special Collections Library, Duke University, http://scriptorium.lib.duke.edu:80/sheetmusic/a/a29/a2969/a2969–1–72dpi.html

8. Harry Williams, "When You Were Sweet Sixteen," 1911. (New York: Jerome H. Remick & Co., 1911.) Rare Book, Manuscript, and Special Collections Library, Duke University, http://scriptorium.lib.duke.edu:80/dynaweb/sheetmusic/1910–1920/@Generic__BookTextView/49393;nh=1?DwebQuery=a6587#X

9. Mooney, 223.
10. Cohen-Stratyner, xvii.
11. "Dixie" is also known as "Dixie's Land" and "I Wish I Was in Dixie."
12. *Grove's Dictionary of Music* defines a "walk-around" as a "secular imitation of the black 'shout.'"
13. Siegmeister, 138.
14. Spaeth, 367.
15. Terry Waldo, *This Is Ragtime* (New York: Hawthorn Books, 1976), 21.
16. Clarke, 58.
17. "Decadence of 'Rag-Time' Music." *Billboard*. Dec 29, 1900, 1.
18. Ibid., 1.
19. Waldo, 21.
20. The term "cakewalk" may have originated from American slaves performing strutting dance steps as competition for a prize of a cake.
21. Southern, 317.
22. Clarke, 56.
23. Waldo, 22.
24. Ostendorf quantified the term by stating that ragtime "identifies that era in the history of American music from 1896–1917." Berndt Ostendorf, "The Musical World of Doctorow's Ragtime," *American Quarterly*, 43, no. 4. (Dec., 1991); 579.
25. Cohen-Stratyner, xix.
26. Cohen-Stratyner, xix.
27. Meyer, 63.
28. See *Dance History Archives* and Streetswing.com for an invaluable list of dances, origins, and variations. http://

www.streetswing.com/histmain/d5index.h
tm.
29. Cohen-Stratyner, 52.
30. Millard, 83.
31. Cohen-Stratyner, xx.

Chapter 16

1. Richard K. Spottswood, "An Introduction," *Ethnic Recordings in America: A
Neglected Heritage*, Library of Congress,
American Folklife Center (Washington,
D.C.: GPO, 1982).
2. Siegmeister, 11.
3. Beethoven's *Third Symphony* was to
be dedicated to Napoleon Bonaparte, "the
hero who was to save the world from
tyranny." As the hero turned into dictator,
a disillusioned [Beethoven] tore off the ded-
icatory page and trampled it underfoot.
When the symphony was published in 1806,
it was called simply *Eroica*, with an in-
scription, in Italian, 'to the memory of a
great man.'" Sigmund Spaeth, *At Home
with Music* (New York: Doubleday & Co.,
1946), 82.
4. During the 1990s, consumer preference for classical recordings represented on
average only 3.2% of the American music
industry. Its decade high was 3.7 (1992,
1994) and its low was 2.7% (2000). source:
Recording Industry Association of America, "2000 Consumer Profile."
5. In the nineteenth century, the pop
ulation center shifted west from Baltimore
to Indiana, a distance of approximately 450
miles. The majority of the population was
still in the eastern United States, and the
recording industry's perception of that
population — their consumer market —
continued to incorporate many immigrant
groups and their second and third generation families. That population was well represented in urban areas, particularly New
York. Source: U.S. Department of Commerce and Labor, Bureau of the Census,
*Thirteenth Census of the United States,
Taken in the Year 1910: Abstract of the Census* (Washington, D.C.: GPO, 1913), 30.
6. In "Chapter 13, "Of Places, Performers, and Songs" I briefly quoted Donald Clarke's explanation for the transition
of local entertainment spots into showcases
for traveling talent. The complete quotation is: "With taverns and 'opera houses'
available as venues for touring talent, and

with the railways making it possible for the
talent to go anywhere, a variety show circuit began to develop all over the U.S.A.
Chanson du vau de Vire originated in a val-
ley in the Calvados, France, which was famous for its satirical songs in the fifteenth
century, and the corruption 'vau de ville'
was used of any light entertainment. The
American music hall tradition came to be
called vaudeville." Clarke, 44.
7. Roger Daniels, *Coming to America:
A History of Immigration and Ethnicity in
American Life* (New York: Harper Perennial, 1991), 121.
8. U.S. Department of Commerce, Bureau of the Census, *Historical Statistics of
the United States: Colonial Times to 1970,
Part 1* (Washington, D.C.: GPO, 1975), 117.
9. Bernard Bailyn, Robert Dallek,
David Brion Davis, David Herbert Donald,
John L. Thomas, and Gordon S. Wood. *The
Great Republic: A History of the American
People* (Lexington: D.C. Heath and Company, 1992), 154.
10. The most likely countries of origin
for those foreign-born residents categorized
as black or Negro were (a) Cuba, Puerto Rico
and the Caribbean islands in general, and
(b) Africa. The 28,000 persons in 1900 and
the 52,000 in 1910 are all the foreign-born
individuals identified as having departed
originally from these two regions.
11. Daniels, 276.
12. For purposes of this research, blacks
are included in Appendix 1 titled *Foreign-
born and Black Population of New York City:
1900 and 1910*. The black/Negro share of the
total *foreign-born/black* population of the
city in 1910 remained flat at approximately
4.5%; blacks represented almost 2% of New
York City's total 1910 population. (*Thirteenth
Census of the United States, taken in the Year
1910: Abstract of the Census.* Table 19.)
13. *Thirteenth Census of the United
States, taken in the Year 1910: Abstract of the
Census.* Table 19.
14. Mario Maffi, *Gateway to the Promised
Land: Ethnic Cultures in New York's Lower
East Side* (New York: New York University
Press, 1995), 108.
15. It is almost certain that within many
if not most of the documented languages
categorized in the 1910 census there existed
additional languages and dialects not accu-
rately identified by census takers.
16. U.S. Department of Commerce and
Labor, Bureau of the Census, *Thirteenth

Census of the United States, taken in the Year 1910: Abstract of the Census (Washington, D.C.: GPO, 1913), Table 4.

17. Robert Ezra Park, *Society: Collective Behavior, News and Opinion, Sociology and Modern Society* (Glencoe: The Free Press, 1955), 165.

18. A contemporary ethnic example, for comparison and understanding, is a recording by singer Gloria Estefan. Her early music with recording group Miami Sound Machine might be categorized as crossover (from a Latin-pop audience to the general-pop audience), but it nevertheless displays her Cuban ethnicity. The song "Conga" (1985) has its roots in Cuban-Latin dance music, the popularity of which — while originating in south Florida — transcended that perceived regional boundary to become generally popular. Contemporary examples of the second field, pseudo-ethnic, include the Elvis Presley and Joe Dowell recordings of "Wooden Heart" (1961). Presley and Dowell adapted a German folk song "Muse I Denn," singing portions of the song in German.

19. Spaeth, 353.

20. Without more accurate and comprehensive lists from the early companies, much of this is based on estimates. The total might actually be significantly larger than 23,500. Sources: Koenigsberg, *Edison Cylinder Records* and *The Online Discographical Project*.

21. Gracyk, *Recording Pioneers*, 11.

22. Lyrics within the Exotic group included references to cities (Cairo, Constantinople, Bombay, and Singapore); countries or regional geographic locations (Siam, Bosporous, Zanzibar, Samoa, Mandalay, Turkey, Hindustan, Arabia, Burma, Egypt, Japan, Borneo, Africa, and South Seas); people (sultans, Gungha Din, Bedouins, Arabs, Fakirs, and Cleopatra).

23. Ann Charters, as quoted by Richard M. Sudhalter in recording liner notes for *Don't Give the Name a Bad Place: Types and Stereotypes in American Musical Theater 1870–1900* (New World Records 80265), 29 compact disc.

24. Cohen-Stratyner, xviii.

Chapter 17

1. In fact, the smaller ethnic groups ran from a low of 1 recording, to a high of 28 recordings. The smaller list of 23 ethnic groups comprised less than 30 recordings each, with most having 10 or fewer. All ethnic groups are, however, included in Appendix 2.

2. Millard, 83.

3. Francis Davis, *The History of the Blues: The Roots, the Music, the People from Charley Patton to Robert Cray* (New York: Hyperion, 1995), 36–7.

4. Waldo, 25.

5. Waldo, 25.

6. "Tutti Frutti": Little Richard was on the charts in November 1955, Pat Boone in January 1956. "When a Man Loves a Woman": Percy Sledge was on the charts in April 1966, Michael Bolton in June 1991. Source: Joel Whitburn's *Top Pop Singles*; *Billboard*.

7. Southern, 89.

8. Millard, 86.

9. Southern, 317.

10. Southern, 236.

11. Siegmeister, 743.

12. Stephen Foster, "Massa's in de Cold Cold Ground." (New York: Armstrong Music Publishing Company, 1902), 2–3.

13. Shelton Brooks, "The Darktown Strutter's Ball." (New York: Leo Feist, Inc., 1917).

14. John Solomon Otto and Augustus M. Burns, "The Use of Race and Hillbilly Recordings as Sources for Historical Research: The Problem of Color Hierarchy among Afro-Americans in the Early Twentieth Century," *The Journal of American Folklore*, 85, no. 338 (Oct. — Dec., 1972); 346. http://links.jstor.org/sici?sici=0021–8715%28197210%2F12%2985%3A338%3C344%3ATUORAH%3E2.0.CO%3B2-Q

15. Richard Corliss, "That Old Feeling: A Berlin Bio-pic," *Time Online Edition*, 30 Dec. 2001, http://www.time.com/time/sampler/article/0,8599,190220,00.html

16. Spaeth, 372.

17. Southern, 309.

18. James T. Maher, as quoted by Berndt Ostendorf in "The Musical World of Doctorow's Ragtime." *American Quarterly* 43, no. 4 (Dec., 1991): 580.

19. The original scheduled air service to Hawaii was provided by Pan American World Airways. Pan Am's first Hawaiian flight by a China Clipper, which was a Martin M-130 Flying Boat, departed from San Francisco and arrived in the Hawaiian Islands on November 23, 1935. Commercial jet service began in 1960.

20. Pekka Gronow and Ilpo Saunio, *An International History of the Recording Industry*, translated by Christopher Moseley. (New York: Cassell, 1999), 14.

21. Ibid., 32.

22. Toni Logan, "Fountain of Uke," *San Francisco Examiner*, 25 Apr 2002, 8 Apr 2003, http://www.examiner.com/ex_files/default.jsp?story=X0425UKULELEw

23. Gracyk, *Recording Pioneers*, 118.

24. Arthur M. Schlesinger, Jr., ed., *The Almanac of American History* (New York: Barnes & Noble Books, 1993), 245.

25. Ibid., 375.

26. Jane C. Desmond, "Picturing Hawai'i: The 'Ideal' Native and the Origins of Tourism, 1880–1915," *Positions: East Asia Cultures Critique* 7, no. 2 (Fall 1999) http://muse.jhu.edu/journals/positions/v007/7.2desmond.html

27. Gronow and Saunio, 32.

28. Review of "The Bird of Paradise," by Richard Walton Tully. Maxine Elliott's Theater, New York. *New York Times*, 9 January 1912, 8.

29. "Brudda Bu's Ukulele Heaven," *A Brief History of Hawaiian Slack Key Guitar (ki ho'alu)*, 2001, http://www.arts.auckland.ac.nz/ant/234/lec3Anotes.htm

30. Daniels, 127.

31. Daniels, 140.

32. Daniels, 140.

33. J. Stanley Lemons, "Black Stereotypes as Reflected in Popular Culture, 1880–1920." *American Quarterly*. 29, no. 1 (Spring, 1977): 106.

34. Gracyk, *Recording Pioneers*, 288.

35. Mick Moloney, "Irish Ethnic Recordings and the Irish Imagination," *Ethnic Recordings in America: A Neglected Heritage*. Library of Congress, American Folklife Center (Washington, D.C.: GPO, 1982), 85.

36. Whitburn, 301–303.

37. Moloney, 87.

38. Moloney, 90.

39. Daniels, 144.

40. The earliest discs, regardless of material composition, established viability of the basic format, from wax, to shellac, to vinyl, to today's aluminum and gold-coated compact discs. The diameter and circumference have changed over time, but the disc concept exists today.

41. Gronow, 4.

42. Gelatt, 105.

43. Gelatt, 201.

44. Gronow, 5.

45. Daniels, 162.

46. Daniels, 188–189.

47. Daniels, 195.

48. Paul Nettl, *National Anthems*, translated by Alexander Gode (New York: Frederick Ungar, 1967), 107.

49. Whitburn, 79.

50. Daniels, 155.

51. Nativism, favoring the original American immigrants from Great Britain, Ireland, and Northern and Western Europe, placed quotas on all immigrants, based on one's country of origin after 1924.

52. Daniels, 226.

53. Spaeth, 290–292.

54. Cohen-Stratyner, 55.

55. Daniels, 245–246.

56. Source: The Polish Roman Catholic Union of America, http://www.prcua.org/news/earlyhistory.htm

57. Source: Polish National Alliance, http://www.pna-znp.org/historybrief.htm

58. Daniels, 222.

59. Spottswood, 134.

60. Gronow, 15.

61. Cohen-Stratyner, 67, 283.

62. Joel Whitburn asserts that "Cohen on the Telephone," "Cohen on his Honeymoon," and "Cohen Telephones from Brighton" were all popular enough to be included on his early popularity charts. A documented popularity suggests consumers from outside of the core audience. See Whitburn, 486.

63. Arthur M. Swanstrom and Carey Morgan, "The Argentines, the Portuguese and the Greeks" (New York: Jos. W. Stern & Co., 1920), 3–6.

64. Gronow, 5.

Chapter 18

1. "Columbia Company," Disc and Cylinder Reviews, *Talking Machine News*, February 1907, 809–810.

2. Whitburn, 7.

3. "Ten Best Sellers," *The Billboard*, 19 July 1913, 15.

4. Ibid., 15.

5. Eisenberg, 16.

Chapter 19

1. Gelatt, 77.

2. Baldwin, 318.

3. Millard, 82.

4. The Consolidated Talking Machine

Company was the precursor of the Victor Talking Machine Company. Victor, which was started in 1900, would later merge with Berliner, and still later — January 4, 1929 — would become a division of the Radio Corporation of America, renamed RCA Victor Records. Victor was also affiliated with the Gramophone & Typewriter Company, Ltd. of London. Fred Gaisberg's relationship with Caruso would benefit both the Victor Talking Machine Company and the Gramophone & Typewriter Company, with Victor ultimately becoming the strongest link to Caruso.

5. According to Enrico Caruso, Jr.'s performance chronology, Arturo Toscanini conducted the performance in Milan.

6. Enrico Caruso, Jr., and Andrew Farkas, *Enrico Caruso: My Father and My Family* (Portland: Amadeus Press, 1990), 82.

7. Ibid., 82.

8. Howard Greenfield, *Caruso* (New York: G. P. Putnam's Sons, 1983), 19–21.

9. Pierre V. R. Key, with Bruno Zirato, *Enrico Caruso: A Biography* (Boston: Little Brown, 1922), 28.

10. Note from Enrico Caruso to Don Antonio Mazzarella of Caserta, January 1895. Source: Key, 58–59.

11. According to Enrico Caruso, Jr.'s biography of his father, the singer had the following number of paid performances during the sixteen years surveyed: 1894:1; 1895: 57; 1896: 20; 1897: 28; 1898: 36; 1899: 68; 1900: 91; 1901: 74; 1902: 69; 1903: 90; 1904: 90; 1905: 90; 1906: 110; 1907: 113; 1908: 91; 1909: 59. These are calendar-year performances, not opera/concert seasons. Source: Caruso, Jr., 655–698.

12. Caruso, Jr., 356.

13. Rev. of *Rigoletto*. Metropolitan Opera House, New York, *New York Times*, 24 Nov 1903, 1.

14. Caruso, Jr., 357.

15. Ibid., 357.

16. "Chronology of Enrico Caruso's Appearances." Enrico Caruso, Jr., and Andrew Farkas, *Enrico Caruso: My Father and My Family* (Portland: Amadeus Press, 1990), 655–698.

17. Greenfield, 72.

18. Caruso, Jr. 358.

19. Ibid., 359.

20. Stanley Jackson, *Caruso* (New York: Stein and Day, 1972), 92.

21. Caruso was paid £100; 1902 value in US dollars was $487.00 ($4.87-to-£1.00); adjusted for inflation $487 equals $10,100 IADs.

22. Millard, 59.

23. Caruso, Jr., 359.

24. Many view Gaisberg's April 1902 recordings as the start of Caruso's Victor recording career. While Caruso recorded exclusively for Victor, he did do two other sessions — some evidence suggests they were earlier than Fred Gaisberg's April 1902 session; another view is that between Gaisberg's second session of recordings in November 1902 and the execution of a formal contract Caruso made ten non-Victor recordings, all of which are listed in Caruso's biography written by his son. Seven were released by the International Zonophone Company, and three by the Anglo-Italian Commerce Company (AICC). Roland Gelatt states that the French company Pathé Frères had been granted rights by AICC for release of the Caruso masters outside of Italy (Gelatt, 104). Regardless the world was introduced to Caruso through the Gaisberg and Victor recordings, and the vast majority of all recorded repertoire was initiated and controlled by Victor.

25. Caruso, Jr., 361.

26. Based on the numbers we know including the estimate of a $90,000 profit cited earlier, one can estimate that the original £100/$487 investment ($10,100 IADs) yielded a relatively quick 8000% profit equal to $1.9 million in IADs.

27. Caruso, Jr., 363–362.

28. Caruso, Jr., 363.

29. Source: "How Much Is That," http://eh.net/hmit/compare/

30. John Frederick Cone. *Adalina Patti: Queen of Hearts* (Portland: Amadeus Press, 1993), 305.

31. Caruso, Jr., 363.

32. Eisenberg, 17.

33. Cone, J., 308.

34. Baldwin, 318.

Chapter 20

1. Henderson, 98.

2. Siegmeister, 635.

3. Michael C Keith and Joseph M. Krause, *The Radio Station* (Boston: Focal Press, 1986), 1.

4. Cohen-Stratyner, xv.

5. Cohen-Stratyner, xv.

Bibliography

A&M Secret. Film director Dir. Chuck Beeson. Los Angeles: A&M Records, 1979.

"The Acoustic Process." *Southern Music in the 20th Century*. Southern Music Network, 5 December 2004. http://www.southernmusic.net/acousticprocess.htm.

Alger, Horatio. "Aunt Jane's Ear Trumpet." *Gleason's Literary Companion*. 6, no. 14 (April 8, 1865), http://www.niulib.niu.edu/alger/auntjane.htm

American Memory: Historical Collections for the National Digital Library. Library of Congress, http://lcweb2.loc.gov/ammem/ammemhome.html

Bailyn, Bernard, Robert Dallek, David Brion Davis, David Herbert Donald, John L. Thomas, and Gordon S. Wood. *The Great Republic: A History of the American People*. Lexington: D.C. Heath & Company, 1992.

Baldwin, Neil. *Edison: Inventing the Century*. New York: Hyperion, 1995.

The Beatles. *The Beatles Anthology*. San Francisco: Chronicle Books, 2000.

Blackburn, Robin. *The Making of New World Slavery: From the Baroque to the Modern 1492–1800*. New York: Verso, 1999.

_____. *The Overthrow of New World Slavery: 1776–1848*. New York: Verso, 1996.

Boulding, Kenneth. *The Meaning of the Twentieth Century: The Great Transition*. New York: Harper & Row, 1964.

Bronson, Fred. "Chart Beat: A Single As British As 'American Pie.'" *Billboard*, 18 March 2000.

Brooks, Shelton. "The Darktown Strutter's Ball." New York: Leo Feist, Inc., 1917. Song.

Brown, Lawrence Guy. *Immigration: Cultural Conflicts and Social Adjustments*. New York: Longmans, Green, & Co., 1933.

Brownstone, David M., and Irene M. Franck, *Facts about American Immigration*. New York: H.W. Wilson Company, 2001.

Camlot, Jason. "Early Talking Books: Spoken Recordings and Recitation Anthologies, 1880–1920," *Book History* 6 (2003): 147–173. http://80- muse.jhu.edu.libdb.fairfield.edu/journals/book_history/v006/6.1camlot.html

Caruso, Enrico, Jr., and Andrew Farkas. *Enrico Caruso: My Father and My Family*. Portland: Amadeus Press, 1990.

A Catalog of Phonorecordings of Music and Oral Data Held by the Archives of Traditional Music. Boston: G.K. Hall, 1975.

Charters, Ann. *Nobody: The Story of Bert Williams*. New York: Macmillan, 1970.

Cimbala, Paul A. "Black Musicians from Slavery to Freedom: An Exploration of an African-American Folk Elite and Cultural Continuity in the Nineteenth-Century Rural South." *Journal of Negro History* 80, no. 1, (Winter 1995): 15–29.

Clarke, Donald. *The Rise and Fall of Popular Music*. New York: St. Martin's Press, 1995.

Cohen-Stratyner, Barbara, ed. *Popular Music, 1900–1919: An Annotated Guide to American Popular Songs*. Bethesda: Gale Research, Inc., 1988.

"Columbia Company." Disc and Cylinder Reviews. *Talking Machine News*, February 1907, 809.

Cone, James H. *The Spirituals and the Blues*. Maryknoll N.Y.: Orbis, 1972.

Cone, John Frederick. *Adelina Patti: Queen of Hearts*. Portland: Amadeus Press, 1993.

Conot, Robert. *A Streak of Luck*. New York: Seaview Books, 1979.

Corliss, Richard. "That Old Feeling: A Berlin Bio-pic." *Time Online Edition*, 30 December 2001, http://www.time.com/time/sampler/article/0,8599,190220,00.html

Courlander, Harold. *Negro Folk Music, U.S.A.* New York: Columbia University Press, 1963.

Daniels, Roger. *Coming to America: A History of Immigration and Ethnicity in American Life*. New York: Harper Perennial, 1991.

Davidson, James West, William E. Gienapp, Christine Leigh Heyrman, Mark H. Lytle, and Michael B. Stoff. *Nation of Nations: A Concise Narrative of the American Republic, Volume Two — Since 1865*. New York: McGraw-Hill, 1996.

Davis, Angela. *Blues Legacies and Black Feminism: Gertrude "Ma" Rainey, Bessie Smith, and Billie Holiday*. New York: Vintage Books, 1998.

Davis, Francis. *The History of the Blues: The Roots, the Music, the People from Charley Patton to Robert Cray*. New York: Hyperion, 1995.

"Decadence of 'Rag-Time' Music." *Billboard*. 29 December 1900.

DeGregrorio, William A. *The Complete Book of U.S. Presidents*. New York: Barricade Books, 1996.

Desmond, Jane C. "Picturing Hawai'i: The 'Ideal' Native and the Origins of Tourism, 1880–1915." *Positions: East Asia Cultures Critique* 7, no. 2 (Fall 1999), http://muse.jhu.edu/journals/positions/v007/7.2desmond.html.

Dichter, Harry, and Elliott Shapiro. *Handbook of Early American Sheet Music, 1768–1889*. New York: Dover, 1977.

Dowd, Doug. *Blues for America: A Critique, a Lament, and Some Memories*. New York: Monthly Review Press, 1997.

Dunaway, David King. *How Can I Keep From Singing: Pete Seeger*. New York: McGraw-Hill Publishers, 1981.

Eisenberg, Evan. *The Recording Angel: Explorations in Phonography*. New York: McGraw-Hill, 1987.

Feist, Leonard. *An Introduction to Popular Music Publishing in America*. New York: National Music Publishers' Association, 1980.

Fink, Michael. *Inside the Music Industry: Creativity, Process, and Business*. New York: Schirmer Books, 1996.

Fisher, Miles Mark. *Negro Slave Songs in the United States*. New York: Russell & Russell, 1968.

Foster, Stephen. "Massa's in de Cold Cold Ground." (New York: Armstrong Music Publishing Company, 1902 Song.

Gates, Bill. *The Road Ahead*. New York: Viking Penguin, 1995.

Geduld, Harry. *The Birth of the Talkies: From Edison to Jolson*. Bloomington: Indiana University Press, 1975.

Gelatt, Roland. *The Fabulous Phonograph: 1877–1977*. London: Cassell, 1977.

George, Nelson. *Hip Hop America*. New York: Penguin Books, 1999.

Glazer, Nathan, and Daniel Patrick Moynihan. *Beyond the Melting Pot: The Negroes, Puerto Ricans, Jews, Italians, and Irish of New York City*. Cambridge: M.I.T. Press, 1963.

Gracyk, Tim, ed. *Companion to the Encyclopedia of Popular American Recording Pioneers, 1895–1925: Rare Items from the Recording Industry's Early Decades*. Granite Bay Calif.: Tim Gracyk, n.d.

_____. *Popular American Recording Pioneers*. Binghamton N.Y.: Haworth Press, 2000.

Greenfield, Howard. *Caruso*. New York: G. P. Putnam's Sons, 1983.

Griffith, R. Drew. "The Origin of Memnon." *Classical Antiquity* 17.2 (1998): 212–34.

Gronow, Pekka, and Ilpo Saunio. *An International History of the Recording Industry*. Translated by Christopher Moseley. New York: Cassell, 1999.

Gronow, Pekka. "An Introduction," *Ethnic Recordings in America: A Neglected Heritage*. Library of Congress. American Folklife Center. Washington, D.C.: GPO, 1982.

Halberstam, David. *The Fifties*. New York: Villard Books, 1993.

Hall, Alan. "Shaping Sound." *Scientific American*, 16 Mar 2004, 21 December 1998; http://www.sciam.com/article. cfm?articleID=00000454–7BF8–ICE2–95FB809EC588EF21&pageNumber=2&catID=4

Hall, Charles, J. *A Chronicle of American Music: 1700–1995*. New York: Schirmer Books, 1996.

Henderson, Archibald. *Contemporary Immortals*. Freeport, (N.Y.): Books for Library Press, 1968.

Herbst, Peter. *The Rolling Stone Interviews. Talking with the Legends of Rock & Roll: 1967–1980*. New York: St. Martin's Press, 1981.

"Historic American Sheet Music: 1850–1920." Duke University, Rare Book, Manuscript, and Special Collections Library. http://lcweb2.loc.gov/ammem /award97/ncdhtml/hasmhome.html

Hodin, Mark. "The Disavowal of Ethnicity: Legitimate Theater and the Social Construction of Literary Value in Turn-of-the-Century America." *Theater Journal* 52 (2000), 211–226.

Horgan, John. "Bill Gates' Apocryphal History." *Scientific American*, February 1996, 32b.

Review of "I Pagliacci." Grand Opera House, New York. *New York Times*, 15 June 1893.

Iger, Arthur L. *Music of the Golden Age, 1900–1950 and Beyond: A Guide to Popular Composers and Lyricists*. Westport: Greenwood Press, 1998.

The Internet Broadway Database. The

League of American Theatres and Producers. http://www.ibdb.com

Jehl, Francis. *Menlo Park Reminisces (Volume One)*. New York: Dover, 1990.

Jackson, John A. *Big Beat Heat: Alan Freed and the Early Years of Rock & Roll*. New York: Schirmer Books, 1991.

Jackson, Stanley. *Caruso*. New York: Stein & Day, 1972.

Jones, K. Maurice. *The Story of Rap Music*. Brookfield, Conn.: Millbrook Press, 1994.

Keith, Michael C., and Joseph M. Krause. *The Radio Station*. Boston: Focal Press, 1986.

Kenney, William Howland. *Recorded Music in American Life: The Phonograph and Popular Memory, 1890–1945*. New York: Oxford University Press, 1999.

Key, Pierre V. R., with Bruno Zirato. *Enrico Caruso: A Biography*. Boston: Little Brown, 1922.

Koenigsberg, Allen, ed. *Edison Cylinder Recordings, 1889–1912*. Brooklyn: APM Press, 1987.

_____. *The Patent History of the Phonograph, 1877–1912*. Brooklyn: APM Press, 1990.

Kubik, Gerhard. *Africa and the Blues*. Jackson: University Press of Mississippi, 1999.

Lemons, J. Stanley. "Black Stereotypes as Reflected in Popular Culture, 1880–1920." *American Quarterly* 29, no. 1 (Spring 1977): 102–116.

Lieberman, Robbie. *My Song Is My Weapon: People's Songs, American Communism, and the Politics of Culture, 1930–1950*. Urbana: University of Illinois Press, 1995.

Locke, Alain. *The Negro and His Music*. Washington, D.C.: The Associates in Negro Folk Education, 1936.

Logan, Toni. "Fountain of Uke." *San Francisco Examiner*, 25 Apr 2002, 8 Apr 2003, http://www.examiner.com/ex_ files/default.jsp?story=X0425UKUL ELEw

Maffi, Mario. *Gateway to the Promised Land: Ethnic Cultures in New York's*

Lower East Side. New York: New York University Press, 1995.

Maken, Neil. *Hand-Cranked Phonographs: It All Started with Edison.* Huntington Beach: Promar Publishing, 1998.

Mattfield, Julius, ed. *Variety Music Cavalcade, 1620–1950. A Chronology of Vocal and Instrumental Music Popular in the United States.* New York: Prentice-Hall, 1952.

Mayfield, Geoff. "Jackson Ends R&B Reign." *Billboard,* 30 August 2003.

"Memnon." *Encyclopaedia Britannica.* Chicago: University of Chicago, 1979.

Meyer, Hazel. *The Gold in Tin Pan Alley.* Philadelphia: J. B. Lippincott Company, 1958.

Millard, Andre. *America on Record: A History of Recorded Sound.* New York: Cambridge University Press, 1995.

Miller, E. Willard, and Ruby M. Miller. *United States Immigration: A Reference Handbook.* 1924. Reprint, Santa Barbara: ABC-CLIO, 1996.

Moloney, Mick. "Irish Ethnic Recordings and the Irish Imagination," *Ethnic Recordings in America: A Neglected Heritage.* Library of Congress. American Folklife Center. Washington, D.C.: GPO, 1982.

Mooney, Hughson F. "Songs, Singers and Society, 1890–1954." *American Quarterly* 6, no. 3. (Autumn, 1954): 221–232, http://links.jstor.org/sici?sici=00 03- 0678%28195423%296%3A3%3C2 21%3ASSAS1%3E2.0.CO%3B2-8

Moore, Catherine. "Work and Recordings: The Impact of Commercialization and Digitalization." In *The Musical Work: Reality or Invention,* edited by Michael Talbot. Liverpool: Liverpool University Press, 2000.

Nettl, Paul. *National Anthems.* Translated by Alexander Gode. New York: Frederick Ungar Publishing Company, Inc., 1967.

The Online Discographical Project. Editor: Steven Abrams. 21 Feb. 2003, http://settlet.fateback.com/discography.html

Ostendorf, Berndt. "The Musical World of Doctorow's *Ragtime.*" *American Quarterly* 43, no. 4. (Dec., 1991): 579–601.

Otto, John Solomon, and Augustus M. Burns. "The Use of Race and Hillbilly Recordings as Sources for Historical Research: The Problem of Color Hierarchy among Afro-Americans in the Early Twentieth Century." *The Journal of American Folklore* 85, no. 338. (Oct.— Dec., 1972): 344–355. http://links.jstor.org/sici?sici=0021- 8715% 28197210%2F12%2985%3A338%3C3 44%3ATUORAH%3E2.0.CO%3B2-Q

Park, Robert Ezra, and Herbert A. Miller. *Old World Traits Transplanted.* New York: Harper & Brothers Publishers, 1921.

_____. *Society: Collective Behavior, News and Opinion, Sociology and Modern Society.* Glencoe: The Free Press, 1955.

Peek, Philip M. *Catalog of Afroamerican Music and Oral Data Holdings.* Bloomington: University of Indiana, 1970.

Poe, Randy. *Music Publishing: A Songwriter's Guide.* Cincinnati: Writer's Digest Books, 1997.

Pretzer, William S., ed. *Working at Inventing: Thomas A. Edison and the Menlo Park Experience.* Dearborn, (Mich.): Henry Ford Museum & Greenfield Village, 1989.

Read, Oliver, and Walter L. Welch. *From Tin Foil to Stereo: Evolution of the Phonograph.* Indianapolis: Howard W. Sams & Co., 1959.

Recording Industry Association of America. http://www.riaa.com

Review of *The Bird of Paradise,* by Richard Walton Tully. Maxine Elliott's Theater, New York. *New York Times,* 9 January 1912.

Review of *Rigoletto.* Metropolitan Opera House, New York. *New York Times,* 24 Nov 1903.

Ritz, David. Recording Notes. *B. B. King's Greatest Hits.* MCA. 1998. Compact disc.

Rust, Brian, and Allen G. Debus. *The Complete Entertainment Discography, From 1897–1942.* New York: Da Capo Press, 1989.

Salaam, Kalamu ya. "It Didn't Jes Grew: The Social and Aesthetic Significance of African American Music." *African American Review* 29, no. 2, (Summer 1995): 351–375.

Sanjek, Russell. *From Print to Plastic: Publishing and Promoting America's Popular Music (1900–1980)*. Brooklyn: Institute for Studies in American Music, 1983.

Schlesinger, Arthur M., Jr., ed. *The Almanac of American History*. New York: Barnes & Noble Books, 1993.

Siegmeister, Elie, ed. *The Music Lover's Handbook*. New York: William Morrow & Co., 1943.

Slobin, Mark. *Subcultural Sounds: Micromusics of the West*. Hanover: Wesleyan University Press, 1993.

Southern, Eileen. *The Music of Black Americans: A History*. New York: W.W. Norton & Co., 1997.

Spaeth, Sigmund. *At Home with Music*. New York: Doubleday & Co., 1946.

_____. *A History of Popular Music*. New York: Random House, 1964.

Spottswood, Richard K. *Ethnic Music on Records: A Discography of Ethnic Recordings Produced in the United States, 1893 to 1942*. Urbana: University of Illinois Press, 1990.

_____. "Commercial Ethnic Recordings in the United States," *Ethnic Recordings in America: A Neglected Heritage*. Library of Congress. American Folklife Center. Washington, D.C.: GPO, 1982.

Sudhalter, Richard M. Recording Notes. *Don't Give the Name a Bad Place: Types and Stereotypes in American Musical Theater, 1870–1900*. New World Records 80265. Compact disc.

Swanstrom, Arthur M., and Carey Morgan. "The Argentines, the Portuguese and the Greeks." New York: Jos. W. Stern & Co., 1920. Song.

"The Talking Phonograph," *Scientific American*, 22 December 1877, 384–385.

"Ten Best Sellers." *The Billboard*. 19 July 1913, 15.

"This Is the Instrument," advertisement, *Atlantic Monthly Advertiser*. June 1899.

Toffler, Alvin. *Future Shock*. New York: Bantam Books, 1990.

"Top 200 Albums." Chart. *Billboard*, 30 August 2003.

Tosches, Nick. *Unsung Heroes of Rock 'n' Roll: The Birth of Rock in the Wild Years before Elvis*. New York: Da Capo Press, 1999.

U.S. Department of Commerce and Labor, Bureau of the Census. *Thirteenth Census of the United States, Taken in the Year 1910: Abstract of the Census*. Washington, D.C.: GPO, 1913.

U.S. Department of Commerce, Bureau of the Census. *Historical Statistics of the United States: Colonial Times to 1970, Part 1* Washington, D.C.: GPO, 1975.

University of Colorado Digital Sheet Music Collection, 2003. Project Manager: Marcelyn H. D'Avis. http://www-libraries.colorado.edu/mus/smp/index.html

Waldo, Terry. *This Is Ragtime*. New York: Hawthorn Books, 1976.

Whitburn, Joel, ed. *Pop Memories: 1890–1954 — The History of American Popular Music*. Menomonee Falls, (Wisc.): Record Research, 1986.

Wright, Donald. *The World and a Very Small Place in Africa*. New York: M.E. Sharpe, Inc., 1997.

Index